THE PHILOSOPHIC HISTORY
OF CIVILIZATION

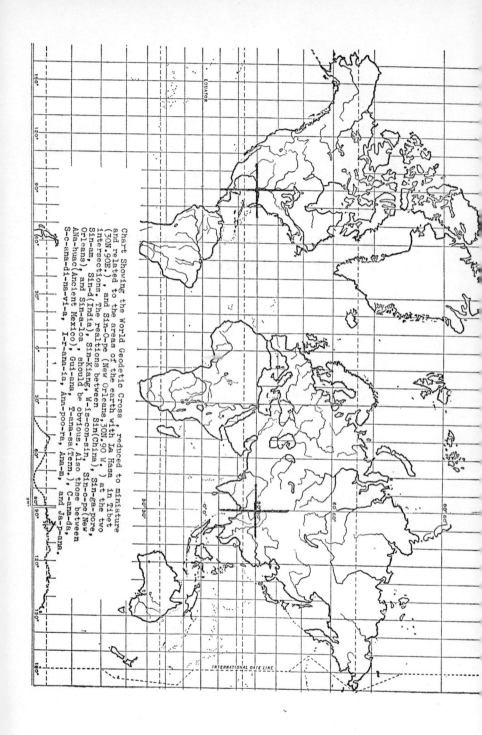

Chart Showing the World Geodetic Cross, reduced to miniature and related to the areas of the earth with Ia Hasa in Tibet (30N.90E.), and Sin-O-pe (New Orleans 30N.90 W.) at the two intersections. The realtions between Sini(China), Sin-ga-pore, Sin-am, Sin-d.(India), Sin-Kiang, W-is-con-sin, Sin-o-pe(New Orleans) and Sin-a-loa should be obvious. Also those between ANa-huac(Ancient Mexico), Gui-ana, T-ana-sa(Tenn.), C-ana-da, S-c-ana-di-na-vi-a, I-r-ana-ia, Ana-poo-ra, Ana-m, and Ja-p-ana.

The PHILOSOPHIC HISTORY OF CIVILIZATION

Showing the Spiritual and Material Factors
Involved in the Evolution of Nations.

by
JENNINGS C. WISE

PHILOSOPHICAL LIBRARY
New York

Aude Sapere
Vive ut cras moriturus
Disce ut semper victurus

"History is philosophy teaching by example."—VOLTAIRE

"I know of no way of judging the future but by the past."
—PATRICK HENRY

"In history truthfully written is found the latitude and longitude for guiding the Ship of State."—THOMAS JEFFERSON

TABLE OF CONTENTS

LIST OF ILLUSTRATIONS

PREFACE

An immense volume might be written on the struggle that led up to the French Revolution and the manner in which at last Science was liberated to some extent from the limitations of Aristotelian philosophy. Here, however, it is sufficient to note that Jean Jacques Rousseau (1712-1778) first acquired distinction in 1749 when chance cast to him the affirmative in the debate whether or not letters and science had tended to corrupt more than to advance morals. Following his brilliant demonstration science advanced rapidly under the incitations of Voltaire and the Encyclopedists to the point, that amid the French Revolution the great German-Jewish astronomer, Wilhelm Friedrich Herschel dared openly to declare to the youth seeking instruction at his hands that there was much to forget as well as to learn. Still so-called historians and mere tyros of science were writing foolishness when to celebrate the centennial of American Independence the first congress of scientists assembled in Philadelphia to consider the revelations of the past century. Asked what he thought would serve best the advance of human knowledge, the great Scotch surgeon who for twenty years had labored to induce the acceptance of anesthetics by the posterity of Galen promptly replied: "Put every textbook ten years old in a dark cellar."

Meantime the relatively young science of Geology had shown that down to about B.C. 10,000 Europe and America and America and Asia had been far more closely connected than at present; Archaeology had disclosed civilizations vastly older than those of which the historians had conceived; Physical Anthropology had carried the human stem back a million years or more into the so-called Archaic Age, which the historians had invented as a convenient catch-all for whatever they did not understand. But if it was evident that the history of civilization could not be written logically without relating the evolutions of man and culture to the human habitat; that the common philosophy of antiquity expressed through similar myths in widely separated areas traced back to universal primordial concepts, still it was impossible for a satisfactory history of civilization to be written. Nor could this be done until the American Bureau of Ethnology founded in 1877, thanks to the Congress of Scientists, under the auspices of the Smithsonian Institute, had digested and correlated the vast researches of a host of expert ethnologists rendering fact rather than fiction respecting the aborigines of America available to historians. When at last in 1907 the magnificent *Handbook of American Indians,* embodying the ethnology of the seven linguistic families including over seventy tribes which in course of the ages had come to occupy that part of America north of Mexico, appeared countless so-called legitimate histories at once became obsolete, including the works of Prescott, Parkman, Bancroft, Fiske, and Winsor, which had been accepted as definitive. Yet, even the teachers of history in the faculties of institutions deemed the highest in the field of education continued to rehash old propagandas, with only now and then the slightest regard to the revelations of science. Worse than this, history continued to be so compartmentalized that the nexus of the present, the child of the past, with that age of which it was born was lost. Instead of being history in its true sense as defined by Voltaire —philosophy teaching by example—what was being taught was a mere rigmarole of names and dates, explaining so little as to be simply a tax upon the memory.

In this situation the author, who had come at the end of forty years of historical research in five continents, to understand the myth of Columbus's having discovered America, as a preliminary to his *Mystery of Columbus* (1947), published his *America, the Background of Columbus* (1946). Not designed to be a narrative history, but a purely critical work unsuited for ordinary readers, in it he undertook to correlate for the first time what modern science had disclosed, with the certain confidence that it would receive the silent treatment from the great majority of "legitimate historians."

Although it received recognition by numerous scholars of moral courage as a valuable contribution to letters, it was not without errors, which fortunately did not prejudice its thesis, even if they were detected by those whose high commendation it elicited. Only lately the great Danish scientist Nils Bohr, by many deemed the foremost in his field, has pointed out that Galileo, Harvey, and other revolutionary thinkers should not be condemned for their errors, since the latter in their correction advanced knowledge. In the face of this highly intelligent attitude by a great thinker, the author is not the least embarrassed by his own mistakes, which he freely confesses. The exact time when this or that ancient monument arose is relatively unimportant as compared with the knowledge of which it was reminiscent. For instance, the great cromlechs of ancient Britain could not have been reared as geodetic markers among other things, without the astronomical knowledge upon which they were based.

In this work, the author will demonstrate, again by resort to all the sciences, and especially to the lance of mathematics, what Raleigh meant when he declared in the introduction to his *History of the World* (1618): "Only Eternity and history have triumphed over time;" what Francis Bacon meant when in his *Advance of Learning* (1605) he wrote: "Knowledges are as the pyramids whereof the base is history." Also he will show why the Irish scholar Dicuil (825 A.D.), after leading the first Celtic monks to Iceland upon visiting Egypt designated the pyramids in his astronomical treatise as "the barns of Joseph." Likewise he will attempt to show what Shakespeare meant when he declared that the sons of Edward lay in the breast of Abraham, and upon what his great mystery play, "The Tempest," was based. Familiar with the great mass of occult literature by which the world has been flooded and the absurdities of self-styled esotericists who have prejudiced occultism in all its forms, he will not be deterred by the latter, nor allow the fear of the uninformed to limit the range of his reason.

The truth is, of course, a clear distinction is to be drawn between Metaphysics, essentially a speculative science, and history. It has not been the truth that has dictated the actions of men and the evolution of their varying civilizations, but what they have either believed or professed to believe. This being so, one who undertakes to interpret the history of civilization in the light of his own metaphysical convictions alone is not an historian, but a mere propagandist of his own convictions.

But what is the need for such a work as this?

The answer is a simple one. Obviously so long as the sacred scriptures are interpreted to youth in their literal sense and made to challenge Science, Agnosticism will pass into the Skepticism of those who see an apparent irreconcilability between holy testaments of the various faiths and the visible facts of life. With the soil of youth plowed and fertilized by ignorant teachers, who more and more in their vanity are relegating faith in a Transcendent Wisdom to the nursery, while proclaiming the "Economic Man" the rightful and sufficient dictator of human destinies, the spread of Atheism can but play into the hands of the enemies of both God and man now ruling the Communist world. Therefore, without religious bias the author has undertaken to show that the best that civilization has produced down the ages has been the product of faith in a wisdom superior to that mortals have so far displayed; that only where faith in Divinity has prevailed has human liberty been possible; that materialism invariably has yielded only misery to those who have departed from the primordial philosophy that lifted man from the plane of tooth and claw to the high estates of the nations of antiquity.

To do this, however, it is not proposed by the author, nor is it necessary, to do more than trace the evolution of civilization down through the so-called Archaic Age, to the point where the nexus between recorded history and what went before the testimony of the oldest works of man can be interpreted in the light of the oldest scriptures. For it is known that they are all essentially esoteric in nature, never designed to be taken literally by those to whom as the initiates of the ancient mysteries alone the keys to the myths embodied in them were entrusted, as pointed out by Plato, Euhemerus, Diodorus Siculus, Josephus, Plutarch, and the Christian Gnostics Clement of Alexandria, Iamblichus, and Lactantius successively. In this way the author will attempt to make science yield a sound basis for faith in a Creative Genius as preferable to the appeals that have long been made to a mystical blind faith in seeming absurdities contravening science and overtaxing human credulity. Thus, in this work the thoughtful, of whatever faith, will find nothing to condemn even though it may not appeal to Fabian Socialists hiding behind the League of Industrial Democracy through which they have gained control of modern education to the delight of the Communists whose ends they are but serving, even when unwittingly.

To avoid the cluttering of the text with a multiplicity of citations numerous appendices have been included, along with a topical bibliography of works not cited in the current cyclopedias, upon which (with those that are readily available to ordinary readers and scholars alike) the author has relied.

Upon this work the author looks as but a pebble cast upon a deep, dark, placid pool of complacent ignorance, that may set in motion a ring of interest among the thoughtful, to some extent contribute to the intellectual revolution from which alone a new school of history may spring, having regard to the warning of Zechariah:—"Not by might, nor by power, but by my spirit, saith the Lord of Hosts."

In conclusion, he does not deem it hypocritical in the least, as some are sure to charge, for a self-confessed sinner, keenly aware of his own weaknesses and shortcomings (and who has refused to prostitute his reason to expediency) to point to more than one sage who down the ages has said: "I was glad when they said unto me, let us go unto the House of the Lord." To those who have made this publication possible he is deeply grateful.

Jennings C. Wise,
Lexington, Virginia
September 10, 1954.

CHAPTER I

SOUND CHRONOLOGY AN ESSENTIAL ELEMENT OF HISTORY

WITHOUT A SOUND CHRONOLOGY historians have necessarily been but wanderers in the sea of time. Yet it has been only natural that Christian historians have been loath to challenge the birth date of Adam, B.C. 4,002, fixed by the Paschal Cycle of 600 A.D. and later by the *Chronologica Sacra* of James Ussher, the Anglican Bishop of Asaph, in 1652, still given in Christian prayer books.

The first Christian chronology, however, was that put forward by the Ante-Nicene Father, Sextus Julianis Africanus in his Chronicon bringing the history of the world down from the creation to the year A.D. 221. According to him the Creation had occurred in B.C. 5,449, or shortly before the highly developed Hindu culture of the Mahabharata Age is commonly supposed today to have begun. Also he fixed the birth of Adam in B.C. 4,004. Having lived in Palestine since 190 necessarily he was familiar with the *Antiquities of the Jews* published by the great Jewish historian Josephus in 77 A.D., with the *Synthesis* of the eponymous Manetho of Egypt to whom the first lighthouse, or that erected at Alexandria in B.C. 315 has been ascribed, and who fixed the founding of the 1st Egyptian Dynasty by the Pharaoh Mena in B.C. 7,500. Also he must have been familiar with the *Chronology* of the Chaldean historian Berossus who about B.C. 250 fixed the founding of the first of the Ten Divine Dynasties of Chaldea in B.C. 432,535, and with the Sanskrit texts of India fixing the passing of the seventh avatar, Rama Krishna, or Chrisna, in B.C. 4,004.[1]

[1] For the Ten Divine Dynasties of Chaldea, according to Berossus, see Appendix "A."

[7]

Modern historians must note that incredible as the chronology of Berossus may seem, it was never challenged by any contemporary of Berossus, even by the great Jewish scholars constituting the Sanhedrin of Judah whose function it was to supervise the alterations and redactions of the Jewish scriptures which in the life time of Berossus were embodied in the Septuagint including the Pentateuch ascribed to Moses and two of the Apochrypha, or secret works of the Hebrews. Moreover it was accepted without question by the Greek historian Apollodorus (c.B.C. 150) as the basis for the *Bibliotheca,* and also by the Roman historian Alexander Polyhistor (c.B.C. 80), upon whom the Christian Eusebius, Bishop of Alexandria, who at the first Council of the Church was appointed official historian, drew for his knowledge. Nor was it challenged by the Christian historian Socrates of Constantinople (c.A.D. 450) and the Neo-Platonist historian Proclus, head of the Platonian Academy of Athens and contemporary of Socrates who insisted that Eusebius had forged much that had been written by Berossus. Before a proven forgery of it by the Dominican Giovanni of Viterbo had been made, two centuries after the Paschal Cycle of Gregory the Great (A.D. 600), the Latin monk George Syncellus adopted it in his Annal of A.D. 800. Not only this but the date fixed by Berossus for the founding of the 1st Chaldean Divine Dynasty concurs with that now commonly ascribed to the Neanderthal cycle of culture in which the gigantic Heidelberg man is supposed to have appeared. Finally by the Encyclopedia Britannica, XIIIth Edition, his chronology was accepted as sound.

Inasmuch as we now know that the Mycenean culture of Greece produced the Palace of Knossus before the date assigned by Africanus to the Creation, common sense suggests that dealing in esoteric dates he was referring to the beginning of a cycle of culture rather than to the creation of the universe, and that this was thoroughly understood by the ancient scholars as well as by Gregory the Great who altered the birth date of Adam, and by Syncellus and Ussher.

To be sure, since James Hutton of England founded the first note of modern Geology in 1785, and soon after this William Smith made possible the division of the geological record into ages based on the rate of stratification, different writers have applied different names to the geological ages and their subdivisions. Recently it has been calculated by Wilkinson with the aid of the radio active clock that the mass of gas thrown off by the sun about 2,500,000,000 years ago of which the earth and moon were formed required 500,000,000 years to solidify, and still it is a moot question whether the moon or the earth came into being first.[1] For the purpose of this work, however, it is sufficient to give here a single classification of the geological ages as the background against which to trace the evolution of man and culture.

GEOLOGICAL CHRONOLOGY[2]

Cycle	Duration: Solar Years
The Primordial Age	171,000,000
The Primary Age, or Age of Marine Life	103,040,000
The Secondary Age, or Age of Reptilians	37,500,000
The Tertiary Age, or Age of Mammals	6,610,000
The Quaternary Age, or Age of Man	850,000

While it is thought by some that the cycle of the Tertiary here given is excessively long, and that the Quaternary, or present Age may have begun as early as B.C. 1,000,000, and by others that it began concurrently with, and as a result of the beginning of the Great Ice Age about B.C. 900,000, when the formation of the ice caps and radical changes of temperature caused the terrestrial spheroid to wobble on its axes. The important thing for the student to note is that the alternate names applied to the Geological Ages merely indicate the characteristic type of life upon the earth in those cycles, and misleading as they have proved to superficial scholars, do not imply that there was no overlapping of Reptilians, or Dinosaurians, Mammalia of the Animal Kingdom, and Man.[2]

In addition to what has been shown, carrying the history of the earth back a total of 319,000,200 solar years, Anthropology has carried the Human Stem back to the Eocene or Nummulitic Period of the Tertiary commonly conceded to have begun several million years ago.[3] But again the student must be warned. Although the radical changes in the form of the earth during the earlier, or Miocene Period, deemed by some to have been of a cataclysmic nature attended by the upheavals which brought into being the successive ranges of the Tertiary Mountains, left many areas of preceding periods unsubmerged, it is impossible to say that man did not exist in the submerged areas of earlier periods.

Whatever the facts may be, so far has the knowledge of the earth advanced that a French scientist has been able to relate the forms of the earth as it evolved towards its present form, to the Primary, to the Jurassic period of the Secondary, and to the Eocene period of the Tertiary, as shown in the four geological charts included in this work.

While the land masses indicated on Chart I are thought by some geophysicists to be the worn down surfaces of a tetrahedron into which the gas first consolidated, the point of which emerged first from the waters precipitated upon it by the surrounding atmosphere, the vast Pale-Arctic-Huronian Continent encircling the North Pole possesses the form of a coronet with a leaf projecting southward from Hudson Bay at the west to the present Scandinavian Peninsula.

But more remarkable than this. The Afro-Brazilian Continent shown below the Coronet possesses the form of a huge bird with closed wings corresponding to the symbol of the Imperial Eagle, and to the fossils of huge winged dinosaurs to which reference will be made later.

From Charts III and IV it appears that the North Atlantic Continent of the Jurassic Period in course of time retracted westward to leave the Scandinavian barrier like an egg dropped in the sea by the land mass of the Arctic Zone above it of which the Spitzbergen group of Islands and all the Zemblas in the present Arctic Sea were formed.

The reader should bear in mind these formations as we proceed.

When, however, scientists come to consider the human record of the past we find them in accord with the ancient Hindu claim that even if the oldest of the Sanskrit texts—the *Rig Veda*, may not have been compiled by Vyaza, "the Arranger," until about B.C. 5,000, what appears in it, the *Upanishads*, the *Brahmana*, the *Puranas*, and the two great Hindu Epics—the *Mahabharata* and the *Ramayana*, had been taught for unknown ages; that the Tamil or Adamic Calendar, the oldest known to man was based on the original twelve signs of the Zodiac to which no scientist has presumed to assign an age since Volney showed it was in use as early as B.C. 15,000 among the peoples of Asia Minor.

[1] See Proceedings of the American Association for the Advancement of Science, London, 1940.

[2] *Philosophy*, LEFEVER (1878).

[3] *The Antiquity of Man*, KEITH (1925).

[4] *The Earth Before History, The Origin of Man and the Evolution of the Earth*, EDUARD PERRIER (1925). The charts here included were reproduced with the permission of the publishers of Perrier's work, Messrs. Tench, Truebner, Paul & Co., Ltd., London, by the author of this work, first in *America the Background of Columbus* (1946).

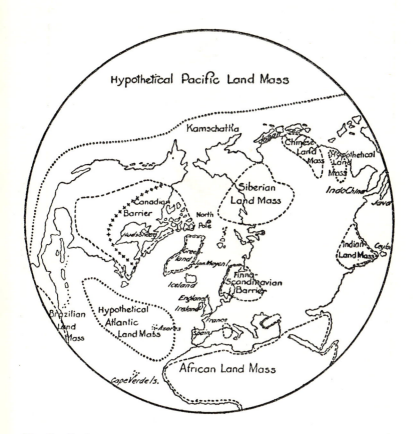

MAP I.—Conformation of Land and Sea in the Northern Hemisphere at the beginning of the Primary Period.

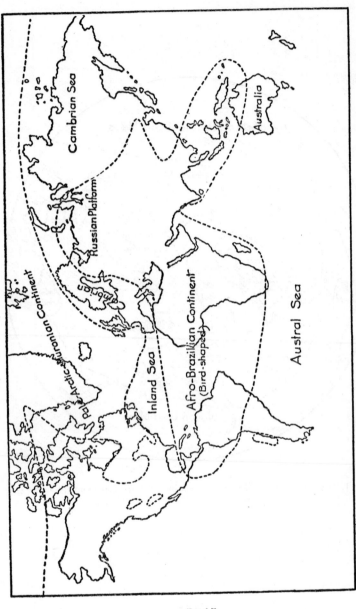

MAP II.—The Continents of the Cambrian Epoch.

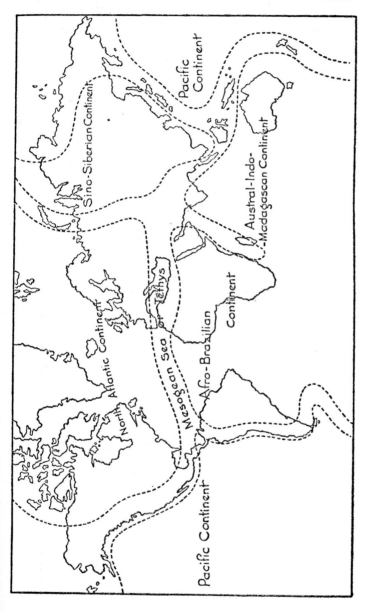

MAP III.—The Earth of the Jurassic Period.

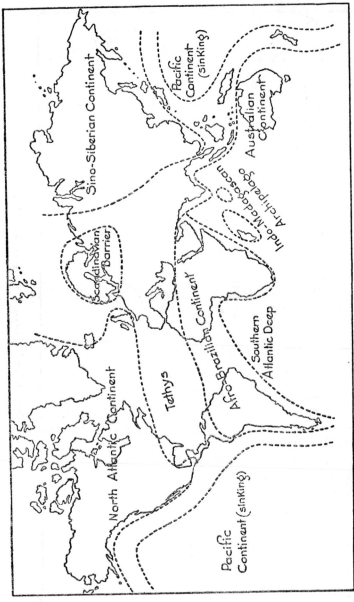

MAP IV.—The Earth of the Nummulitic Period.

(The lower of the dotted lines shows the limit of the area on which the water could encroach.)

CHAPTER II

NATURE THE TEACHER OF MAN—HER TENDENCY TO GEOMETRICIZE—THE PRIMORDIAL WISDOM PHILOSOPHY

BETIMES EVEN THE fowl of the air and the beasts of the field are stirred by the correspondence between the phenomena of the celestial and terrestrial spheres just as were the first sentient beings upon the earth.

As the dawn awoke now and then like thunder from the couch of Eastra, chanticleer would hail it with his din and men, whether in the realm of Norden or in the sultry zones of Sudra, would see Sol roll like a ball of fire through the sky to seek his couch again in the vast beyond their horizon. Then would the orbs of the firmament, as if summoned from the inscrutable deep of Erebus to light the night, fill the heavens with glory, and in periodic turn would be seen by all a woman's likeness in the crescent moon, and in the fulling orb a masculine visage.

Between the ecliptic of the sun and the bright baldric of the sky, studded as it was with the stars that formed the Milky Way; the seven visible planetary orbs; and the horizon where the celestial dome seemed to rest upon the purple rim of Mother Earth, as between the annular rings that marked the growth of trees to which men owed the blessings both of shade and food, and those which a pebble cast upon a placid pool set in motion, also was seen a correspondence. Nor did even the first mortals fail to note in the rainbow's arc the seven cardinal colors of nature's pallette appearing in the gorgeous plume fluttering as the feathery crown of Gaura-sinkar, "the Mother Mountain of the Earth," spread by the frosty atmosphere 70 miles o'er the mystical realm of Ne-pa-la.[1]

At times they beheld the cruciform of light which formed at the sun and moon alike, resembling a mortal with arms outspread; amid recurring eclipses saw the crescent formed by the solar light upon the lunar orb, also form upon the leafy carpets of the forest's shade. And as they counted the seven visible planets, and the colors of the solar spectrum, they also observed that in the cycle of Nature's grand musical scale there were seven notes.[2] Ranging from the deep growling of the thunder in the cosmic sea, or from the bass tremolo of the roaring surf cast by angry waves upon terrestrial shores, the voice of Nature passed through the altos of the windswept reeds, of the waving fronds above their heads, to the swish of leaves by gentle zephyrs stirred on to the high soprano of the cicado. So too did they discover in the calls and cries of the fowl of the air and other insentient creatures of the earth, the seven sounds that man might utter in whatever tongue he spoke, which today we call the vow-els.[3]

Eventually the adepts of nature's magic, comprising the wise men called ma-gicians, or sa-g-e-s, learned that the vibrations of the atmosphere not only produced all sound, but were subject to the same septenary law as color; that between the seven notes of the musical scale, the seven vowels of human speech, and the seven cardinal colors, there is a close relation.[4]

In the frosty atmosphere and in the mineral kingdom alike, they observed crystals displaying triangular, cubical, pentagonal, hexagonal, and octagonal forms that grouped themselves in seven systems according to combined chemico-mathematical laws. In the vegetable kingdom they beheld the leaf of the ivy that evolves through a series of triangles marked by its veins, and came to look upon it as a symbol of eternal life.[5] Also they beheld the water lily, or lotus, of which the leaves form a tri-foil, while the bud and flower depend for nurture not upon the soil of the earth, but upon the water corresponding to the cosmic sea, in which the pendant roots are suspended.[6] Thus, it has ever been deemed the symbol, not of eternity, but of the spiritual origin of man.

In course of time the magicians also discovered that the crystals of the minerals, like those in the frosty atmosphere, would refract the pure white light of the sun into the solar spectrum, and on a screen would cast a cruciform. Thus if a crystal disc were placed before a lens and revolved successively through four cycles of 90°, it would project in turn a black spot, one with a white cruciform, a white spot, and one with a black cruciform. And if the four sides of a cubical box were unfolded, the resulting figure also would be a cruciform with four squares in the vertical and three in the horizontal arm, or seven counting both ways.

All this must have been noticed when the Magicians placed the spots on the sides of the cubes called die, so arranged that the total on the opposite sides is seven.[7] Was this done to remind the gambler that there were principles involved in life beyond the realm of chance?

In time too it appeared that even the chemical elements entering into the matter of crystals arrange themselves according to a law of affinity into seven groups.[8] Also it was seen that in the mortal's head, as in that of many insentient creatures, there are seven apertures,—eyes, nostrils, ears, and mouth, corresponding to the seven senses; that in the human heart are seven chambers; over his body seven layers of skin; beneath the skin seven complexes of lymph; in his body seven ganglia of nerves. If some of these things were only within the ken of the Magicians, the Old Wives did not fail to note that the menstrual period of seven days corresponded to the recumbent phase of the crescent moon, and that a living being might gestate within a mother's womb in seven months. Nor was it only within the sphere of esoteric knowledge monopolized by Magicians that between the Sun upon which all life upon the earth depended, the cosmic sea in which the moon floated, and the crust of the earth, there was a correspondence with the germ, yolk, white and shell of the egg from which various creatures of the earth were hatched. Here let us note particularly that all over the earth grows today the cruciferous plant, commonly known as *candytuft,* technically called *Iberis,* referred to the tribe or plants *Iberis Sin-a-pe-ae,* that grows along with weeds, and that derived its name from the pre-Aryan, Naga-Maya word I-b-e-r, 'the Spirit of Brahma, the earthly son,' implying the cruciform designated in Sanskrit as the *tau,* and by the ancient Egyptians as the *ankh,* 'the Ark, of No, the King of Heaven,' representing the spirit of God upon the waters.

In view of what was visible in nature to early man, it was inevitable that soon or late a philosophy based upon the correspondences between the phenomena of the celestial and terrestrial spheres which have been described should have evolved. Nor do the vast researches which have been made in the field of Philosophy and in the special field of Philology fail to indicate that such a philosophy did appear as the Primordial Universal Wisdom Philosophy, constituting the first known philosophic ark, or vehicle, that found expression in the so-called Serpent Cult of the Maya to which all known religions have been traced.

Broadly stated, it conceived of the unity of the Universe; the fundamental unity of the souls of all mortals with the Oversoul which it held to be Infinite and Absolute and as the Creative Genius necessarily unimaginable in form because Infinite, of which all things, inanimate and animate, were part of the Divine Design achieved through the universality of law and the endless evolution through recurring cycles of birth and death, guided by the laws of cause and effect and, therefore, of all things as the differentiated aspects of one Reality, of all truths as the reflection of the one Truth. Thus it differed from Speculative Philosophy, or Metaphysics, in that it started from a transcendental apprehension of Divinity to explain the manifested universe, and did not generalize from phenomena to the being and attributes of God. Moreover, it differed from pure Mysticism in that it did not content itself with the relations of the soul to the Creator of mortality, but also concerned it-

II. The Largest of the Five Recently Discovered Moon Stones
of Mexico.

Illustration used with the permission of the
National Geographic Magazine.

III. The largest of the Five Colossi of Bamian.
(For occult interpretation see *The Secret Doctrine,* Blavatsky, 1886).

self with the constitution and course of nature in a way well calculated to illustrate to man that all things were the product of a Wisdom superior to his own. Thus it sought to discourage the self-destructive atheism that is born of a colossal and blinding vanity. It did not fail to remind man that he was the inheritor of the earth's bounties, not by virtue of his title of right based on his own perfections, but for some inscrutable reason beyond his ken. Thus it was designed to keep before him the question of whether he was advancing or retarding a Grand Design of authorship higher than his own. It did not conceive of paltry mortals being advanced by forbidding teachings of a superior Wisdom, in the manner of present day materialists who see in the Economic Man the rightful dictator of mortal affairs.

As for mortals, they were the product of a combination of the Divine Essence, or the Adi, transmitted in the Buddhi, or sheaf of matter called by the Hindus the Va, to the lunar matter to bring into being the so-called Trinity of Spirit, Soul and Body. Corresponding to Fire, Water, and grosser matter, it was symbolized by the triangle, and called the Chi, or Divine Lotus. From the Moon this bud, so to speak, was swept over by a cosmic deluge to the earth.

The Wisdom Philosophy did not concern itself with the continents and islands of Geography. Instead it conceived of successive World Continents made up of all the land masses during these cycles, to which presently the names here shown are applied:

I. The Sacred and Imperishable Land, so-called because deemed never to have been destroyed.

II. The Hyperborea, so-called because its cycle was hyper to the knowledge of the Greek myth makers whose Frost God Boreas was supposed to have spread his mantle over the earth at a time anterior to the appearance of the present Root Race, that is in the Secondary, whereas the present, or Fifth Root Race, which is deemed to include all the peoples of the earth, of

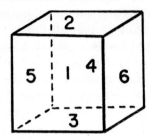

WHAT THE UNFOLDED SIDES
OF THE CUBE REVEAL :

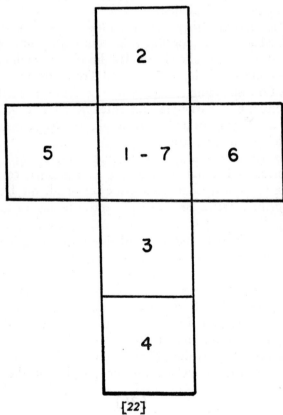

      whatever color, save a few survivors of the Third, appeared in the Tertiary.

III. Lemuria, for which the name of the Latin festival of the Lemuria has been appropriated, just as the Scotch Zoologist Sclater employed it to designate a vanished land mass in the Indian Ocean.

IV. Atlantis, of which the memory is preserved by the Sea of Atlantis at the east of Greece and north of Attica, as well as by the Atlantic Ocean.

V. America, a name which traces not to Americus Vespucci as commonly supposed.

Basic in this primordial philosophy was the doctrine of Reincarnation during the vast cycles of time of which it conceived and upon which the Tamil, Adamic, or Zodiacal Calendar was based. Extremely complex, it is fully dealt with in a concise work that leaves no room to doubt that to it traces the ultimate concept of Resurrection and Judgment by the Divine Father.[12]

Inseparably connected with the concept of Reincarnation was the concept of Karma, or that Divine Law pursuant to which the actions of men earn reward or punishment accordding to a just desert, being properly described in one aspect as the Law of Retribution. In this way was explained the apparent inequalities of reward and punishment meted out to individuals in the brief cycle of what is deemed life on earth. For according to the Doctrine of Reincarnation life is everlasting so that both reward and penalty may be reaped beyond the time when the soul of mortals as the envelope of the Adi is released from the material body. Such teachings could only serve to discourage wrongful and to encourage rightful action upon the earth. In a word it was taught that human action was a force that radiated like the circles set in motion by a pebble cast upon the surface of a placid pool, and though seemingly not extending beyond its area, exerted an influence of incalculable consequence in the grand scheme of the Over-Soul. And as the concept of Resurrection and Judgment Day is to be traced to this concept which in fact is basic in the Christian Creed that has come to be mumbled without the slightest understanding of its implications, so is the Christian teaching with respect to Communion with the Infinite as the ultimate goal of the children of God.

Such in brief were the fundamental tenets of the Wisdom Philosophy embodying what came in course of time to be called the *Secret Doctrine* for a very plain reason. Experience of mankind has shown that few individuals have ever been able to accept a pure philosophy as a guide for conduct in preference to one that ascribes to Divinity the likeness to mortals that found expression in the gods of Pantheistic religions and in Deities of anthropic type. In other words the colossal vanity of mankind is such that the concept of God in the likeness of man has been more acceptable than that of the Creative Genius as transcending in form the human imagination. Consequently the tendency toward idolatry which has persisted down the ages, and the hostility of the Black Magicians who in antique times made capital of it. This compelled the teachers of the Wisdom Philosophy to go under cover, so to speak, and to impart their unpopular doctrines of Reincarnation and Karma through the agencies of the Mysteries to those who after initiation in the lower degrees were gradually and secretly prepared to advance to the higher philosophic concepts upon which were based the myths. In them the gods in fact merely represented the principles they were designed to impersonate to the end of insuring a control by an enlightened minority over the masses intellectually incapable of grasping the Secret Doctrine of the Maya Ark, or Primordial Serpent Cult.

It now remains to consider the vast cycles of time of which the Wisdom Philosophy conceived. An examination of the Sanskrit texts reveals that the larger cycles called Days of Brahma and Rounds embracing millions and trillions of solar years were calculated by resort to the Zodiac. They were multiples of the cycle of 432,000 solar years called the Yuga, ten of which made up the Mahayuga or Great Cycle. This was given the mathematical arrangement of the constituent yugas on four planes as here shown, and which in the Philosophic System of Pythagoras took the form of a triangle formed by ten dots corresponding to the ten yugas, called the Sacred Tetra-k-t-is for reasons hereinafter to be explained.

Here it will be observed that the Hindu cycle of the Yuga of 432,000 solar years was the equivalent of 12 Chaldean sari, since the unit of the saros embraced 3,600 years. Thus, the Cycle of 432,000 solar years allowed the Ten Divine Dynasties of Chaldea in the Chronology of Berossus, as shown in Appendix "A," consisting of 120 sari, was the same in duration as a Hindu Mahayuga.

The Hindus readily explain the persistence of knowledge of which the evidence is found in the Hindu and other ancient scriptures. Thus, according to the Wisdom Philosophy, not only did each Root Race produce seeds of its successor, but there were an overlapping and merging of the sub-races produced by them. On the other hand, Esoteric Buddhism rejects the cataclysmic theory of Reclus with respect to the evolution of the earth. While it conceives of physical convulsions throughout the ages, such as those that brought the mountains of the Secondary and Tertiary into existence, and caused the Magnetic Cataclysm of B.C. 10,000 dealt with by Plato in the Timaeus, it views the transition of the earth from its Primordial to its present form as the result of a gradual and ceaseless evolution during which occurred the series of cosmic deluges that brought into being the successive Root Races. These deluges it distinguishes from the countless floodings of the earth resulting from submersions and upheavals, just as the High Priest Souchis of the Temple of Neith at Säis in Egypt is alleged by Plato to have done as the informant of Solon (B.C. 602). Furthermore, it does not conceive of the earth as having acquired suddenly its present consistency but as gradually evolving to this stage in the manner of the shell of an egg, and of the Root Races evolving in the

THE MAHAYUGA OR GREAT CYCLE
4,320,000 YEARS

CONSISTING OF A DEKKAD OF TEN LESSER YUGAS OF 432,000 YEARS EACH[*]

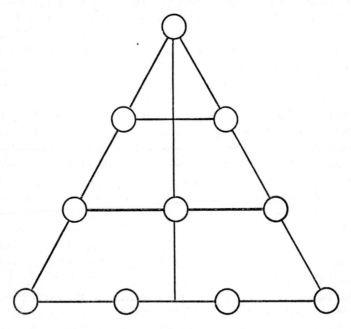

[*]KNOWN TO PYTHAGORAS AS THE
SACRED TETRA-K-T-IS

same manner from an ethereal to an increasingly materialized type of man. In its view, therefore, the Terrestrial habitat of man may be likened to the rind of a certain kind of fruit that thickens and hardens as it ripens.[9] Also it could be argued that each of the World Continents of which it conceives would have preserved in the manner of a negative some of the spiritual light shed upon the preceding one by reason of the fact that the transitions from one to the other did not involve a destruction of all the peoples of the earth. Upon this argument, however, it does not have to rely. For not only does it conceive of the seven Rishi as the Archtype for the seven Pitris of each Root Race, but of a series of major Avatars who eventually will constitute a Dekkad of Spiritual Beings in mortal form endowed by the Over-Soul reflected in them with the wisdom enabling them to uplift mankind by successive spiritual reilluminations. Of these, one is conceived to have appeared to each of the first four Root Races, while three others, or Rama in the aspects of Balarama, Rama Lunus or Chandra, and Rama Crisna or Krishna are deemed to have appeared to the present race. By some, Buddha Gotama is deemed the eighth avatar, and by others Jesus of Nazareth is held to have been the ninth, with the tenth, or the Man on the White Horse, yet to come. Appropriately they were called Ava-tars, 'winged crosses.'

In addition to these major incarnations of the Over-Soul, the Wisdom Philosophy conceived that many minor avatars appeared in the fields of science, education, religion, statesmanship, and as military leaders, all endowed with higher perceptions than the run of ordinary men and held to have been created to serve special ends. Among others who have been held to be avatars of this type may be mentioned Rameses II, Charlemagne, and Napoleon, while Washington is included by the Hindu pundits among the lesser Avatars. By some he was deemed to have been a reincarnation of the Teutonic All-Father Odin, being assigned by the American Indians the spiritual status of Hornandanigius, "the Conqueror".

Although it is not properly within the sphere of the historian as distinguished from the Metaphysician to indulge in comments upon the soundness or unsoundness of the philosophy which has been described, in view of the current misrepresentations of it which have served to divert self-styled "legitimate historians" from dealing with it, it is incumbent upon an historian with regard to cause and effect to note several things.

The vast researches which modern scientists have made in the field of philology have failed to bring to light any other philosophy or any religion that has essayed so complete an interpretation of the visible evidence in nature of a design on the part of the Creative Genius.

In the Wisdom Philosophy there appears nothing that can be construed with reason to do otherwise than encourage belief in the power with which man was endowed by the Creative Genius to save himself in the spiritual even if not in the physical sense. Also in it there is nothing in the way of a premium placed on the accident of fortune that enables one to acquire more knowledge than his fellows. On the contrary it makes a clear distinction between mere knowledge which a human fiend may acquire, and the wisdom which has been ascribed to the humble Cincinnatus, to the lowly cowherd Caedmon, the putative author of the first English Bible, and to the numerous individuals of the type of Lincoln who have appeared upon the stage of history, unfavored by fortune and inherited prestige. In the clear distinction it makes between knowledge as an accumulation through the physical process of the brain, and wisdom as a matter of spiritual perception born of a heart that places a higher valuation upon communion with the Over-Soul than upon mere physical possessions and what they command among men, it is essentially a philosophy of hope; also it conceives of an essentially merciful Creator. Thus it encouraged a belief in the equality of man insofar as human destiny is involved. Plainly this was understood by Plato who pointed out that men are either gods or beasts according to whether their higher or lower beings are allowed by them to rule their actions.

Nevertheless, the doctrine of the Over-Soul incarnating over and over in a series of avatars could not fail to provoke the bitter conflicts that have raged between its exponents and the protagonists of the religions that in course of time have appeared with metaphysical concepts challenged by it. On the other hand, since these conflicts themselves explain many of the events that occurred before the oldest known scriptures were written, there is all the more reason why it is necessary for the historian not to ignore the nature of the oldest philosophy known to man which, as shown, was still so important a factor even in Medieval history that it, like the current ancient history must be radically revised.

1 Until recently the precinct of Gaurasinkar to which the name of its first British explorer, Eve-rest, was given, was deemed too sacrosanct to permit further explorations. When great rumblings from the bowels of the earth occurred in those parts following the great aerial exploration of the British in 1925, the Government of India was compelled to halt further explorations.

2 Planet—Plane-T, "Plane of the Tau."

3 Vows of the gods.

4 *Theory of Color*, HEMHOLTZ (1862).

5 I-v-y, "Spirit of the Va, Ya."

6 Lo-t-u-s, "Logus-Tau-Uratur-Sa" (Wisdom).

7 D-i-e, "Divine Spirit of the Earth."

8 The basis of ancient alchemy ascribed to the mythical Tri-s-ma-gis-t-us.

9 Here it should be noted that the highest mountain ranges on the earth relative to the size are lesser in respect to the smoothness of its surface than the rough of a lemon peeling.

11 Fully demonstrated in the *Mystery of Columbus*, WISE (1947).

12 *Reincarnation*, WALKER (1902).

CHAPTER III

THE INFLUENCE OF THE PRIMORDIAL WISDOM
PHILOSOPHY UPON LANGUAGE
AND LANGUAGE AS THE
GUIDE OF HISTORY

INASMUCH AS language is properly defined as the vehicle
through which the expression of ideas is achieved, and among
humans this is accomplished through speech, signs, and written words, it is inconceivable that the Primordial Wisdom
Philosophy did not exert a profound influence upon the various languages in which the oldest known sacred scriptures
were written. This being so, in view of the theory of the
evolution of man embodied in the Wisdom Philosophy it is
readily understood why the Hindus and other ancient peoples
ascribed a divine origin to both language and mathematics.

While the erroneous concept of the founders of the Science
of Language that language had evolved as a tree, was exposed by Schmidt and it is now generally accepted that like other
forms of culture it evolved through waves superimposing,
as it were the flotsam of one upon another to produce according to local circumstances the varying jetsams of different
languages, there is much that has not been explained.

All the written languages are necessarily based upon alphabets themselves based on sounds. Of the known alphabets
that designated by the Hindus as the Amarakosa is deemed
the oldest. Logically, in accordance with the concept of the
divine origin of language the Aryan name applied to it implies 'signs of the Amara', or letters of the Immortals, just
as the Greek word *alpha-bet* implies 'the first covenant'.

These names themselves plainly indicate that the symbols
of the Amarakosa and those from which the present Greek

alphabet were evolved were hieroglyphs or sacred symbols designed by the Hierophants as the official spiritual teachers to convey common ideas to those speaking different tongues and employing signs or symbols of their own. Manifestly resort to such thought-pictures was the sole way in which the heterogeneity of tongues that would naturally have resulted from the wide dispersion of the earth's inhabitants and the ceaseless churning they received as the surface of the earth was altered, could be overcome while uniting different peoples in a nation, or for conveying to them a common philosophy, or a common religion.

Not only this, but the hieroglyphics were often of a cryptic or secret nature with cryptographs and even words, or cryptograms, possessing meanings known only to the initiated of the Mysteries by whose Hierophants they were designed. Thus, it has been demonstrated by Francois Lenormant that the Alphabet of the Naga-Maya Language upon which the Aryan, or Arya-Maya language was superimposed and from which the Aramean language common to the peoples of Asia Minor in the Mosaic Age was evolved, embodied a record of the climactic events which had transformed in some remote age the surface of the earth.[1]

To facilitate the correlation of the ancient myths embodied in the various hieroglyphic alphabets, the great scholar Karl Richard Lepsius, who as the pupil of Alexander Humboldt conducted the Prussian Scientific Expedition to Egypt in 1842, devised what he called a *"Standard Alphabet for Reducing Unwritten Languages and Foreign Graphic Systems to a Uniform Orthography in European Letters."* However helpful that alphabet may have been to scholars, Lepsius overlooked the fact that the ancient Italics had devised such an alphabet upon which both the Teutonic and Romance languages are based. The Latin alphabet symbols are here described in order that the student of history may more readily discern the common implications of names employed in the ancient scriptures of widely separated peoples.[2]

Symbolism of the Latin Alphabet

A—The Aramaic Alpha: The Divine Lotus: Triangle born by descending wings.

B—The Aramaic Beta. The spheres of Heaven and Earth with the Aramaic Iota common to the two.

C—An arc corresponding to the crescent of light cast by the sun on the moon and earth.

D—An arc embracing the Aramaic Iota.

E—The Aramaic Epsilon. Two planes of matter including all that is within the spiritual and terrestrial spheres.

F—The Aramaic Epsilon with the material plane omitted.

G—An arc conveying matter.

H—An Infinity sign with a plane of matter included.

I—The Aramaic Iota, or the numeral 1.

J—The Aramaic Iota with the phallic hook added by the Hebrews.

K—The Aramaic Iota uniting spread and closed avars.

L—The Aramaic Gamma reversed. An Iota and the lower plane of matter.

M—The Aramaic Mu. Two closed arms implying descended avars, and resembling cosmic waves.

N—The Aramaic Nu. Closed and spread avars.

O—A circle. The visible matter (Serpent Swallowing its tail. No beginning. No end.)

P—The upper sphere and an Aramaic Iota.

Q—A circle with an Iota issuing therefrom.

R—The Aramaic Rho. P with wing added.

S—An uncoiled serpent.

T—The Aramaic *tau,* and the Egyptian *ank,* or cruciform, squared by the Hebrews.

U—Symbol of the principle of the uterus in nature, implying sex.

V—Spread avars representing the Va.

W—Two Va's joined. Waves of life in the Terrestrial Sea, and duality of sex.

X—The Aramaic Chi. Spread and closed avars joined, representing descent of the Va to the earth.

Y—A Va bearing an Iota.

Z—The Aramaic Zeta. Two 7's, one inverted.

Not only does the combination of these cryptic characters produce words of different languages, having the same meaning, but words with the same characters which even though pronounced differently, express the same idea such as *sa, sage, sachem, sapience, sakinoo, serpent, shamen, snake, pasha,* Set, Se-cha, Naga, *tau,* and Tien.

Therefore the thoughtful must be struck by the correspondence between the symbolisms of the Latin alphabetical characters, the Arabic numerals, and the meaning of the words in the following list:

    1. A—Absolute, all, air, atmosphere, arc, angle, azimuth, ark, art, ability, audition, apparent, ancient, ancestor.

2. B—Bug, bud, bloom, birth, brain, boat, body, breath, bard, brand, benignance, blessing, boon, book, blue, black.
3. C—Creator, circle, crown, coronet, carnate, cognizance, conscience, curl, coil, curious, count, celestial, cloud, color, cause, cure, calculation, clear, candor, child, Christ.
4. D—Divinity, dawn, day, dark, duration, distant, do, discern, discourse, donation, deft, differ, danger, display, dazzle.
5. E—Eternity, essence, ether, electricity, energy, eminence, entrance, exit, extreme, earth, evidence, evil, ever, end, example.
6. F—Fire, flame, fate, faint, fail, faith, first, figure, frenzy, furor, father, form, frame, food, freedom, fancy, fame, flower, fly, free.
7. G—Gas, genius, God, Ghost, gorgeous, glory, gravity, gift, gold, ground, great, grain.
8. H—Heat, hinge, hang, high, heaven, holy, house, home, head, heed, hierarch, hope, honor, happiness, health, hour, husband.
9. I—Infinity, incarnate, intellect, intent, integrate, indelible, isolation, issue, image, inaugurate.
10. J—Justice, junior, jot, jet, jealous, Jovus, Jehovah, Jupiter, Jethro.
11. K—Ken, knowledge, kin, kindle, kill, kindness, kiss, king.
12. L—Light, Lord, luminous, line, limit, leaf, love, lust, language, law, last, let, liberty, learning.
13. M—Mist, miracle, marvel, moon, manifest, muster, mind, moral, milk, matter, munificence, money, manager, marine, morn, mate, male, model, motive, music, magic, majestic, Mark.
14. N—Nether, never, none, nay, not, next, note, name, navy, nest, noon, night.

15. O—Origin, orb, over, omnipotent, oracle, obscure, order, odor, oil, ocean.
16. P—Pristine, power, patent, prescience, presence, puberty, plain, plane, planet, paint, philosophy, prayer, patience, patent, pope, priest, papa, poet, pier, prince, power, policy, pattern, purple, pure, Peter, Paul.
17. Q—Queen, queer, query, quest, quiver, quintessence, quote.
18. R—Root, rate, rent, rant, ring, round, real, rest, rule, royal, regal.
19. S—Spirit, soul, spring, sperm, spit, sense, smell, say, sing, sex, sin, saint, sage, save, sanction, syllabus, seem, sure, science, storm, source, stern, satellite, star, sipre, spend, sage, show, seven, sphere, sagacity, stature, statutes, starved, sapience, scintillate.
20. T—Thee, trinity, think, task, touch, talk, tell, turn, trust, throw, take, thank, tree, truth, twin, tall.
21. U—Universe, utter, uterus, unction.
22. V—Void, vapor, vitality, vim, visage, vibration, vanish, virtue, virgin, vagina, vanity, vice, vanquish, visit, visible, vessel, vaccine, vow, voice.
23. W—Will, wander, whither, who, which, what, where, world, wonder, wraith, wind, wing, wave, whole, weal, world, water, wit, will.
24. X—(chi)
25. Y—Youth, yellow, yearn, yawn, yonder, yarn.
26. Z—Zenith, zephyr, zither, zealous.

How the Latin words evolved from the primordial Mayavic is indicated quite plainly by what is here shown of the manner in which the Mayavic tongue evolved from a combination of vowels and of the consonants, together forming many of the two-letter words of that language.[3]

aa	ba	ca	da	ea	fa	ga	ha
ab	be	ce	de	eb	fe	ge	he
ac	bi	ci	di	ec	fi	gi	hi
ad	bo	co	do	ed	fo	go	ho

ae	bu	cu	du	ef	fu	gu	hu
	by	cy	dy	eg			
				ei			
ai				ek			
ak				el			
al				em			
am				en			
an				eo			
ao				ep			
ap				eq			
aq				er			
ar				es			
as				et			
at				eu			
au				ev			
av				ew			
aw				ex			
ax				ey			
ay				ez			
az							

The highly cryptographic nature of the Latin Alphabet appears from the following interpretation which is only one of several that are possible.

A—Of the absolute was born
B—Brahma, the spiritual breath of the Celestial and Terrestrial spheres, and
C—The Moon
D—The Diva or Divine Spirit
E—Of the three planes of matter—Eribus, the visible heavens, and the Earth.
F—Upon which entered the Fire of the Father
G—God
H—The Holy
I—Spirit
J—Jehovah or Jupiter
K—The King, was
L—The Logus or Law
M—Of all matter
N—In the Nether
O—and the Visible World
P—The Philosophy
Q—Pursuant to which from the Moon issued the spirit
R—That Reincarnate Rules
S—The Soul embodying the Septenary Principle
T—Of the Tree of Life
U—Of which the generative principle of sex
V—By the Vehicle of the Va is conveyed
W—To the Womb-Man or spiritual twin
X—and conveyed
Y—By Ya-ma
Z—To the 7 Rishi who transmit it to the 7 Pitris.

As we proceed always it must be remembered that when we come to interpret the nomenclature of the Mosaic scriptures and the place names shown on the graph or Gea, we will be dealing with names of the Alexandrine Greek dialect employed by the Jewish scribes in compiling the Septuagint between 280 and 270 B.C. under the orders of Ptolemy Soter, nearly two centuries after the Greeks had transformed the Aramean alphabetical symbols originally used by them, into their present alphabet; that by this time there was probably not a scribe in Judea, or in Greece who was unfamiliar with the Sanskrit, Zend, and Phoenician alphabets, and with cuneiform hieroglyphics of the trilingual order which the Greek invaders of Persia had beheld at Beniston and elsewhere, before reaching India; and also with the Egyptian hieroglyphics of the Pyramid Texts embodying the *Book of the Dead,* and the runes of the so-called Celtic realms. In a word we will be interpreting them not as the writer sees fit to do, but as the scribes of the *Septuagint* (c. 350 A.D.) did; as did the Goth Ulfilas who based the first Christian bible on the Gothic runes and an early Greek version of the Hebraic texts; as St. Jerome did in the later *Vulgate,* or Latin version; as the alleged Saxon writer Caedom did in the first English version (c. 670 A.D.); as did the Hindus of the Mahabharata Age, supposed to have begun about 5,000 B.C., in the *Veda,* the Brahmanas, Upanishads, Puranos, and their two grand *Epics;* the Persians in their scriptures; the Maya did in their American glyphs; the Chinese and Japanese did in the Sacred books of the East and in the works of Confucius; as was done in the early Irish literature, the Norse *Sagas,* the Germanic and the Finnish scriptures, and those of Polynesia, all in coordination as by the theologian Jakob Andrae in his *Mythologia Christiana* (c. 1535), and by Hugo de Groot, or the mystic Grotius, the alleged father of International Law (1583-1645), his contemporary Spinoza and others, guided by Cardinal Cusa and the latter's successors of the Platonian Academy of Florence.

THE PHILOSOPHIC HISTORY OF CIVILIZATION

[1]LENORMANT, *Topical Bibliography.*

[2] It is to be noted that the V appearing in many of the Latin letters is similar to the Sanskrit letter *var* appearing in the Aryan word *var* implying a sheath of matter, corresponding to the philosophic concept of the Divine Lotus as well as to a pair of avars, or wings.

[3] Should the demonstration be carried on through the other eighteen letters of the Latin alphabet, far more of the two-letter syllables of the primordial language would appear.

CHAPTER IV

THE FIRST AND SECOND ROOT RACES OF THE WISDOM PHILOSOPHY. THE MISSING LINK OF MODERN ANTHROPOGENESIS

THE HINDUS CONCEIVED of Brahma as the Absolute, the Infinite, the Creative Genius, unimaginable in form because infinite, yet finding expression in nature through Brahma. In the visible aspect the Creative Genius was symbolized by them appropriately by a circle corresponding to the horizon and a serpent swallowing its tail, displaying no beginning, no end.

These concepts were derived from the Primordial Wisdom Philosophy to which traces the concept of the Naga who evolved the Serpent Cult from the Maya Philosophic Ark, and who saw in the milky way a natural symbol of the Divine Serpent of Wisdom designated by them as Se-cha, ascribed by them to the Seven-Headed Serpent Narayana finding in mortality the reflection designated by them as Naragana and applied by them to their earliest symbols in stone of this idea.

Eventually from Hinduism evolved the Brahman concept of Brahma, Vishnu, and Shiva as the expression of Divinity in the creative, saving, and destructive aspects, respectively, basic in their theory of evolution of both matter and man. In the form of Vivasat in each of the seven cosmic deluges which they hold to have occurred so far, Vishnu has saved the Manu through which the Divine Spirit has been transmitted by Bramah to mortality from the destructive force in nature impersonated by Shiva, corresponding to the Set of other religions.

Once these ideas are understood it is simple to interpret the deluge myth embodied in the *Catapatha brakmana.* In it Vivasat, in the form of a fish, is shown towing Manu in a boat to the top of the world where at Mount Amaravati, he is said to have created first the Amara, or immortals, called gods, and then men.

In Mount Amaravati, is to be seen, not the top of the earth in the sense of the North, but in the sense of the enveloping sphere of ether. In the boat we see the *Ark Navalis,* in the amara or gods, the Seven Rishi, and the men created by Manu, the Seven Pitris of Esoteric Buddhism.

Inasmuch as each Root Race is conceived to have come into being by similar process, in one of the other Hindu deluge myths, relating to the cycle when already mortals had undergone the separation of the sexes, the King of men is shown placing himself, his wife, the seven sages, and a pair of each of the animals in a boat, and being towed to safety by Vivasat in the form of a fish, by a cable attached to the horns of the fish corresponding to the porpoise, or *Delphin,* of the Greeks.

The persistence of the concept of Vivasat assuming the form of a fish to save Manu in the cosmic deluges, is indicated by the team of porpoises that were often represented in ancient Greek art, drawing the chariot of Poseidon, or the Latin Neptunis, the brother of Zeus and Hades, and "God of the Terrestrial Sea." Also Bel the alleged creator of the earth, the seas, and the deluges, of the Assyrian pantheon, is supposed to have accomplished his teachings through a series of "Fish Men," designated as Dagon. They corresponded to the Chaldean Annedoti of whom the first was the Musaros Oannes, described by Herodotus as presenting the aspect of a fish.

As shown by the studies of Layard, Smith, Lidzbarski, and Jablonski, the old Tiara of Bel Shamen was trinitic in form, resembling the mitre of present-day bishops, symbolizing a fish with an open mouth. Also, his vestment was the sleeveless garment known to the Hebrews as the *chim,* having the appearance of a fish's body. Designed to conceal the sex aspect of the spiritual teacher, also it was worn by the fish men along with the mitre. While the fish is still a sacred symbol of the Christian church, and the high prelates wear the tiara, the clerics of lesser degree still wear the white chasuble over the cassock to conceal the arm.

To those of the First Root Race, the Wisdom Philosophy ascribes an ethereal form, originally sexless and senseless, possessing the aspect of wraiths of huge size in comparison with the stature of modern men, and of the color of the Moon. In consonance with this concept the Brahmins or sacerdotal caste of the Hindus, symbolized the First Avatar, designated by them as Ma-t-s-ya, by the fish appropriate to the cycle when the first mortals are supposed to have floated, as it were, in an ethereal realm.

Of dreams vast studies have been made by modern psychologists. Also many mortals have insisted that they beheld ghosts. This Occult Science explains its concepts of the senseless shell, or astral reflection of departed beings, claimed by them to linger in matter. In view of the Hindu concepts of the evolution of man, and the creator called the 'Living Soul' in *Genesis,* more Psychologists may hold that in the dreams of ghosts there is a reminiscence of the original mortal of which the wisdom philosophy conceives.

The Sacred and Imperishable Land in which the First Root Race appeared, materialized gradually into the Hyper, or Second World Continent, called the Hyper-borea by the Greeks. Gradually too the First Root Race materialized to the point they produced the seeds of the Second Root Race described as smaller than the First, and as Bi-sexuals of a dark moon color who reproduced as do certain trees by spores, and who eventually acquired a coat of hair. In this type of Man the Hindus insist, is to be found the Missing Link of the modern Anthropologists. On the other hand they conceive of the Second Race as far less material than present man, just as the Second World Continent is said by them to have been of a Semi Astral type. Therefore, in their view, the Bi-sexual arboreals left no fossils.

Much has been written by modern Anthropologists about

the arboreal ancestors of men. Plato described them as possessing four arms and four legs. This may be taken merely to imply that the arboreal used four limbs either as legs or arms. This creature also was described as one that by folding its limbs could roll like a ball upon the earth. In this way escape was possible from enemies among the insentient animals, while the bisexual could travel upon the earth plane, as do quad-ru-ped apes of modern times.

Inasmuch as Esoteric Buddhism carries the Second Root Race back into the Secondary, or Age of Reptilians, when according to Geophysicists the earth was still of a semi-astral character, the historian must note the signs of the cancer, or crab, and of the *capricornus*, or goat, appearing in the Zodiac, to which the latitudinal circles called the Tropics, appearing on the earliest graphs of Gea, owe their names. Also he must note that just as the Brahmins symbolized the First Avatar by a fish, they symbolized the Second Avatar, Ku-r-ma by a tortoise, or amphibian appropriate to the form assigned the Second Root Race as amphibious in the true sense of occupying two planes—the ethereal and the material, bearing Mount Mandara on its back.

The question arises, therefore, as to the historical implications of the Tropics. Were they designed to indicate the zones of the terrestrial sphere, in, which first the 'Living Soul' of Hebraic cosmology evolved?

Certain it is, that in the Secondary, when the first uplifts brought into being the Huronian Range of Mountains in the northern zones, where also the first glaciation occurred, within the Equatorial Zone lying between the two Tropics of Cancer, vegetation was more prolific, while the climate would have favored the arboreals more than the two Temperate Zones in which the trace of the first mountains extends from Asia through the Arctic Zone into Canada.

In the gazeteers place names such as Fua-mu-la-ku (Equator, 62 E.), and Ku-i, the original designation of Shang Hai (31 N.22 E.), are given much more frequently in the warm-er climes, than to the north although Kur appears in Kur-a-din-ya in Mesopotamia and in Kur-di-s-t-ana, and the Kur-ile archipelago at the east of Asia, which was once within the Spiritual See of the Grand Khan Ku-b-la-i. Nevertheless in the gazeteers the place names presently applied to important cities of the earth in all parts, such as Kuai Lumpur (Maylasia), Kueling, Kuong, Kuldja, Kumamoto, Kure, Kurume, Kursk, Kutasi, Kuybyshev, in China, Japan and Siberia, and to the realm of the Kuban Cossacks. Just beyond the desert of Kara Ku-m is Ba-ku in the Caucasus. Also there is the Ku-en Lung Range of Asia, while Ku and Kur are more frequent in the synonymy of names in the Handbook of American Indians. Also the implications of the words *Ku-l-t-ur,* or *culture; Ku-miss,* applied to the milk of a mare; and *Kur,* or *cur,* implying a mongrel, are not to be ignored.

In the *Codex* Troano of the Maya wherein the destruction of the lands in the South Pacific is described, the Land of Kui is said to have vanished.

Finally there is the myth common to many peoples, and especially prevalent in the Equatorial Zone, that man saved himself from a deluge on the back of a turtle, while the group of islands on the Equator at 90 W. off the coast of Pe-ru bear the name Ga-la-pa-gos, implying the Tortoise, which both Humboldt and Darwin found to be held in high reverence by the peoples of South America.[1]

The oceanic survey of Sir Charles Ross had evoked a new discussion of Atlantis by Martin and others when in 1859 the Zoologist Sclater applied the name *lemure* to monkeys on the vanished land, known to the Romans as Lemuria. Just five years before Darwin and Wallace had expounded their theory of evolution. Acknowledging a missing link in the anthropogenesis of man, Sclater unwittingly had only encouraged the materialists by reason of the marked structural similarities between the Gibbon and mortals, when Haeckle undertook to localize the origin of his Ape man in the land mass that lay beneath the Indian Ocean.

THE PHILOSOPHIC HISTORY OF CIVILIZATION

Although Darwin and Wallace, as well as Leidy, Agassiz, de Quatrafrages, and others disposed of the Ape-Man as well as of the Monogenist theory of evolution, even today, among so-called educated people, persists the idea Darwin loaned himself to the concept of the Anthropoid Ape as the Missing Link which only the Hindus have undertaken to explain. The Student of civilization is left, therefore, to choose between the Bi-sexual and the Ape-Man or ascribing the Missing Link to the Hyper-borea as did the Ancient Greeks.

1 For Polynesian Mythology see Topical Bibliography.

CHAPTER V

THE ANDROGYNES OF THE THIRD ROOT RACE
THE LAND OF MU, THE ORIGINAL SEAT
OF THE GODS

THE ORIGINAL TYPE of the Third Root Race of which the Wisdom Philosophy conceived, though smaller than the Bisexuals, were gigantic androgynes who reproduced by eggs as did the insentient mammals.

Of a deep red color, and clothed with a shag of hair they were so described by the ancient Egyptians.

It is useless to dismiss all this as fancy. In accord with the description of the First Adam mentioned in *Genesis,* the first Gods of which the peoples of Mesopotamia had any knowledge are described in Assyrian tablets as hermaphrodites to which the following seven names are applied:

1. Zi
2. Zi-ku   'Noble Life, Director of Purity.'
3. Mir-ku, 'Noble Crown, Saviour from death of the gods created by him, and later of the dark race which he had created.
4. Lib-zu, 'The Wise among the Gods.'
5. Nissi
6. Su-hab
7. Hea, or Sa, (The synthesis of the God of Wisdom) identified in the Chaldean and Assyrian texts with Oannes-Dagon, 'the Fish Man', and known to the Hebrews as the mortal serpent, designated in the Hebraic Kaballa, as Sa, Sat, Set, Hea, Wa, etc.[1]

To these rishi of the Third Root Race are to be traced such names as Zend, Zulu, Zuni, Ku, Kui, Kurd, Ku-r-din-ya,

Suez, Tze, Tzin, Lydia and Libya. Also the Zend Language derived its name from Zu-en-d wherein the *Zu-en* or *en Zu* has ever been interpreted to mean 'the first Wisdom.'

The separation of the sexes, according to the Tamil or Adamic Calendar, did not occur until about 18,000,000 years ago. The Hindus carry the appearance of the Androgynes back into the Secondary, or the Age of Reptiles.

In the *Ramayana* it is disclosed that the Maya were great seamen, and that even when the moon was young, implying the infancy of the Serpent Cult, they navigated all of the Seven Seas of the earth, implying the cultural Sees of the Pitris. With this statement the Greek myth of Poseidon as 'God of the Terrestrial Sea', corresponding to the Roman Ne-p-t-u-n-is, is in complete accord. Yet it would be difficult indeed to understand how the Maya Ark was conveyed by the teacher of the Serpent Cult to all parts of the earth even with the charts in Chapter I before us.

It must be fixed in mind, however, that even if these charts be accurate, the most they show is that the areas depicted upon them were above the waters at times indicated. Manifestly they do not show other areas of the same period now lying in the ocean depths.

To understand how culture was spread over the Earth from the common source in the North to which de Quatrafrages traced it, one must envisage the antique earth as it would have appeared in a polar projection.[2]

On this map even the present land masses disclosing the roughly triangular configurations of North and South America, and of India, appear to reach southward like the fingers of a human hand. Moreover it shows how the countless relics of the antique earth dictate the sailing routes of today. The Third World Continent, however, included great land masses of which the present Continents are small remnants.

Although the Romans designated all the vanished realms as *Lemuria,* this name was an evolution from *Le-mu-rumel* which traces to the Mayavic La-mu, 'the Land of Mu' where-

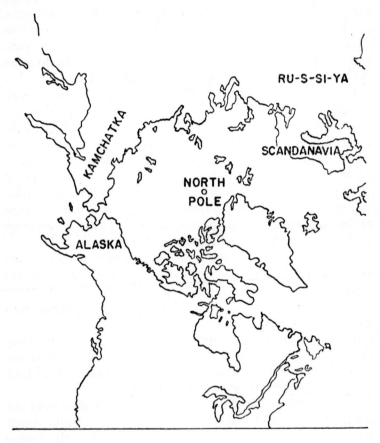

THE EARTH MASS AS VIEWED FROM THE NORTH POLE

in the M and the U are symbols of the Moon as the Mother
of the Earth and of the Divine Wisdom ascribed to the
Rishi, and the Pitris as the offspring of the Heavenly Twins
designated by the Mayavics as the Uratur. Therefore in the
graph of Gea, we find such place names as Ulster U-r-al,
'Uratur, Atlantis,' U-rum-chi; U-n-g-ar-ia; U-z-b-e-k; U-k-ra-
i-ne; Ur; U-g-an-da; Ur-a-gua-y; and U-tah.

From the kult of Uratur evolved the modern word *Kulture*
or *culture.*

As a people with a younger culture than that of the Asia-
tics, the Greek myth-makers before the time of Plato, professed no knowledge of the Hyper Sphere which was by then
the Hyper-Borea.[3] Accordingly they conceived of the Earth-
ark or Ea, having been begotten by Oceanus, implying the
Cosmic Sea, out of Ga-ea, impersonating the Mother Earth.
So this name G-a implies the G-round or ground constituting
the Terrestrial Sphere of the Lotus.

Gods designated as Ce-nu-bis, C-no-ph-is, Mo, Moo, Nu,
Nu-t, Neph, Nech, and by other variants, were the imperson-
ations of the Nether World.

The origin of man was ascribed by them to U-ra-nu-s, ever
identified with the Hindus Va-ru-na.[4] He is said to have begotten out of Ga-ea six sets of Titan twins, each including
a male and female, comporting with the Hindu and Assyrian
concepts of the Androgynes[5]. While the 12 Titans correspond
to the 12 signs of the Zodiac, the 6 sets of twins represented
the androgynes in the 6 zones, each 30° wide, into which the
earlier philosophers who designed the geodetic grid, divided
the surface of the spheroid. Later when the Tropics were
adopted the present 5 zones, Equatorial, North and South
Temperate, Arctic and Antarctic, came into being. But the
twins also implied a combination of the spiritual and material
man.

By Uranus the 12 Titans are said to have been cast into
Tartar-us to which the realm of Tartary and the Sea of Tartary at the Northeast of Asia, the alleged oldest daughter of

Oceanus out of Gea, as well as the Tartar or Tartar forebears of the Turks owe their name.

Said to have resented the cruelty of Uranus, the mythical Gaea is depicted as loaning her youngest son Cronus a sickle shaped knife corresponding to the Scimitar, as a symbol of the Crescent, with which to emasculate his father.

When he had done this and married his Sister Rhea, who he is said to have begotten out of his Mother Gea, he asserted as King Cronus, dominion over the entire earth.

Today the name of Cronus is present in Cronland and Cron-stadt, or Kronstadt on the Baltic, the port near which St. Petersburg was sited by Peter the Great. Often Rhea and the six great Gods of the Greek Pantheon are described as the offspring.[6]

With C-ro-nus in whose name appears, that of Uranus, has ever been associated the Sat-urn, or Sat-uranus 'the Serpent of Atlantis' revered in aboriginal Greece and Italy alike as the patron of agriculture. Appropriately the name Saturn was applied to the reddest of all the seven visible planets.

If we assume that the six cycles represented by the six sets of Titan Twins implied Mahayugas as indicated by the Sacred Tetraktis of Pythagoras, the five Mahayugas preceding the current one which will be shown to have begun in B.C. 2,596,-004, would carry the appearance of the Androgynes back to B.C. 24,196,004, allowing about 6,000,000 years for the evolution of the Androgynes into a fully sexed type of man. The fossils of the Androgynes, if in fact any were left, would be indistinguishable from those of the Gibbon. The remains of the Androgynes assuredly would have been consumed by the Reptilian and insentient mammalians on the earth, just as Cadavers today are devoured by wild beasts and birds of prey.

The tradition persists that there were no mountains on the present earth when men appeared upon it. This account accords with Geology which shows that the Secondary mountains had worn down to a mere trace when the Tertiary uplifts occurred. Since the earth was softer than now it would have been subject to rapid erosion.

Undoubtedly there would have been emissions of gas from the pockets beneath the crust of the earth during both the Secondary and the Tertiary uplifts. The noxious vapors would have pervaded the low places where the reptilians and insentient mammalians would have congregated in preference to the uplifting areas. This fully accounts for the perishing of the countless creatures of which fossils have been found. In this respect the history of the earth is so clear that many writers have seen in the partial clearing of the earth of creatures hostile to the existence of a more materialized man, a providential preparation of it for human tenancy. Whatever the fact eventually the Androgynes came to occupy every part of the Land of Mu. Thus from Mu-s-ko-vi, we pass to U-ru-mu-chi (Sin Kiang) beyond the Kara-ku-mu in the present Turkeystan, or the ancient realm of Syr. At the north of India is Ka-ra-Ko-ru-mu, south of which we find Mu-su and Mu-su-ra.

From Fu-a-mu-la-ku on the Equator (62° E.) east of Mo-za-mu-bi-que in Africa we pass to F-o-r-mo-sa and thence through the relics of the so-called Lost Continent of Mu, including Mu, Mu-lu-c-ca, the island of Moro and Sa-mo-a, to the Mu Stone South of Tasmania.

Crossing the South Pacific we come to Mu-so in Columbia and find the Mu-sos in the Andes to the South and North of the Mu-squi-to Coast. In Nicaragua is Mu-ra-ka, the domain of the Mu-hocks, on the West Coast of North America, and Ka-la-mu-zoo in M-i-chi-g-an. In the Gulf States are found the Mu-s-ko-gi, and in the Adi-rond-ak, the Sha-ta-mu (Hudson River) near which are Mon-tau-k and Mo-na-d-nock. At the East of Savannah and South of Nova Scotia are the Bermu-das. In Spain is the province of Mu-r-cia, and in the Irish Sea near Mu-n-ster, as in the Caribbean, is found an island called Mo-na. In Ireland is Mu-n-s-ter, and in Germany both Mu-n-ster and Mu-ni-ch at the West of Mu-s-ko-vi. To the South in Turkey is Mu-s-tagh, and in Mesopotamia is Mu-ga-ya or Ur, with the port of Mu-s-ca-t in Arabia.

The grand circuit of these names is but a suggestion of what

[49]

the graph of Gea reveals respecting the Land of Mu. To say exactly when the Androgynes occupied any part of the Third World Continent or when the Mayavic names were applied to the localities which still bear them, is, of course, impossible, for still two groups of these pre-Aryans, namely the Pi-sha-cha of Ceylon and the Flat Heads of Australia are found upon the earth. Nevertheless it is possible to see exactly how the instruction of the Androgynes was accomplished.

While Darwin, Wallace, Agassiz and others disposed of the Monogenist theory of evolution which conceived all mortals evolving in a single area and adhered to the Polygenist theory according with the Hindu concept of the seven pitris, the researches of many great explorers such as de Nordenskjiold and Nadaillac and the researches of de Quatrafrages, left no room to doubt that the common seat of human culture was in the Polar Coronet shown on Map II in Chapter I, known as the Qu-en-land to the dark forebears of the Pi-ra-ti who spoke the Queenland language and from whom the Teutonic peoples had evolved.[7]

Thus within the Arctic Circle still lie the relics of the Polar Coronet in the Arctic Z-one, or Ze-land, of which the name is preserved by Zeeland and the Zu-y-d-er Zee of Holland, and Ze-a-land in Denmark. Also formerly the Shetland and the Faro Islands were called Zeland, while the Netherlands owe their name to the fact that once they were part of the Nether, or Northern land mass along with No-r-g-e, or Nor-w-a-y, the Svalbard Islands, Ya-n Ma-y-en Island, and Bear Island between Spitzbergen and Norway, the three groups of Islands called Zemblas, W-r-angel Island at the North of Ka-ma-sha-T-Ka, as well as the so-called Canadian Barrier.

In Z-land, of course, is to be seen the Ah Zhai Land, or A-zi-t-lan, to which the Zuni and other Pueblo groups in A-ri-zo-na, Naguals of M-e-x-a-tla(o), and the Ma-ya-x of Y-u-ca-tan trace back their origin through the seven serpents; nor is it difficult to see that the name of Bear Island, the concept of the Beowulf people of the ancient Teutonic realms, and of the Mu-sko-Vites as the people of the Bear, all trace back to the likeness of the shaggy red Androgynes and the *tlao* or bear.[8]

Before considering further the evolution of civilization, it is imperative to fix in mind the basis of the ancient Greek concept of the Arctic realm which they called the Hyperborea, as one of perpetual sunshine and verdure prior to the present Greek Ice Age. Thus although a glaciation occurred in the Secondary, geology shows that Zeland, or the Queen's Land, was of such warmth that in it flourished palm trees and the magnolias, of which specimens have been found beneath "Greenland's Icy Mountains."[9]

---

1 See *Topical Bibliography; Assyrian Researches*, SMITH (1876). Also works of Sir Henry Rawlinson who also conceived of the First and Second Root Races, and of the Third Root Race, or the first Autochthonous Race, as the first on the present earth.

2 The copyrighted Maps here included are reproduced with the permission of C. S. Hammond & Company, Inc., New York City.

3 Hyper, 'without measure.'

4 U-ra-nu-s, 'Uratur, the creator of the Nether Serpent.' Va-ru-na, 'The Sheaf of Ru—the Nether Ark.'

5 T-i-t-a-n, 'the Tree of Life, the Spirit of the Tau, the ark Navalis.'

6 The name of Rhea—Rhe-a, 'the Rishi-ha the Earth Ark' was preserved by the ancient Kingdom of Rhe-g-i-um which included the Rh-i-n-e and the Rh-o-n-e.

7 The name Queenland was eventually given to the Northern part of Australia which geology traces back to the Secondary Age.

8 At W-y-is-a-ling in W-is-con-sin on the same meridian with Y-en-a-see in northern Siberia, and T-en-nee-se close to which is Ya-ma-see in Georgia, is to be seen one of the oldest effigy mounds in North America, long believed to represent our elephant, but now recognized as the effigy of the bear.

9 Greenland as late as 1505 was deemed by European explorers, a part of Labrador, ever called Greenland until that name was applied to it before the age of Erik the Red who in the year of Millennial Expectations, A. D. 1,000, was appointed Viceroy of the island, for the purpose of attracting colonists. The physical character of the Arctic realms, therefore, fully explains the references in the Odes of Pindar to the Green Isle. The character of modern American history also is shown by the fact that from A. D. 1100 Vinland as a possession of the Islandic Republic found in the Tenth Century was deemed within the Holy See of Rome. See *Catholic Dictionary* (1887). In a word Vinland merely implied a Christian Vineyard corresponding to the biblical vineyard of Noah, indicating the part to which the Monk Leif Ericson had been dispatched as a bearer of the Cross by the King of Norway as a vassal of Rome.

CHAPTER VI

THE FIRST ORACLES OF THE
MAYAVIC PHILOSOPHIC ARK

THE RECENT ATTEMPT that was made to account for the mixed blood of the Punics by creating a race of Mediterraneans, better to explain the so-called Indo-Europeans, and the assigning to this imaginary race of the Egyptians, the Syrian forebears of the Phoenicians, the Hittites, the Pelasgic predecessors of the so-called Celtic Greeks, the Albanians, the Ligurian Gauls, the Berbers, the Ba-squi or Ba-s-ki of the Pyrenees, and the Goidhal migrants to Ireland who produced the Gaels, was but another case of modern fancy.

Although of mixed blood, these peoples had in common the philosophic concepts of the mythical monsters which play so large a part in Indo-European Mythology. Significantly all of them cherished the mythical bird called the Roc of which the Irish Sham-roc is a symbol. A sham in the true sense inasmuch as this green-tri-foil was produced by no actual species of the Vegetable Kingdom, the Sham-roc was a symbol not only of the Trinitic principle of the Sacred Lotus, but green in color corresponded to the mortals of the earth in the cycle of the Third World Continent of Mu, or the Ru of the Third Root Race of which the Serpent Cult conceived. Among the ancient Greeks the Roc was known as the Pi-ro-s, 'the Spiritual Bird of the Serpent,' known to the Punics generally and their Arabian kinsmen, as the Pho-enix, or the red bird said to have arisen immortal out of the fire and the ashes of the past. Because in fact it was a symbol of the primordial Serpent Cult, just as was the Sphinx of S-ph-enix, 'the Serpent Philosophy of the Giants,' the connection between the Phenix and the Sphinx is plain. Thus, eventually the Sphinx was

IV. Two of the largest Colossi on the Grand Rapa (Easter Island) (Illustration from *Voyage autour du Monde*, La Perouse, 1797).

V. The Watcher

Franconia Notch, New Hampshire
Near Mount Washington
Reverse and see the profile of the Celestial Face.

carved in stone by the Egyptians, the Nagals of Burma, and the Naguals of Arizona and Mexico who, all alike, owed their original culture to the teachers of the Maya Ark.[1]

The concepts of the spiritual bird upon which those of the Ark Angels, the Cherubim, and the Seraphim, are based, go far back, into the past. Always man has seen the face of the woman in the moon that, as the light of the sun spread over the orb, appeared to evolve into the visage of a man. This phenomenon accorded with the Hindu concept of the D-a-h-ana, 'the Divine Ark of the Heavenly Mother,' whose spiritual light the Moon as the Diva, or the Queen of Heaven, was supposed to reflect upon the earth by night. The Mayavics, however, designated the ever widening circle as O-r-n-y-t-h.[2]

The vast antiquity of the concept of the Ornyth is indicated by the fact that the Greeks never deemed Athena the off-spring of the philandering Zeus. Instead, they looked upon her as the self-perpetuating Mother of Wisdom who sprang from the head of Zeus in the sense that she was his thought rather than his creation. Therefore, she was not included among the six great gods produced by Cronus and Rhea. Moreover, she was not deemed, as were Ares and Mars, the patron of war, in the material sense. Therefore, in her quiver are seen the arrows representing the shafts of light with which alone wisdom could dispel the darkness of human ignorance, the passions, and the prejudices born of it. Yet, she appears also armed with a spear implying that sometimes wisdom demands that force be employed to defend and advance human enlightenment.

To say the least the philosophic concepts associated with Ornyth were philosophically of the highest order. Nor were they high in the philosophic sense alone.

In the early passages of the *Rig Veda,* with which the Greek Myth of Uranus and the *Hebraic Kaballa* of Lucifer accord, is described the falling of spiritual being into matter. With the myth of Lucifer, the angel said to have sacrificed himself to bring light unto mortals, the mystic Grotius, the alleged Father of International Law, was thoroughly conversant. Like others he saw in Athena, and in the Ark Angel Michael, champions of the law of karma, as implied by their weapons.³ Also he knew that in 1552, Sebastian Cabot, the Grand Pilot of Edward VI, had dispatched Richard Chancellor on an expedition to Muskovy, by way of Nova Zembla. Long since he had escaped from imprisonment in Holland to France when he was appointed by Queen Christina the official historian of Sweden, and published his history of the Low Countries. Knowing the implications of the name Christianna applied to the ancient capital of Norway, as the contemporary of Spinoza and Descartes, he pointed out that the ancient Queenland language was common to Scandinavia and America. In doing so he in effect said to the scholars of the West who, unlike Andreae, VanVondel, and Spinoza, were concerning themselves only with the East: "Look ye to the isles of Sval-bard beyond the Island of the Bear!"⁴

In the Queenland Language *S-val-bard* implies the Serpent Bird of the mystical realm of V-al-halla—the spiritual realm beyond Hell where the Va-l-k-y-r-s were supposed to dwell, while Spitzbergen is commonly translated as 'sharp mountains', spits, 'mouth,' and berg, 'bird,' together imply an oracle of the Rishi, or the Spiritual Birds.

In the La-pa-t-eve Sea appear the three groups of *Z-emblas* which extend from S-val-bard to W-r-angel Island at the north of Ka-ma-sha-t-ka. The word No-va-ya, prefixed to *Z-embla* implies No, or Ce-no-b-is, the Greek impersonation of the nether world from which the Ya, implying the first mortals, were conveyed to the earth. In addition to this, the word *embla* denotes the mythical Ash Tree to which the Norse ascribe their origin. Therefore, *Z-embla* has exactly the same significance as *Tau-X* appearing in the names of countless mountains on the earth ever revered as natural symbols of Divinity. Thus in Assyria we find the Taux Shina, and in Circ-asia, 'the circus of Asia', we find the grand Ten Taux. To many mountains are applied names containing the word *sha,* to which the titles *shaw* and *pasha* are to be traced. Sometimes the *sha* appears as *shi,* 'the Serpent of the Holy Spirit.' Among the most holy mountains on the earth are the Trinity of Ka-ra-ko-ru-m at the north of Ka-shi-mere, including Gu-sha-brun, and Ma-sha-brun, exceeded in height only by K^z, and Guar-a-sin-g-ar, 'the Mother Mountain of the earth', presently called Mount Everest. At the north of Tibet is the great peak of Khan T-en-g-ri, symbolizing the Rishi.

Undoubtedly Roger Williams was guided by Grotius in the compilation of his dictionary of the Indian language in which he interpreted many of the Queenland words. And certainly Francisco Ximines, the Guatemalan convert who compiled the Legends of Guatemala, 'the Queenland' in the *Popul Vuh* (1750), only to have it suppressed for a century, supported all that Grotius had written. As far as we know, therefore, the German Volk was the first modern anthropologist to visit the Sval-bard Group. Soon the Swedish explorer de Nordenskjiold, heeding the words of Grotius, explored these and other Arctic realms including those in Russia and Karelia at the north of Siberia.

Today we know that the island of Puna, off the coast of Peru, the Galapagos Group on the Equator, and the Grand Rapa, called Easter Island, thirteen hundred miles west of Peru and ever claimed by the Peruvians, are all relics of the vanished Pacific continent. Whether or not the Andeans all came from the North, or some from the Pacific continent, the identity of their language and their gods with those of Africa and Egypt has been demonstrated.[5]

The identity of Ornyth, the Sybil of Norse Mythology and the Pythoness of the primordial Greek mysteries, indicates very plainly the implications of Tri-s-ma-g-is-t-u-s, the predecessor of Hermes.[6]

The symbols of T-ris-magistus and Hermes as well as those of Ornyth and Athena are readily interpreted.[7]

The Greek designation of the primordial cycle of culture as the Age of the Mythical Pan, the Python, the Ark of the

North, or Nether, refers to the cycle in which the Mu-s-e-s were the teachers in the land of Mu of the Arts and Sciences.[8]

1 *Die Herabkunft des Feuers,* KUHN (1860).

2 Because Pallas Athena, goddess of Wisdom and War of the Greeks, was ever associated with the Ornyth which was symbolized by her halo, a modern zoologist gave to the owl, or the Ornith, the name Pallas Athena, since the owl, like the woman in the moon, was deemed down the ages to be able to see better by night than by day. *Zoological Notes,* BOLE (1822).

Pa-ll-a-s, 'The Philosophy (para) of the Els (gods), of the Ark of the Serpent.' A-the-na, 'the Ark of the Gods of Ana.'

3 See *The First English Bible,* CAEDMON (675); *Lucifer,* JOOST VON VONDEL (1654); and *Paradise Lost,* MILTON (1660?); *Adamo,* ANDREINI (1654); and *Adamus Exul,* GROTIUS (1611), all based on the Hebraic Kaballa. Also see *Prometheus Vincit,* AESCHYLUS, and *Prometheus Bound,* MILTON, and *Prometheus Unbound,* SOUTHEY.

4 In 1477 while visiting Mecca, Juan Caboto was informed of the ancient trade route from Novaya Zembla to Ka-ma-sha-t-ks. When, therefore, after reaching England he separated from Columbus who went on to Iceland and explored the Gulf stream at the west which English, French, Scandinavian, German, Polish, Basque, and Portuguese fishermen had been following since 1420 to Labrador, while searching out the Northwest Passage described by Roger Bacon in 1266, when the Polos were in Peking writing to Venice of the flow of gold and silver into China from beyond Japan, he may have visited Novaya Zembla. Concurrently with the works of Grotius, the mystic Roger Williams, was compiling a revealing Dictionary of the Indian Language, being an initiate of the Indian Mysteries of Nana-Bo-Za-Ha, which were enshrined at Nara-g-ana-sett. Of these mysteries Ma-sa-soit, 'Yellow Feather,' was the Grand Sa-chem in Ma-si-chu-s-setts. He was the friend of both John Smith and Williams. To the latter it was his subordinate Sachem, C-ana-o-n-i-cus, who gave Rhode Island to Williams.

Here note that John Smith, Roger Williams, and William Penn, were all familiar with the history of America. See the Memoirs of William Penn, *Annals of Pennsylvania.*

The idea that the Colonies planted in the West Indies, Panama, at Rio de Janeiro, Santa Fé, St. Augustine, Fort Caroline, Roanoke Island, Jamestown Island, Kennybunkport, and Plymouth, were founded in a virtual *terra incognita* is without foundation of fact. In 1498 John Cabot had erected a fort at the present site of Ft. Monroe, and in 1528 de Allyon had erected another, San Michael, on Jamestown Island. In 1571 the Spanish Mission of Axacan was located on the Rappahannock.

JOHN SMITH'S *History of New England and Virginia* (1620) has been so altered that the facts known to him do not appear in it. Yet, in an opening passage he refers to the voyages to the West of Prince Madoc of Wales in 1170 and 1171. In vain attempts have been made to trace the name of Ma-t-o-ac, and Appomattox to the Welsh. See *The Welsh Discovery of America,* BOWEN (1885).

In the veins of Ma-t-o-ac was the blood of both the Re-na-pe of Virginia, akin to the Re-na-pe of Massachusetts, as well as that of the Sioux. Consequently her alternate name was the Siouan name Po-ca-hone, 'the joyous one' while her Re-na-pe name, comporting with the falls of the Powhatan, implied 'dancing water.' Among the seven hills on which Richmond is located are Chimborazo and Shako. When Newport and Smith arrived at the Falls of Powhatan in 1607 before founding Jamestown, they found the brother of Po-ca-hontas as the Sachem of the local Powhatans bearing the title of Taux, and as a symbol of friendship and peace carved the cross on the rocks in the rapids. Another brother of Po-ca-hontas was the Sachem of the shrine of Ac-co-m-ac on the eastern shore of Virginia, bearing the same name as the site near Boston where John Smith had located Plymouth near Plymouth Rock. On the Rio Grande is another Ac-co-m-a where a great eagle as the symbol of the Divine Spirit is carved on the rock, just as avars are found in rock carvings throughout the United States. See *Rock Carvings,* GARDNER (1898). Accordingly, the spread eagle appears on one side of the crest of the United States, while the pyramid resembling those found in Mexico, Yucatan, Central America, and Peru, appears on the other side. In his two great works, *The First Republic* (1892) and the *Genesis of the United States,* DR. ALEXANDER BROWN of Richmond, presented material rendering obsolete the *Discovery of America* (1892) and other works by JOHN FISKE, as well as those of Parkman and Prescott. See also *The Forest Primeval,* CONWAY SAMS (1916).

⁵ See *Africa and the Discovery of America,* WEINER (1924) for which the author was figuratively crucified; and the *Origin and Evolution of Man,* JAMES CHURCHWARD, F.R.S. (1911) in which the futile attempt was made to trace the human race to the pygmies. Alexander Humboldt suggested that migrations from the Pacific occurred. Enough has been said to show that the claim by the unscholarly though sensational writer, JAMES CHURCHWARD, in his various works dealing with the so-called *Lost Continent of Mu* respecting the origin of man in the South Pacific, is without foundation of fact.

⁶ T-ris-magistus 'the Taux, the Rishi, Magistus.' Her-m-e-s, 'Ornyth, Mother of en Su, the first Sybil.'

⁷ Magistus implies the Divine knowledge ascribed to those upon whom the titles of Monarch and Majesty came to be conferred. In the royal regalias appeared the mound, a globe surmounted by a *tau,* symbolizing both the earth and the moon. Also the regalia included a sword and a mace. Synonymous with T-ris-magistus was Hermes, the patron of history, the arts and sciences, and the messenger of the gods was shown with casques displaying the avars of the spiritual bird Ornyth, or Athena. Around the staff of Hermes-Trismagistus, or the *caduceus,* is entwined the two-headed serpent corresponding to the Twins of the Divine Lotus.

The *Tri* in Tri-s-magistus corresponds to both the Spiritual Trinity and the cycle of the Third Root Race.

Trismagistus and Hermes were known to the Egyptians as Thoth, and eventually the Assyrians elevated Ea to their upper Triad as the god of history.

⁸ The word *ca-s-que* meaning helmet, derives from the lunar ark of the Queen, as the Egyptian name T-h-o-t-h derives from 'Trismagistus-Hermes-the Serpent Tree, Ha.'

Inasmuch as Mohammedanism traces back to Mosaism, and *Moses* derives from Mu-sha, or Mu-sa, as does the name Je-bul Musa applied to Mount Sinai, the crescent of Islam corresponding to Ornyth, indicates that the Mo-s-lem or Mu-s-lem faith, like the names Mu-sha, Musa, Mo-ham-et, Mu-ham-ed, and Mu-rad traced back to the Serpent Cult. Thus in the Muslim spiritual teachers called Mo-ll-ahs, Mu-ll-ahs, and Mu-e-z-zin, and in the monks or Mu-n-ks of the Buddhists and Christians, we find the counterpart of the Muses, just as the name *mon-key* or *mun-key* traces back to the anthropoids designated by Sclater as le-mu-res. In the L-a-m-a of the Lamaist Hierarchy we see the Spiritual Hierarchs whose name traces back to the Logos of the Ark of the Mother of the Universe-Ana.

The great French scholar, Montalambert, dealt fully with the pre-Christian munks, tracing Mona-chism back to the dim past, because in fact there were organized bodies of spiritual teachers from the time that the Maya-v-i-c-s first embodied their philosophy in the Ark of the Maya common to both hemispheres. A study of the ancient mysteries will show that the first munks were in fact initiates who preserved the knowledge ascribed to the Muses and the Divine magic ascribed to Trismagistus.

What has been shown indicates the human agency through which knowledge was transmitted from age to age.

CHAPTER VII

THE AGE OF PAN AND THE GARDEN OF EDEN
THE ADAMITES

CIVILIZATION had not advanced when the Age of Pan began and stone structures appeared as the temples of the first Mona-chi-s-t-s. It was in sylvan temples called *transparencies,* so-called because the celestial sphere formed their domes, that the first spiritual teachers instructed their flocks. Therefore, to the *Druvyd,* or the oak, still called the Tree of Jove, is traced the name Druid. The *Canastra,* or chestnut, and other sacred trees mark the shrines to which Pan is shown luring the human denizens of the forest with his magic pipe that sounded the notes of the musical scale corresponding to the sounds of the seven vowels, 'words of the gods' upon which all alphabets were based.[1]

The sudden affrights to which the pupils of Pan are described as being subject are readily explicable. Still huge Mammalians existed upon the earth. Inevitably the Androgyne Arboreals would have been a people of marked temerity, hard for their teachers to control since the insentient creatures vied with them for the nuts and fruits of the primeval forests.[2]

The universal concept of Ornyth in the age to which the Greek name Pan, implying universality, appropriately was applied, fully explains the featherations common to the primative peoples of the earth. Moreover in their colorations based on the cardinal colors of the solar spectrum was a form of language. Ornyth also explains the Egyptian conception of Mother Moo, ever associated with the symbol of the Sphinx, and also with the sacred symbol of the winged Scarab that rolls its egg in a ball of mud corresponding to the mortal egg and the terrestrial sphere. Eventually feathers appeared in the crowns of the Pharaohs of Egypt and also in those of the Incas of Peru.

We may safely assume that just as the Scarab concealed its eggs so did the Androgynes.

In accord with the concept of Ornyth-Athena, both the Japanese and the Polynesians ascribed their origin to an egg laid by a great bird, said by the latter to have been a dark tern. As the Greek gods are shown with avars attached to their casques, the Pi-ra-ti from whom the Three Brothers of Scandinavia descended, not only fashioned their larger craft to resemble dragons, but their lesser ones in the form of cranes and serpents. As the Saxons adorned their homes with the wings of the raven, the Vi-kings, or spiritual rulers of the Norse, displayed the dragon's wings in their casques. For the same reason the Nagals of Burma came to be called dragons, while the dragon is a common symbol today among all the Sinitics. Thus in the banner of the Chinese are found five dragons symbolizing the five Root Races of the Wisdom Philosophy. In America the symbol of the Naguals in the time of Cortez was still the Serpent Bird from which they took their names.

Whether or not there were winged dragons on the earth in the Age of Pan, certainly there were fossils of the winged serpent known to modern Zoology as the Archeoptorix.

While it is not proposed to anticipate the metaphysical concepts of the Hebrews who eventually evolved, in *Genesis* is found much of a purely anthropological nature fully supporting the anthropogenesis of the Hindus to which the student of civilization must look as a guide to what occurred in the Age of Pan.

Genesis, however, was never designed to be a detailed history of man as a whole, but instead merely to preserve the record of those from whom the Hebrews were descended. In the great Scripture ascribed to Moses each chapter had reference to a cycle, as do the numbered paragraphs, 'philosophy pictures.' Preceding some of the passages appears the symbol indicating that the following passage deals with a new subject in a new cycle.

The Hebrew scribes were far more logical than the Greeks whose mythmakers plumped the Titan Twins down upon the earth without a cosmological prelude. Thus the Hebrew scribes first described the creation of the universe, then the creation of the Mineral, Vegetable, and Animal Kingdoms in proper order. This having been done *Man* in the plural sense is dealt with. It is to be noted that in paragraph eight of *Genesis* 2 appears the sign denoting the hiatus between the description of the living soul and the instruction of man. Therefore, *Genesis* cannot be construed as denying the Hindu concepts of the bi-sexual as the link between the ethereal creation and the Androgyne.

In the passages dealing with the instruction of the Androgynes the language of the Tree Cult eventually evolved out of the Mayavic Serpent Cult by the Hebrews, inevitably was employed by the Mosaic scribes.

"⁋ 8 And the Lord God planted a garden eastward in Eden."

The *E* in the name E-den employed in this passage refers to the Earth of the Ethiopian Ark, or Ea, ever deemed by the Hebrews the equivalent of the Aryan En-ya-lius and the Italic J-u-p-i-t-e-r and the Mosaic J-e-h-o-v-a-h, all of which traced to the Mayavic En-Zu, 'the first wisdom,' which was the name applied by the Hebrew prophets to Mount Sin-a-i, 'Sin, the Spirit of the Arya', commonly deemed a symbol of the Lofty Head. By the Hindus the seven Rishi, and the seven Pitris, to which trace the septenary names Jupiter and Jehovah, were designated as Nara-g-ana and Nara-y-ana, respectively. By the older Hebrews the Rishi and the Pitris were synchronized in the philosophic concept of Y-a-v-e-y-g-h, implying the serpent in human nature.

The word *den* traces back to the Sumerian word *din,* and implies a human habitation such as the dens of the arboreals.

Eventually it came to imply a sacrosanct place, such as a walled-in close, or reservation.

It is not said in *Genesis* 2:8 that only one garden was planted in the den of E. On the contrary, the planting of *"a garden"* eastward in Eden only indicates that a garden was planted at such a point.

In an esoteric scripture writing such as *Genesis,* the actions of the spiritual teachers of men in their dealings with their flocks logically would be ascribed to "the Lord God."

In the remaining part of *Genesis* 2:8, it is said in reference to the garden:

"And there he put the man who he had formed."

The statement that man was "put" in the garden, like a later one that the man who was "put in the garden" was returned to the earth "from which he had been taken," is conclusive that the Scribes did not intend to convey the idea of man being created in the single garden planted "eastward" on the earth. Therefore, the idea that all men were sprung from an individual born in that part of Mesopotamia which was called E-din-nu by the Sumerians ages before there were any Hebrews, is without Scriptural warrant.

In the particular garden that was located "eastward in Eden," the Lord God, according to the Scripture, "made to grow every tree that is pleasant to the sight, and good for food; the tree of life also in the midst of the garden, and the tree of Knowledge of good and evil."

Vast researches indicate that the *Tree of Knowledge of Good and Evil* was in fact the Tir, 'Tree of the Spirit of Ru', to which traces the name *Din-Tir* applied by the Sumerians to the site which eventually came to be called Babylon, 'gate of the gods,' by the Greeks, and A-r-i-z-z-a-g-a, 'Wisdom Seat,' by the Chaldeans, known to the Assyrians as Ka-dim-ma-ra-h, 'life at the tree.' Also *E-din-nu* came to be called *Kur-din-ya* and *Kara-din-ya.* Therefore, it is manifest that peoples of different tongues successively appeared in the garden which the Hebrews eventually called Eden.

Paragraphs 10-14 of *Genesis* 2 constitute a digression by the Scribes which has proved among the most confusing and misleading parts of this scripture.

"10 And a river went out of Eden to water the garden."

Here the reference is to the figurative stream of magic knowledge embodied in the Maya Ark, that poured into the Din Tir.

"From thence it was parted, and became into four heads."

The reference here is not to races, or peoples, but to the mysteries that sprang from the Mayavic Ark. Therefore, the Scribes continuing in the present tense described the four heads as they existed in their time, naming them as the Pison, the Gihon, the Hiddekel and Euphrates implying respectively the mysteries which had been founded by the peoples of red blood, the Ethiopians of the Nile, the peoples of Irania, and those of Mesopotamia.

Having made this digression, the Scribes returned to their narrative of the past.

"15 And the Lord God took the man, and put him into the Garden of Eden to dress it and to keep it."

"16 And the Lord God commanded the man, saying, Of every tree of the garden thou mayest freely eat:

"17 But of the tree of knowledge of good and evil, thou shalt not eat of it: for in the day that thou eatest thereof thou shall surely die."

Here the plain implication is that some of the Androgynes were initiated in the mysteries to serve as Levites, or guardians of the Maya Ark.

With the Androgynes spreading over the earth as mere nomads, terrified by the uplifting of vast areas out of the sea such as those which occurred in the Secondary, countless witch doctors claiming wisdom as did the Black Magicians, or the evil Daityas of a later cycle, would have instituted the rite of cannibalism which was still deemed a sacred one among many savages in historic times including the Aztecs of the Columbian Age. Thus the inhibition against the eating from the Tir is readily explicable.

We have already seen that the Din Tir cannot be interpreted to imply the only garden planted in Eden. Therefore, Assyria was deemed by its inhabitants the garden of Se-mi-ra-mis, and at Nineva eventually would be reared the wondrous Hanging Garden as a symbol of the garden in which the forebears of the peoples in those parts were instructed. Moreover, the ancient Greeks ever associated Ogyges with a vanished world. Therefore, Sicily and the Atlantic Islands were deemed parts of Ogygia the name of which was applied by Plutarch to Greenland. This leads to the conclusion that the Oak of Ogyges in Hebron in the western part of Canaan where Abraham is said to have reared an altar, was in fact a sacred tree in the Age of Pan, and that a similar shrine existed at the mystical pool of Siloam, 'the lake of Sin,' just east of the Oak of Ogyges where arose Ya-ru-siloam, eventually called Sa-lem by the Hebrews who looked upon it as a place of spiritual salvation long before it became known as Jerusalem. Then, too, from time immemorial Mu-ga-ya which came to be called Ur, was deemed the seat of the Moon God Sin.

"And the Lord said, it is not good that man should be alone; I will make him an help-meet for him."

After pointing out that the Lord God had formed every beast of the field, and every fowl of the air, for the first time the name *Adam,* which was coined by the Mosaic scribes from the adjective *adammah* implying redness, is used. Thus the scripture continues, showing that the animals and fowl were brought to Adam to be named by him. "And whatsoever Adam called every living creature, that was the name thereof." But Adam is a highly cryptic eponym. While ADAM is to be interpreted as the Ark of the Divine Light of the Mother, A-dam implies Ana, the dam, or the Mother of Heaven. Of Adam the metathesis is MADA, 'the Mother Ana, the Divine Light,' while Ma-da implies the Mother, or the Diva of which the Maya philosophic Ark conceived.

Inasmuch as it was manifestly impossible for all the creatures of the animal kingdom to have been brought to the Garden of Eden, some there are who see in the animals to which Adam is said to have given names, merely the animistic signs of the Zodiac upon which the mysteries of the Maya Ark were based. It is not said, however, in the passage quoted, that Adam only appeared in the garden of Eden. Inasmuch as the eponym Adam referred to the teachers of the Maya mysteries at every Tree of Knowledge throughout the world, logically the eponymous Adam could have named all the animals of the earth since the name of the Maya appears in every clime.

The Wisdom Philosophy does not conceive of the avatars as having appeared concurrently with their respective Root Races. Inasmuch as they were deemed the saviors of men in the philosophic sense of spiritual teachers, it would be illogical to conceive of them as appearing before the need for them existed. Because Jesus is said to have gone to the cross, and Mahomet to have died at a specified time no one conceives of the cycles of Christendom and Islam as having expired. Who shall say when the cycle of a spiritual teacher ends? As a pebble cast upon a placid pool sets in motion rings of force that expanding carry beyond the visible bounds of the water's surface, so it is with the teachings of men whose good deeds and bad deeds alike induce effects that cannot be limited to a particular time. Therefore, the cycle of an avatar must be viewed as corresponding to the cycles of influence we associate today with Go-Tau-Ma Buddha, Jesus of Nazareth and Mahomet.

According to the Brahmins, the Third Avatar was Va-ra-ha whose name is well preserved.[3] To him was assigned the symbol of the boar.

All cryptic eponyms in the sacred scriptures of antiquity, are subject to more than one, and often to as many as seven interpretations. Here it is sufficient to note that A-dam, besides its implications of color, was a peculiarly appropriate eponym for the Androgyne who like all the avatars was deemed a helpmate of the primordial peoples. In Adam then, is to be seen but the name applied to the teachers of the Androgynes, or the Dams of men, and in it a mere eponym also derived from A-d-am, 'the Ark of the Diva, the Moon Mother of the Amara, (immortals called Rishi in the Wisdom Philosophy.)'

---

[1] The word *camp* derives from *canastra,* or *chester.* Therefore, Winchester, Sinchester, Chichester, Colchester, Portchester, and other cities owe their names to the chesters or camps around the sacred trees, while the castanet, one of the first musical instruments, like the first bells was employed to scare off evil spirits. The Hippo-canastra, 'horse chestnut,' derived its name from the scar on the twig left by each stem of a leaf, forming a perfect horseshoe displaying the nails. Inasmuch as horses existed in America along with elephants in the cycle of the Ru, as well as in Asia during the cycle of Pan, a spike-team of splendid horses are shown drawing the chariot of Poseidon, or Neptunis, god of the terrestrial sea, and also similar teams of delphins, or porpoises, since the realm of this god included both oceans and continents. Compatible with the spiritual concept of Trinity also the Tri-dent of Neptune included three prongs. The name *Mu-s-t-ang* applied by the Spanish colonials to the wild horses of America traces back to the land of Mu.

[2] Eventually the sacred trees were called by the Aryans *T-ara* so that the Japanese word *tairo* implies 'temple.' To the music of Pan's pipe traces the concept that music has power to soothe the savage breast. In the Satyrs depicted among Pan's pupils one recognizes the symbol of the hybrid male-female of the Androgynes, also symbolized by the sign of the Capricornus in the Zodiac employed by the Greek mapmakers to mark the Tropics of Capricorn beyond the zone of which at the North lay the land of the Z-one, or the Zone of the Spiritual Ark, which constituted the Hyper-borea of the Greeks.

[3] See Va-ra-o at the North Cape of Europe, Varangerford in Norway, Varberg in Sweden, Varde in Denmark, Varingia, Varcar, and Vakrf in Russia, Var, Vrades, and Varennes in France, Varalja, Varanne, and Varad in Hungary, Varos in Bosnia, Varallo, Varazzi, and Varaita in Italy, Varosh in Cyprus, Varna in Bulgaria, Varel in Germany, Vardar in Turkey, Varella in the Malay States, Vara in the Fiji Islands, Vaa in Madagascar, Valparaiso in South America and countless other place names in North America where many similar tribal names appear.

A Roman Emperor bore the name Varus, while Va-ti-c-an is to be translated as 'the Soul of the Cross, the Spirit of the Celestial Mother, Ana.'

CHAPTER VIII

THE SEPARATION OF THE SEXES
THE CULT OF IS-IS, OR THE COW WORSHIP
THE RU INHERIT THE LAND OF MU

IT APPEARS from *Genesis* 2 that after the Androgynes had
been furnished with Adam as a 'helpmate', the Lord caused,
not the Androgynes in general, but Adam to fall into a "deep
sleep."

The implication of this is plain from what follows. During the deep sleep, the rib was taken from man, not from
Adam alone, to form the Wo-man or womb man. The deep
sleep of Adam, therefore, may be taken to imply the period
of evolution during which occurred the physical transformation of the Androgynes into the fully sexed type of man.

To exactly what stage of development the Third World
Continent of Mu had attained during the long sleep of Adam
cannot be shown because of the radical changes which occurred in the earth during the Secondary. Nevertheless, a
great modern geologist has shown what no historian should
ignore. Even though Ziland was broken up before the Tertiary, a land bridge continued down to B. C. 10,000 to con-
nect Labrador with the present Europe even though parts of
it sank, rose, and sank again from time to time.[1] This bridge
was none other than the Land of Is.[2]

Following the statement that "the Lord God caused a deep
sleep to fall upon Adam," and the statement that during his
sleep one of his ribs was taken, and that "the flesh" was
"closed up instead thereof," we read:

"And the rib, which the Lord God had taken from man,
made he a woman, and brought her unto man."

The Hindus hold that according to the Adamic Calendar
of the Tamils, the transformation first occurred in the region

[67]

of Lake M-ana-so-ro-w-ara about 18,000,000 years ago, that is in the third Maha Yuga preceding the current one which began in B. C. 19,776,000. Although this does not mean that all the peoples of the earth suddenly became fully-sexed, since the dawn of history the region of M-ana-so-ro-w-ara has been one of the most sacrosanct known to man, and even today is one of the most mysterious regions on the earth.[3]

The old tradition that the separation of sexes occurred in the region of western Tibet was respected by both Leady and Quatrafrages although the latter showed that man did not originate there. Also it was accepted by Osborne.

In the original text of *Genesis* the man and the woman are designated as A-is-h and A-is-ha, nor is there anything in *Genesis* limiting them to one area, or to one race.[4] On the contrary, the sh and sha appearing in these names, meaning 'head' as in Ka-ma-sha-t-ka, imply not only peoples who based their philosophic concepts upon the two heads seen in the moon, but upon the two heads of man and woman.

One of the great mysteries of history has been the appearance of the Cow Worship of the so-called Archaic Age. It would have been only natural in the cycle of the Androgynes that the woman and the man in the moon should have been deemed twins. The eponymous A-ish and A-is-ha representing the two sexes suggests that already before the transformation of the Androgynes was complete, the concept of Is-Is 'the Twin Spirits of the Serpents', upon which the Cow Worship was based had evolved in the land of Is. Undoubtedly it was to Aish-Aisha that was due the name given the Ash Tree from which the Norse Boreans claimed to be descended. Then too, there were the mystical bull rites of the Druids; the form of the bull which Zeus is shown as assuming at will; the Cattle of Geryon which Hercules was called on to capture as one of his twelve labors; the bull of the mythical King Minos of Crete; the White Heifer into which Hera converted the nymph Io out of jealousy of Zeus by reason of his philanderings with the putative mother of the Ionians; the

Cro-Magnon art of the Middle Stone Age; the mysteries of the Apis Bull in Egypt; the Brazen Calf of the Israelites in the Mosaic Age; the bull which the Persian Mithras is shown assailing, the semi-sacred rite of bull fighting introduced by the Cid in Spain; the names of the bull conferred on the Shamens of the North American Indians who, like the Boreans of Europe, wore horns in their feathered headdresses; and the bull crest of the Spanish house of Borgia.[5]

As the Sphinx that was eventually erected at Gizeh in Egypt, displays in its tail a serpent corresponding to the First and Second Root Races, in the body appears the form of a bull or ox with the legs of a lion and the head of a normal man wearing the cowl of a priest of Isis-Osiris, the whole constituting a symbol of the five Root Races. In addition to this, the stone of the Libyan desert out of which the Sphinx was carved, was colored with a durable red pigment of which some still remains.[6]

Also the Boreans of Europe gave the name W-arsa-W to the city in P-o-land which eventually arose on a huge cave, displaying the Twins in the two W's corresponding to the two races on the earth.

Certainly it is not to be doubted that the name *vache* applied to the cow traces to the *Va,* or spiritual sheaf of mortality and to the Chi, 'Child of the Holy Spirit'. For as the Divine Lotus furnished the spiritual nature of man, according to the Wisdom Philosophy of which the avatar Va-ra-ha was the teacher, the Cow furnished the material nutriment of the Mammalians. Finally, it should be noted that the city of Mo-s-cow or Mu-s-cow, in the realm of Mu-s-co-v-y and Ka-bul lies between W-arsa-W and Ox-i-ana.

These are but some of the things that illustrate the reminiscence in historic times of the cycle of Aish and Aisha.

Following the description in *Genesis* of the separation of the sexes, Adam III is made to refer to the womb-man as follows: "This is bone of my bone, and flesh of my flesh: she shall be called woman, because she was taken out of man."

After the separation of the sexes, man was to beget his progeny by phallic process. Therefore, it is said in *Genesis* that henceforth man was to "leave his father and mother," in the genital sense, while the male was to cleave to his wife and with her to be of one flesh since the inception of mortals was to occur through the action of the male sperm upon the female ovum.

A-is-ha, however, was not the first wife of Adam III as shown by the Ta-l-mu-d of the Jews in which his consort is named as Lilith.[7] Her reputation is an evil one indeed for just what logically would have occurred upon the separation of the sexes is said to have followed. Thus Lilith is described as a vile sorceress, corresponding to the persisting traditions respecting the Pythoness of the Greek myths.[8]

In the Theogony of the Greeks the first fully sexed Titan appropriately is designated as I-a-p-e-t-us, 'the Spirit of the Ark, the philosophy of the earthly Taux, Uranus'. Moreover, it is quite plain that Sa-t-urnus in whose name appears that of Uranus, and who as a patron of agriculture was associated with Cronus by both the Arcadian Greeks and the Italics, was of an earlier age than the gods of the Olympian Pantheon. The same is true of the Italic O-p-s, 'the God of Plenty', indicating the origin of the word *opulence*. It was these older gods who were worshipped by the forebears of the Greeks and Italics in the Age of Pan when Aish and Aisha appeared. Appropriately, the name of Sa-t-urnus, 'Sa, the Taux of Uranus', was applied to Saturn, the reddest of all the planets.

Here it is imperative to have regard to the evolution of the earth. The charts in Chapter I show that in the course of time parts of the Polar Coronet, or the Queenland, came to be included in the Sino-Siberian and the North Atlantic Continents. As the latter changed its form, there came into being two land masses at the west of Asia which was said by the Greeks to be the oldest daughter of Oceanus. The one at the west became the Greek Atlas, and the one at the east the Greek Libya, said to have been begotten by Poseidon,

'God of the Terrestrial Sea,' out of the nymph Clytemnestra, implying the Polar Coronet.⁹ Libya in fact was an evolution from the Scandinavian Barrier shown on Chart 4. Gradually expanding westward, it connected with Atlas through the land of Is, and expanding southward and eastward brought into being both the Eurasian and the Eufrician land masses, and of the latter the Medi Terre formed the connecting link between the present Africa and the present Europe.

The great land mass which came into being when Libya united with Atlas and Asia and also the present Africa, extending almost entirely around the earth in the form of a pair of widely spread wings, included the Dekkan of India that came to be called Gond-w-ana. Therefore, modern geology gives to the world mass of the Tertiary the name Gond-w-ana-land.¹⁰ This was the land mass for which the zoologist Sclater borrowed the name *Lemuria* from the Romans.

To the Hindus, however, A-is-h and A-is-ha were known as the Ru, a name implying the reincarnated Uratur, and also the red Twins as the word ruby implies redness. Therefore, they called Gond-w-ana-land *Ruta*.

Eventually the M-ana-x of Britain would vanish in the process of evolution as would the Cor-n-is-h who, like Cor-n-wal-l, and the mythical Corenus, the alleged brother of Python to whom W-al-e-s, 'the Twins of the Ark Land, the first Serpents', owes its name. Eventually too, the An-g-l-es, or the spiritual teachers of the invaders from Ju-t-land, or Y-u-t-land, called J-u-t-e-s, 'the First Twins, the Taux, the First Serpent', and also of the Arian Sa-x-o-n, 'Sa, the Chi of the Nether Serpents,' would divide B-ri-t-annia into the Seven Kingdoms of the Saxons. Still, however, would survive among the I-r-is-h, Bri-t-is-h, and Scot-t-ish, the posterity of D-is in the land of Is-Is, the name of the Ru. Thus numerous islands of the Irish Sea bear the name Rhu. In Insuliae Britanniae, are found such place names as Ru-y, Ru-de, Ru-no, Ru-sh, Rush-well, Ru-s-s-ell, Ru-s-kin, Ru-th, Ruth-ven, Ruth-er-ford, Ru-g, Rug-b-y, Ru-x-t-on, Ru-m-ford, Ru-t-gers, Ru-t-ledge, Ru-m-ford, Run-n-y-mede, Ru-ri-k, Ru-p-er-t, and Ru-p-re-ch-t, some of which we find in ancient Franconia and Germannia, and in Scandinavia. In France also there are countless place names such as Ru-e, while Ru-y is a characteristic name in Spain and Portugal.

At the east coast of the Te-u-t-on realm of P-ru-s-sia is Ru-s-koi, Ru-s-sa-ya, or Ru-s-sia, of which Ru-the-n-ia, and Ru-m-el-ia are part. In Italy is the ancient realm of E-t-ru-ria, the city of Pe-ru-g-ia, and the river Ru-b-i-con. In that land which was originally a part of the Medi Terre and was called Ru-m-el, or the Land of Ru-m, is cherished the memory of the twins, Ro-mu-lus and Re-mus, who are said to have been nurtured by the she wolf implying the Androgyne progenitors of the E-t-ru-s-ka. In the present Libya evolved the Tri-poli of Mo-roc-co, Al-ge-ri-a, and T-u-n-is, the predecessors of the Greek U-t-i-ca, and the Phoenician-Isrealitic C-ar-t-ha-go which was converted by the Romans into the Province of Ma-u-ri-t-anna-ia, and by the Christians into H-y-po-l-y-t-u-s. Nevertheless, as a relic of the Medi Terre, the present Libya was known to the Hebrews as Ru-m-el.[11]

Because the present Asia Minor was attached to the Medi Terre, or Rumel, 'the land of Rum', in which eventually fifteen Romes arose, Palestine originally was called Ru-ten-nu, being connected at the south with the region in Arabia now called the Desert of Ru-b. The latter, like the present Red Sea, lay within the Mare Ru-br-i-con of the Romans. But the land that produced the Ru-b-ya-t of Omar K-ha-ya-ma, and the present E-ri-t-r-ea at the south of the Red sea, both lay within the sea to which the Chaldeans eventually applied the name *E-r-y-t-h-rea,* like the Mare Rubricon implying redness appropriate to the color of the Ru inhabiting that area.[12]

From the Pass of U-ru-mu Chi, through the K-u-en L-u-n-g Range of Sin Kiang, separating Siberia from the Celestial Empire of ancient Chi-na, and the Kara K-u-m at the west, one passes to the region of Kara-ko-ru-mu at the north of Kash-mir, southward through Mu-su-ra, and Mu-sa to Sin-ga-la, or the present C-e-y-lon. The only relic of the vanished land mass that bore the name Sin-ga-la, it came to be called L-an-ka, or L-ana-ka, by the Hindus. Above it looms Adam's Peak that bore the Mayavic name Pi-di-ru-ta-sa-ga-la.[13]

In the Gobi desert is another Kara-ko-ru-mu. For the reasons hereinafter to be shown, it would become the capital of the Mongols who from the Ya-l-u, separating Moon-go-la from M-ana-chu-r-ia, would overrun Chi-na.

Inasmuch as down to B.C. 10,000 the Western Hemisphere was connected with Libya by the land bridge of which Islanda (Iceland) and Froi Islanda (the Faro Islands) were parts, in North America we find the name of the Ru preserved in countless tribal and place names.[14]

Although in the course of time the Ru came to occupy the whole earth, fully explaining the concept of Lemuria, according to the Hindus the evil Daityas, or the Black Magicians, became ever more bold in their disregard of the spiritual teachings of the Mayavics. In view of the physical circumstances to which they were subject in the cycle of Varaha and Lilith, this was inevitable, and also that they should go from bad to worse amid the frightful ordeal in which they were involved with vast areas being constantly uplifted from the sea.

In the retrospective passage found in *Genesis* 6 we read:

"And it came to pass, when men began to multiply on the face of the earth, and daughters were born to them,

"2 That the sons of God saw the daughters were fair, and they took wives of all which they chose."

Here were veiled references to the debased Adamites, 'the sons of God,' who it appears at an early date developed the practice of claiming as part of the first fruits constituting the tithes of the priesthood, young virgins as well as the portion of the crops of nature which they deemed their due.

"3 And the Lord said, my Spirit shall not always strive with man, for that he also is flesh. . . ."

In a word, the sons of God like men in general were deemed the spirits of the Lord in the flesh.

Because the third Root Race was limited in the span of life of the individuals to 120 Solar years, in the remaining part of the passage quoted above, we read: "Yet his days shall be an hundred and twenty years."

---

[1] See Map in *Prehistoric Europe,* JAMES GEIKIE (1892).

[2] With its inhabitants the medieval scholar, Florence of Worcester (1112), dealt as intimate realities. The fact also is established that the coast of Normandy underwent radical changes as late as 800 A. D. when Mont St. Michele was isolated as an island. Nor did Iceland, "the Land of Fire," and Greenland, attain their present forms until about 1400 when their flourishing civilizations were wrecked by seismic disturbances that for some ten years cut off communications between Europe and Iceland save by pirates, leaving it separated from Greenland by an open sea of 160 miles.

[3] T-a-m-i-l, 'The Taux, the Ark of the Moon, the Spirit of the Lotus.' M-ana-s-o-ro-w-a-ra, 'the Mother, Ana, the Serpents of the Moon, the Roc, the Twins, the Ark of Ru.' Here it is that modern occultists place the Sages of the mythical *Sha-n-g-ri-la.*

[4] Here it is interesting to recall the novelistic pursuit by ANTHONY HOPE HAWKINS of the mythical *She, King Solomon's Mines,* and *Aisha.* The writer as a member of the Author's Club in London, knew him well. Undoubtedly he had obtained a lot of mystical material from Slatin Pasha, and also from Abruzzi who had explored Kilimanjaro after Slatin's release by the Mahdi.

[5] The crest of the Orsini (Bears) who were the allies of the Medici in their struggle with the Borgias (Bulls), was the *bear,* while the crest of the Medici was first 7 spheres and then 3. To this struggle among the Italian bankers traces the idea of bull and bear markets.

[6] *Die Herabkunft des feuers,* KUHN (1860).

Mother Moo and the Egyptian Sphinx, LE PLONGEON (1881).

[7] In Lil-i-th, 'the lily, the spirit of the Taux, Ha,' just as in Soma-li, appears the Divine Lotus.

[8] Back to this cycle may be traced the concept of the Sumerians with respect to El lil, 'the God of Lilith,' the first god known to them, as a great magician who issued from the bowels of the earth beneath a great mountain near Ni-p-p-ur where he was wont to work all manner of magic.

[9] Li-b-ya, 'the lily of Brahma, the first mortals.'

[10] Gond-w-ana, 'the land of the twins of Ana.'

[11] Here a thoughtful philosopher must wonder at the name applied by the Na-zis who, claiming as the offspring of the mad Nietzsche to see in strong nations no more than big fish for whom the small ones were created as the rightful prey, applied the name Rom-mel to the Marshal whose task it was to conquer Ru-mel.

[12] Eventually at the south of Soma-li-land, 'the essence of the Moon, the Lotus,' the name of the mythical Mount Me-ru, was applied to the actual Mount Meru near the Equator in K-en-ya, 'the King, En Zu, Ya,' K-i-l-a-m-ana-ya-ro. Not far to the east, and marking exactly the equator, in U-g-ana-da stand the Seven Mountains of the Moon among which the Nile finds its source, known to the Egyptians as the Ru-w-en-z-o-ri, 'the Ru, the Twins, the First Z, the Lunar Rishi.' They bear a name comporting with Somali and Kilimanjaro.

13 Pi-di-ru-ta-sa-ga-la, 'the Spirit of the Diva, Ru, the Taux Ark, Sa, the God Land.'

14 See *Gazetteer,* and the *Synonymy in Handbook of American Indians,* Bureau Am. Eth., Bulletin 30, Smithsonian Institute (1907).

Although the Mo-hawks, 'Moon Hawks' of the Sha-ta-mu in the Adi-ron-d-ac, were eventually incorporated by the Serpent peoples called Iroquois by the French, they were different and darker than the other members of the linguistic family to which the ethnologists applied the name Iroquoian. Therefore, it may be that they were of the same primal stock as the Mu-hocks of Mu-ra-ka on the West Coast of America. Whatever the fact, they were similar in color and other ways to the five tribes of the Mu-s-ko-gi who were grouped in the Mu-s-k-h-o-gean linguistic family, and who represented an older people than the Iroquois who, being of the Serpent Cult, like the Siouans, were designated by the Chi-pe-w-a as "Adders." Also the Sho-sho-nes of the Rockies were called serpent people.

From the Mu-s-qui-to Coast of Nicaragua where the Spaniards found the pygmies among the aborigines of America, it is but a step to Pe-ru, 'the house of Ru.'

CHAPTER IX

ATLANTIS AND THE FOURTH ROOT RACE.
THE MOON GOD SIN, THE FIRST SOLAR DEITY.
ANA, THE INSCRUTABLE UNIVERSAL MOTHER.

NOTWITHSTANDING all the foolishness that has been written about Atlantis, the Fourth World Continent is no longer deemed by Science a mere fiction of the imagination, but is looked upon as one of the ever-changing forms of the geological Gondwanaland.

Up to the evolution of Aish-Aisha the anthropogenesis of the Mosaic Scribes has been abundantly clear. From now on, however, it becomes confused to such an extent that even a Christian commentator as editor of *Westminister Commentaries* impatiently declared the geneaology and the chronology in *Genesis* to be so contradictory that it affords no material for historical interpretation.[1]

It is true that in respect to anthropogenesis the passages in *Genesis* are confused, but it is not true that they are contradictory, nor is it difficult to understand why they are confused when the situation in which the Scribes found themselves is envisaged. To do this, it is necessary to clear away a lot of historical fog.

Back in the Mosaic Age so-called Celtic Boreans designated in the ancient records as the *peoples of the sea,* who had come to occupy the Isles of Israel in Europe, had overrun the Mediterranean world, and as will be shown, in their veins was the blood of Hebrews. By B.C. 1,000 they had brought to an end as allies of the Israelites, themselves Danitics, the Rameside Empire. Thereupon Egypt passed into the hands of a Phoenician Pharaoh. Concurrently the Phoenicians established themselves at Cadiz in order to dominate the Pillars of

Hercules as the gateway to the Atlantic. About the same time the so-called Gadhels, the forebears of the Gaels, migrated from Iberia to Ireland, and the Trojan war was ended. Now too, the Philistines were overthrown by Saul thanks to the aid of David who as the Lion of Judah succeeded to the kingship of the Israelites and established his seat at Jerusalem. David was succeeded by Solomon whose ten thousand wives merely represented the peoples to whom Hebraism had been extended before the age in which the mythical Zoroaster, representing the Ma-z-di, or wise men of Persia, had embodied their wisdom in the *Zend Avesta* and in the *Vendidad*.

With the Greeks now in complete control of Ionia which had come to include the part of Asia Minor at the north of the Agean Sea, and the mysteries of the Cabiri established at Sin-o-pe on the Black Sea, inevitably the Greeks exerted a profound influence upon the redactions of the Mosaic Scriptures. Certain, too, it is that the Sarku, or the White element of Asia Minor, who in course of time had evolved from the dark Z-al-ma-t Guar-g-ar-di, or the Aryan Ethiopians who had given their name to the Black Sea, had no idea of allowing their descent from the Ethiopians to be stressed by the Mosaic Scribes. The same was true of the Ma-z-di of Persia, and the eponymous San-chi-o-no-i-th-on of Syria, or the Scribes of the Kabira to whom the *Book of Chon* is to be traced. Therefore, nearly a thousand years before the Judaizers of the Christian church dictated the Creed of Nicaea (A.D. 325), the Hierophants of the Hindu, Iranian, Hebrew, Syrian, Egyptian, Greek, and Borean Mysteries were determined to draw the veil over the history of the past which had been revealed to Plato before the Goth Ulfilas compiled the first Christian Bible. The Dark Age of Christendom ascribed to Constantine was in fact but part of the policy which the Judaizers had adopted as the disciples of Philo Biblius. This being so, it requires a measure of detective work to interpret in chronological order the passages in the Vulgate.

Eventually, according to the Hindus, the Pitris of the Fourth Root Race appeared in the old Ziland to which the names Zeland, Queenland, Atlao, Atala, Ita-land were applied by different people in different cycles.

This race is described as fully-sexed giants of a brown color and smaller than the Ru.

For the reasons shown neither in *Genesis* nor in the Theogony is this race referred to in explicit terms. Yet, in the retrospective account embodied in *Genesis* 6 in reference to the Fourth Race, it is said:

"4 There were giants in the earth in those days; and also after that, when the sons of God came in unto the daughters of men, and they bear children to them, and the same became men which were of old, men of great renown."

Here is an explicit reference to the Fourth Root Race coupling them with the sons of God, or the Adamites of this cycle.

We have seen that the first fully sexed Ti-t-an was described as Iapetus. Accordingly, it is said in the Theogony that he begat Atlas, Prometheus, the alleged bearer of fire, in the sense of sexual consciousness, to the peoples of the earth. Another brother was Epimetheus, whose name indicates a person wise but always wise too late.[2]

Although in course of time the great land once known as Rut-a by the Ru, had been transformed so that now three land masses existed in the North—Asia, Libya, and Atlas, all included in the Fourth World Continent which came to be called Atla-n-t-is by the Greeks, in fact the name applied to it was a mere evolution from Atlas which itself was an evolution from A-tlao-s, 'the Ark of the Bear Serpents.'[3] And here it is especially important to note that the Italic word *A-ta-la-ya* implied 'watch tower', while *Atlas* is the name today given to the top bone in the human spine.

Inasmuch as the land masses of the North included the relics of the Queenland, of Zeland, and constituted the antipodes of the Austral realms to which eventually the names New Zealand, and the Land of the Southern Cross, or Aus-

tralia, were applied, with Queenland at the northern part of
the latter, the inhabitants of the southern climes referred to
the northern realms as Hell, which was derived from H-el-l,
'Ha-elohim-land,' having exactly the same significance as *pa-
ta-la,* or the Hindu word for antipodes.

Included within the southern antipodes was the so-called
Lost Continent of Mu including the present C-el-e-b-e-s, that
were still called "the land of Heaven and Earth" when they
were visited by the Portuguese explorer deQuiros about 1640.

The Pacific Continent which included the countless relics
of the Land of Heaven and Earth, lay above huge gas pockets and, as shown on Chart 4, Chapter I, was a gradually
sinking one. Inevitably in those parts the witch doctors or
evil Daityas, would have thriven more than in more perma-
nent areas. Nevertheless the names of the Mayavics who had
reached all parts of the Austral realms is preserved throughout Oceanica, Polynesia, and is found in New Zealand well
preserved by the Maiori, just as it is preserved in the Hawai-
ian Islands by Ma-u-na Loa and by Ma-u-na Kea as symbols
of the Divine Ark. Also we find it in Mau-ri-t-i-us, in Ma-da-
ga-s-ca and in Ma-ta-b-el-a on the mainland of Africa.

It was because the Hindus believed that the original Rishi
had appeared in A-ma-ra-va-ti at the top of the earth that
originally they conceived of Mount Me-ru as the successor of
A-ma-ra-va-ti, and placed it in Hell or Patala at the north.

Of Hell the memory is preserved by the Island of Hel-i-
go-land north of Holland, or Helland, with Hel-sin-g-fors,
'the ford of Hell, the God Sin' in Dan's Mark, just north of
Heidelberg, 'Hell's Oracle', and of Ha-mu-burg. At the south
is Hel-ve-t-ia (Swyzland). To the west in Britanny is the
mystical pool of Hel-goat, and in Spain is the shrine of Hel-
lin. In the Channel Islands once attached to Holland and the
east coast of England where Hull is found, appears Helland.
And in the Shetlands is Hellini while the Island of Mu-ll appears in the Irish Sea. The first name given Labrador in the
Icelandic sagas was Helluland.

At the east of Swy-den, or Sweden is Hel-sin-ki, the present capital of Finland, while the original name of Greece was Hellas from which the Hellespont, now submerged, once passed to Hellicarnassus in Ilios, or the Troja close to the Olympus of the Ionians in Mo-e-si. Close to this Olympus stands a second Mount I-da, 'Spirit of Diva,' in Crete and others in Ida-ho, 'Ida, the Moon,' near the Olympian range of Washington.

The terrestrial Hell does not fail to give the thoughtful pause. Eventually the name of this realm in which dwelt the red Ru, would be applied to the imaginary realm that was peopled with red devils, or the Nether realm of which Pluto, or Hades, the brother of Zeus, originally was deemed the ruler. In the Hebraic Kabala of Lucifer this angel is depicted as the bearer of spiritual light to mankind. Moreover it was to the terrestrial Hell that he descended and not to the imaginary realm of Satan. Nor was it until a very late time that Satan was born of mortal hypocrisy to serve as a scapegoat for human weaknesses. The alleged descent of the Christian Christ into Hell may be taken, therefore, to have implied his appearance upon the earth.

The Greek myth in which Deu-c-a-lion, 'the God of the Celestial Ark of the Lion,' the putative ancestor of the Hellenes, and his marriage to Pyr-r-a, 'the spirit of Ru, Atlantis,' said to have been the daughter of Epimetheus out of Pandora, simply implies the cross between the Ru and the Lion Men of the Fourth Root Race.

Inevitably, of course, the evil Daityas, or Black Magicians among the Ru would have perverted the younger race. To explain what occurred in the cycle of Lilith and Atlas it is said that Zeus ordered Hephestus, corresponding to the Roman Vulcan, to fashion out of clay a woman of divine beauty with all the charms and weaknesses of the female sex. The vast antiquity of the concept of Athena is indicated by this myth in which she is shown instructing the new creation in the industrial occupations of women. It was Aphrodite who gave her grace of manners, and taught her all the arts of beauty, while Hermes was qualified for the part of flattering and soothing. With the help of the Graces and the Horae, Athena robed her with costly, beautiful garments, decking her with flowers so that when all was done, the woman Pan-do-ra, with a name appropriate to the age of Pan, might be irresistibly attractive to gods and men.[4] Hermes then conducted her to Epimetheus, who though warned by his brother Prometheus to accept no gift from Zeus, yielded to his besetting weakness. Receiving Pandora into his house, and making her his wife, he discovered that she had brought with her a vase, the lid of which Hermes had explained was to remain closed. The curiosity of her husband, however, tempted him to open it. Thereupon escaped from the vase all the troubles, weariness, and illnesses, from which mankind thereafter was never to be free.

Concubinage, sexual perversion, and disease is what the Greek myths dealing with various hybrids, fail to suggest mythical Pandora as well as Lilith brought to man. We know that bestiality soon or late became rampant upon the earth just as it is today.[5]

In view of the decadence of the two sets of giants on the earth designated in *Genesis* as the Gaur, nothing would have been more vitally important to the welfare of mankind than to overthrow the Black Magic and the vice implied by the myths of Lilith and Pandora. Therefore, the Fourth Avatar who ushered in the cycle of the Moon God Sin, was symbolized by a lion-man, and to him was ascribed the mission as the ruler of mortals, just as the lion is the king of beasts, of tearing to pieces the earth in the manner that it actually was torn to pieces by the convulsions which brought into being the successive uplifts of the Tertiary.

While it was said that Sin, 'the first Solar deity,' was born at Mount Sin, this did not imply the actual Mount Sin, or Sin-a-i, any more than the mythical Mount Amaravati, Mount

Mandara, and Mount Meru were actual mountains, but only that it was the spiritual high place of the Sinitic Cult.

We need only look to Io-Sin-Fa-Zembla in the Arctic Sea, Hel-Sin-Ki in Finland, and Hel-Sin-g-Ford in Denmark, to see the meaning of Mount Sin where all the subsequent solar deities—the Greek Zeus, the Ionian Dionysus, the Latin Bacchus, and the Egyptian Osiris, and Horus also were said to have been born.

The name applied to the first Solar deity indicates very plainly the character of the Serpent of Indra who was called the Moon God because Indra symbolized the metaphysical principle of which the man in the moon was deemed the expression. Thus, just as Uranus and Athena were the Greek forms of Va-ru-na and Ornyth respectively, Z-e-us was the Greek form in a late age of the Hindu Indra.

In the case of Indra, the strife was with the demons V-ri-t-ra, 'the Surrounder'; A-h-i, 'the confuser', and Shu-s-na, 'the parcher', implying the elements of nature hostile to man's advance.[6]

Because the philosophic concept of Sin corresponded to that of Indra in Franconia, ancient France, we find the province of Indra and the city of Ma-in-z, and in the present Western Hemisphere, not so far west of Franconia Notch in the White Mountains the State of Ind-i-ana and the City of Indianapolis.

Together, Sin and Indra fully account for the origin claimed by the great Al-gi-c linguistic family of North America, one of the oldest and the largest group, of the seven linguistic families of modern ethnology to which the name Al-gon-qui-an has been applied. While this name was coined from the characteristic Al-gon-k-in tongue of the Algics of Labrador, whose domain extended along the Atlantic seaboard as far south as the River Neuse in North Carolina, or the original boundary of the Canadian barrier shown in Chart 3, Chapter I, the Algonkins were but one group of the Re-nape who trace their origin to the Al-goo-a-ma-kin, and through them to the Eren a peu, 'real men', as did the Erie of the same family. And here it will be noted that Erie is the metathesis of Eire, the name of ancient Ireland.[7]

It is to the Sinitics, or the propagators of the solar cult, that the Zend language of ancient I-r-ana is to be traced.[8] As it spread over the East the concept of Va-ru-na gave way more and more to that of Indra.

The fundamental innovation of the cult of Sin was its denial of the phallic concept that the man in the moon begat by phallic process mortals out of the woman in the moon. According to it mortality was born of the Divine Lotus transmitted to the moon in whose fecund matter it was germinated by the action of the sun. Thus S-i-n also may be interpreted as the Sun, the spirit of the Nether World which, we have seen, was impersonated by the Greek Cenobis and the Egyptian Cenubis, No, Nu, Nut, and Kneph, and of which Hades and Pluto were deemed the rulers.

In course of time many claims have been advanced that the American aborigines were descended from the Welsh, and so held General Custer. The misconception arose from the joinder of Labrador and Britain through the Land of Is. Thus, just as Caesar found the pre-Celtic Druids of Britain worshiping D-is, whose most sacred shrine was on the island of Mona, the name Mona is that of one of the seven Welsh Witches, and is found in Mona-d-nock, Mon-tau-k point, Mona-su-ka-pa-nough and Mona-sa-ha-s-sa-nough near Charlottesville, Virginia, and the Island of Mona in the Bahamas which was given to Diego, the brother of Christopher Columbus, by Isabella. Surely the Welsh did not found the civilization of Mona-co in the Riviera, or that of Mona-a-s-tir, in Greece.[9] Neither did they produce the Mona-physites of the early Christian Phrygians who as Pythagoreans and reformers, under the lead of Montanus, resisted bitterly the early form of Latin-Greek-Byzantine Christianity, and who, as rebels wore the red cap of liberty, while being persecuted as the K-ar-ta of Phrygia.[10]

[83]

While the Solar Cult denied the phallicism connected with Mother Moo, it was necessary to explain the creation of the Moon and the other planets. We have seen that the Wisdom Philosophy conceived of the Creative Genius as the Inscrutable Absolute, and of the Divine Lotus as the *Ark Navalis* through which the essence of Divinity was said to be conveyed in the sheaf of the Soul to the matter of the moon and thence through the monad called Manu by the Hindus, to the Rishi as the archtype of the Pitris, or mortal progenitors. To this concept traced that of *A-Na,* 'the Ark Navalis,' as the inscrutable Mother of the Universe.

No one understood better than Leonardo da Vinci, the great scholar who succeeded the astronomer Toscanelli in the Faculty of the Platonian Academy of Florence, the intimate of Lorenzo the Magnificent and the associate of Pico or Mirandola, the foremost exponent of the Wisdom Philosophy of his age, the implications of Ana. Therefore in his *Mona Lisa* is found his imaginative picture of Mother Ana, or M-o-ana, 'the Mother of the Universe, Ana.'

From Yana Ma-y-en Island now called Jan Mayen (80 N. 10 E.) between Greenland and Spitzbergen the name of Ana may be traced all over the earth. From there it is but a step to Fra-n-con-ia, or ancient France. In Fran-con-ia, we see a contraction of Frau-Ana, as in the Young Frau of the Alps. At the south of the grand natural symbol of Mont Blanc is Mont Al-b-ana overlooking the Seven Hills of the T-iber, 'the Taux of Iberia.'[11]

Among the Seven Hills of Rome is the J-an-iculum which derived its name from J-an-u-s ever shown with two heads symbolizing among other things the Rishi and the Pitris of the Queenland to which the Qui-ri-n-al owes its name.

At the east of Italy is Al-b-an-ia in the B-al-k-ana, and in Asia Minor is Ana-t-o-l-ia. There we find Kur-d-is-t-ana, and beyond the T-i-g-ris, 'the Taux', the spirit of the gods, the Rishi is Lu-zi-ana in I-r-ana. At the east is Bal-u-chi-s-t-ana, Afgh-ana-is-t-ana, O-x-i-ana and M-ana-so-ro-w-ara or West-

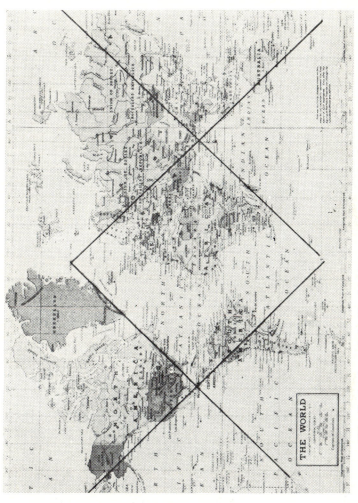

VI. Projection of the Earth, Mercator System, as today, showing how the two Geodetic Chi or Twins were surveyed.

VII.   E-E-Ops-I-Chi-Pe

At the Oracle of Winnewassa in the Mountain of the Prairie near the
Sacred Red Pipestone Quarry in Rock County, Minnesota.

ern Tibet. In India is the G-ana-ges, and there we also find Raj-pu-t-ana, and K-an-sa, with Mount Amara-k-an-t-a-ka and God-w-ana in the Dek-k-ana.

From Ana-r-ya-poo-ra in Ceylon we pass to the An-da-m-ana islands and up the Ira-w-a-d-dy to Ana-pu-ra near Ana-m at the South of Chi-ana and Ja-p-ana. On the Equator at 150° E. is P-ana-pe and in the Philippines P-ana-y.

From Tripoli-t-ana in Libya one passes Southward to B-e-chu-ana-land and An-gola, and on the Equator we find U-g-an-da and Kila-m-ana-ja-ro.

C-ana-da is entered by way of the islands of Ana-co-s-ti and An-ti-fo-gi-s-ti. At the West are Mi-chi-g-ana and Sa-s-ka-t-chi-w-ana. At the South of the former are Ind-i-ana, and Ta-ana-sa (Tennessee).

From Se-qui-t-ana in Maine one comes to M-an-ha-t-t-ana, Ra-ri-t-ana, the Su-s-que-h-anna, Ana-cos-tia (Washington), near which is Ana-polis. Close by are Kicko-t-ana, Ana-m-essex, N-an-dua, Qu-ana-t-i-co, Ke-gho-t-an, and the ancient Shrine of Po-w-ha-t-ana (Richmond), overlooking the falls of the Pow-ha-t-ana into which flow the North and South Ana. At the West of Richmond is Mona-su-ka-pa-nough, an ancient site on the Ri-v-anna (near Charlottesville), and close by is the grand height of S-w-anna-no-a. From the Blue Ridge the Ro-ana-w-k-e flows to Albemarle Sound where are found Se-c-t-ana and Ro-an-o-ke Islands as well as N-an-ti-coke. South of Savannah are the An-t-illies at the North of Gui-ana.

In the vast domain of I-ana to which the name King Louis was prefixed to form Louis-i-ana, lie Mont-ana, and numerous ana-con-das.

Ancient Ana-huac, 'the ark of Ana' included Arizona in which is found Te-x-a-c-ana in Texas. In Mexico are Te-o-ti-hu-i-c-an, Pa-p-an-t-la, and Ax-a-c-an while Co-p-ana is the capital of Honduras.

In view of this worldwide concept of Ana, plainly trace-able to the Maya of the Sinitic age, not unnaturally the ancestors of the Pi-ra-ti of S-c-an-di-na-v-ia looked upon Ana as the wife of Balder, the son of Light and Love for whose reincarnation as Christ they prayed, just as the early Christians held Anna to be the Mother of the Virgin Mary.

From Franconia we come to Germ-anna, the land of the Ana-glaes, at the east, Bri-t-anna at the West, and to A-qui-t-anna, Lu-si-t-anna-ia, E-s-p-anna, and Mau-re-t-anna-ia which was formed out of Tri-polit-ana.

Mo-ana Lisa's realm was indeed a vast one.

---

1 See CHEYNE in *Encyclopedia Britannica* (13th Ed.), "Genesis."

2 See *Prometheus Vincit*, AESCHYLUS; *Prometheus Bound*, MILTON; *Prometheus Unbound*, SOUTHEY.

3 Atla-n-t-is, 'Atlas, the Nether, the Taux of Is.'

4 Pan-d-o-r-a, 'Pan, the Diva, the Rishi, the Ark.'

5 Today the great cities of America present shocking spectacles of bestiality which are staged as in Asia, Africa, and Europe in the manner of plays with admission charges.
Following the revel of materialism during which the ape-man was held to be the ancestor of mortals, a German anthropologist pointed out that the likenesses between the man and the gibbon were due to the descent of the latter from the man instead of the reverse. Today, however, no anthropologist accepts as sound the old tradition that still-born freaks were produced by bestiality.

6 S-in, 'the Serpent Indra.' Z-eu-s, Zu-en, 'the Serpent.' I-n-d-r-a, 'the Spirit of Noo, the Divine Ruler, the absolute.' In "the parcher" may be seen the origin of the concept of Satan.

7 The Irish monk Marianus of the Fifth Century upon whose writings concurrently with the mysterious voyages of St. Brendan to the West, were based by the Latin Monk Nennius (800) the Arthurian Romances, referred to the realm of Bram as the Western Ireland.

8 Z-en-d, "Zu-en, the Divine Wisdom,' En, 'Enyalius,' a Narayana.

9 Mo-na-s-tir, "the Ark of the Serpent Tree." The Bureau of American Ethnology professes its inability to translate the name of Mona-su-ka-pa-nough and Mona-ha-s-sa-nough, two of the five Monacan towns in Virginia found by Captain John Smith on the James, and Ri-v-anna, now Virginia. A Sacred Tree nearly 500 years old still stands beside the circular mound at Mona-su-ka-pa-nough in sight of Monticello. M-ona is contraction of M, Chon, and Naragana. Therefore Mona means the Lunar Cult of the Chon, Naragana. Thus Mona appears in the French word mon-t, implying a high place. Mona-su-ka-pa-nough means the high place of the su-ka-pa, while nough means a nut tree, or food. Su-ka-pa is a form of the Sioux Ka-sa-pa "the King, Sa, the Papa," meaning "a wise father." Thus Ka-ya-pa-ya-pa is the name applied to Rama as one of the Seven Sages of the Veda. Ka-sa-pa had the same implication.

10 Although most of the descendants of Montanus eventually were herded into the Church, in 541 Jacobus Baradaeus of Syria set up the Mona-physite cult with its patriarch at Edessa in Syria. They were the original Jacobites back to whom trace the Quakers, and from their mysteries William Penn derived his knowledge of ancient America.

[11] I-b-e-r-i-a, 'the Spirit of Brahma, the earth of Ru, the Spirit of the Ark.' Thus, there were many Iberias in historic times such as Si-beria, a contraction of Sin-Iberia, while both the Caucasus and the present Iberian peninsula bore this name as did the Tiber. And here it is noted that as the various realms of the earth were brought into the Sinitic fold, the suffix *ia* implying the 'Spirit of Ana,' sometimes euphonized as *ea,* 'the earth of Ana,' was merely added to the preceding name.

CHAPTER X

THE KINGDOM OF ATLAS
"THE WATCHER"

WHILE THE MISSION assigned the avatar Na-ra-sin-g-ha not only testifies to the geological knowledge possessed by the Hindus, Geology shows that the seismic disturbances of the Tertiary did not begin prior to B.C. 6,000,000. Therefore, it is not to be presumed that before this time the two races inhabiting the earth became involved in the new terror incident to the tearing of the earth to pieces. In short, there was a period of 12,000,000 years between the separation of the sexes and the new ordeal of man, affording ample time for the evolution of the brown giants into a potent race.

Of the second race and the Sinitic Cult of which it became the head there would have been the same jealousy among the evil Daityas of the Ru as in the case of Cain and Abel. To this fact traces the myth that Zeus had to be secreted by the nymph Ida, implying the region in which eventually arose Mount Ida in Crete, so that the cries of the infant would not be heard.

In this myth is found the key to the Platonian myth of the Kingdom of Atlas who, we have seen, as the mythical Son of Iapetus represented the Fourth Root Race.

In the Dialogue of the *Critias,* wherein Plato caused his kinsman *Critias,* to relate the story of the mythical Kingdom of Atlas, he merely employed the younger gods on the island of Posidonis at the West of the Medi Terre as blinds. In it Critias tells how as an assemblage of the great gods of the Olympian Pantheon, Zeus, Poseidon, and Hades were selected to rule the visible celestial sphere, the terrestrial sphere, and the incognizable realm of Erebus, or the nether world, to which spirits departed from the mortal body, respectively. Critias then went on to show just how the Teachers of the Sinitic Cult undertook to safeguard against a repetition of the tragedy of Cain and Abel. Thus Poseidon, as the ruler of the Terrestrial See of Sin, is made to beget out of the mortal woman Cleito, 'Clymene, the Spirit of the Taux, Ornyth,' the daughter of Eve-n-o-r and L-e-u-c-ippe, the five pairs of twins as here named:[1]

Atlas	Eumelus
Ampheres	Evenon
Mneseus	Autichthon
Elusippus	Mestor
Azaes	Diaprepes

To each of these twins Poseidon assigned a kingdom, and over all ten of them placed Atlas as the supreme ruler of the league to enforce peace upon the earth in accordance with the laws given the Ten Twins.

As yet no one has explained the philosophic concept of Plato with respect to these so-called twins. With full regard to Cardinal Cusa, Spinoza, and the theory of Walter Russell, the present day philosopher, it is possible to interpret the Kingdom of Atlas in its historical aspect as shown on the accompanying diagram. In a word the energy bringing into being by cosmic deluges successive types of man, would act upon matter in the manner of a pebble dropped into a pool, setting into motion rings like the racial cycles that eventually would merge, while the centripetal force revolving the Universal Dodecahedron of Pythagoras, would bring into being the five constanabius spheres of which Plato conceived with their twins.

Before Plato published his myth, certainly subsequent to the appearance of the Phaedra in 399 B.C., however, as shown by Volney and others who have dealt with the Zodiac and the frame of the Greek maps, including Mackey and more lately Nunn, Wright, and Heidel of the American Geographical Society in their works of 1917, 1924, and 1937, respectively, the Greek geographers as early as the time of Herodotus (484-

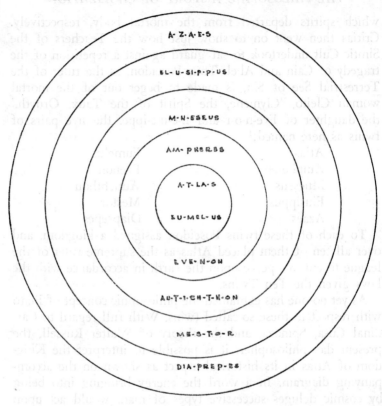

THE TWINS OF ATLAS

424 B.C.) in whose cycle the present Greek alphabet was adopted, had conceived of the Tropics of Cancer and Capricorn with which they divided the spheroid into five zones instead of six, throwing the two old middle zones into the Equatorial Zone. Therefore the 5 sets of twins of which Plato conceived had reference to the five climatic zones to which the 10 signs of the younger zodiacs referred. On the other hand the twinships referred to the combination in mortals of the spiritual and the material man, or the higher and lower beings, of which Plato conceived as the expounder of Hebraic and

Hindu philosophy. Since his myth was designed as a protest, not against any single race, any single nation, any single religion, but against the philosophy of the Anarchs such as Xenophanes and Zeno, of the so-called Eleatic School, and the Greater Vehicle of Buddhism that was evolving in India from the Lesser Vehicle of Arhat of which the Buddha Gautama had been the exponent while trying to reform Brahmanism and bring it back to the Hinduism of which it was sprung, accordingly he selected the earth in its Atlantean form as the terrestrial background of his myth. In other words he began it in the age before the mythical Ogyges was supposed to have brought the earth to its present form with the relics of his realm known to the Greeks as parts of Ogygia such as Ortygia (Sicily), the islands of the Middle Atlantic, and those beyond the *Insuliae Britanniae of the Romans.* Since the land mass of which the Ridge of Teneriffe had been the nucleus, was known to have vanished during the Magnetic Cataclysm of 10,000 B.C., leaving the Azores, and the Madeiras as relics, the attempts to limit the Kingdom of Atlas to this region have persisted. Nevertheless the true historical basis of the myth was known to Hipparchus, the Hierophant of the Pythian mysteries enshrined at Rhodes, who referred to the opposite earth as Autichthon; to his successor Posidonius, the tutor of Cicero and Pompey; to Sertorious who referred to America as Antillia; to Strabo, Diodorous Siculus, Seneca, the Plinys, Pomponious Mela, Josephus, Proclus, the great scholars of the Platonian Academy of Florence, Sir Thomas More, Raleigh, Bacon, Montaigne, Madame Blavatsky, Sinnet, Judge, and others, despite the confusion of countless other writers on Atlantis. But as we proceed it will be seen that just as the four lettered eponym Adam referred to the people in all four quarters of the earth, Plato's twins like the Titans of Greek mythology had reference to the giants in both hemispheres as well as in the North and South of both in the cycles of all five Root Races.

Although Plato conceded great respect for the laws given the

League by Poseidon, in obedience to which the ten kingdoms enjoyed great happiness and prosperity for many years, eventually as the spirituality of the subjects of Atlas faded away, they fell victim to materialism and craving empire set out to conquer the earth.[2]

To repeat, no historian can afford to brush aside as mere fiction what Plato wrote. Hereinafter the meaning of the myth will be mathematically demonstrated. Meantime, it is sufficient to note that the demand upon the two races that the phallicism of the Cow Worship be abandoned was one which, as shown by the myths of Lilith and Pan-dora, unhappily still the serpent of human nature could not meet. Therefore, a tremendous conflict at once began between the male and the female cult which had evolved from the Mayavic Ark. This fully explains why the teachers of the Solar Cult were compelled to go under cover, and found the Eleusinian mysteries, commonly deemed to have been the oldest in Greece although the Python was of world-wide extent.

While *Genesis* 3 does not deal explicitly with the Fourth, inasmuch as it existed co-equally with the Third Root Race, dealing with the two races collectively it shows just what occurred among the ancestors of the Hebrews.

"1. Now the serpent was more subtle than any beast of the field which the Lord God had made. And he said unto the woman, yea, hath God said, Ye shall not eat of every tree of the garden?"

The serpent to which reference is here made implies both the weakness of female nature ascribed to Lilith and Pandora, and the serpent of human nature within each mortal frame to whose temptations the man, as well as the woman, are shown in the same chapter to have been subject. On the other hand the eating of the fruit of the forbidden tree implies that the forbidden cannibalism had appeared along with many other evil things, possibly including sex perversions, bestiality, scalping and other barbaric rites, and possibly also addiction to narcotics, or the traditional lotus eating of the ancient peoples that like bestiality is rampant on the earth today.

But the serpent dealt with in *Genesis* 3 also refers to the degraded mysteries of the evil Daityas, or Black Magicians such as the countless witch-doctors by whom mankind have ever been beset, and who in all ages, as shown by the deep studies of Herbert Spencer, have ever deemed themselves wiser than God.

In the light of what has been shown, including the appearance of the avatar Nara-sin-g-ha, and the reformative teachings of the solar cult, the import of the following passage, is plain:

"13. And the Lord said unto the woman, What is this thou hast done? And the woman said, the serpent beguiled me, and I did eat."

Here, of course, is a plain implication that the nature of the female was just as represented in the myth of Lilith and Pan-dora. But if woman had not yet advanced to the point that she could abandon promiscuity, the Serpent implied the Pythoness as well.

Because the family relation was deemed vital by the solar cult, the imports of the next passages also are clear.

"14. And the Lord God said unto the Serpent, Because thou hast done this, thou art cursed above all cattle, and above every beast of the field; upon thy belly shalt thou go, and dust shalt thou eat all the days of thy life."

In other words those of the Cult of the Python who had perverted the Wisdom Philosophy, sanctioned cannibalism, sex perversions, and bestiality, were to be cursed as long as they should live, and as degenerates be compelled to crawl upon the earth, figuratively on their bellies, as do actual serpents.

"15. And I will put enmity between thee and the woman, and between thy seed and her seed."

Just as moral perverts always would be the enemies of women, women eventually would come to despise them. The remaining words of this paragraph, however, are among the most abstruse in *Genesis*.

"It shall bruise thy head, and thou shalt bruise his heel."

Here the implication is that the eventual enmity of women to moral perversion, would bruise the head of the perverts in the sense that they would come to be looked upon with the loathing normal people have for actual serpents as things to be destroyed; that eventually the Wisdom Philosophy, restored to its pristine virtue, would bruise the heel of the perverts in the figurative sense of making it difficult for them to walk in the light.

It appears, however, that as time went on, even the Adamites, or the initiates of the mysteries, fell victim to the lunar cult, just as indicated by *Genesis* 6. Accordingly the Lord God is quoted as saying to Adam: "Because thou hast hearkened unto the voice of thy wife, and hast eaten of the tree, of which I commanded thee, saying, Thou shalt not eat of it: cursed is the ground for thy sake; in sorrow shalt thou eat of it all the days of thy life."

The word *wife* as here used implies the whole earth in the Fourth World Continent. During the appalling ordeal attending the impending upheavals, the earth was to bring forth "thorns and thistles" for the Adamites; they would find themselves harried by the terrified peoples of the earth, as they, themselves, were compelled to live, not upon the fruit and nut trees which had provided food for men, but like animals upon the herbs of the fields.

"In the sweat of thy face shalt thou eat bread; till thou return unto the ground."

Eventually man would have to labor to live, instead of existing as the arboreals had been able to do, thanks to the bounty of nature, upon fish, fowl, and the bounty of the fruit and nut trees. In other words even the Adamites would have to resort to agriculture in order to produce the grain for bread out of the less abundant earth. For inevitably the mountains would effect changes of temperature producing seasons of growth, of which only some would yield an abundance of food. Then follow words in complete accord with the Hindu idea that the Fourth Root Race vanished from the earth: "For out of it (the ground) was thou taken; for dust thou art, and to dust thou shalt return."

Eventually began the uplifts of the Tertiary and the appalling ordeal of which the proof is found in geology.[3]

In the face of what geology discloses, it is useless to imagine that during the several million years which saw the Tertiary mountains attain their approximate present form, countless mortals, as they rushed hither and thither over the earth, did not fall into savagery. Still the descendants of the Ru who had occupied Somali Land, and back to whom the Bantu among the Zulu trace their origin, preserve the tradition of how their forebears fled in terror to South Africa when the equatorial mountains arose. Also deep studies have shown that a form of hysteria still exists among the peoples of the Siberian Ranges who were involved in the terrifying ordeal that brought these mountains into existence. In fact, it was an age of tooth and claw, of witch doctors and black magic, which eventually produced such barbarities as cannibalism, scalping, and burning at the stake. The mountains that arose in Spitzbergen and Greenland indicate very plainly why the peoples of the land of Is, would have streamed southward out of the northern realms.

One who fails to point out what the survivors of this ordeal have beheld upon the earth as it was torn to pieces, and fails to point to the names applied to the natural symbols of the earth that came into being at this time, is not an historian.

Behold Gaur-ra-sin, 'the Great Ark of Sin', later called Gaur-a-sin-k-ar, implying 'the King of the Arya.' In its name appears *Gaur* implying the giant in the Aramaic tongue of the Hebrews.

In Nepal at the north of India had appeared the seventy peaks at the west of which stand the mountain Trinity including K², Ma-sha-brun and Gu-sha-brun, of which the first was exceeded in elevation only by the Mother Mountain. In the old Gond-w-ana to which they gave the name of India, forming a natural triangle, was to be seen the Vidya Range forming a natural "V" corresponding to the Dekkan or triangle.

Beside the great peaks of Khan Ten-g-ri and T-i-ri-chi Mir were the Ten Taux in Cir-ca-s-sia, and west of them were the Olympii, and Mount Blanc with the Yung Frau bearing a name similar to that of a range in China. Now, too, was to be seen the actual Mount Sin in Su-e-z. Similar amazing peaks had arisen in the western world where the Co-r-d-illera, 'the Serpent, the reincarnation of the Diva, the Isles of Ra,' extended from Alaska to the Falkland, and including many Ana-condas.

In the region of M-ana-so-ro-wa-ra at the west of old Burma was the lake from which trailed, like the roots of a Lotus, the three great rivers called the Indus, Brahma-p-o-o-t-ra, and Ganges, of which the last had broken through the H-i-ma-la-ya to join the Brahmapootra in a common delta.

Amazing as this must have seemed to those who beheld the Trinity of the three great ranges forming a triangle at the north of India, there was also the Euphrates and the Tigris uniting in the triangle of Mesopotamia to form a third stream, and together resembling another lotus to which traces the name E-u-phrates, 'the earth of the Twins, the flower.'

From the fourteen Olympii to the peak of Mount Sin-ai was but a step. Just as Mount Sin-ai had appeared as a natural symbol of Sin and as EnZu, was ever after revered as the lofty head, in K-en-ya, 'the king, the first, ya', had arisen close to Ki-li-man-ya-ro, the mountain near the Equator named Me-ru.[4]

Wonder of Wonders! On the equator in Uganda, had arisen in the land of the Ru the seven great peaks forming a natural swastika, or circle of six with one at the center. From it the Nile trailed northward like the root of another lotus, to the Aegean Sea.

Inasmuch as these grand peaks, called the Mountains of the Moon, still bear the name Ru-w-en-zo-ri, it is plain that the Ru had held on to the source springs of Egypt as well as to C-y-p-ru-s in the Aegean. It is equally plain that the Sinitics of the Fourth Root Race had occupied most of the regions of the earth, including the present South America, and in the end had asserted their sway over all but a mere handful of the Ru, who they had not destroyed, or absorbed.

No one pretending to be an historian, philosopher or metaphysician should argue seriously that the natural symbols which have been described, in their forming and in their naming, played no part in the evolution of civilization.

In view of the terrible ordeal through which the two races had evolved, it could have been no easy matter for the spiritual teachers to extend the new Solar Cult to the older peoples of the earth. While it is impossible to say when the shrines of Sin were established, the graph of Gea leaves no doubt as to the eventual reach of the Solar Cult. Thus, from Io-sin-fa Zembla, the trail of the Solar Cult leads straight south to Hel-sin-ki in Finland, Hel-sing-ford in Denmark, numerous places in Hel-ve-t-ia, Mount Ca-sin-no in Italy, Me-sin-na in Si-c-i-l-y, and Sin-tra in Portugal. To the east of Crete lies Sin-o-pe at the high point of Asia Minor. From there the trail leads to Mount Sin-ai, and to Sin-a-t-ra in Egypt. Thence it passes to Sin-i-ya that came to be called A-by-sin-ia in the Aryan cycle.

From Io-sin-fa Zembla also the trail leads in Si-beria to the pass of U-ru-m Chi in Sin-Kiang, thence southward to Sin-d and Sin-ga-pa-tam in India, and to the great land mass of Sin-ga-la in the Indian Ocean upon which Pi-da-ruta-sa-ga-la, or Adam's Peak, looms above the present Ceylon. In the ancient Burma stands Gaura-Sin, now called Everest. Beyond is Sin-am, Si-am, Singa-pore, and Mount Does-sin, or the Grand Rajah, on the equator in Borneo. In the land called T-zin, before it was called China, we find Tien-t-zin, 'God's Ford,' indicating quite plainly the port from which the cult of

Sin was conveyed to the Cainites and the other peoples of the Austral realms.

From Hel-sin-g-ford in Denmark, it leads westward to Sin-chester in Britain, and thence to the present Western Hemisphere. There the Sha-ta-mu (Hudson) became the Ta-s-wa-sin-tha, on which O-sin-in-g and Sin-g Sin-g are found. Westward the trail leads by W-is-con-sin on the antipodal meridian of Sin-Kiang in Siberia. There, too, we find W-y-is-si-l-in-g.

From various Sin Kings to the south of the Tawasintha, the trail of the Sinitics passes to Sin-ope in the Delta of the Mi-s-sip-pi where New Orleans now stands, and to S-el-os, at the site on which St. Augustine was erected.

Undoubtedly the Sinitics also entered North America from Asia, as we find at the south of Alaska, the domain of A-sin-a-bo-ia, due south of which is Sin-a-loa in Ana-huac. Eventually, at Lake Ti-ti-ca-ca near the present Rio da Sol in southwestern Brazil, Mama Sin-ya-cu would bear to the sun, implying the Solar Cult, the first Inca, Manco Copax, 'the ever widening circle of light.'

It was inevitable that during the churning of the peoples of the earth, which occurred during the Tertiary the Ru and the brown giants should have mixed to form the Punics, or so-called Mediterraneans. Only recently the anthropologist Bowers of Harvard reported that about eleven percent of the population of Tibet consisted of a reddish-brown people almost indistinguishable from the early Lapps and the older groups of North American Indians, who, according to him, had come from the northwest and they had been hidden away for ages in the gorges of the H-i-ma-la-ya, 'the Holy Spirit, the Maya, the Land of Ya.' We may assume that to these red-brown peoples trace the peculiar Iota, Lhota, and eight other tribes of Naga who down the ages have inhabited the Maya Hills in the Dekkan of India, and who insist that they are descended from King Se-cha, half-serpent, half-man, whose capitol, they say, is still in the west. Se-cha, however, was the name they applied to the Zodiacal band of light in the firmament. Therefore the implication of the serpent is plain.

Among the Naga who gather annually to worship at Mount Amara-k-an-t-ka (19° N. 81° E.), marking the meridian of the La-p-t-eve Sea, Lake Mana-so-ro-wa-ra in Tibet, and Adam's Peak in Ceylon, may be seen pipes similar to those of the Irish and Scottish Celts, and of the Ba-ski and the Italics. Also they possess shawls of wool resembling in their coloration, and mathematical designs the Tartans, dear to the Gaelic peoples as symbols of the mythical Tartarus. Among their gods is Amaraka, after whom their holy shrine was named. Furthermore, like the red Tibetans, they are all but indistinguishable from the older Indian types of America.

The ultimate fate of the Fourth Root Race which is said by the Hindus to have vanished from the earth, has been taken by many besides Plato to indicate the price of empire.

"What profiteth it if a nation gain the whole world and lose its soul."

How odd that today the English speaking people whose forebears claim descent from the Lion, should be expending their blood in a contest with the Communist Bear of Russia. Perhaps in the future men will dismiss this present conflict as incredible, just as many dismiss the strife between the Lion Men of Sin and the Bear Men of Atlantis. Yet the thoughtful must wonder just how much those who had adhered to the Cult of Python, reflecting the serpent in human nature, had come to be like the present Communists.

The persisting tradition that the Lion Men eventually turned black with sin, suggests that in the age of Sin, they not only turned morally blacker, but darker in complexion. On the other hand, the fact that none of the Fourth Root Race remained on the earth along with the few thousand Ru who survived the ordeal to which the two races were subjected, indicates that the Fourth Root Race vanished through absorption. However that may be, before the passing of this race, it had produced the seeds of the present race.

In this atomic age men are so much engrossed in marvelling at their own inventive genius, few have time to note one of the wonders of the world which no mortal hand could have fashioned, even though it is conceivable that nature may have been aided by human art.

Chart III, Chapter I shows that within the leaf projecting southward from the Polar Coronet, originally was included at the east Ireland, the British Isles and that part of France which came to be called Na-va-r-re. Within the leaf at the west lay the Canadian barrier. Upon passing from Plutarch's Ogygia (Greenland), a relic of the Polar Coronet, designated in the Queenland language as La-bra-d-o-r, one comes to the present Labrador, 'the Land of Brahma, the Diva, the Mother of Ru.' Adjacent to it is the province of Quebec, 'the Queen's Nose,' forming the eastern extremity of Canada. There stands the grand height, originally called Sha-ka-conia, 'the head of the King, the ark of the Serpent of the It-za', presently called Quebec. Moving due South one comes to the White Mountains where is found the group called the Presidential Range, of which the original Sha-ka-conia, now bears the name Mount Washington. A few miles to the west is the Sha-ka-conia Range. There is found Fra-an-con-ia Notch, in which one of the cliffs forming the pass displays the profile of Shaka, 'the head of the great spirit,' shown in the accompanying illustration.

Amazing as it may seem, the reflection of the cliff in the waters below displays the profile of Ana, the mother of the Universe. Thus this extraordinary symbol expresses the concept 'as above, so below.'

This was indeed one of the most extraordinary natural symbols upon the earth. The sanctity in which it was ever held is conclusive that for ages it was deemed a symbol of the great spirit. Here, indeed, was the cathedral of the American aborigines upon whom its influence was profound.[5] In view of the images to be seen in Christian cathedrals and pictures of God delivering the decalogue to Moses on Mount Sinai, it cannot be said with reason that 'the Watcher' was merely the idol of savages. Certainly George Washington, the Patriot Father who was thoroughly familiar with 'the Watcher' and its implications, had no such idea. Were he upon earth today, possibly he would advise his countrymen not to get rid of the teaching of the Bible in their schools, but to put a picture of 'the Watcher' in every Christian home, in order to encourage more respect for the Great Spirit of aboriginal America than is being shown by many of those who have forgotten the motto eventually placed on the coins of the Republic—"IN GOD WE TRUST."

Here it should be noted that Labrador lies on the meridian of Bra-zi-la, and that just as Sha-ka-conia or Mount Washington, marks the meridian of Lake Titicaca in southern Peru, 'the Watcher' marks the meridian of Cu-x-co, the ancient capital of Peru, where the first Inca is said to have inserted his golden wand in the earth at the crest of the Andes. In addition to all this, we know that the Serpent Cult common to all the tribes of America, bore the name N-ana-bo-za, to which A-sin-a-bo-ia and the God Set-i-bos of the Andes, as well as the tribes of Set-e-bos in Pa-ta-gon-ia, owed their names.

Also it must be noted that the meridian of Z-u-el-a, 'the Serpent, the Twins of Hell, the Ark,' which came to be called Venezuela, and is adjacent to Gui-ana and Bra-zi-la, was eventually marked by the great serpent mount on Lic-king Creek in Adams County, Ohio, displaying two coils in the tail of the serpent corresponding to the O's appearing in Ohio, and symbolizing the western and eastern hemispheres. Moreover, the natural symbol of a serpent holding in its mouth the egg formed by the island of Ma-Pa in Para, just as the serpent in Ohio holds a similar egg in its mouth, is formed by the Amazon.

Manifestly, therefore, 'the Watcher' was known to Plato when he penned the two Dialogues of Timaeus and Critias.

On the other hand, the mission which the H-ind-oo philosophers ascribed to the avatar Narasingha offers a full explanation of why the subject of the Lion-Men is avoided in *Genesis* inasmuch as it would challenge the idea of the omnipotence, the all-wisdom, and the all-mercy ascribed to God, since many men would say that if God possessed all these qualities, it would not have been necessary for Him to experiment with man. Such an argument has ever been held a specious one by the sages, ignoring utterly the philosophy embodied in the *Zend Avesta* and the *Venidad*. Only by darkness is true light known. Without the night there could be no day. Without evil there could be no measure of good. Perfect men would be mere automatons.

Why the ultimate perfection bringing men into communion with God, was deemed one of the motives of the Absolute, lies in the field of Metaphysics and, therefore, beyond the sphere of the historian who, has fulfilled his part in pointing out the arguments with which the sages among men, including Plato, have ever answered the atheist.

---

[1] Note that in the Theogony the Titan Atlas is said to have been begotten by Poseidon out of the Nymph Clymene, implying the Polar Coronet, and that in the name of L-e-u-c-ippi appears the *ippi* in Mississippi.

[2] It is to be noted that in the *Organon* of Aristotle it is recorded how the Phoenicians dispatched a colony to the land beyond the Azores at the height of the greatness of Carthage; that in the age of Aristotle red men from the West had visited Germany. That Hipparchus, the Hierophant of the Pythian Mysteries at Rhodes (B. C. 225) in referring to the antipodes used the name Autichthon: that Posidonius (c. B. C. 100), also the Hierophant of Rhodes, and the Tutor of the elder Cicero and Pompey, had no doubt that the Platonian myth was based upon fact: That Serterius, the Governor of Spain, wrote in B. C. 80 of the land of Antilles at the West: that Strabo, (B. C. 30) referred to the realms in the west: that in 8 A. D. there were five Maya at the Court of Augustus to whom the correction of the Julian Calendar was ascribed: that both Seneca and his nephew Pomponis Mela also referred to realms in the West. That Diodorus Siculus explained that Atlas was the name of the ancient astronomers who had surveyed the heavens and the earth: that the elder Pliny told of the dealings which the Emperor of Rome, had had with the King of the lands beyond Ultima Thule (Iceland). That Plutarch, the contemporary of Josephus and the elder Pliny, ever noted for his sagacity and veracity, deemed the Platonian myth an historical account, and referred to the Colony which the Greeks had long been maintaining in the land beyond Ogygia, (Greenland).

3 Just before the priesthood of France began appealing at the great monastery of Cluny for moral reform appeared the *Volsunga Saga,* also the Mu-spilli or the old High German epic of Bavaria. In the latter was contained the legubrious account of an earth destruction by fire in the past that was well calculated to encourage the unprecedented popular demand for reform attending the Cluniac Revival. Everywhere the freemasons whose Grand Lodge recently had been founded at York in England were whispering that the earth as it had existed was going to be destroyed in 1000 A. D. Consequently men were praying as they had never prayed before, deeply impressed by the revelations of the punishment visited upon the evil peoples of the past. Surely something of the kind is needed today.

4 Ki-li-mu-ana-ja-ro, 'the king, the lotus of Mu, Ana, the Mother of Ya, the Roc.'

5 Mount Washington stands due north of Salem, near Boston, and the shrine of Ac-co-ma-ac, at which Plymouth was founded, 'the Watcher' marks the meridian of Providence near which is Nara-g-ana-sett. We may assume, therefore, that the sacred shrines of Massachusetts were sited by the Re-na-pe in respect to "the watcher." The first French and English Colonists to visit the Coast of Maine were informed of the mysterious mountain at the north. Be it noted that John Smith had been made a Werowanwace of the Powhatan Confederacy at the instance of 'Pocahantas or Ma-ta-oca whose brother, Na-an-t-a-qu-a-s, was Sachem of the Ac-co-macs in Virginia.

In 1790 after Washington had submitted to Congress the treaty negotiated by him with the Six Nations of the Long House, prompting the Extended Lodge, implying the Freemasonry of the Indians still embodied in the Cult of Nana-bo-z-ha, and declared that so long as the grass grew and the waters flowed their rights would be respected, he was proclaimed by them H-o-r-n-ana-dan-i-gi-us, 'the Conqueror,' not in the sense of a mere vanquisher of the Red Man, but in that of a Spiritual Conqueror. Thus Hornandanigius in the Queenland language means the 'Holy Odin, the reincarnated spirit of Nu, Ana, the Mother of Heaven, Dan, the Spirit of the Gihon, the Chu.' That same year he caused to be placed on the official stationery of the Republic the spread eagle found carved on countless native rocks in America as a symbol of the Great Spirit of the Red Man, and with it in the Seal of the Republic the pyramid. Still in India Washington is held to have been an avatar.

CHAPTER XI

THE FIFTH ROOT RACE
THE ETHIOPIANS
THE GIFT OF TRISMAGISTUS

THE WISDOM PHILOSOPHY conceives of the present or Fifth
Root Race, as sprung from the seeds provided by the brown
giants of the Fourth Root Race and as having appeared like
the two preceding races in the land mass of which the North
Atlantic continent shown in chart 3, chapter I, was a relic.
Therefore, it is also said to have been born in Atlas.

Deemed to have appeared about five million years ago
while the Tertiary upheavals were taking place, like the Lion
Men, they are described as smaller than the parent race.
Nevertheless, they were still gigantic in stature. Consequently
on the earth today there are countless men nine feet tall and
more, while there is a whole tribe in Mongolia averaging
eight feet, six inches tall, and even larger than the Giants
of Northern Japan. Like the hermaphrodites on the earth,
they are throwbacks to their forebears.[1]

In *Genesis* 2 the description of the four heads having reference to the types of the mysteries existing in the Mosaic Age,
designated as Pison, Gihon, Hiddekel, and Euphrates, gives
the clue to the original color of the Ethiopians. Thus, while
Pison implies the red Ru, Gihon said to be that which "com-
passeth the whole land of Ethiopia", did not refer to the
Punics, or the red-brown mixture of the Ru and the Lion
Men, whose subraces remained upon the earth, but to actual
negroids presently inhabiting the earth. Moreover all the
peoples on the earth today, including the Yellow Subrace of
the Lion Men, are deemed the descendants of the negroids
called Ethiopians, who are known to the Greeks as Melas, save

the Pi-sha-cha and the Flat Heads of Ceylon and Australia, respectively.

The Melanesians of the South Pacific, and the Dravidians of Malaysia, their kindred constituting the Sudra of India, the dark peoples of Saudi-Arabia, Abyssinia, the Sudan, Nubea, and the yellowish Hottentots of South Africa in whose name the four t's represent a quadruple mixture, are all a mixed people with Punic and negroid blood in their veins.

To the negroid traces the name of the Black Sea, which a modern botanist undertook to trace a dark colored lotus' growing profusely in those parts.

Although *Genesis* makes no reference to the end of the Fourth Root Race, and no explicit reference to the Fifth, in Chapter 3, relating to the latter, it is said:

"20. And Adam called his wife's name E-v-e; because she was the mother of all living."[2]

Following this reference to the Ethiopians it is said:

"Unto Adam also and to his wife did the Lord God make coats of skins, and clothed them."

The coats of skins which *"also"* were furnished the teachers of the Solar Cult, of the present race, may be taken to imply the sacerdotal garb which in the past had been worn by the Adamites.

In the tablets of the Aryan Assyrians a distinction is made between the white Sa-r-ku and the older darker peoples referred to as Z-al-ma-t Guar-g-ar-di.[3]

For the reasons shown the Greeks do not explain explicitly anymore than do the Hindus and Hebrews, the appearance of the Ethiopian. Nevertheless, Atlas is described as begetting the ten Pleiades who were borne by Zeus in the form of a bull out of the cosmic sea. Including Maia, Merope, and Europa, eventually their names were applied to the astronomical pleiades. Because they were unintelligible to the Ru and Punics, the product of the Fifth cosmic deluge are described as chatterers.

As Maia implied the Mayavic teachers of the philosophy of

Atlantis, embodied in her name is found not only the name of the Maya, who applied it to the great plain of India, to Mesopotamia, a part of Irania, to the ancestors of the M-an-x, the island of Mona in the Irish Sea, the river, Meuse, M-i-lan, Mi-chi-g-an, Mi-n-ne-so-ta, and Mi-n-ne-ha-ha. The name of the Melas, however, also appears in Mesopotamia and Mede, as well as in Medi Terre, and Cu-m-me-ria on the Black Sea.

Because the Ethiopians, designated in *Genesis* as Eve, produced all but a few of the antedeluvians, they were collectively referred to along with the surviving Ru and the Punics as the E-ni-x, 'the Ethiopians of the Nilus, the Chi'. And as we find the Shat el Nil in Syria at the north of Asia Minor, we find Ni-c-a-ea at the west of Ni-nus, or Nineveh. Eventually the Enix would produce the *Book of Chon,* or *Khon,* tracing to the Ethiopian God, K-hon-su, in Egypt, who was enshrined at Giza, where the mysteries of the Gi-hon were established.

Known to the Mosaic scribes as the Chus, the second son of Ham, to the Hebrews of antiquity they were known as Ch-u-si-tes. According to Josephus, their history was so antique that much of it was lost. Apparently, however, Josephus was not anxious to revive it.

The first culture in Egypt is ascribed in the *Book of the Dead* embodied in the pyramid text to the Shezoo H-o-r, to whom Ho-ru-s, the alleged son of Osiris-Isis, owed his name. Just above Mount Sinai in Suez, we find Mount Hor, while Osiris and Horus were both said to have been born at Mount Nis-sa, ever identified with Mount Sin. The mysterious San-chi-o-nu-i-t-hon, to whom the *Book of Chon* is ascribed, merely implied the Hierophants of the Syrian mysteries.

Among the oldest scriptures in Greece is an inscription on the Lion Gate forming the adit of the Colossal circle of M-y-c-en-ae in Argos, just south of the present Gulf of Corinth in the region to which was first applied the name Europa. Significantly over the Gateway two lions rampant, facing each other appear as a symbol of the two gigantic races on the earth, back to which the present British Crest may be traced through the Manx. In this inscription we are told that the civilization of the Nilus was due to M-i-z-r, a wandering priest of Atlantis. Thus we have a complete explanation of the name Me-m-ph-i-s, 'Melas, Moo, the phoenix, the spirit of the Serpent,' and also of the name The-ba, common to Greece and Egypt. Properly interpreted as 'Melas, the Spirit of the Serpents, the Ru,' the name Mizr appears in the name Mizraim applied by the Mosaic scribes to Egypt, whose people were not called Egyptians by the Hebrews of antiquity, but were known to them as Mesraites.

To Chon, the Hibernians of the mythical E-r-in and the British traced back their culture, the latter through the Cimbrians, descendants of the Manx. For the Iberians or cross bearers, hence called Hibernians by the Greeks. The Cimri and Cimbrians were kinsmen of the Cimmerians.

Nowhere, however, is the name of the Chon better preserved than in America where we find it in the White Mountains as in Cho-cu-ra. In Maryland are the Cho-p-ta-n-k, in North Carolina the Cho-w-ana-oc, and in Mississippi the Cho-c-taw. In Ida-ho the Nez Perces of the French were called Cho-pu-n-ish, while the Sho-sho-n-es of the Rockies also were called the Cho-cho-ne, and the Comanche bore the alternate name of the Cho-un-man. In California were the Cho-lovone, to which traces the euphonic Ca-la-for-ni-a of the San Joaquin Valley, a name eventually converted into Ka-li-fa. In Nicaragua and Guatemala were the Chon-t-als, while in Mexico we find the Cho-lu-lu, in Colombia the Cho-cos, and in Chi-le the Cho-r-illos. So is fully explained the darker color of the older, long-haired aborigines of America, of the Algonquin, Mu-s-ko-gi and the Zu-ni types, and the pure Negroid Mu-sos and Setibos inhabiting the Andes.

In accord with the ancient records modern anthropologists conceived of the White Race as an evolution through the Caucasians in the region of the White Sea, from a melange of red, black and brown peoples whose blood along with yellow blood entered into the Eskimo, who circulated around the Arctic Circle from the Yellow Sea at the north of Asia.

The idea that the new Negroids evolved in the southern climes because they were more favorable to the black man than the northern climes is without warrant or fact. Still one of the most carefully veiled facts of ancient history is the terrific struggle that raged down the ages between the Borean predecessors of the Negroids and the ancestors of the present race. Holding in contempt the black man, the Ru and the Punics had no idea of surrendering their tenure of the northern realms to a younger race upon whom they looked, as all older peoples do upon younger ones, as their inferiors.[4]

To be sure the Negroids differed greatly physically from the Boreans especially in the texture of their hair and by reason of a peculiarity of the epidermis, which gave them a characteristic odor, offensive to the Boreans.[5] Yet, there is no evidence of inherent inferiority in an intellectual sense of the Negroids.[6]

No other race has been subjected to such continuous physical strain as the Negroids, and particularly the Melanites, by reason of the terrifying mutations of the earth in the southern climes where the Negroids who were not absorbed by the older races were eventually driven. This ordeal coupled with the inveterate prejudice of the Boreans readily accounts for the relative backwardness of the race at the beginning of historic times. Yet, the Negroids varied greatly according to their environments.[7] This being so, the rational conclusion is that the Negroids today are what their environment and the circumstances to which they were subject have made them.

About two million years were to elapse between the appearance of the Negroid and the beginning of the current Mahayuga (B.C. 2,596,004).

The names assigned the four ages of the Mahayuga have no reference to material culture in the sense of the Stone, Bronze, and Copper Ages of modern anthropologists. Instead they accord with the Hindu concept that as civilization ad-

MAHAYUGA BEGINNING IN B.C. 2,596,004

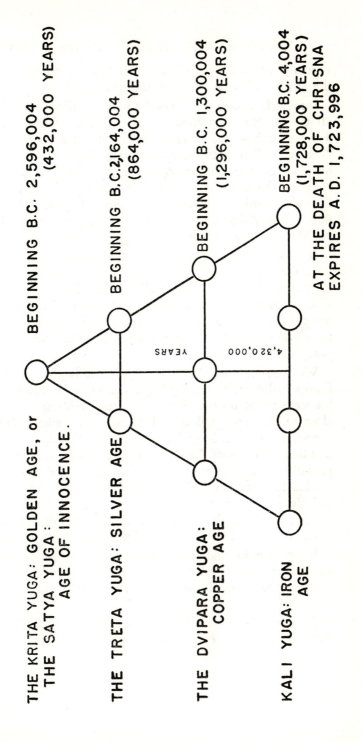

THE KRITA YUGA: GOLDEN AGE, or
THE SATYA YUGA:
AGE OF INNOCENCE.

BEGINNING B.C. 2,596,004
(432,000 YEARS)

THE TRETA YUGA: SILVER AGE

BEGINNING B.C. 2,164,004
(864,000 YEARS)

THE DVIPARA YUGA: COPPER AGE

BEGINNING B.C. 1,300,004
(1,296,000 YEARS)

KALI YUGA: IRON AGE

BEGINNING B.C. 4,004
(1,728,000 YEARS)
AT THE DEATH OF CHRISNA
EXPIRES A.D. 1,723,996

4,320,000 YEARS

vances it becomes ever darker with the materialism of which the strife and wars of economic man are born.

Inasmuch as *Genesis* offers the most detailed chronology of all the esoteric scriptures, it will be relied upon hereinafter. Tracing back to the Hebrews who did not appear until B.C. 783,000, well on into the cycle of the *Diva Para,* 'Lunar Philosophy,' of the Copper Age, corresponding to the copper color of the first Caucasians who appeared in B.C. 950,000, *Genesis* affords no chronological guide beyond B.C. 2,506,-000 in the Krita Yuga, or the Age of Innocence, which is readily explained by geology.

It was not until about the beginning of the current Mahayuga that the Tertiary uplifts had brought into being all the present mountain ranges, and had abated to the point that civilization in its present sense could begin. It is to be noted however, that the current Mahayuga begins at just the time to which the human stem is carried back by modern anthropologists.[8]

We may be sure, however, that already the Ru and the Punics had come to occupy the Medi Terre in which the Melas were to set up the Sinitic mysteries at Me-sin-na in Sicily close to the active volcano of Mount Etna, where Vulcan is supposed to have forged for Zeus the thunderbolts corresponding to those of Indra.[9] Therefore, just as the Italic Enya-li-us corresponds to the Roman Ju-pi-t-ur and to the Seven-headed Serpent Nara-ya-na of the Hindus, we find in Vulcan and Vesuvius, names implying the destructive forces in nature impersonated by the Hindu *Vitra* and the Brahmin *Shiva,* representing Vishnu in the evolutionary aspect of Brahma.

If we are to understand what next appears in *Genesis,* we must bear in mind the world of Ana and what lay at the west of the Medi Terre as part of the Kingdom of Atlas, when Adam V appeared.

Even though the uplifts may have ceased by B.C. 2,596,004, the earth was still discharging gas through the countless ac-

ANOTHER ARRANGEMENT OF THE MAHAYUGA

Showing cycles of 432,000, 864,000, 1,296,000, and 1,728,000 years, bearing the relations of 1, 2, 3, and 4, contained within a theoretical triangle. Corresponding spheres would be contained by either a truncated tetrahedron or a truncated pyramid. The four cycles here shown constitute the Krita, Treta, Dvipara, and Kali Yugas of the current Mahayuga which is conceived to have begun in B. C. 2,596,004.

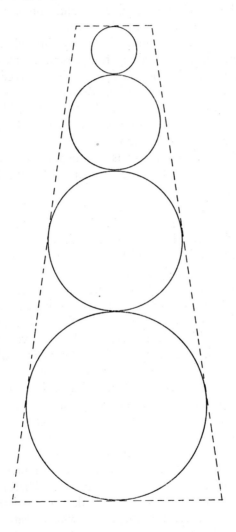

It should be noted that while a sphere is deemed in the Wisdom Philosophy to have evolved from the Universal Dodecahedron of Pythagorean Philosophy, W. Lothian Green in his _Vestiges of the Molten Globe_ (1875), evolves the earth in its present form from a tetrahedron of primal rock of which he conceives that the points which arose out of the seas were worn down to form the present continents.

tive volcanoes such as Etna, Vesuvius, and those in Oceanica and Polynesia.

While the Black and Red Seas and the Gulf of Persia did not exist, the waters of the great rivers of Russia, like those in the Caucasus, found their way through the vanished land of Samo-thrax, and along the present course of the Dardanelles to a small inland sea from which evolved the present Aegean, that was known to the Romans as the Mare Internum because of its former inland nature. Possibly even Cyprus like the Cyclades were not yet islands. Certainly Crete was still attached to Grecaland.

From this small sea also passed the waters of the Nile, by a stream passing between the present Sicily and Tripolitania, which carried the waters collected from the rivers of Libya to another small sea just inside the present Pillars of Hercules.

At the west of the present Iberian peninsula we find Port-u-gala, which derived its name from 'Port of Gallia', implying that from the harbors of Lisbon and other cities of the Lusitani, intercourse was had with Posidonis.

It had been over 15,000,000 years since the separation of the sexes when the current Mahayuga began and certainly several million years more since the first Adamites appeared. To argue some things is unnecessary. In the accompanying diagram appears the magic upon which the concept of the Mahayuga itself was based, or the mathematical learning which had been handed down by the mythical Trismagistus.

About what appears in the accompanying diagram, as in the phenomenon of light, there was no black magic. From the forms shown evolved a whole hexagonic system of mathematics, pursuant to which the period of the rotation of the earth was fixed at 24 hours, each of 60 minutes, while each minute was divided into a second minute. Therefore an hour consists of 60x60, or 3600, and a day of 86,400 seconds.

Observe, however, the magic to which mathematics owe their name. The 8, 6, 4, 0, 0 in 86,400 gives 14 — 2×7, or the septenary principle common to the celestial and terrestrial

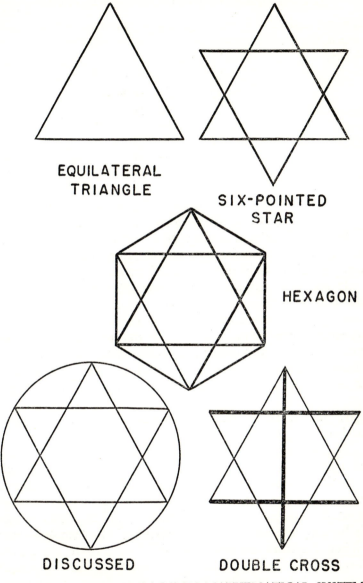

EQUILATERAL
TRIANGLE

SIX-POINTED
STAR

HEXAGON

DISCUSSED

DOUBLE CROSS

THE BASIS OF THE HEXAGONIC MATHEMATICAL SYSTEM
Note that the Pentagon in the Pythagorean Philosophy is derived by
placing together the apeces of five triangles, or by connecting five
equal lines each forming with the other an angle of 120°.

spheres. Indeed, there was magic in the ten numerals with which the Arabic symbols here shown were designed to indicate.

$$1 \times (3 + 3 + 3) = 9$$
$$2 \times (3 + 3 + 3) = 18$$
$$3 \times (3 + 3 + 3) = 27$$
$$4 \times (3 + 3 + 3) = 36$$
$$5 \times (3 + 3 + 3) = 45$$
$$6 \times (3 + 3 + 3) = 54$$
$$7 \times (3 + 3 + 3) = 63$$
$$8 \times (3 + 3 + 3) = 72$$
$$9 \times (3 + 3 + 3) = 81$$
$$10 \times (3 + 3 + 3) = 90$$

In the left column starting at 1 and reading down to 10 and then upward in the right column from 0 to 9 is found a complete circle which no mathematician can explain.

It was observed that it required 365 days designated as the year, for the poles, or points at which the band of celestial light intersected the ecliptic of the sun, to complete an apparent circuit around the sun. Therefore, the year was divided into twelve months, constituting four seasons of three months each, and here note that the 1 and 2 in 12 yield $1 + 2 = 3$, the number corresponding to the trifoil. Also 365 gave $52 \frac{7}{+}$. Therefore, the year was divided into 52 weeks, and in $5 + 2$ we find 7.

The septenary principle upon which the hexagonic system of mathematics was based, was common to the band of light resembling a serpent swallowing its tail, implying no beginning, no end, and to the ecliptic of the sun. Therefore, both were divisible into a Dek-kad made up of the decimus symbolized by the numeral 10, representing one complete cycle. When, therefore, the two arks were divided by 10, the unit 36 was derived. Here note that $3 \times 6 = 18$, while $1 + 8 = 9 = 3 \times 3$. On the other hand $3 + 6 = 9 = 3 \times 3$.

To obtain a practical unit of circular measure, the entire

circle was divided into 360 units called degrees, each symbolized by a circle, while each degree was divided into 60 minutes,
and each minute into 60 second minutes. Thus in a degree
there were $60 \times 60 = 3600$ seconds, and in each circle there
were 360 degrees; $360 \times 60 = 19,600$ minutes; and $360 \times
60 \times 60 = 129,600$ seconds. Just as 360 yields $3 + 6 + 0
= 9 = 3 \times 3$; the total of 19,600 yields 16 whereof $1 + 6
= 7$; also that 129,600 yields $18 = 6 \times 3$, whereof $6 + 3 =
9 = 3 \times 3$, and $6 \times 3 = 18$, while $1 + 8 = 9 = 3 \times 3$.

Let it also be noted that in the 365 days into which each of
three years were divided, and the 366 days into which the
fourth, or leap year, was divided so as to give four years an
average of 365.25 days, we find $3 + 6 + 5 = 14 = 2 \times 7$;
$1 + 2 = 3$. Moreover $3 + 6 + 5 + 2 + 5 = 21 = 7 \times 3$.
Also, 52, the number of weeks, yields $5 + 2 = 7$, and $5 \times
2 = 10$.

Also it will be observed that the band of light is 16° wide,
and that 6 yields $1 + 6 = 7$.

To be sure it was possible to establish a standard of lineal
measure with which to measure the lines forming the triangles,
squares, and hexagons of plane geometry, but when it came
to measuring the spherical arcs man was completely baffled for
the simple reason that a circle is formed by an infinite number
of polygons, and infinity by definition is immeasurable. Therefore, those who formulated the science of trigonometry were
compelled to resort to the mathematical factor found in nature of 3.141599 + that carries on to infinity, in order to approximate the measure of a circle. And here it is to be noted
that $3.141.159 + 29 + = 2 \times 9 = 18$, while $1 + 8 =
9 = 3 \times 3$.

Inasmuch as the mathematical constant was one that no mortal could explain except by its ascription to an Infinite Wisdom,
it was symbolized by the Pi (Philosophy of the One) in the
primordial alphabet, and presently by the Pi displaying the
sign of Infinity, called the para-ll-el, in conjunction with the
plane of matter.[10]

Pythagorean philosophy conceived of a sphere evolving from the so-called Universal Dodecahedron, a solid form possessing 12 triangular faces as when two hexahedrons are placed with their bases together. If the number of faces, 12, corresponding to the signs of the zodiac, should be expanded to an infinite number the sphere would result.

The plane of joinder of the hexahedrons, however, being a hexagon, would intercept the circumference of the sphere at six points, giving the six arcs into which Hipparchus divided the circle.

It was upon the concept of the Universal Dodecahedron that the signs of the zodiac were based. Thus each of the twelve was included within a segment of the zodiacal band of light, 30° × 16°, each including a constellation of stars in which were seen signs of the Divine Design. To each sign was given an animistic name although the constellations do not in fact in some cases possess animistic forms. Yet, one of them, or the constellation of the Southern Cross, forms the *tau,* or the Egyptian *ankh* which was deemed to have been the symbol of the Spirit of God upon the waters.[11]

As yet the mathematician has not lived who has explained the magic reflected in the hexagonic system of mathematics which by early man was ascribed to an inscrutable wisdom transcending human imagination. Only that wisdom could have placed the ten visible planets in the mathematical relations of Bode's Law.

Verily does magic handed down to the present race by the mythical Trismagistus in the transparencies, or Sylvan Temples, present to modern scientists a mystery that no atheist may solve by ignoring it. Until it is explained as the invention of man, it would seem that there is in fact a force superior to that which Lion and Bear Men may develop, a wisdom transcending the imagination of man. So far no self-styled scientist has ever denied this without sooner or later being discredited by Science itself.[12]

1 Pausanias (c. 150 B. C.) tells of the remains seen by him of a man thirty feet tall, while the Spanish historian, De Vega tells of the remains found in the Andes of other giants.

2 E-v-e, 'the earth (Ebba), the vehicle of the Ethiopians.'

3 Z-al-ma-t, 'The Z of Atlantis, The Maya, Taux.' Guar-g-a-r-di, 'the Giants, the gods of the Ark, the Rishi, the Divine Spirits.'

4 See *Hermeneutic Interpretation of the Origin of the Social State of Man,* D'OLIVET (1814), Putnam Reprint (1914).

5 Even today the Indians of North America look askance on the black-red Zambos as white men do upon mulattos.

6 The odor of the Negroids was no more offensive to the Boreans than that of the latter to the Negroids. The famous big game hunter White told the writer it was difficult to keep the Safaris in the same tree with the white man, that they would risk their lives in preference to the sickening smell of a white man.

One of the worst punishments that can be meted out to a Japanese soldier is to place him on guard over Russians.

All races have distinctive odors. In the first World War the British and French soldiers claimed to be able to distinguish dead Germans in the dark by their smell.

Much remains to be discovered by Science with respect to odor in the matter of personal attraction between peoples, some of whom are highly offensive to horses and dogs, while others are especially pleasing to these animals.

7 Of the three families of Negroes among the southern slaves were the highly intelligent chocolate-colored Senegambians, with high foreheads and large eyes, undoubtedly with arabic blood in their veins and also that of the Berbers of Morocco to the north of Senegambia. They were the most highly prized as household servants and artisans, and often won their freedom because of their loyalty and efficiency. The Zulu type from the Congo were gigantic warriors, dangerous and intractable, and were sold off to be worked in gangs under whip on the indigo and rice plantations of the south. The least prized were the ill-shapen, relatively small Negroes from Guinea, with small eyes, low foreheads, pot bellies and bandy legs. Because of their communal habits acquired in the bush of Africa, they had little idea of property and were often treated as thieves by nature, seldom being used as household servants. While the Negroes of today have little idea of all these things and have become mixed, still distinct types are found among them.

8 See *Antiquity of Man,* KEITH.

9 E-t-na, 'the Enyalius, the Taux of the Mother Ark.' En-ya-l-i-us, 'The First Ya, the Logus, The Spirit of Uranus.'

10 Para-ll-el, 'the Philosophy of the two lines of God.'

11 T-a-u, 'The Tree of the Ark, the Divine Twins.' An-k-h, 'Ana, the King, Ha.'

12 The United Nations would serve mankind well if representing Hindus, Buddhists, Jews, Christians and Moslems alike, it would invite the Polit Bureau of Moscow which is claiming for Russia all the inventions of man, to explain what has been shown in this Chapter.

CHAPTER XII

THE EXPULSION FROM THE GARDEN OF EDEN
THE FOUNDING OF GOD'S HOUSE
THE ABYSS OF LEARNING
CAIN AND ABEL

WHEN THE generations of Adam V as given in *Genesis* 5 are calculated in Biblical years, each of 1,000 Solar years, the beginning of the Adamic cycle carries back to B.C. 2,560,000 as shown in the accompanying design.[1]

The names of the generations, of course, are those employed by the Mosaic scribes and imply nothing of blood as do the alleged sons and daughters of Adam V that appear in the successive cycles. In other words, they are the names, implying the degree of the mysteries in the cycles given.

To the Adamic cycle must be related the events described in *Genesis* 3 following the appearance of Adam V, and Eve, who as shown, merely represented the Earth in the Ethiopian Cycle.

"22. And the Lord God said, Behold Man is become as one of us, to know good and evil."

In other words the spiritual teachers of the mysteries had brought the enlightenment of the selected Adamites of the Fifth Root Race to the point where they had nothing more to teach these aids.

With the Ru, Punics, Ethiopians and the Sub Races of the Lion Men, including the yellow Sinitics, all inhabiting the earth coevally, it would have been inevitable that a new reign of tooth and claw would have continued, had not the people of the earth been stabilized and disciplined by agriculture in the manner indicated in *Genesis* 6:17, and would have lived forever as mere warring nomads. Therefore, with re-

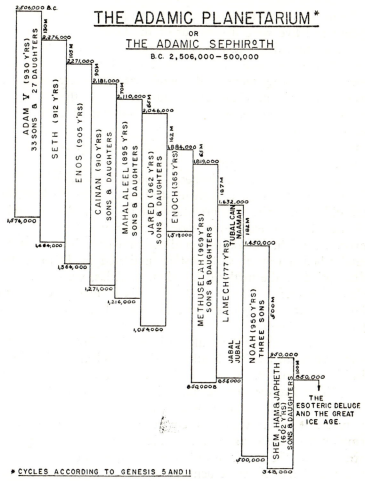

THE ADAMIC PLANETARIUM*

OR

THE ADAMIC SEPHIROTH

B.C. 2,506,000 — 500,000

* CYCLES ACCORDING TO GENESIS 5 AND 11

spect to the Ethiopians who had come to occupy the Garden of
Eden, as well as the Ru and the Punics, it is said:

"And now, lest he put forth his hand, and take *also* of
the tree of life, and eat, and live forever; Therefore the Lord
God sent him forth from the Garden of Eden, to till the
ground from whence he was taken."

"23. So he drove out the man."

Here, however, it is not said, as commonly assumed, that Adam and Eve were driven out of the Garden of Eden.

Agriculture demanded a permanency of tenure, and to insure this, even more than the teaching of man to set apart their holdings by metes and bounds was necessary. Families would expand into clans, clans into tribes, and then into nations. Still, therefore, warfare would continue if domains or isles were not set apart to the larger groups to be held with the sanction of the spiritual authority. This required that the whole earth be surveyed.

Inasmuch as both hemispheres were now occupied by different types of men, a more central place than Zealand, or the old Mount Sin, was necessary for the hierarchy of God's House. To this end, even though the seats of the various mysteries might be located in different parts, there must be established a central seat, just as indicated by Plato in his description of the mythical kingdom of Atlas, with laws proclaimed therefrom corresponding to those Plato ascribed to Poseidon. In no other scripture are these laws so well dealt with as by Plato.

It has been shown how the various Oracles of the Zealand were established in the Svalbard Islands and at the Zemblas. In historic times the Pi-ra-ti of the Dracontia Cult, from whom the Three Brothers of Scandinavia, were descended, as adherents of the doctrine of Karma still taught that the magic imparted to men would surely turn against them were it employed to serve material ends alone. Of this concept their symbol was the magic sword they call the Ch-er-u-b possessing the shape of the cruciform sword of Ares and Mars.[2] Moreover, the Norse Arians in the time of Charlemagne still were praying for the return of Bal-d-ur, who they predicted would be resurrrected as the Son of Light and Love, and whose memory was preserved through the Festival of Chris, to which the Christian Christmas traces. Nor is it to be overlooked that the common concepts of the Christians and the Arians were due to the fact that the Peoples of the Sea had overrun Asia

Minor and Egypt during the Mosaic Age, before the Scriptures were compiled. Therefore, the Cher-ub, 'the Divine Lotus of the Ethiopians and the Ru, Brahma', to which the Pirati ascribed the divine magic of the mythical Trismagistus was ascribed by the compilers of *Genesis* to archangels, to one of whom, Michael, as the Avenger, was given a sword. This like the Spear of Athena indicated an enforcer of the Law of Karma. Accordingly, after the statement that the man was driven out of the garden, it is said in *Genesis* 3:

"24. And he placed at the east of the garden of Eden Cherubim, and a flaming sword which turned every way, to keep the way of the tree of life."

In this passage, it is not declared that the "Cherubim and a flaming sword" were placed in the eastern part of the garden. Instead they were said to have been placed "at the east of the garden". Therefore one must look beyond E-din-nu, or the Hebraic garden of Eden, for the Flaming Sword.

At the north of the part of Siberia called Kar-e-lia, spread the K-ara and La-pa-t-ere Seas in which lie the I-o-sin-Fa, No-va-ya, and S-eve-r-n No-va-ya Zemblas. Due south of the last lies the realm of Mon-go-la wherein today is found the great desert of G-o-b-i. Geology shows that from the Sea that once covered it the waters were swept during the cataclysm which began in B.C. 10,000, southeastward upon the realm today called Chi-na, submerging for many millenniums the land to which long since the Ru and Lion Men had conveyed the Maya Ark.³ In this Sea were islands of which the great dunes to be seen today in the Gobi are the relics.

In the Gobi twelve of the islands, including the present dune of Kara-ko-ru-m or Cha-ra-chota (104° E.), centered at 40° N. 100° E., and together constituted a terrestrial zodiac. Here, according to the Hindus was the Abyss of Learning; also known to them as Mount Meru. In a word the Abyss of Learning implied the spiritual high place of the Ru which actually had fallen into a terrestrial abyss.

Here it is to be noted that the Cherubim and the Flaming

Sword, implying in fact the Christoes of the Kabira, and the Magic of Trismagistus embodied in the Philosophy of the Zodiac, were enshrined on the latitudinal circle of Mount Baris (40° N. 44° E.) or Mount Ararat, in the Ararat Range, just 56° E. of the holy height revered by the Hebrews. In Mount Ararat, however, is to be seen but a natural symbol as the high place known successively to the predecessors of the Hebrews as Mount Amaravati, Mount Mandara and Mount Sin.

The human agency through which God's House was established is plain. In the Rama-y-ana it is recorded that the Na-ac-als, 'Nara, the Light of Atlantis', a secret brotherhood of the Maya, arrived from Patala, or Hell in the west, in Burma, and from there, as missionaries of learning and religion conveyed their cult successively to the Dek-ka-ana of India, Chaldea, and Egypt.

Dayanand Saraswati, the great Hindu pundit and leader of the Aryan reform movement during the excitement in the west over the ape man, pointed out that Burma originally included all that part of Asia beyond India. Thereby he explained what is indicated by geology. Burma evolved from the head of the bird-shaped continent shown in Chart II, Chapter I, wherein India appears at the mouth.

It does not take much imagination to see that just as the Sinitics of India and Nara-sin-g-ha, derived their names from Sin, N-a-ac-al implied the 'Nether Ark, the Light of Atala,' and that to the Naacals traces the name of the red H-ak-ka of whom the present peculiar red peoples of China and Formosa are the descendants, and who produced the Ak-ka-dians, or the first Arcadians of Asia and Asia Minor whose language was common to China and Mesopotamia. In a word, the Naacals were the Adamites who established the Erythrean Ark in the Abyss of Learning which was called Mount Me-Ru by the Hindus because of the red Adamites. To them, of course, also traced the wise men called Na-g-als. 'Dragons', and 'Devils', in Burma, said to have been great magicians, or Daityas, just as the Naguals of Arizona and Mexico, to whom the Maya of those parts traced their culture, were known as serpents. The Hakka of Asia, of course, explained the Hakka of America, with whom the Skidi Pawness of Texas were associated. Also to the Naacals may be traced the once sacrosanct area of Korea, 'the Kings of the Serpent Cult, the Ru, the Erythrean Ark', known as the Hermit Kingdom until the Russians overran Siberia and gained access to Korea through Antung. Likewise is explained the concept of the Japanese, among whom appears Ha-kai-do, and who conceived of themselves as the Sons of Heaven and of the Mi-ka-do as of divine origin.[4] In the mythical B-u-shi-d-o of the Japanese, we see 'Bird, the Twins, the Spirit of the Diva, the Moon,' deemed the Soul of Nippon.

Following the reference to the Abyss of Learning in *Genesis,* is the story of Cain and Abel, in which the so-called esotericists have found especial delight because of its abstruse implications. Yet this myth too is subject to a rational interpretation.

The first and second sons ascribed to Adam and Eve following the expulsion from the Garden do not imply races, but merely two variants of a similar philosophy.[5] Here, no attempt will be made to deal with the many possible implications of the myth. Suffice it to say that naturally the first converts made by the Naacals would have been among the yellow Subrace of the Lion men in the region of the Yellow Sea, whose spiritual seat ultimately became Pe-kin, 'the House of God'.

According to Josephus, the eponymous C-a-in, 'the Celestial Ark, Indra,' was the first to employ weights and measures, and to set apart their lands by metes and bounds. This, of course, enabled them to develop the trade and commerce for which the Chinese have ever been noted, and who are said to have been the first to develop the prismatic compass as well as gunpowder.[6]

Abel, however, is assigned the character of a shepherd, implying that they were pastorals of the first Ethiopian Adamites in the region of the Abyss, and also missionaries in the spiritual sense.

As time went on, the Cainitic Adamites became ever more materialistic, and therefore, despite their alleged professions, did not find favor with God's House by reason of their superficial sacrifices.

The result of these two types of Adamites coming into contact with each other was inevitable. Just as always those who have preempted a domain, resent intrusions by a pastoral type of man, just as always the pastors of a new cult are odious to the devotees of an older one, the Abelites incurred the jealousy and enmity of the Cainites. In vain, "the Lord" pleaded with the latter to mend their ways, pointing out that "sin" lay at their door, which implied that the people of Asia generally were Sinitics. If only they would obey their teachers, Sin would do their bidding. They must beware, for already the earth was opening its mouth, crying for the blood of evildoers. These pleas were vain. The Cainites had what they wanted and did not propose to yield it up. Undoubtedly there was actual strife between them and the Abelites. Eventually Cain lay in wait for his brother Abel and slew him with a stone. This does not alone imply that the slings of primordial warfare such as the bola employed by modern savages to destroy men and beasts, were used by the Cainites, but the stone of idolatry as well. For as the sacred books of the east show, the concept of Tien whose name appears in Tien Sin, 'God's Ford', the port of Pe-king, was preceded by that of an evil moon goddess corresponding to Lilith, and the Pythoness.

Pursuant to the law of retribution, Karma, despite their protests and pleas, the Cainites could not avoid responsibility for their brother. When at last they were called to account by the hierarchy of God's House, the inevitable penalty was meted out to them. The exile of Cain and the mark said to have been placed on his forehead by the Lord so that none would kill him, are readily explained.

It was not the function of the spiritual teachers of God's House, to punish men by executing them. As yet the rite of crucifixion had not been instituted by the Iranians. Instead the Black Magicians, or evil Daityas of the Cainites, were to be confined to the island of Daitya at the east of Burma. The Naacals furnished the human agency for the herding of the exiles. Any who slew the latter while they were migrating were to suffer "seven-fold," that is, they would pay the unavoidable penalty which murder invoked pursuant to the law of Karma and during the process of reincarnation through the circuit of the seven planets, even if the murderers were not detected and punished according to man-made law. The mark said to have been placed on the brow of Cain may be taken to imply the yellow color of the Cainitic Adamites. The name Nod coined by the Mosaic scribes to designate the island which was set apart to the exiles is but another cryptic eponym, implying a realm that had vanished from the earth into the Nether World long before the Mosaic Age.[7]

It would be ages, as shown by Josephus, before all the banished Cainites reached Daitya. For, in fact, the earth *was* actually opening its mouth just as indicated in *Genesis*.

It was about B.C. 2,500,000 when as shown by geology, the appalling catastrophe occurred of which Adam is said to have given warning. Therefore, just as Adam is said to have prophesied that the earth was to be destroyed by fire, now began the seismic disturbances attended by volcanic action, during which the great insular land mass of Sin-ga-la, known to the Hindus of a later cycle as La-n-ka, 'Land of the Nether, King of the Ark,' which had come to extend from near Madagascar eastward to Malaya, was destroyed with the sole exception of the present Ceylon, upon which Adam's Peak, or Pi-di-ruta-saga-la has arisen. Only a handful of the Pi-sha-cha, or non-Aryan Ru in Sin-ga-la survived this awful earth destruction.

Recent explorations by the American Bureau of Hydrography, in collaboration with the world-wide Oceanic Survey for which Lord Ross of England made financial provision through the Royal Academy, have enabled the mountain range that once connected the Punjab of India with Persia and Arabia, to be mapped with precision, just as the two Rosses had long since mapped the vanished part of Gondwanaland that formed the connecting link between Africa and Brazil. Later, too, the Bureau of Hydrography of the United States Navy remapped the vanished realms of the Atlantic, and those of the Pacific. Not only are the mountain ranges, and their peaks known today, but the valleys and the river courses of the vanished lands of both La Mu Ra and Atlantis.

In view of these vast researches we may conclude with reason that it was the earth destruction of this time that enlarged the Gulf of Persia and the Arabian Sea approximately to their present forms, and that it had much to do with the exile of the Cainites.

Inasmuch as the geologists have fixed no age for the severance of the Afro-Brazilian Continent shown on Chart IV, Chapter I, it seems highly likely that it was now this earth destruction also occurred, of which the record is preserved in the old high German Epic of Bavaria, called the Muspille of unknown origin, which appeared about 900 A.D., during the Cluniac Reformation when the free masons were predicting an end of the world in 1000 A.D.

Whatever the facts may be the relics of the old Afro-Brazilian Continent are found in the C-ana-r-y, Ma-d-e-i-ra, and Cape Verde Islands, the islands of Fernando Po and Saint Helena, and also in the Roc of Sao Paulos, and in the Island of Tri-na-da-d, both off the west coast of Brazil.

The destruction of Sin-ga-la and of the South Atlantic land mass connecting Gui-n-ea with Gui-ana could not have failed to exert a tremendous psychological influence upon the Ethiopians just as the equatorial mountains in Asia had done. Because of the effect of the great uplifts that brought into being the Altai, Tian Shian, Kuenlun, Hindu Kush, and Himalaya Ranges, still today a form of hysteria is found among the inhabitants of the Altai.

In the case of the Afro-Brazilian land mass, more than the civilization which had existed in the connecting link was wiped out. If a map be examined, it will be seen exactly why the upper part of Africa above the triangular part below the Sahara is largely a desert. When the connecting link was submerged, the zone of the Sahara was drained, either into the Nile Valley at the east or into the Atlantic through the Sen-e-ga-l and Niger Rivers and their tributaries. Moreover the waters of the equatorial zone in which is to be found the great system of the Congo, continued to flow southward from the highlands. Inevitably in course of time a once verdant land, parched by the Sirocco, became a desert with only oases here and there. It is to be noted that the present Sahara Desert has the same name as the Sahara Sea which receives the waters of the Ganges and Brahmapootra. This suggests that the name traces to the Ru, and that the present Sahara was at one time covered by a sea of which the Jebels are relics.

Nevertheless the Medi Terre, or the Land of Rum, was still a part of the Greek continent of Libya, while the land mass of Posidonis was evolving into the huge island described by Plato. Possibly in the end it came to include the Caribbean, which did not exist in the early Eocene, as shown by Chart IV, Chapter I.

Certain it is that before the Afro-Brazilian Continent was severed, the Punics had found a land bridge to Brazil, and also to Zuela, which eventually came to be called Venezuela.

Notwithstanding the coming into being of the Gulf of Persia, and the enlargement of the Erythrean Sea, the present Turkeystan, all the ancient realm of Syr in which is found the great Desert of Kara Kum, was connected with the present Persia and through it with Asia Minor, Arabia, Egypt, and the Medi Terre. Thus the whole of Asia Minor was originally called Syria, while Egypt was never deemed to be a part of the Eurafrican land mass. Consequently, Asia Minor and Egypt together were known to Josephus as Siriad.[8]

The myth of Cain and Abel and the great earth destruction

described, do not fail to explain why the Chinese, ever deemed a peculiarly wise people, and who originally worshipped a vile Moon Goddess, came to possess no gods, but instead looked upon Tien, whose name is preserved by the Tian Shian Mountains, and by Tien Tsin, merely as a benevolent teacher who moved among men to counsel and guide them.

1 Between the calculations of Josephus and the dates given in *Genesis* 5 and 11, there are slight variations as to the earlier cycles. Upon these, in all probability, would be due the corrections made by Gregory I in the Paschal Cycle.

2 From which arose the concept of the Excalibur dealt with in the Arthurian Cycle of Romances common to Britain, France, Scandinavia, and Germany, and also wielded by the Greek Hercules and the Hebrew Archangel Michael. The name Cherub is derived from Chi-Eros-Uratur-Brahma.

3 In the je-bels, or high places found in the deserts of K-ara-K-um eastward of the Caspian in Syr, and in the deserts of I-r-an, Ara-bi-a, the Libyan Desert, and the Sahara, we find similar relics.

Jebel, 'the First Ethiopian, Belus.' Belus was the name given the mythical first King of the Nilus, implying Khus.

In the age of Ghengis Khan, the Mongols who hailed from beyond the Yalu, made their capital at Karakorum. The oldest Maya symbols were discovered there by Koslov along with Dinosaurian eggs at Karakhota.

4 Mi-da-d-o, 'Maia, the King, the Diva, Ornyth.'

5 In the Korean alphabet is found the Phi of the pre-Phoenician script.

6 It is a strange turnabout in history that following the first known use of gunpowder in warfare by the Mongols against the Japanese, atomic bombs destroyed H-i-ra-shi-mo, and Naga-sa-ki (32° 30' N.) marking the exact latitude of Babylon, and San Diego, on the coast of Queen Ka-li-fa.

7 N-o-d, 'The Nether World of Daitya.' Compare Nod with the fable Winken, Blinken, and Nod.

Here is to be noted that in 1883 a large island near Java and the former Daitya, blew up overnight with the loss of 50,000 people. Daitya did not vanish according to the Hindus until B. C. 70,000.

When the Allies banished Napoleon to St. Helena, just as the British and Burgundians banished the French banker and agent of the Medici, who had financed for Giovanni Medici, the father of Cosmo, and the great-grandfather of Lorenzo, the Magnificent, who financed Columbus, to the Island of Chios where Jacques Coeur spent the rest of his days, the Biblical story of Cain furnished the idea for the confinement of the would-be ruler of the earth.

8 S-y-r, 'Sin, Ya, the Ru.'

Si-r-i-ad, 'Sin, the Spirit, the Rishi, the Ark of the Diva.'

CHAPTER XIII

THE SETHIC PLANETARIUM
THE SEVEN SPHERES OF THE KABIRA

JOSEPHUS RELATED THAT after Cain had killed Abel, their father, Adam, was anxious for more posterity, and among his many children, begat Seth. In *Genesis* IV, following another sign implying a hiatus, in a section obviously out of chronological order, we read:

"25. And Adam knew his wife again: and she bore a son, and called his name, Seth, for God, said she, hath appointed me another seed instead of Abel, whom Cain slew."

In S-eth, 'the Sinitic Ethiopians,' as in Cain and Abel, is to be seen a Mosaic eponym corresponding to the Greek Saturn, applied to the ancestors of the Hebrews, who by the Naacals were brought into the fold of God's House, the Erythrean Ark. So is explained the mysterious EA to which constant references appear in the tablets of the Mesopotamians. Not until EA appeared as a god in the upper triad of the Assyrian Pantheon, along with Bel and his consort Belit, who corresponded to Cronus and Rhea, to Zeus and Hera, and to Jupiter and Juno, was it ever deemed that there was ever such a god as Ea. Instead, like the Chinese Tien, he was supposed to have arrived out of the Erythrean Sea, and as the author of the first book, to have been the patron of all the arts and sciences, a mortal healer and pacifier of men. In other words he was exactly the same as the Naba-th-ea-n-s described in the Chaldean *Book of Q-tamy* as the patron of agriculture. So, we may mark "solved" another mystery.[1]

Josephus gives a very clear picture of the eponymous Seth, describing him as a godly man who devoted himself to the study of the heavenly bodies and their movements. Also he credited Seth with seven equally virtuous sons, who inhabited the same land in peace and amity until they died, and invented "the peculiar religion having to do with the stars." This implies that the eponymous Seth whose cycle began in B.C. 2,376,000 just 30,000 years after the cycle of Adam V began, founded the mysteries of the Kabira, 'The Seven Spheres of Heaven and Earth', represented by the seven sons ascribed to Seth.

In the diagram hereinbefore included the losenges were employed to illustrate the overlapping of the ten cycles constituting the Adamic Dekkad. Here the cycles corresponding to the ten spheres in the current Mahayuga are shown emanating in the manner described by Plotinus in the *Enneads,* as one soap bubble is formed out of another by the mortal breath.

Also in this diagram is illustrated the manner in which the Kabira, representing successive degrees of the mysteries transmitted by the eponymous Ea, emanated one from the other.

It will be observed that the ten cycles beginning with that of Adam, and ending with that of Noah, constitute a Sephiroth, similar to the one beginning with the cycle of Shem-Ham-Japheth, and that upon the expiration of the Cycle of Enoch, the cycle of Shem-Ham-Japheth filled out the antedeluvian Dekkad. Accordingly, among the Hebraic apochrypha, or Ka-b-ala, implying the secret testaments of the Kabira in the cycle of Atlantis, is found the *Book of Enoch,* from which it appears that upon the Seventh Mountain, implying God's House, dwelt the Se-ra-p-h-i-m and the Cherubim.

As shown in Chapter I, the spheres enabled the records of the corresponding cycles to be preserved. To them the Sepher Y-e-t-z-i-r-a dealing with the seven spheres of the Kabira and the Sepher Se-phi-roth, dealing with the ten luminaries of the Dekkad are to be traced.[2]

The Adamic Dekkad shown in the diagram, like the arrangement of the Hindu Mahayuga and the Sacred Tetraktis of Pythagoras, comports with the fact that civilization is never

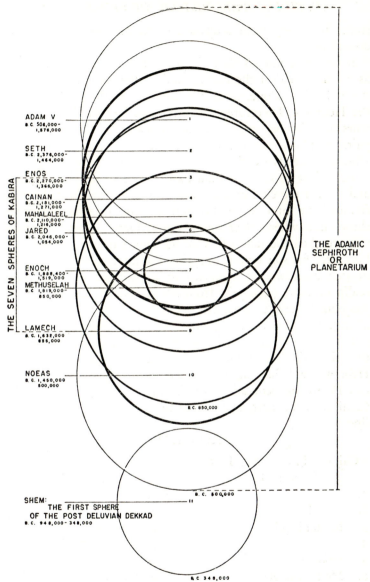

THE SEVEN SPHERES OF KABIRA

ADAM V
B.C. 506,000-
1,576,000

SETH
B.C. 2,376,000-
1,464,000

ENOS
B.C. 2,270,000-
1,366,000

CAINAN
B.C. 2,181,000-
1,271,000

MAHALALEEL
B.C. 2,110,000-
1,216,000

JARED
B.C. 2,046,000-
1,054,000

ENOCH
B.C. 1,888,400-
1,519,000

METHUSELAH
B.C. 1,819,000-
850,000

LAMECH
B.C. 1,632,000-
856,000

NOEAS
B.C. 1,450,000-
500,000

THE ADAMIC
SEPHIROTH
OR
PLANETARIUM

B.C. 850,000

B.C. 500,000

SHEM:
THE FIRST SPHERE
OF THE POST DELUVIAN DEKKAD
B.C. 948,000-348,000

B.C. 348,000

THE ELEVEN SPHERES EACH ARE TO BE VIEWED AS EMANATIONS OF THE
PRECEDING ONE. (FOR ELABORATION OF THE PRINCIPLE SEE ENNEADS,
PLOTINUS (250 A.D.); LIBER OF MYSTERIES: IAMBLICUS (300 A.D.))

THE COLORATION OF THE KABIRA IS AS FOLLOWS: VIOLET, ORANGE, RED, GREEN, GREEN, YELLOW, BLUE,
CORRESPONDING TO THE SACRED HEBDOMAD.

⌈131⌉

static: It either advances upward in the manner of a spiral, or downward.

It would be impossible to interpret the history of civilization as a whole against the background of the Adamic Dekkad of the Sethic line alone, since it relates only to the progenitors of the Hebrews. Therefore, not only must be considered the six pairs of twins begotten by Uranus out of Gea, and Plato's five pairs of twins, but the Cainitic line of Adam V, all representing successive cycles.

According to *Genesis* Cain took a wife in the land of Nod and named the city, in the sense of the spiritual see, that was founded by him, after his son Enoch. Josephus, however shows that when, after many wanderings, at last the exiled Cain reached the land of Nod, he named the city founded by him after his son En-o-s, implying the mysteries of the Kabira of that cycle were transmitted to the peoples in the eastern realm of Nod (Daitya), from among whom Cain is said by Josephus to have taken a wife. And, of course, this implies that already the lands in the South Seas were inhabited.

If the two Adamic lines be set side by side, it will be seen that there is no contradiction in the anthropogenesis of the Hebrews, and that the Mosaic scribes merely referred in *Genesis* IV to the generations of the mysteries among the exiled Cainites in the East, and not to the generations of the Sethic line.

ADAMITES

Cainitic Line of the East (Genesis IV)	Sethic Line of the West (Genesis V)
1.	En-o-s
2. I-r-a-d	Cain-an
3. Me-hu-j-a-el	Maha-la-l-e-el
4.	J-ar-ed
5. En-o-ch	En-o-ch
6. Me-t-hu-sa-el	Me-t-hus-el-a-h
7. La-me-ch	La-me-ch

While it appears that the Cainitic Kabirs of Irad and Me-hu-j-a-el did not evolve in the same order as those of the Maha-la-l-e-el and J-ar-ed in the Sethic line, beginning with the Kabirs of En-o-ch, the mysteries were the same.

While the cryptic names applied by the Mosaic scribes to the seven Kabirs which evolved from Cain and Seth alike, have many implications, astronomical and otherwise, some of them seem plain. Thus, just as Cain, C-ain, or C-a-in, implies the first cult, or the Serpent Cult embodied in the Ark of Indra, or Sin, and S-eth implies the Sinitic Ethiopians, En-o-s implies 'the First, or Lunar Cult, of Selti.' Moreover the studies that have been made of the mysteries have enabled the Sethic Kabirs to be identified with the Italic Kabirs designated as Saturn, Vulcan, Neptunis, Mars, etc.[3] Therefore, in the Cycles of the Seven Kabirs, the cryptic names of the Mosaic scribes and their corresponding cycles afford a guide to history even though the text of *Genesis* is jumbled in respect to chronology.

---

[1] See the works of Abrabanel, Herbert Spencer and Chowlson on the Nabatheans.

[2] Se-phi-r-o-t-h, "Set, the Philosophy, Reincarnated of the Moon, the Taux of the Hebrew."

[3] See Topical Bibliography, Mysteries, especially the works of Plotinus, Lactantanius, Iamblicus, Skinner, Eaber, and Welcker, and also the work of Mackey on the astronomy of Ptolemy, in which the names of the Roman Kabirs apply to the seven planets.

CHAPTER XIV

THE FORESHADOWED DOOM OF THE MAYAVIC
CIVILIZATION · THE IMPLICATIONS OF ENOCH ·
NOAH AND THE ARYAN ARK

NOTWITHSTANDING THE EFFORT made by God's House to enlighten the peoples of the earth through the Mysteries of the
Kabira, gradually as indicated by the Cycles of the Seven Sons
of Seth, the expiration of the Cycle of Enoch in B.C. 1,519,000
indicates that it had been impossible to extirpate the worship
of the old Moon God of the Python, and the idolatry that went
with it. Accordingly, in *Genesis* V, it is said:

"22. And Enoch walked with God after he begat Methuselah three hundred sixty and five years."[1]

"4. And Enoch walked with God: and he *was* not; for God
took him."

The meaning of this passage is explained in *Genesis* VI, in
another chronologically jumbled passage:

"5. And God saw that the wickedness of man was great on
the earth and that every imagination of the thoughts of his
heart was only evil continually."

Here, of course, reference is made, not to the thoughts of all
men, but to those whose imagination had produced the graven
image of the Black Magicians and idolaters.

"6. And it repented the Lord that he had made man on the
earth, and it grieved him at his heart."

"7. And the Lord said, I will destroy man whom I have
created from the face of the earth; both man, and beast, and
the creeping thing, and the fowls of the air; for it repenteth
me that I have made them."

Here the scribes merely gave expression to the concept of the
law of evolution, pursuant to which would occur another cosmic deluge bringing into being another type of man.

[*134*]

"8. But Noah found grace in the eyes of the Lord."

Josephus went out of his way to explain how the Greeks had changed many of the older Mayavic names to suit themselves, and that *Noah* was a Greek perversion of the Aramaic N-o-ea-s, 'the Naacals, Brahma, the Erythrean Ark, of the Sethites.' Moreover Noah is also but a contraction of No-a-chi, wherein appears the Aryan *chi,* 'the celestial ark of the Holy Spirit.' Also it will be observed that in *Genesis* VI Noah is described as a just man, perfect in all generations, who walked with God, just as Enoch is said to have done.

From all this we argue back that Enoch was a Greek contraction of *En-o-chi* derived from En Zu, 'the Great Wisdom' with the O or symbol of Brahma substituted for the Mayavic Zu, 'the Seven Serpents, Uratur,' and the Aryan Chi added. Thus in Me-t-h-us-el-a-h, the emanation from En-O-chi, we see the Greek word *melas,* implying the Ethiopians, combined with the Hebraic T, the h in Ha, implying the Seven Principles of Mortality, while *us* is a contraction of the Aramaic *Chus* implying the Punics, to which is added the Aramaic *elohim,* 'the gods', and the *a* and *h,* implying the Ark of the Hebrews. Likewise, L-a-me-chi, the emanation from the sixth Kabir designated by the composite name applied to it, may be taken to imply 'the Logus of the Aryan Melas, the Chi.'

The conclusion is, therefore, that Enoch, ever associated with the Seven Mountains, or the Seven Kabirs, by the Hebrews, in fact was but the eponym applied by the Greeks to the cycle in which appeared the posterity of J-ar-ed, 'the First Ark of the Ethiopian Diva,' who derived their name from A-r-ya, 'the Ark of Ru-Ya,' wherein, as already shown, *Ya* implied the first mortals to whom traces the M-a-ya, or Mother Ark of Ya.

Also we conclude that in course of time had appeared the mysterious Uighurs, who by Speigel were held to be the first and only true Aryans, consisting of the descendants of the T-a-t-ars and the yellow peoples of Mongolia, whose spiritual see came to extend not only from the Gobi to Japan and southward into Chi-na, M-ala-ya, and M-el-en-e-sia, but westward through the Sinitic realm of S-iberia, had come to be the human agency through which the new ark of the Arya was superimposed upon that of the Maya ark.[2]

Here it is to be noted,however, that the *Arya* was in no sense a repudiation of the old Sinitic Ark, but merely an evolution from it involving the concept of *K-ar-ma,* the law of retribution coupled with that of reincarnation through the circuit of the seven planets, as distinguished from the concept of the old degraded Lunar Cult which had conceived merely of man being the off-spring of the phallic process ascribed to the man and woman in the moon.

Such a complex concept not unnaturally was beyond the grasp of those who had perverted Sin in the philosophic sense, into the Moon God whose immemorial seat was at Ur or Mu-ga-ya in the delta of the Euphrates, and to whom the short cycle of Enoch may be ascribed. On the other hand, the mysterious Uighurs as the conveyors of the Aryan Ark fully explain why the Aryans were deemed not only reformers but warriors. In truth they were in all respects not only like the Monachists of later times, but like the Knights Templars and the Portuguese Order of Christ who like the mythical knights of the Round Table of King Arthur, were more than mere monks. Inevitably as they spread over the earth the name Aryan lost all implication of blood and race which originally it possessed as shown by Speigel, but came to imply merely 'wise men', including all those who accepted the new ark. Consequently, the language of the Arya is found superimposed upon that of the Maya in every clime.

A glance at the Sethic Planetarium will show that the Noachean cycle did not begin until B.C. 1,450,000, that is 69,000 years after the expiration of the cycle of Enochi. The reason for this also is plain. As already pointed out, an avatar as the reincarnation of Vishnu, the Aryan impersonation of the saving aspect of Brahma, did not occur as conceived by the Wisdom Philosophy, until the need for the avatar arose. From *Genesis* VI it clearly appears that the old civilization was doomed. Moreover, in accord with this it was pointed out by Josephus that just as Adam had warned in the past that the earth was to be destroyed by fire, implying the seismic disturbances of which the record is preserved in the *Muspilli,* and to which Plato referred in the *Timaeus,* Adam now warned the peoples of the earth that next it was to be destroyed by weight of the waters which we shall see implied the consequences of the ice cap that was formed when the earth was transformed from the Tertiary to its present or Quartenary form.

In the Wisdom Philosophy of the Aryan Hindus the fifth avatar, or the first of the three who are deemed to have appeared to the present Root Race, is designated as Rama Balarama, deemed the first incarnation of Vishnu in the three successive forms of Balarama, Rama Lunus, or Chandra, and Rama Chrisna, or Krishna.

Of this avatar the symbol was a dwarf, corresponding to both the cycle in which the pygmies had come to inhabit all parts of the earth, and to the infancy of the new Ark of the Arya, designated in the current Mahayuga as the Age of Innocence, or that in which the Seven Virtuous Sons of Seth appeared. As R-ama implied the Amara, or immortals, of the Ru, who had enshrined the Erythrean Ark at the Abyss of Learning, B-a-l-a implied 'Brahma, the ark, the logus of the Arya,' designated by the Arameans as *No-ea-s,* and by the Greeks as *No-a-chi.*

From the Gobi the trace of Bala, or Bal, leads to Borneo, Batavia, the island of Bal-i east of Java, Bal-an-gi-ga in Samar, B-an-kok in Siam, B-harata-sa-v-ar-sa, B-en-ar-e-es, Bal-pur, and Ba-ro-da in India, B-h-u-t-an at the north, B-a-mia-an in the Hindu Kush, B-ela in Bal-oo Chis-t-an, and to both T-a-b-ri-z, and B-o-k-ha-ra in Syr, beyond which are numerous Bal-ks in the region east of I-r-an and Ba-c-t-ri-a. Beyond is Mount Ba-ris, (Ara-ra-t), Mount El-b-ru-z, and Ba-ku in the Caucasus (Iberia). In the Crimea we find Bal-i-c-la-va and in Greece E-u-b-o-ea and The-ba below the Bal-k-an Mountains in which we find Bel-g-ra-d. In Syria are B-e-i-ru-t, Ba-al-b-e-k and Ba-sham, and on the Euphrates B-o-r-si-p-pa and K-e-r-bel-a.

From the Baltic the trail leads to Norway in which appeared Bal-d-ur, the Son of Light and Love peculiar to that realm. At the south are B-er-lin, B-r-e-men, Bel-g-iu-m, B-ru-x-el-les, Aix-la-Ba-ins, B-on-ne, B-e-thune, Ba-s-t-iogne, B-ur-goyne, B-r-e-s-t, and B-o-r-d-eaux. In the British Isles and Ireland we find Bal-na-gowne, Bal-mo-r-al, Ba-th, Bal-b-ri-g-g-an, Bal-l-y-shan-non, Bar-row, Bal-ti-more, Bal-l-an-t-y-ne, B-e-r-i-nice-ea, and B-la-r-n-e-y, while the original name of Dublin was Bal-le-Atha Gilath.

In the Iberian Peninsula we find the Ba-s-que, of whose realm originally the Bal-e-ar-i-c Islands were a part, as well as B-ur-go-s and Bar-ce-lona, in Spain. In Italy we find B-r-e-sc-ia, and to the South, the B-ar-b-ar-y States, or the Land of the B-e-r-b-e-r-s.

While the mythical first King of Egypt was B-el-us, who set up the god B-u-ba-s-t-es, the mythical Queen She-ba of Arabia was also called Bal-k-is. So, there is no mystery about the name applied to the countless j-e-bels in the deserts of Arabia and Africa, and the name Je-bel Mu-sa applied to Mount Sin-ai, and to A-b-y-sin-n-ia, and the names B-an-t-u, Mo-za-m-b-i-que, D-ur-b-an and B-e-ch-u-anna-land, or about the The-ba in Egypt. Plainly the Mesraites had been aryanized when the eponymous Mizr applied the name The-ba to the city on the Nile.

In the west we find B-ra-t-hell in Greenland, the Ba-ha-mas, the B-er-mu-das, B-ar-an-cas, B-ra-cu-da, B-ra-zos, B-ra-zi-l, and Ba-gota.

Because the Aryans in fact brought Mesopotamia into their fold, in *Genesis* 4, following the symbol indicating another chronological jumbling, we read:

"19 And Lamech took unto him two wives; the name of the one was Adah, and the name of the other Zillah."

By Josephus these two wives were designated as A-d-a and

S-illa. In the former is found the eponym applied by the ancient Greeks to Asia Minor.

The only place where Z-illa is found on the Graphs of Gea is in Northern Asia Minor, while S-illa appears only in Somali. But just as the *li* in Somali, implying the lotus, appears in Lilith and in the Sumerian El lil, it appears in L-a-p-t-eve, Li-t-hu-an-ia, L-at-vi-a with the two Ts in Latt indicating the mixture of the Ru and the Ethiopians. As in L-a-t-ium, Il-li-ri-a, and I-li-um, also it appears in Indra-la-Lois in France, and in that part of North America called Illinois by the French.[3]

It is to be concluded that Z-illa or S-illa was the eponym applied to those domains set apart to the Japhetics which became known as the Isles of Israel.

Undoubtedly the Greek Myth of Ch-ar-i-b-d-is and Sylla traces back to the trouble that occurred between the Aryans and their predecessors in Sicily and Southern Italy.

In view of what had befallen the Aryans in the cycle of Enoch, the following passages in *Genesis* 6 also are readily understood:

"23 And Lamech said unto his wives, Adah and Zillah, hear my voice, Ye wives of Lamech, hearken unto my speech: for I have slain a man to my wounding, and a young man to my hurt."

The implication of this passage is that the Ethiopians in the cycle of Lamech and the Tatars had become involved in a bitter strife in which they had brought to an end the cycle of Enoch.

"24. If Cain shall be avenged seven fold, truly Lamech seventy and seven fold."

This is but an esoteric reference to the law of karma pursuant to which a penalty for the warfare which had caused an end to the cycle of Enoch would be exacted.

Knowing the implications of the cycles of Kabiri, of the Uighurs and of the Kara, it is now possible to find on the Graph of Gea the proof that pursuant to the purpose of God's House to pacify and enlighten the peoples of the earth, and to protect the Tree of Life all ways, the terrestrial sphere was surveyed by the Aryans.

[1] 365 yields $3 + 6 + 5 = 2 \times 7$.

[2] So is explained the fact that the name Ar-men appears in the Peak of Ar-men in Kamashatka, and also in Armenia, while both the Caucasus and the peninsula at the west of the present Europe, and the river T-iber in Italy preserved the name I-beria as did S-iberia.

U-i-g-h-u-r, 'Uratur, the Spirit of God, the Heavenly Twins of the Ru.'

I-b-e-r-i-a, 'The Spirit of Brahma, the Ru, the Spirit of the Arya.'

[3] Prior to the Black Hawk War of 1832, the Sax and Fox of the Algonquian, linguistic family had been forced out of Illinois into I-O-w-a. Note the name *Black Hawk* borne by the Sa-ch-e-m.

CHAPTER XV

THE ORIGIN OF THE PRESENT GEODETIC SYSTEM AND THE ORIGINAL SURVEY OF THE EARTH

MUCH COULD HAVE HAPPENED during the 1,056,000 years between the beginning of the cycle of Adam V (B.C. 2,506,000), and the beginning of the Cycle of Noah in B.C. 1,450,000.

Of course it had been possible to furnish a planter of seed with lineal measures that would enable him to lay off his land by metes and bounds from some landmark, such as the Cainites are said to have possessed before their exile. But how was the whole earth to be surveyed from the Abyss of Learning?

The answer to this question is found in the Hindu myth of the dwarf Va-ru-na. It was a shrewd bargain which the dwarf Varuna corresponding to the age of innocence is said to have driven with the Daitya B-a-l-i, 'Brahma, the Ark, the Logus of the Spirit,' pursuant to which he was to have all the world he could pace off in three strides. In conformity with this agreement Varuna proceeded to set off the firmament, and to claim the earth below, as well.

It was a simple matter for those possessed of the trigonometric science to calculate the circumference of the earth by recourse to wells with cross hairs, and the formula here given:

Circumference of the Earth is to 24 hours as a measured arc on its surface is to the time it takes the image of the sun to pass from a cross-hair in a well at one end of the arc to a cross-hair in a well at the other end.

Once the factor C had been determined henceforth the elapsed time gave the length of any arc.[1]

When the obliquity of the spheroid had been determined, a celestial globe could be enmeshed with circles of longitude and latitude giving 360 triangles in each hemisphere each with a base of 1° at the equator. The 360 circles of latitude intersecting the 360 meridians would form theoretical squares of 1°, or so small that the Che-las recruited from among the Naacals, by travelling over the world under the direction of Chichens of God's House could instruct others how to map the features within the squares. When these were put together the Graph of Gea would be complete.

Certainly it would take a vast amount of time to accomplish this task. Moreover, in an ever changing world, the work of remapping would have to be continued. Nevertheless, once the grid had been adopted, the work could proceed. Yet it was imperative that the initiates of the Sinitic mysteries, who would have to be relied upon by the Chichens and Chelas should be individuals of the highest integrity and proven physical as well as moral courage, just as in the case of the Monks of the Buddhists and Christians of later days, in order that they might bring the peoples of different tongues, including the savages on the earth, into the fold of God's House.

Let those who would challenge what has been said, place on the terrestrial sphere pins marking the sites of the oldest known centers of culture. At once it will be seen that they could not have arisen at the sites bearing symbolic geodetic symbols and names, both according with the concept of the Wisdom Philosophy, save at Trees of Knowledge planted by the surveyors.

In view of the name of the Cherubim found at Chara Chota, or Kara-Ko-ru-m in the Gobi, and the name Kara-ko-ru-m also applied to the region at the north of Kashmir in India, and the fact that Ceylon and Australia are still inhabited by the Pi-sha-cha descendants of the Ru, the survey of the world is readily explained. Moreover, the name *Maia,* 'the Maya, Spirit of Atlantis, the alleged daughter of Atlas, whose name is preserved not only in Mesopotamia and by the plane of India, but by two Mi-a-mi-s in North America, and by the Maiori in Australia, indicates the cycle of the survey.

GEODETIC TABLE

Showing how the Great Circle 100° East—80° West on which was located the Abyss of Learning at 40° N. 100° E. prior to the Magnetic Cataclysm of B. C. 10,000, was marked in both Hemispheres at important sites bearing modern names.

		Eastern Hemisphere		*Western Hemisphere*
North	80°	Severn Novaya Zembla	North 80°	Ellsmere Island
	75°	Lake Tamyr (Mongolia)	75°	Devon Land
	49°	Muren Kure (")	70°	Cockburn Land
	41°	Maomu (Inner Mongolia, Gobi)	62°	Mansel Is. (Hudson Bay)
	40°	Abyss of Learning (Inner Mongolia, Gobi)	60°	Ottawa Islands (Hudson Bay)
	37°	Lake Koka Nor	45°	Toronto Area (Ontario)
	30°	Litang (Tibet)	42°	Erie Area (Penn.)
	28°	Likiang (" ")	40°	Pittsburgh Area (Penn.)
	26°	Tali (" ")	39°	Morgantown Area (W. Va.)
	25°	Shunning Area (China)	38°	Roanoke Area (Va.)
	24°	Mienning Area (" ")	36°	Winston-Salem Area (N. C.)
	23°	Chenpien (" ")	33°	Charleston Area (S. C.)
	20°	Chiang Sen (Siam)	23°	Sagua la Grande (Cuba)
	18°	Ultaraditra (" ")	22°	Trinidad (Cuba)
	14°	Bankok Area (" ")	10°	Canal Zone (Panama)
	13°	Singora Area (Malaysia)	Equator	
Equator			2°	Quito Area; Chimborazo (Ecuador)
South	55°	Pariaman Area (Sumatra) Mt. Ophir	South 25°	Guayaquil (Ecuador)
		Antarctica	25°	San Felix Arch. (S. Pacific)
			35°	Juan Fernando Arch. (" ")
			55°	Antarctica

[143]

It is to be noted that at Centerville in Washington County, Penn., lies the intersection in the Western Hemisphere of the Great Circle 100 E.—80 W. with the Latitudinal Circle 40 N., and that Washington County until recently was a part of O-h-i-O. The obvious geodetic relations of the effigy, geometric, and religious mounds in the area between the Great Lakes and the Ohio River, the Mississippi and Che-sa-pe-ake Bay, which has been erected before Columbus unveiled America, with dunes in the Gobi Desert, will readily appear if they are indicated by pins on a globe. This relation readily explains the statements of both Columbus who explored the mainland south and west of the Caribbeans from Brazil to Yu-ca-tana, and of John Cabot who explored the Atlantic Seaboard from Greenland to Florida (see map of Juan Cosa, 1505), that America was within the realm, or Spiritual See, of the Grand Khan of Asia. The successors of Cabot in the Northwest Passage Foundation of which Sir Humphrey Gilbert's son John, the half-nephew of Sir Walter Raleigh, including the great Magician who was Queen Elizabeth's teacher, believed the same thing. When William Penn explored the Wilderness beyond Philadelphia he recorded that he had found much to indicate a very ancient connection between the aborigines of America and the Peoples of the Old Testament. It is upon that belief that the Book of Mormoni is based.

GEODETIC TABLE

Showing the marking at important points of the Latitudinal Circle, 40° North, on which the Abyss of Learning, the mythical Mount Meru of the Hindus, or the Flaming Sword and the Cherubim of the Mosaic Scriptures, was sited in the present Inner Mongolia on a group of islands constituting a terrestrial Zodiac centering at 100° East, prior to the Magnetic Cataclysm of B. C. 10,000.

East	100°	Dune in Suchow-Maomu Area	West	30°	Ridge of Teneriffe: Mount Atlas
	117°	Peking (China) God's House		9°	Sacred Precinct Coimbra, Portugal
	125°	Antung (Manchuria-Korea Boundary)		4°	Sacred Precinct Toledo, Spain
	140°	Akia (Japan)		0°	Castellon, East Coast of Spain (Al-ma-go-r-za)
	141°	Morioka (Japan)		4°	Menorca, Balearic Islands
West	124°	Point Delgado (California Coast)	East	10°	Sardinia
	120°	Pyramid Lake (Cal.-Nev. Boundary)		16°	West Coast Calabria (Italy)
	112°	Santaquin (Utah near Salt Lake)		18°	Galipolis (Apulia, Italy)
	109°	Utah-Colorado Boundary		20°	Ginokoster (Albania)
	105°	Denver and Anacondia (Pike's Peak)		22°	Area of Olympus, Thessaly
	102°-95°	Kansas-Nebraska Boundary		24°	The Chersonese
	95° 30'	Missouri Boundary near St. Joseph		26°	The Troja: Hissarlik
	91° 30'	Quincy (Illinois, West Boundary)		30°	Area of Mount Olympus (Moesia)
	90° 30'	Sanganon (Illinois, Springfield Area)		30°	Mount Ararat: Area of Erivan
	86°	Indianapolis Area (Indiana)		44°	Baku on West Shore of Caspian
	83°	Columbus Area (Ohio)		50°	Krasnovodsk, E. Shore Caspian
	82° 30'	Newark Area (Ohio) Complex Religious Mounds		53°	Bokhara in the Kara Kum (Ancient Syr)
	81° 30'	Moundsville on Kanawha (W. Va.) Great Cone		65°	Samarkand (Ancient Syr)
	80°	Brownsville, Washington County (Penn.)		67°	Kokand (Ancient Syr)
	76° 30'	Lancaster (Penn.)		71°	Mount Turgat: Holy Mountain (Syr Boundary)
	75°	Philadelphia: Sacred Elm of Shakamaxon		75°	Tunhwang (Sin Kiang)
	74° 45'	Mount Holly (N. J.)		95°	Kiayukwan-Kiu Choan Area (Gobi)
	74° 15'	Lakehurst (N. J.)		98°	Complex of Dunes; Dinosaur Eggs
	74°	Normandy Beach, Atlantic Coast		100°	Abyss of Learning: Dune men Remains.

It is to be noted that Washington County, Penn., exactly 180 degrees West of the Abyss of Learning, was once a part of O-h-i-O in whose name appear two O's symbolizing the two Hemispheres, and that in Ohio more effigy and geometric mounds were eventually erected than in any equal area north of Ana-Huac (Mexico).

What is here shown could not be accidental. No more could be that which appears on the latitudinal circle 28° N.

Just east of Gaura-sin-kara (28° N. 86° E.) is Pu-na-ka (28° N. 90° E.), the capital of Bu-tan, and to the west of it is Kat-man-du, the capital of Nepal; while Indraphrasthra, the capital of Rajputana, stands at 28° N. 76° E. Next one comes to Mount Sin (28° N. 35° E.), near which in Su-en-zu or Su-ez, is the sunken city of Pe-t-ra in the desert of T-i-n (35° E.). Beyond it is Mi-n-e-h on the Nile, the oldest city in Egypt. This same circle passes through the Ca-na-ra Islands, the Bahamas, close to Tampa (83° W.), Corpus Christi (100° W.) which marks the antipodal meridian of Ceylon and of Lake Manasorowara in Tibet.

The meridian from the Peak of Ar-m-en (60° N. 150° E.) in Kama-sha-t-ka wherein the *sha* implies the 'head of the God Land', passes through New Gui-nea, and close to Sydney in Australia, while the antipodal meridian is marked by hypothetical Mount Atlas (30° W.).

The meridian from Mount El-i-as, "Enyalius, the Spirit of Atlas" (60° N. 150° W.) in Alas-ka, 'Atlas, the King of the Ark', passes through the fragments constituting the realm of O-ta-hi-ti (50° S. 150° E.) of which the island of Ta-hi-ti was a part, while the antipodal meridian 30° E. passes through Mount Olympus in Mo-e-si, the Delta of Egypt, the Mountains of the Moon, and D-ur-b-an (30° S.), in South Africa. Note also that Khan T-en-g-ri (42° N.) in the Altai Range, with a name implying the Taux of Atlantis, marks the latitudinal circle of Rome, while Chung King marks the meridian of Chara Chota.

The accompanying Chart explains the origin of the name Tibet, 'his Covenant', since the sacrosanct area of La Ha Sa, "God's House", marks at 30° N. 90° E. the intersection of the Geodetic Cruciform, while the intersection of the antipodal cruciform is found at Sin-o-pe, or New Orleans (30° N. 90° W.).[2]

The Geodetic Cross, explained, of course, how the names

THE WORLD TRUE CROSS

SHOWING TWO ANTIPODAL CROSSES

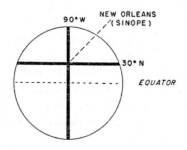

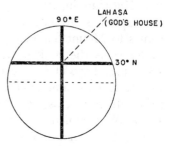

WESTERN HEMISPHERE
VERITICAL ARM OF CROSS MARKED BY:

PEORIA (ST LOUIS) 38° 30' N (KAHOKIA MOUND 90° W)
MEMPHIS (TANASA) 35° N (CIRCLE OF MOUNDS)
JACKSON (MISS.)
BOGALUSA (LA.)
NEW ORLEANS (SINOPE) 30° N (△ MOUNDS)
UXMAL (YUCATAN) 19° N   "   "
COPAN (HONDURAS) 16° N   "   "
TOWER ISLAND (GALAPAGOS), EQUATOR

HORIZONTAL ARM OF CROSS MARKED BY:

ST. AUGUSTINE (SELOY) 81° W
APPALACHICOLA   85° W
NEW ORLEANS (SINOPE) 90° W
SINALOA (MEXICO) 115° W

EASTERN HEMISPHERE
VERTICAL ARM OF CROSS MARKED BY:

KARA SEA, NORTH OF SIBERIA   80° N
LA HA SA (GOD'S HOUSE)   30° N
PUNAKA (BHUTAN) 28° N
DACCA (DELTA OF THE GANGES) 23° 27' N
(TROPIC OF CANCER)

HORIZONTAL ARM OF CROSS MARKED BY:

MIDWAY ISLAND 180° E
HANCHOW (DELTA OF YANGTZE) 114° E
CHUNG KING 107° E (PYRAMIDAL MOUNDS)
PERSEPOLIS 52° E
UR, OR MUGHEIR (DELTA OF EUPHRATES) 47° E
GIZEH-FAYOOM (DELTA OF THE NILE) 30° E
GADAMES (TRIPOLITANA) 10° E
CANARY ISLANDS 18° W

All of the points mentioned are not sited exactly on the cross.
No consideration is given a distance of less than 25 miles in-as-much as the
configuration of the terrain and the water supply would have caused the siting
of the original town that far away from the bench mark, in some cases.

Ma-u-na Loa, and Ma-u-na K-ea came to be applied to the two great volcanoes in Hawaii corresponding to the two Yamas in Japan, also revered as sacred symbols. [3]

But what is this?

Also it explains the names S-iberia, Iberia in the Caucasus, Tiber in Italy, and the Iberian peninsula through which the arm of the cross passed.

Mount Amarka-ka-n-ta-ka (19° N. 81° E.), not only marks the meridian of Lake M-ana-so-ro-wa-ra (31° 30' N. 81°E.), but that of Adam's Peak (70° N. 81° E.), while the antipodal meridian is marked at 19° N. 99° W. by Me-x-tla, 'the Malas, the Chi of Atlantis', in Ana-buac, 'the Ark of ana'.

In the face of this geodetic cruciform, there is no mystery about the immemorial cruciform symbol of the Che-yenne of W-is-con-sin, since the Y-en-n-e in their names implies 'Ya, Enyalius, the Naacals of Erythrea, also being found in Yenne-si at the head of Siberia and in T-ennes-see. But the word *venne* implies 'yellow'. Therefore the presumption is that some of the yellow people of Mongolia were among the Naacal surveyors.

In their grand journey over the earth the directors of the world-wide survey would have noted many wonders. When they came to plot the outline of Alas-ka they would have noted a marvel indeed. Not only does the name of the bear, *tlao,* appear in A-la-s-ka, La-bra-dor, and Bear Island, but the outline of Alas-ka forms on the graph of Gea an exact figure of a bear rampant with his paws raised against Ka-ma-sha-t-ka.

How Asia was surveyed by the Kara is quite plain. An isosceles triangle with its apex in Nova-ya Zembla (70° N. 60° E.) an altitude of 32° and a base of 50° rests its apogees at Mount Sin (28° N. 35° E.), and near Gaura-sin-kar (28° N. 85° E.). Another with a base of 90° and its meridian passing through Mount Atlas, would find its apogees at Sha-ka-ma-x-on (40° N. 75° W.), and at Mount T-ur-g-a-ti (40° N. 75° W.) marking the boundary between Syr and Sin Kiang at the junction of the Pamir and Kuen Lun ranges.

From the Kara Sea the trail of the surveyors leads straight through the Kara Kum to Ka-shi-mere adjoining the region of Kara-ko-rum at the east. From there it leads to Kara Chi in the realm of S-ind which includes the delta of the Indus. As the Kara surveyed India they also located the body city of Ka-shi (24° 30' N. 84° E.), now called B-en-ar-es, on the G-ana-g-es.[4] Also they located Indra-prasthra, 'the Flower of Indra', and the capital of Raj-pu-t-ana, on the meridian of the 'Trinity of Kara-ko-ru-m' (76° E.).

Even if it be assumed that by some accident of nature the Abyss of Learning was located at 40° N. 100° E., no mortal can explain the geodetic symbols here shown, in all of which the concepts of the Wisdom Philosophy find expression:

La Ha Sa, 30° N. 90° E.

Gaura-sin-kar, 28° (2 + 8 = 10) N., 86° E. (8 + 6 = 14 = 2 × 7).

No-va-ya Z-embla, 70° N. 60° E.

S-ammara on the Volga, 50° N. 50° E.

Olympus, 40° N. 30° E.

M-ana-so-ro-wa-ra, 31° 30′ N. (3 + 1 + 3 = 7), 81° E. (8 + 1 = 9).

Mount Amarakantaka, 19° N. (1 + 9 = 10), 81° E. (8 + 1 = 9).

Adam's Peak, 7° N. 81° E. (8 + 1 = 9).

Ya-ru-siloam, 31° 30′ N., 34° 20′ E. (3 + 1 + 3 = 7; 3 + 4 + 2 = 9; 7 + 9 = 16; 1 + 6 = 7).

Benares, 24° 30′ N. 84° E. (8 + 4 + 2 + 4 + 3 + 0 = 21 = 7 × 3).

The delta of the Yangtze, 28° N. (2 + 8 = 10), 120° E. (1 + 2 + 0 = 3).

The delta of the Euphrates, 30° N. 47° E. (3 + 0 + 4 + 7 = 14 = 2 × 7).

The delta of the Nile, 30° N. 30° E. (3 + 0 + 3 + 0 = 6 = 2 × 3).

The delta of the Mississippi, 30° N. 90° W. (3 + 9 + 0 = 12 = 4 × 3).

The Peak of Armen, 60° N. 150° E. (6 + 0 + 1 + 5 + 0 = 12 = 4 × 3), while 4 + 3 = 7.

The Mountains of the Moon, Equator 30° E. (3)

The delta of the Amazon, Equator 50° W. (5)

Mount Elias, (60° N. 150° W. (6 + 0 + 1 + 5 + 0 = 12 = 4 × 3).

Mount B-ar-is or Ara-ra-t, 40° N. 44° E. ($4 \times 4 = 16 = 1 + 6 = 7$).

Mount T-ur-gat, 40° N. 75° E. ($7 + 5 = 12 = 3 \times 4$).

Ana-ti-o-chi (Rhodes), 36° N. 36° E. ($3 + 6 + 3 + 6 = 18 = 6 \times 3$).

Mount Albana in La-t-i-um (Italy) 42° N. 13° E. ($4 + 2 + 1 + 3 = 10$).

"The Watcher," in Franconia Notch, 44° 10′ ($4 + + 4 + 1 + 0 = 9 = 3 \times 3$).

Surely all this, and countless other geodetic symbols expressing the septenary principle of the Taux, cannot with reason be set down to accident, even though the atheist may continue to deny the divine magic reflected in nature.

Put in another way, the magicians might have devised the geodetic grid, and they might have dictated the sitings of their holy shrines upon it. No man, however, could so have placed the natural features of the earth that they would have marked the Taux.

When viewed in the light of what mathematics discloses, history does indeed become a grand romance. One fails to find today those more devoted to the service of God than the surveyors who enclosed the whole warring earth within the mathematical arc of the geodetic grid.

Verily did Walter Raleigh declare that History survives along with eternity. Verily did Francis Bacon declare history lies at the base of the triangle called the P-y-r by the Graekos and the Pi-ra-m-is by the Egyptians. Since it was the triangulation of the earth by the surveyors of God's House, or the dwarf, called Varuna, that made possible the world survey and the upbuilding of civilization against the background of the geodetic taux, the meaning of Bacon is plain.

1 This method was still employed by Eratosthenes on the plains of Shinar in Mesopotamia. See the Geographica of Eratosthenes (225 B. C.).

2 The Creoles of Sinope and of Selos New Orleans and St. Augustine, were not fond of the implications of the aboriginal names of their cities.

3 Ma-u-na-Loa, "the Mother Culture of the Naga, the Lotus."
Ma-u-na- K-oe "the Mother Culture, the King of the Erythrean Ark."

4 Benares marks the great circle passing through Winnipeg in Manitoba, the Houston-Galveston Area in Texas, and Vera Cruz in Mexico.

CHAPTER XVI

THE TRUE CROSS OF EGYPT

IT APPEARS THAT from time immemorial the surveyors of the earth have been visiting the mountains of the moon to observe the zodiacal poles. In medieval times the map of the world was enclosed in a disc surrounded with colored bands in which appeared the signs of the zodiac.[1] Still appear in the ancient observatory on the Summit of Chi-m-borazo the holes in the rocks through which the planets were observed. For this observatory like Tower Island in the Galapagos, like Qui-to, and the Island of Ma Pa contained within the mouth of the Amazon, the island of Sao Tome off the coast of the Congo, and the Ru-w-en-zo-r marked the Equator.

Vital in the history of civilization is the veritable Jacob's Ladder here shown:

30° E. 80° N. Spitzbergen on the Sval Bard in the Archipelago.

70° N. Va-ra-o at the North Cape of Fin-land.

60° N. Cronstadt on the Bal-ti-c Sea in Va-ra-n-g-ea.

50° N. Ki-e-fa in the U-k-r-i-ne.

40° N. Olympus in Mo-e-si.

30° N. The Fa-yoo-mu in Miz-r-a-i-m.

20° N. Argo at the 3rd Cataract preserving the name of Argo in Graekos Land.

10° N. J-e-bel T-e-l-l-u-m in D-ar Nu-ba.

Equator. Mountain of the Moon, Ru-w-en-zoo-ri.

This Ladder explains, of course, how Memphis 49° 47' N. came to mark the exact latitude of La Ha Sa, while K-ar-n-ac-k was sited at the The-ba on the Nile marking the exact latitude of Kash-i or Benares in India, and also why Sa-k-ka-ra or, Saq-qui-ra, close to Memphis was ever held to be a place of great sanctity.

When Livingston came to Uganda, he found living there near the natural S-w-a-s-ti-ka formed by the Seven Mountains of the Moon, whose summits are only visible in the moonlight when the mists raised by the sun are cleared away, the pygmies who called themselves Akka. Also known as the Ti-ki Ti-ki, in whose name appears the Ti in Ti-ana-ya-ni-ka, and the Ki in Ki-li-m-ana-ja-ro, they are highly peculiar in that they alone of all the peoples on the earth today forbid the possession of domestic animals save game chickens for which they are famous.

Had the Akka, 'the Ark of the King, the Kara', been taught by the first faros of the Nilus to adopt this evident safeguard against bestiality? However that may be, Dr. Livingston preferred to die among them rather than to return to so-called civilized society.

In the name *Akka* as in Dacca in the delta of the Ganges, and Accra and Akka in Guinea, is to be seen but a form of Na-ac-al.

The Aryans conceived of the Pitris or the progenitors of men, as the inspired Fathers of Mortals, and as reincarnation of the Divine Lotus, symbolized by the Celestial Roc. Therefore, islands in the North Sea, and also an island in the Baltic bear the name Fa-r-O which is preserved by the F-in, 'the Faro of Indra' as in Finland, and also as in F-a-yoo-mu. We, also, find it in the Irish Fin-bo-ga, Fin-lo-ga, and Fin-g-al.[2] To this concept traces the title Faro, assumed by the early kings of Egypt as the successors of the mythical King B-el-us, implying the Ethiopian Aryans of Egypt called Chus, known to the Hebrews as Ph-ara-o-h-s, who styled themselves Kings of Egypt and Princes of Kash. Compatible with the feathers in their crowns, they looked upon their higher beings as the *Ba,* and upon their bodies as the *Ka.* Accordingly they had their remains mummified and placed in the tombs of the Kings, carved out of the Libyan Desert across the river from K-ar-n-ac, so that the Ba might reincarnate in the beautiful bodies they possessed because of the care with which they were bred. [3]

Continued southward from the Mountain of the Moon, the

meridian 30° E. passes through Mo-z-am-b-i-que in which is preserved the name of the Queenland, and on through D-ur-b-an 30° S., while the antipodal meridian (150° W.) passes through Mount El-i-a-s, (60° N.) now called McKinley, and through the relics of the land of the Southern Cross in the Archipelago of O-ta-he-i-i-t-e (50° S.) including Ta-hi-ti, and there we find the two-headed peak, O-ra-h-en-a, resembling Mount Sin-a-i.

Verily, in the age of the sons of Seth, the earth was a small place in the eyes of God's House.

In the geodetic ladder which has been shown, there is a world of history, since it forms with a latitudinal circle 30° N., another geodetic cross with its intersection at Fa-yoo-mu (30° N. 30° E.) a second World Taux, or *Ankh* as shown in the hand of the Egyptian God Cenobis, representing the spirit of God upon the waters.[4] Around this geodetic cruciform known to the Egyptians as the true cross, would revolve the whole of Egyptian history from now on.[5]

Those who eventually overran the Land of the Lotus Eaters which derived its Homeric name from the natural lotus formed by the Nilus, and furnishing the lifeblood of Egypt, might forget many things, but they would never forget the true cross. [6]

But the meridian 30° East formed with the latitudinal circles 40° N. and 30° N. the form of the cross with two arms which often appears in modern symbolism. (‡).

---

[1] See *Leardo Map of the World*, WRIGHT (American Geographical Society).

[2] See also F-u-ji- Yama, F-ua Mu-la-ku, and Fal-k Land, and F-u-e-r-e-n-t-e-s in Sicily.

[3] The Pharaohs only married their sisters, and only those who were without physical blemish. The idea that in-breeding of men is fatal to health is due to the fact that it multiplies defects; in the same way, however, it perpetuates beauty of form and other qualities, just as in the case of animals. Thus, dogs and horses are both bred back to an outstanding individual.

[4] A-n-k-h, 'Arc of Nu, Kneph, Ha.'

[5] Ages later would be the labyrinth of Fa-yoo-mu, 'The Faro, Ya, Heaven and Earth Mother,' in which as in the nearby Sphinx at the pyramidal Trinity of Giz-e-h, the mysteries of the eponymous M-an-e-t-h-o would be enshrined near Cairo which arose on this site called Babylon, originally designated as 'C-akè.'

6 The true cross would be reestablished by Saladin following the pact enforced on him by Richard of the Lion Heart. Sa-la-din, 'Sa, the Land of the Garden.' S-u-l-t-an, 'Sa, Uratur, the Logus of the Taux, Ana.'

The ransom exacted of Christendom by Saladin was in the nature of a guarantee that the rights of Egypt and the true cross would be respected henceforth by the Knights Templar.

In the name Faro-u-k, the late Khedive, as 'King Hierophant of the Dive,' preserved the ancient title of Faro as the spiritual father of the Ark of the Roc, symbolized by the crescent displaying the profile of Isis, the Ornyth, or the Roc.

CHAPTER XVII

THE THREE SONS OF NOAH
THE ARYAN POSTERITY OF LAMECH

IN THE PRECEDING CHAPTER it has been shown that already
had appeared the K-ara, 'Kings of the Aryans', to whom such
names as Khan T-en-g-ri, Yangste Kiang, Chung King, Pe-
King, Ka-ma-sha-t-ka, K-o-r-ea, K-u-r-ile, as well as K-o-b-e,
K-y-o-t-o, and K-y-us-shu in Japan, K-ea in Hawaii and Ka-la-
ma-zoo in North America are to be traced just as Shang-hai in
Chi-na and in Japan and Hakka in America are to be traced to
the Red Hakka of the North, who had taken their names from
the Na-ac-als. Inasmuch as their language was similar to that
of the Aka-ka-dians who would eventually appear in Mesopotamia, we may assume that they too were pupils of the Na-acals,
who in China and Burma came to be called *Nagals,* in India
Naga, and in Mexico *Naguals.*

By B.C. 950,000 Balarama, or Noah, had brought into the
Aryan fold the three groups in Syria, or the present Meso-
potamia and Asia Minor, Arabia, and Egypt, named by the
Mosaic scribes as here shown:

1. Ch-e-m or S-h-e-m: the Chus, or Shus, of Ethiopia
   and Mesopotamia, implying the peoples of Shumer
   and Suzianna, or E-la-mu.
2. H-a-m: the H-i-t-t-i-t-i of Armenia and Mesopotamia.[1]
3. J-a-ph-eth: The First of Arya, the Phut of Ethiopia,
   the Punic Ancestors of the Philistines.

Despite the virtuous sons of Seth, however, the civilization of
Mesopotamia could not be saved by the three groups of Aryans
designated as the sons of Noah.

In *Genesis* VI, 20, 21, it is said that Adah, the first wife of
Lamech bore Ja-bal, "the father of such as dwell in tents, and
of such as have cattle."

Written in the present tense of the Mosaic scribes, this passage refers to the nomads of Syr, Asia Minor, Arabia, the Sahara, and adjoining regions.

The brother of Ja-bal 'the first of the ark of Bal,' who is described as the father of all who handle the harp and the organ, is credited by Josephus with having invented the psalter. Therefore, it is to be inferred that the Aryans of this cycle invented sacred music, and in the organ, of course, we see merely wind instruments.

Out of Z-illah Lamech begat Tu-bal Cain, implying the Tatars who had appeared in Syr and Irania as the ancestors of the Turanians or the Turks. By Zillah also he begat a daughter, Naa-mah, an eponym appearing on the graph of Gea in Syria, undoubtedly implying the Nabatheans.

Tu-bal Cain is credited in *Genesis* with being the instructor of every artificer in brass and iron and with being the first to invent armor and to employ war elephants. By Josephus this group is also described as being of a violent type, caring only for material things, and given to robbery, rape, ceaseless warfare and the enslavement in their harems of the women who were seized by them as desired.

Moreover, stone weapons and tools have been found in East Anglia which have been traced to the Old Stone Men of the Tertiary. Certainly they were not fashioned to no purpose. Furthermore the history of Su-zi-ana, the 'Land of the Cedars' shows that in that country just beyond the Tigris there were countless magic trees ascribed to the tyrant Khu-m-ba-ba, who is said to have been conquered by the hero G-i-l-g-a-sh.[2] Thus, we also find evidence in the Hebraic E-la-mu of the warfare that was raging in the cycle of Lamech.

Noeas is shown by Josephus as pleading in vain with evil ones who, although claiming to be angels like the giants of old, were taking unto themselves women and committing all manner of sins. But, he tells us in as much as these black magicians threatened to kill Noah he departed from their land. - It is utterly impossible, of course, to understand the evolution of civilization in the Noachean cycle unless it be borne in mind that when the Aryan Kara were surveying India and Egypt, the posterity of Cain were mingling with the yellow peoples of Polynesia, and also with the Melenesians of Oceanica over which spread the vast Pacific Continent.

There were now upon the earth the Ru, the Punics, the yellow sub race of the Fourth Root Race, and the Ethiopians of the Fifth Root Race. Who shall say which one of these groups produced the Tertiary men of Java and the Tertiary men of East Anglia who fashioned the tools and weapons found there? And who shall say what group produced the people whose artifacts have been found in Arizona and Nevada along with elephants such as those Tubal Cain is said to have employed? The inference is that in the present America there was a strife going on between the Ru and the Ethiopians.

Whatever the facts may be, the earth had now reached the point of evolution where skulls such as the one of the Tertiary Man of Java, were being deposited in the soil. Nevertheless there is a limit to just how much history can be based upon cephalic indices.

Different types of skulls were found in the same strata of many parts concurrently. A million years hence the finding of the skulls of long head savages who now occupy the Austral realms, along with those of the British and American soldiers recently buried among them, could prove nothing as to the time when the peoples of their respective races appeared. Where a type of skull is preponderant in a particular area, however, it is to be inferred that man of a type indicated by the skull was the characteristic one. Thus, the Pale Alpines of modern Ethnology may be taken to represent the Ru, and the Pale Negroids the Punics who inhabited the earth before the true Negroids appeared.

[1] Here it is to be noted that the Delta of the Nile came to be called **Chem-i,** implying the Red Land of the Ru, as distinguished from T-o-s-ri, 'the Black Land,' beyond Memphis.

[2] T-i-g-ris, 'the Taux, the Spirit of the gods, the Rishi.' In **Gi-l-ga-shi,** 'Gihon, the land of the Gaur, the Shi,' we see the Biblical Gihon, the "second head," representing the mysteries of the Ethiopians. S-H-I- 'Sa, Ha, the Spirits.'

CHAPTER XVIII

THE PILLARS OF THE SONS OF SETH
THE OLDEST MONUMENTS ON THE EARTH

WHEN THE THREE alleged sons of Noah appeared (B.C. 950,-
000) there were still in being two of the sons of Seth—the
Kabirs of Me-th-u-se-la-h and L-a-me-chi with names reflecting
the name La-Ha-Sa which was still being applied by the Turks
in the form El-Ha-Sa to Mesopotamia, until recently.

By Josephus it was said that in his time still were to be seen
on the plain of Siriad two pillars erected by the sons of Seth in
which they embodied their wisdom in order that it might be preserved to their posterity. The first, he described, as one of brick,
and the second as one of stone "lest it be washed away by the
waters."

In that part of Mesopotamia at the South of Babylon, or an-
cient Sumer where are to be seen today the ruins of H-illa 'the
Hebrew-illa, G-ur-su, Ki-shi, and La-ga-shi,' close to which
eventually the Chaldeans erected the city of E-re-chi on the
Euphrates (31° 30' N. 44° E.), we find the great pillar of
T-el-l-o, 'the Taux, the Elohim, the law of Brahma.'

It consists of a wall of sun burned bricks, thirty feet high,
surrounding an egg-shaped area with an axis of 2½ miles oriented to the North and an axis of 1½ miles oriented to the
East, the two forming a perfect *tau* of seven units since two
overlap. Upon the top of the wall as well as within the vast
area inclosed by it, seeds might be cultivated for use following
the floods to which this area was subject. Certainly it would
have been logical for the sons of Seth to heed the alleged
warning of Adam that the earth was to be destroyed by "weight
of the waters."

Just across the Tigris is the land of El-a-mu, or Su-zi-ana
where the present Su-sa-is is found. Here is to be seen covering

an area 3½ miles in circumference, a great mound forming a six-pointed star at 32° N. 48° 25′ E., whose geodetic symbols yield $3 + 2 + 4 + 8 + 2 + 5 = 24 = 8 \times 3$.

At the northwest of Su-zi-ana, in the region of E-c-ba-t-ana, stands the amazing height B-e-h-is-t-ana. On this sheer wall of rock, rising to an elevation 1700′, we find inscribed in cuneiform script, the tri-lingual texts of three successive cycles—Maya, Akkadian, and Zend.

The ancient complex of ruins at K-e-r-m-en- shaw is found at 34° 18′ N. 47° 12′ E.

Keeping on eastward we come to Shi-ra-z at 29° 48′ N. 52° 10′ E. Here is to be seen a great complex of circular mounds, or pills.

Slightly at the northeast is Perse, 30° N. 52° 40′ E., and there we find a huge rectangle of polished marble, 940′ × 1550′, with projections 43′ high. Of it the axes form a *tau,* marking exactly the horizontal arm of the geodetic *tau* of Asia.

Next we come to Yezd at 31° 54′ N. 54° 22′ E., marking the latitude of Lake Manasorowara. Here the outstanding feature is the citadel called the Ark, and we note with interest that the sum of the numbers in both the latitudinal and longitudinal symbols is the most mystical of all numbers—13.

The geodetic symbols of all these sites and the measures of their monuments, however, will bear careful analysis. And what historian will say that the mathematical knowledge reflected in these grand geometrical symbols was not possessed until the monuments described themselves were fashioned?

Have we found among them the pillar of stone to which Josephus referred, in fact a clue to the identity of the so-called lost Book of Numbers upon which the Hebraic *Sepher Yetzira* was based? Let the Archaeologists determine what monuments may have evolved at the points mentioned into those presently to be seen there, mere embellishments, possibly, of older ones. Possibly in the great wall of Belristan just East of Silmer is to be found the pillar of stone, rather then in the sunken red city of Petra in the shadow of Mount Sinai.

Moving on towards La Ha Sa we pass through the region of M-ana-so-ro-w-ara in the sacrosanct area of western Tibet. We gaze in wonderment at the lake (31° 30′ N.) from which flow the roots of the lotus, or the Indus, Ganges, and Brahma-pootra which furnish life waters of India, while the Oxus rises in the same area and flows northwestly through Syr into the Caspian. It seems obvious that the Tello in Sumer, Ya-ru-siloam (Jerusalem) and Sais, the oldest city in the delta of the Nile, were all sighted to mark the lake, just as Mount Carmel, Babylon, Naga-sa-saki, and San Diego at the south of California, all mark the region of western Tibet.

From Lake M-ana-so-ro-w-ara we pass on to LaHaSa (30° N. 90° E.). In that sacrosanct area we find just west of P-o-tala (91° E.), a plain at the elevation of 11,000 feet, forming a natural half moon out of which arises at 29° 45′ N. 90° 55′ E. a pyramidal height also called P-o-t-al-o, 'the Philosophy of the Moon, the Taux of Atlantis, the Serpent.' It marks as nearly as the terrain permitted, the intersection of the Cross to which Ti-bet, 'the Cross Covenant,' owes its name.

Who shall say when the first serpent temple was reared on the P-o-tal-o? We only know that there today one is found of which the geodetic symbols yield $3 + 0 = 3; 9 + 0 = 9 = 3 \times 3; 5 + 5 = 10$, or one 0, the symbol of the Heavenly Serpent.

To the west of the P-o-tal-o lies Shi-ga-t-ze, 'the Spirit of the Gaura, the Taux, Za En,' marking almost exactly the intersection of the Cross of which, as shown, the symbols yield $3 + 0 + 9 + 0 = 12 = 4 \times 3$. While 12 corresponds to the 12 signs of the Zodiac, $12 = 4 + 3 = 7$.[1]

---

[1] In the World Almanac of 1932 a strange statement appeared. In the list of the highest mountains of the world Ma-shin-shan, said to stand near Lhasa, was listed as higher than Everest. The statement was omitted from the next edition and has never been repeated. Apparently the compilers were gulled into interpreting the mythical mountain implying God's House, as an actual mountain.

Still another mystery remains to be solved. During World War II American aviators flying from India to Chung King, reported having seen a pyramid of Cheops, at Gizeh on the Nile. At the time the writer analyzed the measures given by the aviators. Nothing more has been heard of the pyramid and it remains to be seen whether in fact the aviators merely mistook one of the triangular mounds in the area of Chung King for a pyramid.

We find in the area extending from the present Lhasa to the province of El Hasa in Mesopotamia no monument that suggests the brick pillar referred to by Josephus more clearly than the great rectangle, 140′ x 550′ at Perse, or 'the Mount of Grace,' marking the horizontal arm of the World Cross at (30°N. 52°10′ E.). It is quite possible, however, that more than one of the monuments we have examined in Irania, were erected by the virtuous sons of Seth. Certainly these monuments must be fixed in mind against the time when we come to consider the post-diluvian civilization that arose in Mesopotamia. For certainly we have found in the hero Gi-l-ga-shi, the founder of both Shi-ra-z in Su-zi-ana and of La-ga-sh in Sumer.

Beyond this the writer does not care to go in the attempt to identify the stone pillar referred to by Josephus, except to point out that there is still another antique monument of which no one has attempted to fix the age. Thus at Pe-t-ra, 'the House of the Taux, Ra,' (28°N. 35°E.) we find in the shadow of Mount Sin-ai, the Lofty Head of the Hebrew Prophets, carved out of the red stone of the desert of Tin in Su-ez, a wondrous subterrain city, marking exactly the latitudinal circle of Mount Everest, 'Gaurasinkar,' and Mount Sin-ai and the meridian of Mount Sin-ai, Mount Carmel, and the Shrine of Sin-o-pe, or sin-u-b, which was eventually sighted at 42°N. marking the head of Asia Minor on the Black Sea, and the boundary between Armenia and Ionia, as well as the latitude of Kham Tengri, Mount El-b-ru-z in the Ararat Range, and the Seven Hills of Rome, on the Tiber, and here it will be noted that the antipodal meridian of Petra passes through Alaska and through the relics of the Pacific Continent which today constitutes the Society Archipelago including the islands just east of Tahiti.

It may well be, therefore, that the pillar of stone referred to by Josephus was in fact this wondrous city which no waters could have washed away. Certainly in the color of the stone, just as in E-e-ops-i-chi-pe, carved by the Cheyenne out of the red cliff at the Mountain of the Prairie, in Minne-sota, 'the land of sky tinted water,' is found a symbol of the Ru. The fact that additional carvings at Petra, of the Greek type, may have occurred later, is in no wise conclusive of the age of this sunken city which, though certainly existing when Moses is said to have gathered the refugees from Egypt in the Desert of Tin, is not mentioned in Genesis. Yet in it may be seen the well at which it is said he met his second wife, the daughter of J-e-t-h-ro. Perhaps we will not err if we take it that Jethro simply implied the mysteries enshrined in Petra.

CHAPTER XIX

THE ARK OF NOAH
THE REIGN OF THE FROST GODS,
HEIMDALL AND BOREAS

NOTWITHSTANDING the World Cross and the Egyptian Ankh, it was a vile earth upon which the eponymous Shem, Ham, and Japheth appeared in B.C. 950,000. Thus in *Genesis* 6 we read:

"11. The earth was corrupt before God, and the earth was filled with violence.

"12. And God looked upon the earth, and behold, it was corrupt; for all flesh had corrupted his way upon the earth."

In the last passage "flesh" is used merely in the sense of the world of Lamech with men of the type of Tubal Cain and those who had converted Sin and Baal into the Moon God.

"13. *And God said unto Noah, The end of all flesh is come before me; for the earth is filled with violence through them; and behold I will destroy them with the earth."*

Manifestly this passage implies what the Aryans as the Shepherds of God's House, were saying to the peoples of the entire earth.

To repeat, once the ice cap had been formed and the reigns of Heimdall and Boreas, the Frost gods, had begun, sudden fluctuations causing glaciation by alternate meltings and freezings, would cause tremendous local floodings of all the low places of the earth, just such as the Adamites had foreseen.

But how were those who were not to be destroyed, to be saved from the cold? A mere boat floating around on a worldwide sea, such as that in which even to-day it is taught that men saved themselves from a flood, would not save them from the cold.

[*162*]

SHEMTIC PLANETARIUM OR DEKKAD

(ACCORDING TO GENESIS 11-25)

EMANATIONS FROM NOEAS (B.C. 1,450,000 - 500,000)

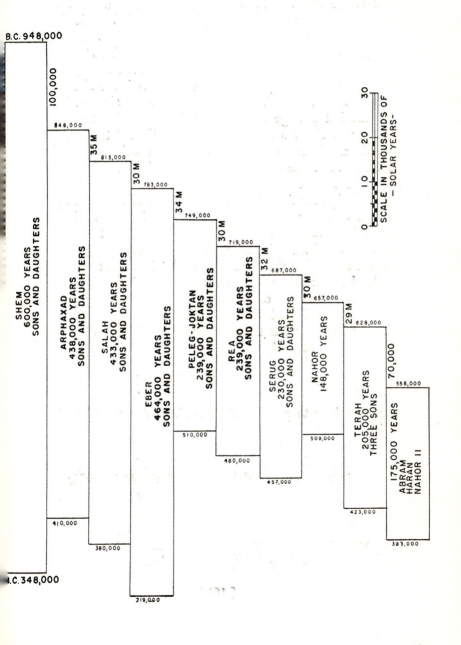

"14. *Make thee an ark of gopher wood; rooms shalt thou make in the ark, and shalt pitch it within and without with pitch. And this is the fashion which thou shalt make it of; the length of the ark shall be three hundred cubits, the breadth of it fifty cubits, and the height of it thirty cubits. A window shalt thou make to the ark, and in a cubit shalt thou finish it above; and the door of the ark shalt thou set in the side thereof; with lower, second, and third stories shalt thou make it.*"

In the last passage quoted there is nothing indicating that the ark was either a ship or a structure limited to the Mesopotamians. Moreover, no such thing as a universal flooding of the earth at one time has ever occurred, since first it arose above the waters.

The design for the ark given the peoples of the earth by the teachers of God's House, was ideal for a fortress against the wild animals that would go on the rampage from hunger, and the enemies of the spiritually minded sons of Noah, and also as a shelter against the impending cold. Then too, there would be cloud bursts that would occur when glaciation induced by radical alterations of temperature, began, and evaporation of the waters overloaded the clouds with moisture. In truth the ark described was but the pattern for the first castles of the chosen people of God, such as other peoples who have erected castles have claimed to be.

On the other hand, those who had carved out of the rocks the sunken city of Pe-t-ra, had shown the Chrestoes of all the mysteries, how to preserve their seeds in the great labyrinths which soon appeared all over the earth.

But the word ark is capable of many constructions. It implies among other things a container or vehicle. Therefore, just as the Arctic Zone contained Ziland, and the Philosophic Arks were the vehicles of spiritual enlightenment, the whole earth had been converted by the surveyors and shepherds of God's House, into the philosophic ark of the geodetic grid. Thus, men were to save themselves by both the arks or castles of gopher wood, and by bringing themselves into the spiritual

ark, or the See of God's House symbolized by the geodetic
tauxs in both hemispheres. The earth ark contained not only
mortals but all the other creatures of the earth.

"17. *And, behold, I, even I, do bring a flood of waters upon
the earth, to destroy all flesh, wherein is the breadth of life,
from under heaven. And everything that is in the earth shall
die.*"

Plainly it was the flesh of the earth that was to perish.

"*But with thee (Noah) will I establish my covenant; and
(if) thou shalt come into the ark, thou and thy sons, and thy
wife, and thy sons' wives with thee.*"

The covenant was made, therefore, with all who should
come into the spiritual ark or See, God's House.

"19. And of every living thing, of all flesh, two of every
sort, shalt thou bring into the ark, to keep them alive with
thee; they shall be male and female."

The meaning of this is fully shown by the next passage.

"20. *Of fowls after their kind, and of cattle after their
kind, of every creeping thing of the earth after his kind, two
of every sort shall come unto thee, to keep them alive.*"

Inevitably these creatures would seek out the parts of the
earth ark where they could escape the cold and the waters.

"21. *And take thou unto thee of all food that is eaten, and
thou shall gather it to thee; and it shall be for food for thee,
and for them.*"

In the great strongholds for which the pattern had been
furnished, were to be stored by the Noacheans, not only the
food necessary to maintain life during the floods, but the seeds
for future planting.

"22. *Thus did Noah, according to all that God commanded
him, so did he.*"

There is no evidence of upheavals and submersions caused
by seismic disturbances during the 100,000 years previous to
B.C. 850,000. On the contrary the mutations of the earth were
in fact those caused by the weight of the waters in the sense
of its glaciation.

The facts are well preserved in the wondrous eddas of the Norse peoples whose mysteries were enshrined, among other places, in Fingal's Cave on the islet just south of the Giant's Causeway leading from Scalp Mountain at the summit of Ireland, to the region of the Scalpa Floe at the head of Scotia. From them it appears that the present Ice Age has included three winters between which have been the first and second glacial periods. How much the scientists are indebted for their findings to the mysteries of the Kabira with respect to the Great Ice Age, as well as for their theories of evolution of the earth and man, the reader must decide.[1]

The first winter of which the ancestors of the Pi-ra-ti tell, was that when the great serpent J-o-r-h-o-r-gu-mund, implying the ice cap arose from the waters encircling the earth. The second was the winter of the Wolf when men fought with famishing wild beasts for the carcasses of their dead. Then at last came the third—the winter of the sword. Then it was that the All-Father O-d-in, "the offspring of the Moon, the Diva, Indra," summoned the Champions of V-al-ha-lla from their castles to route the evil giants and recover the dominion of the earth. When this had been done the younger gods would assemble on a great mountain at the center of the earth where was located the wall of the wise one-eyed giant Mi-m-r who had guided O-din, or the Teutonic W-o-din. Contemplating the past, they would watch the new race of men take up the fresh grass lands of the earth.

For the present, however, we need only consider the Paleolithic age of the old stone men who had come to inhabit the earth when the first winter began.[2]

While the Ice Cap extended in the Eastern Hemisphere down to 60° N., in the Western Hemisphere it spread down to 40° N. This difference is readily explained by what the atheist ascribes to accident. There was an immense mass of warm water in the Arctic Zone at the North of the Eastern Hemisphere although not in the Western Arctic. Therefore, the present Europe was tempered, more than America beyond the coasts of the Atlantic. Consequently, notwithstanding the almost complete desolation of the region, in America, over which the ice cap extended, along the seaboard from Labrador to the Gulf of M-e-x-atla, a remnant of the Re-na-pe, thanks to the caves in the mountains, survived even in the North, as well as in the A-pa-la-chi. Yet, they survived exactly in the manner of the present E-ski-Moo, "Earth spirits of the Moon," whose ancestors continued to circulate around the earth in the Arctic Zone, and in the undestroyed· part of the Land of Is.

At the west others survived in the caves of the Cor-d-ill-e-ra, 'the Great Serpent,' which had arisen out of the sea and that extended from Alas-ka to the Fa-l-ka Land at the southern extremity of the Western Hemisphere, furnishing the backbone for the link of Pa-na-ma, which link connected the two western continents. Most of the civilization that survived in the western world, however, was that in Arizona where the Zuni and other Serpent people burrowed out great cities in the cliffs.

All over the earth, however, there were caves such as that of Fin-ga-la, close to the Giant's Causeway ascribed by the Irish to F-in, their alleged progenitor, similar to those in the Maya Hills of the Dek-k-ana.

According to the Greek myth of Deucalion, he had been advised by his wise father-in-law Pro-m-e-t-h-eus to save himself from a deluge which Zeus was preparing. Accordingly, he placed himself and his wife Pyrra in a cubical box which eventually landed them at Mount Parnassus, due South of Olympus or close to Mycenae in Argos.

The Cube whose four sides unfolded displays the Taux, implied, of course, the Aryan Ark.

Although the Deuca-Lion and Pyrra had been told not to look backward, and to throw away the bones of their mother, on arriving at Parnassus they cast stones instead of bones. Those cast by Deucalion became men, and those cast by Pyrra, became women. The implication is that from the descendants of Deucalion representing the E-nix or sub-race of the Lion

Men, evolved the peoples of the solar cult, while those who evolved from Pyrra representing the Ru, were the peoples of the lunar cult, who subsequently appeared among the Aryan Graekos, or the Hellenes sprung from Deucalion and Pyrra.

In the Greek myths also it is shown how thanks to the cow that fed them, implying the Cow Worship, the ancestors of the E-s-ki-moo survived. The Pirati of the North who in medieval times still worshipped Bal-d-ur, 'the Son of Light and Love,' tell how he was killed by the evil Loki 'God of the Fickle Winds,' with a lance of mistletoe thrust into his heel. Yet, they insisted that he would return to them as Chris or Kris, and looked expectantly for his resurrection.

In the myths of the South Seas, also is found a record of the Ice Age. There, the Tu-ra-ti also knew the cold. Thus, had it not been for the cold, the great black spider, implying the Melanesians, would have spread all over the earth.

Inevitably, of course, the cold drove many peoples southward from Hell. Undoubtedly it was in the first winter that the great labyrinths upon which the cities of Pa-r-is-i, Rome, W-ar-sa-w and Ya-ru-si-loam arose, were burrowed out of smaller caves, along with the labyrinths to be seen at Chi-u-z-zi and Mount Ca-sin-no in Ita-la-ya as in Crete, the islands of Lemnos and Samnos, in which the mysteries of the Cabiri ultimately were enshrined, just as in the holy cave of Mount C-ar-mel (32° 30' N. 35° E.) on the meridian of Pe-tra and Mount Sin, and of Sin-o-pe at the summit of Syria (42° N.). Another labyrinth was constructed at Fa-yoo-ma in Egypt.[3]

Also at P-ana-pe, the 'Philosophy House of Ana' (Equator 150° E.), was erected a labyrinth—one of the grandest in the world, which is readily explained.[4] For if one should inscribe on the graph of Gea an isosceles triangle with the Mountains of the Moon (30° E.), and Pa-na-pe, as its apogees, both on the Equator, with an altitude of 30° and a base of 120°, the apex will rest at 30° 90' E. in the Forbidden Realm of God's House at La Ha Sa.

On the Grand Ra-Pa or Easter Island, in Oceanica (12° S.

120° W.) some 1,300 miles West of Peru, are to be seen the miniature rock houses in which the Pygmies of that island found refuge. In the Andes as throughout Ana-huac in M-e-x-tla, and in the islands of Ka-rib-da, are found countless caves. One of the grandest caves in the world, however, is that of L-u-ra-ya in the Ap-pa-la-chi not far from the Tau where the red cruciform crystals of Rialite, called Fairy Stones are found, though nowhere else on the earth.

So vanishes the mystery of the Cave Men, as also that of the E-ski-Moo who are merely the descendants of those who continued to survey the earth as messengers of God's House.

But if in the post-diluvian cycle of Shem-Ham-Japheth, the Eskimoo were not the same as they are today, neither were the so-called cave men all brutal savages as modern science depicts. Among them as there have been in all ages, were men of inspired enlightenment—the true elders of mankind corresponding to Japheth "the Elder."[5]

What became of the thousands of caves in which the peoples of this age survived in addition to the crude ones presently known?

The answer is a simple one. The cities of the future arose upon many of the caves which became cellars and sub-cellars, such as the catacombs beneath Pa-ri-si, Rome, W-ar-sa-w and Ya-ru-si-loam.[6]

During the immense period over which the First Winter and the first glacial period extended, began to appear upon the earth, not only the labyrinths, but the amazing world-wide system of mounds that radiates from the Abyss of learning to every clime, which were designed to serve both as seed beds above the local floodings and as geodetic markers. Consequently they bear geodetic symbols corresponding to their symbolic names. Along with them began to appear in both hemispheres the symbols called the S-w-a-s-t-i-ka, ascribed to the people of that name, and also to those called J-an-s, who had come to occupy the Hi-ma-la-ya. Undoubtedly the Swastika and Jans were both the offspring of the Red Men in Tibet.

THE PHILOSOPHIC HISTORY OF CIVILIZATION

The civilization which the She-zoo Hor had founded in Egypt was less affected than any other in the world by the new physical ordeal to which men had been subjected. Therefore Egypt was to be the most enlightened country in the world in the post-diluvian cycle, and there would appear the great mound of Jebel Tellum in the Susan and the one to be seen at El Obeir.

---

1 Author's Note: See the *Great Ice Age*, GEIKIE (1888). Also the works of Darwin and Wallace who after visiting India, put forth simultaneously and independently in 1852, their theory of evolution. Modern science divides the culture of man into Paleolithic, Megolithic or Middle, and Neolithic Cycles, corresponding to the Three Glacial Periods of the Great Ice Age now recognized to have begun concurrently with the present or Quaternary Geological Age. In fixing the beginning of the Quaternary Age at between B. C. 1,000,000 and B. C. 850,000, undoubtedly the Geologists were guided by the Chronology in *Genesis* shown by the spheres of the Noachean Planetarium, although they do not admit the fact. Their Stone, Copper and Iron Ages have no reference to time, and merely relate to the stage of civilization. Thus, in the same cycle of time one people might be in the Stone Age while another might be in the Iron Age. Per example, many savages today are still in the Stone Age, side by side with visitors of the Iron Age. Roughly speaking those who divide the Stone Age into the Old, Middle, and New Stone Ages, concur with the concept of the Paleolithic, Megolithic, and Neolithic cycles.

2 Author's Note: The Megolithic Age of the second winter is usually fixed at about B. C. 500,000 when the Noachean Cycle came to an end, while the Neolithic Age of modern man of the Third Winter ordinarily is fixed at about B. C. 30,000.

3 Antioch was the original name of the Island of Rhodes. There were numerous Ana-t-i-o-chi, one of which, Ma-zi-acca, came to be called Caesarea. It was in the Labyrinth of Samnos that Pytha-gora received his primary instruction from Pherecydes, a sage of the Orphic mysteries. It was at the Holy Cave of Mount Carmel that El-i and El-i-sha, the first Hebrew prophets, appeared as the exponents of the Wisdom Philosophy.

4 Panape is located in the present Caroline Islands.

5 El-d-e-r, "Enyalius, the Divine Euseues Reincarnated."

6 Author's Note: Also the catacombs of Rome.

CHAPTER XX

THE NOACHEAN DELUGE
THE MONGOLOID MAN APPEARS
THE BIBLICAL FLOOD

CONCURRENTLY with the terrestrial changes which had occurred during the transition from the Tertiary to the Secondary a new cosmic deluge brought into being in the North the Mongoloid type of man from which evolved the various groups of Caucasians including the Dana of Greece. From Dan-ne-mora in Norway where these Borean Danitics appeared, they may be traced on the graphs of Gea to Dan's Mark, and from Dan-t-zi-g straight down the Dan-u-b-e to the area of the Black Sea from which the Dar-dan-elles now lead to the Ionian Sea. Also they appeared in Ireland as the T-u-a-ha-t-i de Dan-a-an. Undoubtedly also they had appeared in Circassia and the Caucasus as well as in the Hindu Kush where the Aryan Caucasians appeared from whom the Hindus evolved. Because the Caucasians as they spread down the Urals through Circassia into the Caucasus merged there with the Ethiopians and the Ru the antediluvian Japhethics are designated in *Genesis* as the "Elder."

In North America also a Mongoloid type of man appeared among the Siouans and Iroquoians of the North, who were of a lighter color than the older Algonquians, Muskhogeans, Caddo, and Shoshoneans.

By B.C. 850,000 the fluctuations of temperature had caused the waters in the great inland lakes, including Lake Va-ana in the Caucasus where Ti-f-l-is, Ba-ku, and Ta-b-r-i-z are found today between the Caspian and Black Seas, to swell as did those seas to the point of overflowing. To this flood the melting ice in the highlands of I-r-ana at the east, and those of the Syrian desert at the north of Rub, would have contributed.

In Genesis 7, we read:

"In the six hundredth year of Noah's life, in the second month, the seventeenth day were all the fountains of the great deep broken up, and the windows of heaven opened."

Thus, the first winter came to an end in Mesopotamia with a sudden rise of temperature and the evaporation of that resulted in a cloud burst of forty days and nights.

"In the self same day entered Noah, and Shem, and Ham, and Japheth, the sons of Noah, and his wife, and the three wives of his sons with them into the Ark. They, and every beast after his kind, and all the cattle after their kind, and every creeping thing that creepeth upon the earth after his kind, every bird of every sort."

In other words, it was on the date of 2-7-601 of the cycle of Noah, that the peoples and insentient creatures of the earth found themselves upon the terrestrial ark. So, we note the mystery in 1-7, and in 601, or $6 + 0 + 1 = 7$, corresponding to the Scripture in which the event is recorded. But the date in solar years is B.C. 2:17: 850,000, while the sum of these numerals is 32, the basic figure of the Sepher Y-e-t-zi-ra.

Therefore, if one should visit the seven hills that loom above the river Po near Mount Al-ba-nus, he would find on one of them called the Janiculum at 42° N. 12° E., a four-way arch oriented to the points of the compass just as in the case of the Palace of K-no-s-sus on the present island of Cre-ta. On the face of this so-called Temple of Janus where the mysteries of the Kabira were enshrined by the Italics, appear 32 notches.[1]

The Italics named the first month of the solar year after Ja-n-us, a contraction of Ya-Cenubis. With acquired logic they gave the name Feb-ru-en, implying second, since F-e-b implies "Faro the Ethiopian Bal" or the Second Race on the earth claimed by the Punic ancestors of the Italics.

Because the water congealed upon the heights, it is said: "And the waters prevailed exceedingly upon the earth; and all the high hills, that were under the whole heaven were covered."

Inasmuch as this did not mean that all the hills were submerged, next it is said: "Fifteen cubits upward did the waters prevail; and the mountains were covered." In other words, although ice formed on the mountains, the flood did not rise above the walls of the Tello which are 30′ high, that is 360″, while 15 cubits each of 20 inches, was but 300 inches.

Due to the cold, all those who had not entered the arks, perished. Thus, "all flesh died that moved upon the earth, both of fowl, and of the cattle, and of the beast, and of every creeping thing that creepeth upon the earth, and every man; all in whose nostrils was the breath of life, of all that was on the dry land, died . . . : And Noah only remained alive, and they that were with him in the Ark."

From this it is obvious that those who did not enter the earth arks, which the people in the cycle of Noah had been directed to build, had perished.

"And the waters prevailed upon the earth an hundred and fifty days." That is, the low places were submerged that long as a result of the enormous downpour and the melting ice on the hills.

Inasmuch as those in the arks survived, "God remembered Noah, and every living thing, all the cattle that was with him in the Ark; and God made a wind to pass over the earth, and the waters assuaged."[2] In a word, a cold wind halted the meltings and the flooding of the low places. So "the waters returned from off the earth continually: and after the end of the one hundred and fiftieth day the waters were abated." With the low places drained, "the Ark rested in the seventh month, on the seventeenth day of the month, upon the mountains of Ara-ra-t."[3]

Ju-la-i, 'Jupiter, the Septenary Law of the Spirit,' or July,

'Jupiter, the law of Ya,' implying 7, gives the month, fixing the date of the abatement of the flood as B.C. 7:17: 850,000, of which the numerals aggregate 874, while 8 + 7 + 4 = 19, and 1 + 9 = 10.

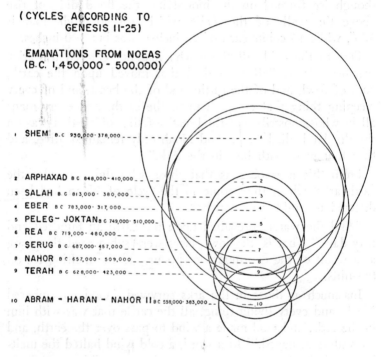

THE SHEMITIC PLANETARIUM OR DEKKAD
B. C. 948,000

(CYCLES ACCORDING TO
GENESIS 11-25)

EMANATIONS FROM NOEAS
(B.C. 1,450,000 - 500,000)

1 SHEM B.C. 930,000 - 378,000

2 ARPHAXAD B.C. 848,000 - 410,000

3 SALAH B.C. 813,000 - 380,000

4 EBER B.C. 783,000 - 317,000

5 PELEG - JOKTAN B.C. 749,000 - 510,000

6 REA B.C. 719,000 - 480,000

7 SERUG B.C. 687,000 - 457,000

8 NAHOR B.C. 657,000 - 509,000

9 TERAH B.C. 628,000 - 423,000

10 ABRAM - HARAN - NAHOR II B.C. 558,000 - 383,000

In the passage quoted it is not said that the ark came to rest on Mount Ara-rat. The Ara-ra-t mountains where the ark rested, cover a large area in which there are many exalted heights. Near that range are the Kara Dag, and the Taux Shina in the Caucasus, to the south of Mount Ara-ra-t.[4]

Undoubtedly when the flood began in Mesopotamia in B.C.

850,000, many persons fled the low grounds in vessels, finding refuges in the highlands.[5] It seems certain too that some of the arks of gopher wood were erected on Mount B-ar-is, or Mount Ara-ra-t.[6] Yet it is utterly absurd to imagine that all the peoples of Mesopotamia would have sought out that one spot when countless high places were close at hand, such as the Tauxs in the Caucasus, the mountains at the north of Ru-b, and the high places east of the Ti-gr-is. For if the waters never rose in Mesopotamia above the walls of the Tello, surely there was no reason for the Mesopotamians to breast a current hundreds of miles into the very region where the flood was originating, in part, at least, in the great lakes of the Caucasus. Certainly that region would have been the last in which the Mesopotamians would have sought a refuge.[7]

"And the waters decreased continually until the tenth month: in the tenth month, on the first day of the month, were the tops of the mountains seen." This implies that the ice had vanished on October 1, 850,000 giving the figures $10 + 1 + 850,000 = 861$, wherein $8 + 6 + 1 = 15 = 5 \times 3$ corresponds to the Trinity of the Fifth Root Race.

Further it appears that at the end of the forty days of rain, from the earth ark, a raven went forth to and fro, until the waters were dried from the earth, and that also a dove was sent forth, but the dove found no rest. The raven and the dove simply imply the scouts sent out, and soon the dove returned although the raven did not, doubtless having perished among the wild beasts prowling the hills. Seven days later the dove was sent out again, and that evening returned bearing an olive leaf, ever the symbol of peace.

At last in the 601 year of the Noachean cycle, on the first day of the Italic Ya-u-en or the Hebraic January, or 1:1:601, the covers of the arks could be removed for the face of the earth, or the mountains, were dry. But as $6 + 0 + 1 = 7$; $1 + 1 + 601 = 9 = 3 + 3 + 3 = 3 \times 3$. The year 601 of the Noachean Cycle, however, was the solar year B.C. 849,000. And $1 + 1 + 849,000 = 851$, while $8 + 5 + 1 = 14 =$

7 + 7. And on Feb-ru-en 27, was the earth dried, that is on 2:27:601, whereof 2 + 27 + 601 = 36, as 3 + 6 = 9 = 3 + 3 + 3 = 3 × 3, in the solar date 2:27:849,999 appears 2 + 2 + 7 + 8 + 4 + 9 = 32, or again the basic number of the Sepher Yetzira.

Amazing as the magic in the dates which have been analyzed may seem, the date B.C. 849,000 shows that those who in the cycle of Noah had been saved by the earth ark, had remained in it 1,000 solar years lacking 10 days when, according to the Scripture, God commanded the survivors of the flood to go forth from the ark, multiply and reseed the earth, and also designated the rainbow as the symbol of the covenant with man that neither the earth, nor *all* flesh, were to be destroyed by another flood.

There is no deduction here that the process of evolution would end, and that there would be no more cosmic deluges. In the rainbow displaying the seven cardinal colors of the spectrum is merely to be seen the token that the septenary principle of nature would persist; that in accord with it man might uplift himself; that his soul would reincarnate during the circuit of the seven planets in the manner specified in the Wisdom Philosophy.

So came to an end the First Winter—the Winter of Jorhorgum and the flood, which in fact but attended the Cosmic Deluge during which the Mongoloid type of man appeared.

Enough has been said to show that the Hebrew Scriptures dealing with the flood were not copied as assumed by some, from the Assyrian account in which Ha-si-a-t-ra is made to play a role similar to that ascribed to Noah, nor from the latter Chaldean account.[8]

---

[1] The present Temple of Janus, or the Arch Triomphens is an evolution from an older temple of which the material was used.

[2] Genesis 8:1.

[3] Author's Note: July was not named after Julius Caesar as commonly taught. The gens Julius of which Caesar was a member took its name from Enyalius, the Immortals who came to be designated by the septenary name J-u-p-i-t-er

after the Hebrews had coined the J appearing in Janus, J-ovus, and Jupiter. The clan Julius claimed to be descended from Jupiter.

4 S-h-i-na "Sa, Ha, the Spirit of Naragana."

5 Note how people today in the floods of the western rivers bring their possessions in boats to high places.

6 Eventually Dionysius, a great historian of Helicarnassus, would declare that timber relics of wood treated with bitumen were found on Mount Ararat. See also Heraclitus of Damascus.

7 Author's note: Dore's imaginative pictures of the Ark, strange to say, have exerted more influence on modern thought, than reason.

8 Ha-si-a-t-ra, "Ha, Sin, the Arya, Taux, Rama."

CHAPTER XXI

THE AKKADIANS

The Post-Diluvian Planetarium of Noah.
Nimrod The Mighty Hunter
And The Rise of Egyptian Imperialism.
The Tower of Ba-Bel.
The Confusion of Tongues.

INASMUCH AS THE physical environment of the post-diluvians in the two hemispheres differed radically by reason of the climates, it was inevitable that civilization in the relic of the Greek continent of Atlas, which came to be called Libya, would evolve more rapidly than the civilization in the Western Hemisphere that continued to be called Atlas. Meantime, however, just as the names *Atala* and *Atalla* had appeared in the present America, that of *Atalla* had appeared in Asia Minor.

It was the function of God's House to protect the weak against the strong. Still the Eskimos were able to move around the Arctic Zone. Therefore, soon or late the peoples of the more favored parts such as Egypt, Chaldea, and China, would become a menace to their weaker fellows, since it is the nature of man that stronger nations will loot, rob, enslave, and even kill weaker peoples so long as the latter have anything to yield. Moreover, because of their material superiority, they will claim the God-given right to do so, even though in doing it they degrade themselves as well as their victims.[1] In view of this sociological principle, and the fact that men are not as fishes, whereof the big were made to feed on the small, the helpless peoples of the earth had to be protected.

More than this, however, lies behind the secrecy with respect to the Western Hemisphere. Experience with mankind had shown bestiality to be a dreadful curse. The Western Hemisphere with relatively retarded peoples, afforded the opportunity for a great experiment. Thus like the Akka pygmy, they came to have no domestic animals. Although eventually they developed the high civilizations of Mexico, Central America, and Peru, these civilizations would be unique in that still in the time of Columbus there were no domestic animals save the llama which had appeared among the Andeans as a beast of burden.

Either bound by the oaths of the mysteries, or fearing to violate the inhibitions of God's House, the scholars of antiquity dared not mention the Western Hemisphere. Therefore, it was mentioned cautiously by them. Nevertheless, it is obvious that those who erected the terrestrial spheres before the time of Columbus, were not ignorant of the so-called new world of the West to which the ancestors of the Eskimos had ready access.

These things having been explained, let us now return to those who, in obedience to God's alleged command in January, 849,000, descended to the plains of Mia between the Euphrates and the Tigris. Although as shown by the Hebraic Planetarium, they were the tenth generation of those who had entered the earth ark near 1,000 years before, during all that time they had continued to receive spiritual enlightenment and had not, therefore, fallen into savagery such as the brutal cave man commonly depicted. But certain it is there were at this time many thousands of savages and near savages on the earth. On the other hand in Mesopotamia and other parts there were many worshippers of the Moon God such as the Chon of Canaan, and the posterity of the Cainites in the realms of the South Sea, called the Land of Mu.

"18. And the sons of Noah, that went forth from the ark were "Shem, and Ham, and Japheth," and "of them," that is by their posterity, "was the whole earth overspread."[2]

The overspreading of the earth, by these Adamites, however, was to require ages, so that the absurdity of imagining the three sons at once spread over the whole earth is on a par with the idea that all the peoples of the earth, along with the gnats and elephants, the lions and tigers, had floundered around in a boat 580 feet long for near 1,000 years. Nor do the child-like minds capable of entertaining such a fancy, consider what became of the wives of Noah, and of his three sons.

Inevitably when the alleged sons of Noah with their wives descended to the plains these Aryan peoples like the missionaries spoke the Aryan language. This did not mean, of course, that the non-Aryans did not have countless varying tongues. Therefore in the Hebrew Scriptures it is correctly declared that when the post-diluvian civilization began, "the whole earth was of one language, and of one speech." In proof of this is found the antediluvian geodetic grid with the tauxs that spoke to men in every clime.[3]

Meantime, just as in China, the Akkadian language had come to be spoken in Irania by the Caucasian offspring of the Tatars in Syr, and we have already seen the nature of the great symbols which were erected in the *Land of Cedars* where the Mount of Grace appears.

Not having been flooded out naturally the civilization of Irania was in advance of that in Mesopotamia, just as was that of Egypt. Inevitably too God's House would have employed the Caucasian Akkadians of Irania to re-enlighten the Mesopotamians.

"2. And it came to pass, as they journeyed from the East," that is in the course of their journey, "they found a plain in the land of Shinar, and they dwelt there."

Naturally the Akkadians picked the highland of Shinar on which to erect Akkad at 33° N. 44° E. in the Euphrates. Marking exactly the latitude of Yezd in the land of the Parsee east of the Tigris whence they had come, it also marked the meridian of the Taux Shina, Kara Dagh, and Mount Ara-rat, the Ten Taux of Circassia, and Io-sin-fa-z-embla in Ziland, upon which T-i-f-l-is eventually was sited.

So arrived the Akkadians on the high plain of Shi-n-ar at

the North of S-h-u-m-er. With an eye for strategy they did not establish themselves in the low region of Nu, E-din-u, Hilla, Gursu, Kis, Tello, Ni-p-p-ur, and Ur, or Mu-ga-ya, but at Ak-ka, (33° N.) on the Euphrates at the point where it comes nearest to the Tigris. Thus, they were able to command absolutely the intercourse between Shinar and Shumer, or Su-me-r.[4]

But in vain the Mayavic Shemites, and Hamites, and the Caucasians represented by the Japhethics, who had been brought into the Aryan fold since the flood, urged the non-Aryan peoples to descend to the plain and resume the planting in which the Nabatheans could help them. Still, however, they were too fearful of more floods, and of each other to abandon their caves. Therefore, they continued in the hunter state of culture which had evolved during the past 1,000 years.

In this situation Noah, it is said "began to be an husband-man, and he planted a vineyard." To be sure the Nabatheans had undertaken to restore agriculture, but the planting of Noah also implied the human vineyard that sprang up upon the earth, thanks to the spiritual cultivation of the Aryan missionaries.

Among the three groups, however, there were the three different types of Adamites who had evolved among those who had found refuges in the Arks erected in different parts of the earth ark. Nor is it to be doubted that many of them had fallen victim to the Moon God in their primitive stage of culture. Accordingly it is said that Noah drank of the wine, became drunk, and "lay uncovered within his Tent." This simply implies that the Ethiopian Sinitics in a spiritual sense had fallen into such confusion they were unable to understand and profit by the Wisdom Philosophy.

According to Josephus they were all urged to send forth colonies. "God desired that they spread over the earth that they might not raise seditions among themselves, but instead might cultivate it and enjoy its fruits after a plentiful manner. But in truth they were so ill instructed that they did not obey his commandments for which reason they fell into calamities, and were made sensible by experience of what sin they had been guilty."

The Chon who had occupied the present realm of I-ra-q at the north of R-ub, saw the spiritual nakedness of the people who had evolved from the vineyard, and it is said Ham called the attention of Shem and Japheth to the plight of their father.

The inevitable had happened. More and more of the Ethiopians in Sumer and Ru-b had fallen victim to the Moon God Sin. They did not mean to allow the Akkadians whom they deemed intruders, to dominate Mesopotamia. Therefore not only a political but a religious schism was the result. Accordingly it is said that after Ham appealed to the Shemitics, they took a garment and laid it upon their shoulders and went backward, and did not see the nakedness of their father. In other words, instead of allying themselves with the Ethiopian Chusites represented by Ham, they repudiated them. Taking the Aryan cloth, so to speak, "their faces were backward," because they accepted principles of the Wisdom Philosophy. In a word the Sumerians and the Caucasians had united against the Ethiopians.

Such was the situation when, according to the Scriptures, God a second time urged the Mesopotamians to send forth colonies, but again in vain. Plainly all of them were far more interested in saving themselves than in missionary work among savages of the Scythian type with their scalp knives. Consequently the schism was enlarging when the human vineyard came in B.C. 848,000 to include sixteen different groups.

Inasmuch as eventually these sixteen groups did spread over the earth, carrying their philosophy to other peoples, what appears in *Genesis* respecting their philosophy is of vital importance to the student of civilization. Therefore it is necessary to understand the post-diluvian planetarium, or Sephiroth of Shem of which the cycles are co-eval with those of the peoples who are described as the descendants of Ham and Japheth.

One must not be misled by the names assigned to the sixteen groups which indicate the regions in which eventually they settled, rather than those where they had evolved.

Because the post-diluvian Caucasians called Ja-ph-eth were a trinitic mixture implying the first Caucasians to appear in Asia Minor, were in fact issue springing from the antediluvian Japheth called 'the Elder,' their descendants are named first in Genesis 10, while those of Ham are the next, and those of Shem are the last to be named. The reversal of the prior order indicates very plainly the Ja-ph-ethics had evolved in the North of Ana where the Caucasians had merged with the Ethiopians, while the Shemitics had evolved in Sumer at the South of Shinar, and the Hamitics in the intervening areas of Syria. And here it is especially important to note that Canaan upon whom such stress is put as the first son of Ham, is an eponym derived from C-ana-a-n, 'the Lunar Ark of Ana, the Ark of the Nilus,' implying that the Canaanites as distinguished from the other sons of Ham were pure Negroids, while the other three sons of Ham were Punics.

Those who, according to *Genesis,* evolved during the first 35,000 years of the cycle of Arphaxad, are here shown.[5]

Ja-ph-eth. 1. Gomer, 2. Magog, 3. Madai, 4. Javan, 5. Tubal, 6. Mesheh, and 7. Tiras, of whom the last two also were called Mesa and Thorbel, respectively, by Josephus.

Ham. 1. Cush, 2. Mizraim, 3. Phut, 4. Canaan.

Shem. 1. Elam, 2. Asshur, 3. Arphaxad, 4. Lud, 5. Aram.

To be sure the Aryan Akkadians called Arphaxad, had brought both the Japhethics and Shemites into their fold. Meantime, however, the Hamites, represented by Canaan, had converted Baal, or the Greek Helios, into the Moon God. Therefore it is said that when their grandfather Noah awoke from the stupor produced by the wine of the vineyard, and saw what his younger son, implying the Caucasus, had done to him, he cursed Canaan.

"And he said, cursed be Canaan; a servant of servants shall he be unto his brethren." But the Lord God of Shem was blessed by him, and he declared "Canaan shall be his servant," implying that eventually the Cushites or the Ethiopians descendants of the Ru and the Lion Men, to whom Canaan had fallen victim, would be brought into the fold of God's House. Also Noeas is made to say that God would enlarge Japheth; that he "would dwell in the Tents of Shem," and that Canaan also would be the servant of Japheth.

In other words the Caucasians were to be welcomed by the older Sumerians. Together they were to subject the Canaanites who did not accept the Wisdom Philosophy, but had fallen victim to the Old Moon God Sin, as the mythical Cain had done.

As we have rationalized both the myth of Cain and Abel, and that of the two Pillars reared by the Sons of Seth, now must we rationalize the myths of Nimrod and the Tower of Babel.

To repeat, Egypt had been the least affected country on the earth by the climatic events of the cosmic deluge. Therefore, when in B.C. 873,000 began the cycle of Sa-la-ha, bearing a name that is an Hebraic inversion of La-Ha-Sa, the Chusites of Egypt had converted the cult of Is-Is into the cult of Isis-Osiris.[6] Moreover, the Punics designated as Cush, the son of Ham, who had come to occupy the Syrian desert at the north of Ru-b, as well as all the others named as the Sons of Ham, naturally cherished not only the memory of the world their Lion Men ancestors had ruled, but deemed Mesopotamia the rightful inheritance of the Punics. Also they looked upon the Caucasian Akkadians from I-r-ana as interlopers. Nor were they unaware of the curse which Noeas is said to have placed upon C-ana-an, and the prophecy that Shem and Japheth together would rule Syria; that Japheth or the Caucasians would enlarge, dwell in that land, and make servants of the Punics. Also the Cush were fully aware of the vital importance of Mesopotamia as the middle land lying between Asia at the east, and Rumel at the west, Circassia at the north, and Rub at the south. Accordingly it is said that Cush, the son of Ham, and the brother of Canaan, in the third cycle, or that of Sa-la-ha, begat the mysterious Ni-m-rod, "the Mighty Hunter," who has ever proved a great mystery to the historians of the West. *Nimrod* was merely an eponym indicating the spirit of imperialism which had evolved among all the Hamites, who deemed themselves descended from the first men of which the Man in the Moon was deemed the symbol, ever known as the Hunter Moon. Thus their purpose to conquer Mesopotamia with the backing of Egypt, implied by eponym of the 'Mighty Hunter' *applied to the Cushites.*[7]

To be sure the Asshurites had erected Asshur on the Tigris (35° N. 44° E.) beyond Akkad (33° N. 44° E.), thereby manifesting their purpose to preempt Shi-nar. Against the Chusites, however, they were helpless. Sweeping down from the jebels in the Syrian desert, soon the backers of Nimrod brought the whole of Sumeria under their sway. Also they subjected not only Asshur (35° N. 44° E.) which had been erected by the oldest son of Shem, but Akkad.

Having achieved this great conquest, Nimrod is represented as saying to the peoples of Mesopotamia: "Go to, let us build us a city, and a tower, whose top may reach unto heaven; and let us make a name, lest we be scattered abroad upon the face of the whole earth."[8]

This does not mean that the Punics of Egypt had any idea of rearing a tower to heaven. One may raise his eyes and hands *unto* heaven without thought of entering that realm. But it does *show*, however, that the Punics were fearful that unless they united with the Ethiopians, they would be subjected by the Shemitic-Japhethic-Akkadian combine. In a word, it was politics on the grand scale to which imperialists such as those represented by Nimrod, have ever had resort. Accordingly the character of Nimrod is well described.

"He persuaded the Mesopotamians not to ascribe to God, as if it were through his means they were happy, but to believe it was their own courage which procured their happiness. He also gradually changed the government into tyranny, seeing no other way of turning men from God but to bring them into a constant dependence upon his power.⁹ He also said he would be avenged against God, if he should have a mind to drown the world again; for that he would build a tower too high for the waters to be able to reach! And that he would avenge himself against God for destroying their forefathers."¹⁰

This same scripture goes on to say: "The multitude were very ready to follow the determination of Nimrod, and to esteem it a piece of cowardice to submit to God; and they built a tower, neither sparing any pains, nor being in any way negligent about the work; and by reason of the multitude of hands employed in it, it grew very high, sooner than anyone could expect; but the thickness of it was so great, and it was so strongly built, that its great height seemed, upon the view, to be less than it really was. It was built of burnt brick, made of bitumen that it might not be liable to admit water."

Nevertheless those obedient to God's House were not to be challenged with impunity.

"5. And the Lord came down to see the city and the tower which the children of men builded. And the Lord said, Behold the people is one, and they have all one language; and they begin to do; and now nothing will be restrained from, which they have imagined to do. Go to, let us go down, and there confound their language, that they may not understand one another's speech."¹¹

Nothing, of course, so confounds a civilization as religious conflicts. The Ethiopian Canaanites had anthropomorphized the philosophic concept of Sin, known to the Greek as Helios, or the Syrian B-a-al, 'Brahma, the Ark of Atalla,' into the Moon God, and were worshipping the idols called Beths. The Sumerians had set up the Moon God at Ur. While some of the posterity of the Akkadians still clung to the Wisdom Philosophy, among others had appeared the concept of Anu as the creator of the earth and man, with Anu-it as his wife, a perversion of Ana to whom the creation of the Great Gods was ascribed.

With all these co-extant concepts, inevitably the utmost confusion of tongues in the philosophic sense occurred, since none accepted the religion of the others. So we are told by Josephus that the place eventually called Ba-b-y-lon by the Greeks, by the Hebrews was called Ba-bel, implying the babel of confused voices. He also declared that when God saw how madly the peoples of Babel were acting, he did not resolve "to destroy them even though they were not grown wiser by the destruction of the former sinners." Instead, "He caused a tumult among them, by producing in them divers languages; and causing that, through the multitude of those languages, they should not be able to understand one another."

This myth of the Tower of Babel, therefore, affords many lessons for the posterity of Nimrod. In the first place it was utterly useless for the Chusites to imagine that they could unite peoples of such varying ideologies as those of the Shemitics, Hamitics, and Japhethics, under a single government, no matter how tyrannical the ruling caste might be. The political structure reared upon a foundation of such shifting sand, was doomed to fall. Secondly, the whole concept of Nimrod was based on the utterly false assumption that man with his paltry knowledge was self-sufficient. Also it ignored the fact that the waters of another flood in Mesopotamia might not be the only force against which the inhabitants of those parts might have to contend.

"8. So the Lord scattered them abroad from thence upon the face of the earth: and they left off to build the city. Therefore is the name of it called Ba-bel: Because the Lord did there confound the language of the earth: and from thence did the Lord scatter them abroad upon the face of all the earth."[12]

In one Hebrew scripture it is recorded that the Lord sent a great wind that toppled the Tower to the earth, and the tradition of this has persisted.[13]

Let the skeptics say, if they will, the tower of Babel was a mere mythical tower implying an over-reaching civilization that inevitably collapsed because of the discords of those who reared it. For otherwise why are there no remains of it?

In answer it may be said that the Tower and all it represented from the first would have been anathema to the House of God. Nevertheless its reality is indicated by the countless Ziggurats, or Towers of Babel, created at later times. Naturally the last vestige of it would have been obliterated by those who remained in Mesopotamia. The stones and the bricks used in its construction inevitably would have found their way into other structures that eventually arose. Therefore, even if the tower may not have been toppled to the earth by the winds of a storm, it would have been cast down, soon or late, by the winds of human passion aroused by the tyrannical attempt of Nimrod to dominate the earth with the false philosophy of the Cushites. Perhaps that is what Moses Charenenses meant.

What kind of an actual storm could have dispersed the peoples of Mesopotamia besides one of religious panic?

We have seen what one storm had done in B.C. 850,000. Yet in that case the mountains afforded asylums. Also we have seen how the Lord sent a wind to dry the earth. There have been cases of wholesale migrations from both denuded areas, and those in which unseasonable cold, or even excessive rains, destroyed, both the seed beds of the crops and the natural fruits.

So came to an end, temporarily at least, the Kingdom of Nimrod.[14] Nor is there lack of evidence to indicate that this occurred in the cycle of Sa-la-ha.

As the thoughtful consider the myth of Nimrod, the Tower, and the Confusion of Tongues, one cannot fail to marvel at the logic of events upon which the myth was based, and the extraordinary perceptions of those who framed it. Indeed like all myths based upon the spheres of the Kabira, it testifies to wondrous power of reasoning that well may be deemed intellectual magic.

According to Josephus twice the spiritual teachers had urged in vain the forebears of the peoples who are said to have scattered, to disperse voluntarily in order to avoid among other things the overcrowding of an area seen to be too small to support a large population. According to the myths of the Confusion of Tongues, and the dispersion by a storm, at last nature had intervened to enforce God's will.

Was the actual migration that occurred the result of mere accident? If there had not been some strong impulse, why would it have taken place? To what extent had the urgings of the peoples who actually scattered, been due to the desire that they should bring intellectual enlightenment to the less fortunate among the smitten peoples of the earth?

It is not for a mere historian to ascribe this to God. Yet he must point out what was believed to have caused it by those who suddenly departed from the land of their birth, and by their posterities who, since the dispersion, have reared so many monuments designated by them as Towers of Babel.[15]

How the Wisdom Philosophy came to persist also is indicated by Josephus. Thus he pointed out that the priests of the Sybil preserved the sacred vessels, or the symbols of Enyalius, or Jupiter. And certain it is that the Ark of Ea was enshrined at *Sephervaim* close to the City of Si-p-para, which eventually was erected in Shi-nar by the Chaldeans.[16] Thus, in the Sybil we see the teachers of the Erythrean ark.

---

[1] According to Gen. Robert E. Lee (1856), the major evil of slavery which conceivably might benefit the Negro of the Dark Continent, was not the wrong to the Negro but the harm it did the master.

[2] Genesis 9.

[3] Per example the Latin-speaking missionaries of the Dark and Middle Ages, and the English-speaking peoples of today in all parts of the world, speak the same language.

[4] A-k-k-a-d 'The Ark of the K, the King of the Ark of the Diva.'
S-h-i-n-ar, 'The Serpent, Ha, the Spirit of No, the Arya.'
S-h-u-m-e-r, 'The Serpent, Ha, Uratur, Mia, the Ethiopians, the Ru.'

[5] Ar-ph-a-x-ad, 'the Aryans, the Philosophy of the Ark of the Chi, the Ark of the Diva.'

[6] O-s-iris, "the Circle of the sons of Iris (Divine Lotus)."
O-s-r-i-s, "the Circle of the Serpent, the Reincarnated Spirit of Sin."
O-s-r-i-s, "the Circle of the Serpent, the Spirit of the Rishi."

[7] Ni-m-r-o-d, "Nilus, Mesopotamia, 'the Ru, the Ark of the Diva.'"

[8] This is exactly what the friends in the Kremlin are doing today.

[9] Josephus.

10 Compare the materialists of today who hold the Economic Man to be the true ruler of the earth.

11 Genesis 11:5-6.

12 Genesis 11.

13 Moses Charenenses, the Armenian Historian of the Fifth Century, says a terrible storm overthrew the tower. *History of Armenia*, edited by Lauer (1869). See also *Ueber die Glaubwurdiket der arminischen Geschichte, des Moses von Khoren* (Leipsig, 1876).

14 The writer predicts exactly the same end to Communism. See his epic: *The Flaming Sword*, (1950), and his *Challenge to Communism* (1950).

> "For verily is it writ upon Revelation's warning scroll
> That whate'er may fall before the Marxian horde,
> The gilded domes and spires that gleam
> Where once was heard the voice of God,
> Shall topple to the ground as did the tower,
> Immured in the dust that accumulates inevitably memories
> Over all discarded trash. And soon or late
> Another Dante will enlarge the list
> Of souls forever damned by godless Self."
>
> *Three New Year Poems*, J. C. WISE (1950)

15 Author's note: Pictures of many of these towers are included in *The Conquest of Civilization*, BREASTED (1932).

16 Sepher-va-i-m, the 'Book of Varcha, the Spirit of Mu.'

S-i-p-para, 'The Serpent, the Spirit of the Papa, Philosophy.'

CHAPTER XXII

THE MATHEMATICAL PROOF
OF THE KINGDOM OF ATLANTIS.

Chi-Chi, or The Twins of Plato

WE HAVE ALREADY seen that as the *Book of Enoch* conceived of the Seraphim and the Cherubim residing upon the Seventh Mountain or High Place, dealt with by the Prophet Ezekiel. Thus in the Book of Revelation in the Bible wherein *mountain* was employed to designate the high places of the spiritual teachers of the *Sephervaim*. The *Sepharim* of the Hebrews was in fact the Chi-Chen of the Aryan Uighurs; while the Cherubim of the Mosaic scribes was none other than the Chi-elas, or holy men of the Mysteries of the Ka-bi-ra common to God's House, or the Erythrean Ark, and to the Ethiopian Ark also designated as EA, to which the Hebrew name *No-ea-s* and the Greek name No-a-chi, both trace, as well as En-o-chi, and La-mi-chi.[1] And the same is true of T-i-ri-ch Mir, the great peak in the Tian Shian Range, Chi-na 'the Chi of Ana.' There the Uiguirish language preceded that of the present Sinitics, and, therefore, explains the affinities between the Chinese and the Akkadian languages, just as do the red H-akka of China and Formosa.

The Kara surveyors who had brought the whole earth into the geodetic ark of Noeas before the flood of B.C. 850,000, had known, of course, a vast amount about astronomy and geodesy as indicated by the spheres of pillars constituting the ancient symbol of the mythical Atlas. Certain it is that in the cycle of Peleg-Joktan, the twins of Plato were able to plot the earth on what today is called a Mercator Projection, supposed to have been first employed by the Medieval cartographer Mercator. In the system of this projection, all compass directions appear as straight lines. Therefore, either great circles, or even other circles with diameters of less than 180 degrees, when projected on a chart not only appear as straight lines, but the arc of the circle in one hemisphere has a corresponding straight line projection in the other hemisphere.

Mathematics, of course, is an exact science and leaves no room for doubt as to the meaning of what appears on the projection of the whole earth here included.[2]

If this map be examined, it will be seen that Mount Amarakantaka (19° N. 81° E.), stands on the great circle that passes through Mexico City (19° N. 99° W.), and also on the same latitudinal circle, just 180 degrees to the east of Mexico City. While it would be impossible for two great circles to intersect at both of these points, lesser circles could be inscribed on the globe that would do so. It was not necessary, however, to do more than erect on a projection in the Mercator manner of the entire earth, a triangle with the arc of 80 degrees between Mexico City and Mount Amaraka-n-t-a-ka, 'Amaraka, the Naga, the Taux of the ark of the Kara.' Erect a triangle with its apex in the Land of Is near the present J-an May-en Island, and on the same inverted triangle with its apex in the B-o-u-v-e-t Islands of the South Atlantic. This having been done by prolonging the sides of the two triangles, two geodetic Chi will be formed intersecting at two points.

It will be observed that the line passing from Is through Mt. Amaraka-n-t-a-ka, Sumatra and Onslow in Australia, at the north passes through Norway, Sweden, Finland close to Helsinki, Cronstadt in Russia on the Baltic. Continued through Syr, Afghanistan, and Rajaputana, it intersects at Mount Amarakantaka with a line passing from the Arctic Sea at the North of W-r-angel Island, through Mount Amarakantaka straight through the Abyss of Learning (40° N. 100° E.), and from the Dekkan through Madagascar.

Of the Western Chi, however, the line from W-r-angel Island passes through Alaska, close to Mount Diablo overlooking the Golden Gate in the realm of Queen Kalifa, and thence through Te-x-u-ana at the mouth of the Colorado River just east of the San Diego, through Sin-a-loa in Mexico it passes to X-o-chi-calco just south of Mexico City, southeastward close to Gua-ya-gui-l in Ecuador, through C-u-x-co, the ancient capital of Peru, LaPaz and Ascunsion, the capitals of Bolivia and Para-gua-y, respectively, and on through Porto Allegre on the coast of Brazil to the Bouvet Islands.

The line from the North Sea, however, passes through Greenland, Labrador, Que-bec, "The Watcher" in Franconia Notch, New York, Mount Mitchell in Ya-d-kim County, North Carolina (36° N.). Thence it proceeds to New Orleans, and on through X-o-chi-calco and A-x-a-ca-n to the relics of the Pacific Continent.

What is here shown, could not, of course, be accidental. Obviously just as the Uighur Chelas ran the line from W-r-angel Island to X-o-chi-calco, the Danitics ran the line through "The Watcher," which marks the meridian of Cu-x-co, through Mount Mitchell which, according to the Englishman Williams who visited Fort Caroline in 1565, was sacred to the local nations as Mount O-la-y-mi. So is explained the fact that just as we find Dan-ne-mo-ra in Norway, we find it on the Shat-a-mu or T-a-s-w-a-sin-t-ha which found its source in the Adi-ron-d-ac-k, 'Adi, the circle of the Diva, the light of the King,' or the river now bearing the name Hudson. And as there are numerous Dan-villes as in New England, New York and Virginia, the River Dan in the latter state finds its source at the grand Pinnacles of Dan just beyond the Meadows of Dan where the cruciform crystals, or Fairy Stones of red rialite alone are found.[3]

But it also explains the cryptic name O-hi-o implying the Twins of the Holy Spirit, or the two hemispheres, and the cruciform symbol of the Ch-e-yenne in which appears the name yenne also appearing in Yenne-si at the North of Siberia, in T-ennessee, and in T-ana-see in the Malay Peninsula.

The Ch-e-yenne, of Algon-qui-an linguistic type, however, were found merged with the Siouans at the East and the Sho-

sho-n-es, or Cho-cho-nes at the west, one of the oldest and
darkest peoples in America who produced the Utes of U-tah
where Bright Angel's Pass is found near Salt Lake City not far
from D-en-v-e-r (40° N. 105° W.) and Pikes Peak or Ana-con-
da, 'The Mother of Heaven, the Circle of En Zu, the Diva'.
And it was in the Black Hills of the Dakotas just to the East
of W-y-o-min-g in which Che-yenne appears on the meridian
with Denver, that Gutson Borglum carved his great national
mountain, displaying the Sages of the United States of America. Moreover, it has been said that the Mountain on which this
monument appears was originally called Sphinx Mountain.[4]

It will be noted that Sho-sho-nes, or Cho-cho-nes, implying
Two Serpents, is pronounced exactly like X-o-chi appearing at
the intersection of the geodetic Chi of America. In it the
X represents the *Chi* of Heaven and the *Chi* of mortality, being
coupled with the O as the symbol of the Python, or Serpent
cult of the Ru, who long since had appeared in Pe-ru. On the
other hand the vertical arm of the True Cross, south of the
Galipagos on the Equator, is lost in the South Pacific just as is
the part of the antipodal True Cross, beyond the delta of the
Ganges and Brahmapootra. This being so the Chi of America
enabled all the major cities of South America to be sited more
readily with respect to the True Cross as shown on the accompanying map.

The Western Chi fully explains the appearance of the name
applied to Li-ma, 'the Lily of the Mother Ark,' the port of
Cu-xco, or the ancient capital of Peru, at which the first Inca
is said to have fixed his golden wand, in Ma-da-g-a-s-ca-r, while
the Puna of Peru, and the Island of Puna off the coast, is plainly but another form of the Naga realm of P-oo-na in the Dek-k-
ana of India. In the latter name as in Brahma-p-oo-t-ra appear
the two O's in O-hi-o, in Ka-li-ma-z-oo (Mi-chi-g-ana) in the
Egyptian Fa-y-oo-ma, and also in Mai-oo on the Red Sea, which
preserves the name of Maia, the daughter of Atlas, just as do
the two Mia-mis in North America.

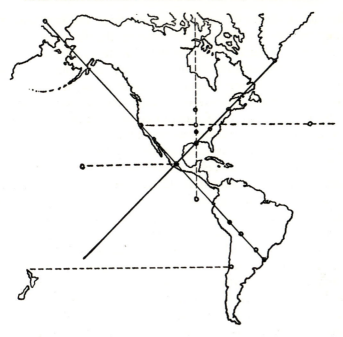

X-O-CHI

Gnomonic Projection of the Western Hemisphere showing the Western Twin or geodetic Chi, and also the True Cross, with relations to both of the ancient centers of culture.

Let it be noted also that Adam's Peak (7° N. 81° E.) in Ceylon, marks the meridian of Mount Amara-kan-taka, and Lake M-ana-so-ro-w-ara, of which the antipodal meridian passes through North and South Dakota, the land of the Da-ko-ta, 'the Seven Serpents,' Ne-bra-s-ka, K-an-sa-s corresponding to the Hindu province of Kansa and carved out of the original Ark-Kansas, as was O-k-la-ho-ma at the west of the O-z-ark Range, and finally through T-e-x-as and Chi-hau-hau, 'the two arks of the Chi,' to X-o-chi, also implying Chi-o-chi. Moreover it marks the latitudinal circle 7° N. on which is sited in Pe-ru the sacred shrine of Ca-ja-ma-ra at which the Inca was murdered by the Spaniards in the time of the Pi-za-r-ro-s.⁵

But if in what has been shown, the reality of Plato's Twins has been mathematically demonstrated, and the background for a real history of America has been given, it behooves the student of history to note even more than already shown. For in truth at the site of X-o-chi in course of time arose what is perhaps the most stupendous monument on the earth which suggests what the Tower of Babel may have been like.

We have seen the Tello erected by the Sons of Seth in Sumer. If such a monument could have been erected before B.C. 850,000, one of similar design could have been projected in the cycle of Peleg-Joktan even though the labor on it may have extended over thousands of years.

While it is estimated upon good authority that the population in North America, above the Rio Grande, by reason of climatic conditions there, all told, including Canada and Greenland, never exceeded 2,500,000 at any one time prior to 1492, by 1,200 A.D. the population of Mexico, Central America, and South America is said by Spinden to have been not less than 50,000,000. This itself indicates that conditions south of the Rio Grande were quite different from those in the North.

The first essential following the survey of North America during the cycle of Peleg-Joktan to insure the civilizing of its people, and their stabilization in the domains set apart for them by the teachers of God's House, was to provide the posterity of those who had survived the appalling disaster attending the break up of the Afro-Brazilian Continent, and then the denudation of North America of almost its entire population by the cold and the ice cap of the First Winter, with the seeds for maize and other foods that might be grown under the direction of the Nabatheans. To this end a great ellipse with a perimeter of three miles, center at X-o-chi was surveyed on which to rear the largest mound in the world that eventually rose to a height of 450′ upon which in Neolithic times a stone temple, egg shaped, like the ellipse, was erected bringing the whole to an elevation of 500′ and furnishing the model for the Pyramid of Cheops.

Manifestly a symbol of the Fifth Root Race, the so-called Cal-co, or Castle of Flowers, was also a symbol of the Wisdom Philosophy. Thus its summit was reached by the terraced spiral, revetted with colossal stones, with a stone gutter for drainage purposes, resembling exactly the spiral formation in the shells called nummaliths constituting the earlier form of marine life, in the same manner that some of the sunken dolmens of Iberia possessed.[6]

How long it took the Chelas and Danitics to realize their dream of a mound that would furnish seeds for an immense population is a matter that must be imagined. Here it is sufficient to note that *ma-i-ze,* possessing a Maya name, implying a gift of the God, was unknown in Europe as a crop, before the Columbian Age. Furthermore, in every case the local place names such as Chi-ca-gu in the Aleutian Islands, Sa-s-ka-t-ch-w-ana, Mi-chi-g-ana, Chi-ca-go, Chi-li-co-the, Ap-pa-la-chi-a, Chi-ka-hominy, Chi-ra-kee, Chi-sa-peake, Chi-n-co-teague, Chi-ka-sa, Ap-pala-chi-co-la, Chi-hua-hua, Chi-m-bo-ra-zo, and Chi-li, wherein the *chi* appeared, the word implied not only a spiritual teacher, such as the original Ch-e-yenne, and Co-m-an-chi, but a sower of seed.[7]

Inasmuch as the line from the Arctic through "The Watcher," passed through New England, it is not difficult to see the origin of the name Ma-s-sa-ch-u-setts, and of the sacred shrine of the Na-ra-gana-setts which marked exactly the meridian of 'the Watcher.' Naturally agriculture would have been re-established in the natural mound of the southern Ap-pa-la-chi sooner than in the north. The same is true of the region of the Pueblo groups who laid off not only their cities but their domains in great circles resembling Zodiacs.[8]

Enough has been said to show why in 1656, Carlos de Siguenza, Professor of Mathematics, University of Mexico, which had been founded by the Emperor Charles V, the first institution of Learning in America, ascribed the civilization of Mexico to the Egyptian Naptuhim whose cycle, current with that of Salah, did not expire until B.C. 380,000 while that of Shem continued until B.C. 348,000. For the evidence is found in Egypt that in B.C. 400,000 a great worldwide survey was taking place.[9]

We have already seen the origin of the name Ana-huac, 'the Ark of Ana,' applied to the region that embraced Mexico, Texas and Central America. Inasmuch as Me-x-ico traces to M-e-x-atla, in view of the names Atal, Atalla, Atlanta, Tala-ha-see, and similar names in North America, we may safely conclude that M-e-x-atla, implying "Mia, the earth of the Chi, Atlas," traces to the Chichens of God's House, just as does M-ana-x or M-ana-chi, and M-ana-ch-u.[10]

With the Danitics and the Chelas both surveying the earth we need not be surprised to find the name of the Amara well preserved in the realms of Plato's Twins as here shown.

Amar	Ireland
Amorica	Britanny
Ameria	Portugal
Ameria	Italy
Amara	Syria
S-am-arra	Volga
S-amari	North Siberia
S-amarkand	Syr
A-o-mari	Japan
Amora	Japan
Amara-pura	Irrawaddy
S-amara-i	Australia
S-amoa	Polynesia
S-amar	Philippines
Amara-go-za	Nevada
Ama-rilla	Texas
Amar-illas	Cuba
Amara-cao	Venezuela
Ama-z-on	Brazil

To ignore the spiritual factor of history in face of all this is worse than silly. Here we must note the magic of the geodetic symbols of X-o (19° N. 99° E.) $1 + 9 = 10$; $99 = 33 \times 3$; while $1 + 9 + 99 = 109$ in which 10 and 9 appear giving $10 + 9 = 19$. Moreover, $1 + 9 = 10$, corresponding to the complete cycle of the O in X-O.

On the other hand the geodetic symbols of Mount Amarakantaka are 19° N. + 81° E., yielding $1 + 9 = 10$, and $8 + 1 = 9 = 3 \times 3 \times 3$.[11]

---

[1] And also the name of Queen Ch-e-ops of the Third Egyptian Dynasty who erected the Great Pyramid of Gi-z-a, 'Gihon, the Seven Serpents of the Ark.'

[2] The Projection is reproduced with the permission of C. S. Hammond & Co., map-makers, New York City.

[3] It is possible, of course, that some of the Danvilles trace to the Islandingas who included Vinland in their Republic. See the *Mystery of Columbus*, (1947).

[4] *Believe It or Not*, RIPLEY, the King Syndicate. The writer knew Borglum intimately and often discussed with him the Watcher of Franconia Notch which gave him his idea of his grand monument.

[5] In order to pry into the Inca mysteries Martin Loyala, the nephew of Ignatius Loyala, who founded the Society of Jesus, married the daughter of the Inca, for which in 1577 he was killed.

[6] Of the Castle of Flowers more will be said in chronological order.

[7] Here it is to be noted that Ch-e-m-u-n-g in New York, and Ch-e-n-an-go in Pennsylvania, take the form of Ch-en-an-do or Shenandoah in Virginia, and Ch-e-ra-w in the Carolinas.

[8] Note the detailed description given by Plato of the capital of the Kingdom of Atlantis as a circle, surrounded by impassable moats of water, implying the cosmic sea.

[9] See *The Origin and Evolution of Mankind*, ALBERT CHURCHWARD, F.R.S. (1911).

[10] In an Appendix the story of Columbus and the way in which the history of America was concealed, will be given. For more detail see *The Mystery of Columbus*, WISE (1947).

[11] Vast studies of Peru have shown that the oldest civilization there of which there is any record is that of the Ha-t-ru-na, which preceded that of the In-cas. Also they have shown that this was Sinitic culture to which the name Ti-ti-ca-ca, wherein appear two T's implying the superimposition of the Ethiopian culture upon that of the Ru. Means and others have been unable to fix any beginning of the Ha-t-an Runa culture. Ha-t-u-n, 'Ha-taux-uratur-naggals'; Ru-n-na 'Ru-ark-navalis.' The western geodetic Chi fully explains the map of Hylacomulus not brought to light until 1902, after the works of Winsor, Bancroft and Fiske were published, showing that in 1505 the Pacific Ocean was well known in Europe before its alleged discovery by Balboa's exploit in Panama. It also explains the name *America* placed on that long hidden map by the mystic Waldsemüller, and the map which appeared soon after it, appearing in Bancroft's History of Columbus (1892), on which South America bears the name *Land of the True Cross*. In a word the discovery of Waldsemüller's

map rendered obsolete all the speculations of Winsor, Bancroft, and Fiske, of Parkman and Prescott about America and its discovery. Yet, Professor Morison of Harvard, commonly accepted today as the definitive authority on Columbus, would have us believe that Columbus discovered America when a map showing the Western Hemisphere was in existence in Germany and France when Columbus died, showing the Pacific Ocean which Magellan is supposed first to have traversed. Waldsemüller's map seems conclusive that apocryphal voyages of Amerige Vespucci, were apocryphal not in the false but only in the secret sense. When Waldsemüller credited him with first having visited the mainland of America in the Columbian Age (1497), the year that John Cabot visited Newfoundland, one year before Columbus made his third voyage, only lately had the charter granted by Edward IV in 1585 for the colonization of America, been replaced by the one granted Cabot by Henry VII in 1797. In a word Edward IV had authorized the colonization of America seven years before the sailing of Columbus on his first voyage under a commission from the Pope recently discovered in the Vatican, and under the temporal auspices of Ferdinand and Isabella. Waldsemüller did not say that America was named after Vespucci. He merely said it was appropriate that since Amerige Vespucci, who had come to be called Americus, had visited America, the Western Hemisphere should bear the name of the goddess America just as Asia and Europe bore the names of a goddess. Thus, we see the whole fable put out about the discovery of America in the Columbian Age was a hoax from start to finish, born of the rivalry between the Medici principals of Columbus and Vespucci and Cabot, on the one hand, and of the Borgia or Spanish party on the other.

CHAPTER XXIII

THE GREAT DISPERSION

MUCH OF THE misunderstanding with respect to the dispersion that followed the overthrow of the Tower of Babel and impelled the abandonment of the City which Nimrod had founded, in the sense of the philosophy represented by the Punics, is due to a fundamental misconception.

We have seen that the cosmic deluge which had brought into being the Mongoloid type of man who from the first meant to rule the Borean realms, had produced the Danae designated in the Homeric myths as the Ar-g-i-v-e-s, and who eventually come to constitute the Danitics, whose name would appear in the names of those who were dispersed from the Land of Babel. Therefore, the peoples who were scattered by the storm did not spread over the earth and occupy vacant areas, as some have assumed that the scriptures imply. It was clearly pointed out by Josephus that although the alleged grandsons of Noeas went forth in colonies to find new homes they located in the realms of other peoples. He also shows why they planted both maritime and inland colonies. Some went overseas in ships and occupied the islands. In some of the parts where they settled, he declared, the names given them remained, but in others they were changed by the inhabitants. This would have been only natural on the part of the Hellenic and Danitic Greeks. Undoubtedly the same thing occurred in Italaya, the Western Iberia, Franconia, and the western part of the Greek continent of Atlas to which the present Europe was still attached.

Inasmuch as the Medi Terre was eventually submerged, along with the areas where now spread the Black, Red, Ionian, and Adriatic Seas, and much of the Land of Is, at the north, as well as Posidonis, it is impossible to do more than indicate the general distribution of the migrants, as shown by Josephus.

1. The Gomerites occupied the Taurus Range in which Mount Amarna marks the meridian of Amarna in Egypt, as far as the river T-an-a-is at the east of the Delta. Keeping on across the Medi Terre at the North of the Aegean Sea, they passed through Libya to Ca-di-z in the western Iberia beyond the harbor of which are today to be seen the islets of Gades, from which Ca-d-iz derived its name.

From the Gomerites evolved the West and the East Gauls along the Rhine. From them also evolved in the Taurus Range of Asia Minor, the Ash-k-e-na-z or A-s-che-n-a-x, the R-i-phath, and the T-o-r-ga-ma-ha. Of them the first spread over the presently submerged area of the Black Sea where the civilization of Sa-mo-t-h-r-a-x evolved. The Riphath laid the foundations of the civilization that evolved in the region north of Grecaland. The Torgamaha, or Thorogramma, settled in the Eastern Iberia or the Caucasus at the west of the Caspian.

2. Ma-gog went far afield into Syr and produced the Scythians, who eventually extended clear across the north of Libya beyond the Gomerites to the British Isles where the mythical giants called the Gog-Magog appeared and produced the Manx.

3. The Ma-dai spread into the land south of the Caspian, and their descendants came to be called the Medes.

4. The Ja-va-n occupied Grecaland which included Crete, and to them are to be traced the name of Ja-ni-na or Ya-ni-na, the realm at the west of Mount Olympus. Their offspring were E-li-sha-h, and Tar-shi-sh, Ki-t-t-im, and Do-dan-im. The Elishahs occupied the Aeolian Islands in the Aegean Sea, while Tar-shi-sh occupied the Medi Terre, and also northern Syria where they founded the city of Tar-sus (36° 56′ N. 34° 58′ E.). The Ki-t-t-im occupied Cy-p-ru-s, and the Do-dan-im settled the archipelago of the Dodecanese close to Syria. Thus the offspring of Javan provided the Caucasian ancestors of the Ionians.

5. The Tu-balites, or Thobel, the descendants of Tubal Cain and who were the ancestors of some of the Turks, occupied the north of Assyria, and were the ancestors of the Georgian Cossacks.

6. The Me-schech, or Mesa, furnished the peoples who settled Ma-zi-ac-ca (Caesarea) 38° 41' N. 35° 20' E. and also T-ar-su-s (36° 56' N. 34° 58' E.), both virtually on the meridian of Sin-o-pe, Mount Carmel, Petra, and Mount Sin.

7. The Ti-ras settled in Thrace which included much of the vanished Samothrax in the area of the present Black Sea.

The Sons of Ham

1. From the Cushites who had occupied northern Rub, were sprung Se-ba, Ha-vi-la-ha, Sa-b-tah, Ra-a-ma-ha, and Sa-b-t-e-cha-ha, who occupied southeastern Rub below the Gulf of Persia.

2. The Mizr-a-i-m spread from the Delta of the Nile up that river as far as Karnack. They produced the Lud-im, Ana-mi-m, Le-ha-bim and the Na-ph-tu-him, the last with a name corresponding to the Italic N-e-p-t-u-n-e. Also they produced the Pa-th-ru-sim and the Ca-s-lu-him.

3. The Ph-u-t, or Punics who claim descent from Phoenix, spread from Syria into Mizraim, and from there through Libya beyond Egypt to the Atlantic Coast. There they mingled with others to form the ancestors of the Atlantides in the regions of Tri-poli, Tu-n-is and Mo-roc-co, from whom sprang the Berbers. Undoubtedly many of them kept on into the Cana-ry and Ma-d-e-i-ra Islands, and thence into Posidonis.

4. The Canaanites took up the East coast of the Aegean. Their progeny were the Heth, Je-bu-site, Am-e-rite, Gir-ga-site, He-vite, Ark-ite, Sin-ite, Arva-d-ite, and the Ha-ma-thite. On the Aegean Sea they erected the port of Si-d-on, while their southern boundary was close to Suez. At the East their realm extended to So-dom and Go-mo-r-rah near the Dead Sea, A-d-mah, Ze-bi-im, and La Sha.

The Sons of Shem.

1. The El-am-ites occupied the realm of E-la-mu, or Su-z-i-ana, at the east of the Tigris, as far as the realm of the Madai.

2. The As-sh-ur-ites who erected Asshur at 35° N. 44° E. the city to which they gave the name N-in-u-s that came to be called Ninevah.[1] They also erected between Asshur and Ninus the cities of Calneh, R-e-i-s-en, and R-e-h-o-b-o-e-h far to the West on the upper Euphrates. Thus they laid the foundations of As-syria, which they carved out of Syria.[2]

While it is said by Josephus that the Assyrians were the most blessed of all the Mesopotamians, in the founding of Assyria by them is found the beginning of the conflict that was to rage down the ages between them and the Punics of Egypt over the possession of Syria which the Egyptians as the posterity of Nimrod claimed as their rightful heritage.

3. The peoples who had appeared in Sumer during the cycle of Ar-ph--a-x-ad, remained at Akkad and in Sumer where, according to Josephus, the priests preserved the sacred vessels of Enyalius.

4. The Ludites occupied the Medi Terre, and also a part of Egypt. Eventually they would produce the Laudians or Lydians at the north of Asia Minor, and furnish the original Etruskans.[3]

5. The Aramites spread from Aram just east of Sumer and occupied the region of Amara west of the Syrian desert at the north of Rub. Out of Aram evolved Aramea in the Libanos Range, which was once connected with the mountains in the vanished Medi Terre of Libya. From the Aramites were sprung the Uz who founded in Aramea the cities of Da-ma-s-cus, and also Tri-chon-t-is or Tyre, to which is to be traced the *Book of Chon*. Also they produced Hul, or Ul, from whom evolved the Armenians.

It was the Getherites, sprung of the Aramites, however, who occupied Ba-c-t-r-ia at the east of I-r-a-n. In that realm they were in close touch with the Madai of Syr, and the Caucasian ancestors of the Hindus in the Hindu Kush, and were not far from the Naga in the Dek-k-ana of India.

Thus it is seen how the dispersion over the earth of those who entered the ark of Noah in B.C. 850,000 was begun.

Although the tendency is to gaze only at that part of the graph of Gea south of Mount Ararat, because of the abundancy of the Assyrian and Chaldean scriptures and those of the Hebrews, a land of almost unknown history lies in the realm of Circassia where Tiflis stands today, and in the region of Baku, Er-ze-ru-m and Ta-b-r-i-z in the land of Tu-bal Cain. Te-h-e-r-an in the land of the Madai, and B-o-ka-ra, Sa-ma-r-kand also stand in an area of fruitful research. Perhaps no other part of the earth affords a better opportunity for modern archaeologists than the region of Old Merv (42° N. 62° E.), not far from the Ara-l Sea, at the latitude of Khan T-en-g-ri in the east, Mount El-b-ru-z in the Ararat Range, Sinope, and Rome.

In the names of the people who have been mentioned appears over and over that of the Caucasian Dan, who eventually would appear in the Sudan and in America, also they occupied the Tigris, across the Euphrates. There they erected S-amarra,

---

1 N-in-us, 'the northern Indra, Uratur, Sin.' In Va-ha is preserved the name of the Third Avatar, Varaha.

2 A-s-syr-ia, 'Asshur-Syria.'

3 In all probability the mythical Lud of England, was their descendant inasmuch as Hector is said to have migrated from Troy to Great Britain.

Chapter XXIV

THE ORIGIN OF CHALDEA
THE CYCLE OF EBER, "THE COLONIZERS"
THE HEBREWS FOUND THE TREE CULT

No HISTORIAN has ever been able to point to the time when the Akkadians who had appeared at Akkad in the cycle of Arphaxad first came to be called Chald-eans. Yet the origin of that name seems clear.

The word *Chald* was applied to the measure of the bushel, a volumetric measure holding a quantity of water at the mean temperature of 70° F. equal in weight to the body of a normal man. Implying a container it played a part in the initiation into the mysteries that was conducted in the King's Chamber of the Pyramid of Gizeh. It may be traced to Che-a-l-d, 'the Chi of the Ark, the Logus of the Diva'. Therefore, Chald-ea was simply the name applied to the Spiritual See of the Akkadians.

Although the tradition persists that in course of time the Akkadians became no more than black magicians, such as the Sumerians conceived El lil to have been, it is certain that the Chaldeans were their offspring, and that they had appeared in Sumer before the cycle of Sa-la-ha came to an end. Moreover according to the Sumerians, they arrived in the Delta of Euphrates from beyond the Tigris, and first established themselves at E-ri-du (31° N. 48° E.) due south of Su-sa in E-la-mu.[1]

This, of course, would have ended the monopoly which Ur or, Mu-ga-ya, one of the oldest known cities on the earth, and the most favored seat of the Moon God Sin in Mesopotamia, had enjoyed as the entrepot of that section. Soon, however,

they founded the city of E-r-e-ch on the Euphrates at 31° 30′ N.
44° E. close to the old Sumerian cities of G-ur-su, Kis, H-illa,
La-ga-shi, and T-e-llo where the sons of Seth had erected their
pillar of brick.[2] Moreover it marked exactly the meridian of
Mount Ararat, as did the Din Tir (32° 30′ N.) Akkad (33°
N.) Sephervaim or Si-p-para (34° N.) Asshur (35° N.), and
Nineveh (36° N.). The mere fact that all these cities were
located on the meridian 44° E. is conclusive that Mesopotamia
had been surveyed. At E-re-ch, the Chaldeans established Is-
h-t-ar, 'the Moon Goddess,' who was said to be the daughter
of Sin, and whose counterpart was the Assyrian Ashteroth.

In addition to all this Josephus declared that from Arphaxad
were descended the Chaldeans, while Snorre Sturleson, the last
of the saga writers, pointed out in the *Elder Edda* (c.1225
A.D.), shortly before he was murdered that Ur marked the
beginning of the Third Head referred to in *Genesis* 2 as Hi-
d-dek-el, and described as that which "goeth toward the east
of Assyria."

The conclusion seems inevitable, therefore, that Hi-d-dek-el,
of which no interpretation has been offered by the Biblical
commentators, implied 'Ha, the Spirit of the Dekkad, the King
of the Elohim,' and that Dekkad implied the Ten Signs of the
Zodiac upon which was based the Chaldean mysteries, and the
decimal system of mathematics ever associated with the wisdom ascribed to I-s-h-t-a-r.[3]

Once the mystery of the third head, Hi-d-dek-el, has been
solved it is readily seen why in *Genesis* 14:1 Ti-dol, the King
of the Chaldeans as the ally of the Elamites and others
against the Sodomites is described as the King of Nations. In
accord with the original Chaldea, of which no bounds have
ever been fixed because it was in fact a spiritual see instead of
a political entity, the name "King of Kings" indicates a spiritual ruler. The conclusion from all this is that the Chaldeans
did in fact convey to Mesopotamia, just as in the Ramayanna
declared, the cult of the secret brotherhood of the Na-ac-al, af-

ter these missionaries of wisdom and religion had appeared in the Dek-k-ana of India.

So is to be accounted the fact that the Hindu Anu became the Chaldean Anu whose consort eventually became Anu-it, to whom are to be traced Bel-shamen and his consort Belit, of the Assyrian pantheon. The importance of all this as a matter of world history is the occupation of Sumeria by the Chaldeans produced a revolt, not merely by the devotees of the Moon God, Sin, who had been enshrined at Ur or Mu-ga-ya, but of the descendants of the Arphaxadites and Aramites in Sumer. Thus in B.C. 813,000, the cycle of Eber, 'the colonizer,' evolved out of the cycle of Salah.[4]

The actual colonizers of the new cult were the H-eb-er-r-e-w, of which the abbreviation was H-ebr-e-w, implying the Hierarchs of the Iberites, 'Cross Bearers.'

Refusing to subscribe to the pantheism of the Chaldeans, the Hebrews simply inverted the old vehicle of the Maya into the Tree Cult, which they set out to propagate through the agency of their converts among the Noacheans, who had been dispersed over the earth, and thereby to replace the primordial Serpent Cult with the monotheistic concepts of their cult. Accordingly they synthesized the 7 Rishi and the 7 Pitris in the philosophic concept of Yaveygh, implying the tree of life.

Rejecting the Hindu concept of avatars in their esoteric teachings, they inserted the T, or the squared tau of the Maya alphabet in their hieroglyphics, and added an iota with the phallic hook to form the J, (Jod). Thus, the Enyalius of the Chaldeans became Yaveygh, which took the form of I-an-nus, among the Boreans and from J-anu-s evolved into J-u-p-i-t-e-r.[5]

Especially sacred to the Hebrews was the Hebdad (7), ever symbolized by the seven-branched candelabra representing the seven luminaries or Elohim of the Sephiroth, or Dekkad, of which the first three constituted the upper triad representing the Divine Lotus—spirit, soul and body, which the Hindus held was conveyed from the Moon to the Rishi. Of the seven lower luminaries the Hebrews conceived as the mortal serpent, and this they symbolized by the Sacred H-e-b-d-o-m-a-d formed by the triangle over the square.

But even if these ideas were only taught by the Kabalists, or teachers of the secret doctrine, based on the wisdom philosophy, even in *Genesis,* they did not express the idea that man, in his present form was born in the image of God. Thus in *Genesis* 1:26, it is declared:

"And God said, let us make man in our own image, after our likeness: and let them have dominion over the fish of the sea, and over the fowl of the air, and over the cattle, and over all the earth, and over every creeping thing that creepeth upon the earth."

The plural pronoun *them* employed in this paragraph shows that *man* was used in the plural sense.

"27. So God created man in his own image, in the image of God created he him; male and female created he them."

This is no contradiction of the preceding paragraph. It merely holds in the first phrase that there was one creation, and in the second phrase that out of it evolved another. In other words the first creation was the product of what the Kabalists call the Ain-Soph, or the first thought of the creative genius corresponding to the Divine Lotus, or the Ark Navalis of Esoteric Buddhism. Accordingly the Kabalists depict Lucifer as the Angel of Light sacrificing himself to bring spiritual enlightenment unto the earth, or to the mortal serpent Yaveygh.

In *Genesis* 2:7, it is pointed out that there was no man in being when "a mist went up from the earth, and watered the whole face of the ground." The mist implied the atmospheric envelope of the earth, or the Va, the sheath. In the g-round may be seen the gas sphere in which there was the dust of matter. Therefore it is said, "And the Lord God formed man of the dust of the ground, and breathed into his nostrils, the breath of life; and man became a living soul." Here indeed was the Chi introduced into Yaveygh. So, in the "living soul," not in the man in his present form, the Hebrews saw the likeness of God.

1 E-ri-d-u, 'Ethiopia, Rishi, the Diva, Uratur.'

2 E-r-e-ch, 'Ethiopia, Rishi, Enyalius, the Chi.'

3 The Spirit of the Sephervaim, the Taux of the Ark of Ru.

4 Note that the year 813,000 yields $8+1+3=12$, the number of the original Titans and of the Zodiacal signs, while $12=4\times3$, and $4+3=7$.

5 When eventually Zeus appeared the peoples of the tree cult designated him as J-ov-us, 'the first egg.'

CHAPTER XXV

THE REAPPEARANCE OF EGYPTIAN IMPERIALISM
THE ORIGIN OF THE PHILISTINES
AND OF PALESTINE

IT WOULD BE IMPOSSIBLE to understand what followed the appearance of the Hebrews, if certain great events in the cycle of Eber were ignored.

We have seen that in the cycle of Mizraim the alleged brother of Kush evolved from the people of lower Egypt called Mestreans by the Hebrews, because they were sprung from the Eponymous Mizr, the N-a-ph-t-u-h-im, Pa-t-h-ru-si-m, and Ca-s-bu-l-im. As we see in the first a correspondence to the Latin Kabir, the God N-e-p-t-u-n-is, and to the Greek Poseidon, 'God of the Sea,' in the last we note the name of Canaan, Sin, and the God Bubastes. Moreover in the third cycle of the Dekkad of Shem - Ham - Japheth, the Eponymous Cush had begotten Ra-a-h-ma-h, representing a Punic group in northern Rub (Arabia), during the cycle of the Hindu Bala-rama. Thus either to the Mizraim or to the Ra-ah-ma-h may be ascribed the name Sa-la-ha applied to the Lake at the south of Mizraim, and in the name of that lake is found the verification of the *Ramayana,* wherein it is said that the cult of the Dek-kana of India came first to Chaldea, and then to Egypt.

In the cycle of Eber, however, Ra-a-h-ma-h who preserved the name of Balarama, begot De-dan and also the She-ba of Rub, to whom the mythical Queen of She-ba, or Bal-kis, owed her name. Concurrently the Mestreans of Mizraim begat Phi-l-is-tim, 'the Phenix, the Logus of Isis the taux, the spirit of Mu.'

Although Nimrod had been overthrown the spirit of Egyptian imperialism had survived. Determined to repossess themselves in southern Syria so as to safeguard the approaches to Egypt by way to Suez against the Canaanites, Arameans, Aramites, Assyrians and Chaldeans, and at the same time give Egypt ports on the Aegean Coast as Entrepots of the Egyptian trade with Asia Minor, undoubtedly the mythical King Belus of Egypt entered into an alliance with the Danitics of Grecaland and Cyprus as well as with the De-dan in Rub to whom the name Su-dan is to be traced, and also with the She-ba, against the Canaanites. For be it remembered, the Sin-i-t-es, or the off-spring of the Canaanites, had come to occupy the region of Suez, where Petra had been erected in the shadow of Mount Sin-a-i.

Passing through Suez the Philistim seized the southern coast of Syria below Sidon, just east of the island of Cyprus on which the Danitic Ki-t-t-im had settled and erected there the great port of G-a-z-a, with a name similar to Giza. Thus, they laid the foundations of the kingdom of Phi-li-s-t-ia, and of Pa-l-e-s-t-in-e wherein at the pool of Si-lom had appeared the Shrine of Ya-ru-Siloam, eventually to be called Salem by the Hebrews. So began the enduring union between the Egyptians and the Danitic ancestors of the Arabians that gave rise to the concept of the mythical giant, Goliath.

To this union traces the myth that King Belus gave Libya and Asia Minor to Danaeus, the elder of his twin sons, and the realm of Rub, eventually to be called Arabia to Aegyptus, the younger twin. For be it remembered still there was no Red Sea, while Philistia extended eastward into the northern part of Rub, between Canaan and Mesopotamia, which is now call-ed the Desert of Syria, wherein Mount Ea and Mount Nebo, or Mount Pisgah, upon which Moses is said to have died, are located just beyond the Dead Sea.

By cutting in two the Kingdom of Canaan, and also intruding upon the region claimed by the Assyrians, the mythical King Belus opened a veritable Pandora's Box of future wars between the children of Isis-Osiris and those of Ishtar and Ashtoreth.[1]

The Mestreans had in fact deliberately occupied the strategic region between Ur, or the seat of the Moon God Sin, and Ya-ru-siloam, thereby dominating absolutely the caravan routes from Suzi-ana beyond the Tigris, and the Aegean. Moreover, by their alliance with the Danitics of Rub, they had possessed themselves of control over that part of the present Arabia in which Me-din-a, 'the Mesraite Garden of Arabia,' and also Me-c-ca, 'the Mesraite Circle of the Canaanite Ark,' were to arise on the meridian 40° E. due south of Archangel on the White Sea, (60° N.) with Medina at the exact latitude of Kara Chi in the delta of the Indus, close to the tropic of Cancer (23° 30' N.) and Mecca, at the exact latitude of Su-ra-t on the Gulf of Kambay, just north of Bombay, on the west coast of India, and also at the latitude of the Nubian Desert between Wadi Haifa at the second cataract of the Nile, marking the southern boundary of Egypt and the Je-bel Tellum (20° N.), at the third cataract of the Nile. Thus, we see how far back were laid the foundations of Islam by the posterity of the Biblical Ham, whose descendants in the Cycle of Moham-et would unfurl the green banner of Islam, displaying the crescent as a symbol of Isis.

---

[1] These wars would only end when following the rest of Islam the Turks of the Shi-i-te sect of Islam became the dominant factor of Islam and dominating the A-ba-s-sid-s or Sin-it-e sect of Mecca, established the Ottoman Empire with its seat near the present Constantinople which they eventually conquered.

CHAPTER XXVI

THE CYCLE OF THE ABRAMITES

INASMUCH AS IT HAS BEEN SHOWN that during the cycle of
Peleg-Joktan a great survey of the earth was taking place and
the nations of the earth were being allocated to their original
and traditionally God-given domains, while the Egyptians in
cahoots with their Danitic allies were endeavoring to fix their
hold in Asia Minor, the meanings of the names applied to the
cycles of R-ea and S-e-ru-g, or Se-ra-gua, are plain.

R-Ea, 'ru, the Erythrean Ark,' or 'Reisen, the
Ethiopian Ark.'

Se-ru-g, 'The Seraphim, Ru, the Gua, or the God
of the Uighur Ark.'

Because the Danitics were surveying Libya we find their
name in the Su-dan, and that of Serug in Se-ru-k in Mesopotamia, Lake Serug crossing from Lake Salsk at the East of the
delta of the Nile, Seruk in Uganda, and Serual in Morocco,
Seruti in Russia, while Serua Island appears at 6 S. 130 E.
south of the Mo-lu-c-cas includes the island of Naga.

Genesis leaves no room to doubt that already a tremendous
conflict was in progress between the Hittites and Philistia
when the cycle of Te-rah and the concurrent one of H-aran, the
alleged brother of Te-rah began, and it is quite plain that H-aran
(36° N. 40° E.), just up the Euphrates from Rehoboth (35°
N. 40° E.) marked the meridian of Mount Ca-r-mel and
Mount Sin-ai, and Petra.

Against this background the mythical history in *Genesis* of
the evolution of Israel is to be interpreted. Moreover, in view
of the strategic position of Asia Minor, located as it was between Mesopotamia at the East, Circassia and Russia at the
North, Rub at the South, Egypt at the Southwest, and the

Medi Terre at the West, what occurred there possessed an importance in world history out of all proportion to the relatively few peoples involved. For the control of it involved the vast trade between Asia whose caravans from time immemorial streamed across Asia Minor to the Medi Terre and made of Damascus not only the 'Pearl of the Orient,' but the 'Watch' of the Libyan desert to the east that depended upon this great inland port and the river leading from it to Tyre as entrepots of the trade between Asia and the Medi Terre, just as the more southern stream of trade flowed to Gaza and the Canaanite ports on the Aegean. Moreover Asia Minor was in a sense a well at which all the peoples of the world must drink.

What followed the appearance of the Hittites as a power in Asia Minor, therefore, is to be interpreted with intelligent regard to the economic situation of the Hebrews whose Tree Cult was so similar to the old Serpent Cult. Inevitably the two became almost as one in that part of Libya at the north of the Medi Terre over which the Danitics had extended their sway, and in which evolved the Dracontia Cult and Druidism, apparently at a date very much earlier than commonly supposed. Thus, just as indicated by Josephus, in many cases the names of the peoples who had been dispersed over Libya and the islands overseas from Mesopotamia, gradually became lost, as did the trace of the Hebrews who colonized the Tree Cult among them. The South Pacific Island suggests that the Cainites in the East also had a cycle of Serug. Nor can it be forgotten that while the events which have been described were taking place in the West, the Cainites had been expanding and may be taken to account for many of the similarities between the myths and languages of the Pacific Continent and those of their kinsmen.

At the time when the cycle of Na-hor began in B.C. 657,-000, the Hi-ti-ti-ti who, as shown by the three tauxs in their name, were a mixed people, had become a factor in Armenia. Inasmuch as there was no Black Sea their domain which spread at the North into the region of Aschenax at the west of the present Caucasus and that of Samothrax adjoining Thrace at the east of Grecaland, was cut off from the West by the Graecos, from the North by the ancestors of the Scythians in Russia, from the East by the Assyrians, from the South by the peoples who had settled in Rub, and from the Aegean Sea by both the Syrians in the Tracontis who had founded Tyre, and the Arameans with their capital at Damascus. Moreover, between Aramea and Samothrax there were the Ionians with their centers of culture at Ma-zi-ac-ca and T-ar-sus. Eventually, to be sure, Sin-o-pe, or Sin-ub would appear at the boundary of Ionia and Armenia but that would not occur until the Black Sea had appeared ages hence. Coming close at the south to Rub, the Hittites undoubtedly had merged with the Raamaha, the Sheba and the De-dan, as allies of the Philistim and like the latter were hostile to both the Canaanites and the Assyrians who had been pressing westward up the Euphrates as shown by the city of Rehoboth erected by them between the Armenians and Canaan. Therefore there was every reason why the Hittites should have accepted Hebraism as indicated by the name Na-hor in which is preserved the name of the Nabatheans coupled with that of the H-o-r, 'the Hittites, Osiris, the Ru.' By B.C. 618,000 had evolved the cycle of T-er-rah, 'the Taux, the Eberites, Raamaha,' indicating the close alliance between the Hittites and their Punic kinsmen. Containing the blood of the Melas as well as that of the Ru and the Caucasians, as shown by the Negroid Cimmareans who in historic times dwelt along the Black Sea, and also the Carians of Lydia, undoubtedly one of the T's in their name implied the biblical Lud, or Laud, the putative son of Shem, to whom the E-t-ru-ska and the Danitic Trojans are to be traced. Just as the Melas produced the Cimmareans also they produced the peculiar Cimri of Belgium and their kindred, the Cimbrians of Britain among whom was the mythical King Lud who gave his name to London and Londonderry and also to Bel-fast, 'Bel's Fort.' So is explained the known Negroid ancestors of the British who traced their culture back to Corenus, an older god than Apollo, implying the Python of the Sinitic Age. And it was to the Corenus that the M-ana-x and Cor-n-ish as well as the W-el-sh culture of prehistoric Britain is to be traced as well as that of Cor-in-th. In a word the Corydeans, or giants of Britain who were eventually bleached, were Melas as indicated by the name M-ana-x. And it was because the Tree Cult was conveyed to them by the biblical Lud that we find the Island of Colon-sa-y bearing the name of the Eberites or colonizers, along with the Island of T-e-x-a marking the western line of the geodetic Chi of the Eastern hemisphere, just as the eastern line of the Chi in the Western Hemisphere passed through T-ana-sa and T-e-x-a-s, 'the Land of Peace.' Also be it noted that near the Island of Texa appears Tree Island. In other words the British trace back to the mixture of Nagas and Melas to whom the Hebrews introduced the Tree Cult ages before the Prophet Jeremiah who knew this, predicted that a great nation would arise in the West, and to contribute to it, visited Ireland, Britain, Britanny, a former part of the land of Is, and Scandinavia before his death as a contemporary of Solon. So, all the mystery of the predecessors of the white sub-race, or the T-a-ha-t-i de D-a-ana-n, of the Aryan Ark, vanishes since they were simply absorbed in the course of time just as were the Itza from the Land of Is by their Mayavic predecessors in what became North America.

From the scriptures it appears that from the cycle of Terah evolved the cycle of Abram in B.C. 558,000, and that the eponymous A-bra-mu in whom is to be seen a mixture of Aryan Hebrews in Sumer, had two brothers, Haran and Nahor, like Abram said to have been born in Ur over which the Chaldees had asserted their spiritual dominion when they erected Eridu and Erech and set up the Moon Goddess Ishtar to replace her alleged father, the Moon God Sin. Also it is said that Abram married Sarai, this being an eponym for the peoples of Samarra which appeared at 32° 30′ N. 44° E., immediately west of the old Tir of the Sumerians in the Din called E-din-nu by them, and the Garden of Eden by the Hebrews, finally A-ri-z-za-ga by the Chaldeans. It seems evident that Aramea had been in fact but a western evolution from Amara wherein S-ama-r-ra had appeared. This being so the affinity between the Sumerians and the Samarians, and the Arameans, and the connections between the last and Aram at the east of the Tigris is manifest.

Also we are told that Haran died, having begotten Mi-l-ca-h, or Mi-l-chi, Is-ca-h and Lot, these names also being mere eponyms applied to the peoples with whom the Hittites had merged. After Haran passed, Abram and Sarai adopted Lot.

It will be observed that the cycle of Nahor, a very short one, had come to an end 30,000 years after that of Abram is shown as beginning (B.C. 558,000), although the other cycles of the Shemitic Dekkard were still evolving. This merely indicates that there had been a merger of the Hebraic Hittites with the Samarians. On the other hand the barrenness ascribed to Sarai, the wife of Abram, indicates that the alliance of the Sumerians of Ur and Samaria had produced no Hebraic progeny.

While *Genesis* resumes its story of Abram in B.C. 483,000 with the departure of Abram from Haran for Canaan, and tells nothing of what occurred between that date and the departure, and how Abram, Sarai and Lot came to that part in the land of the Hittites beyond Samaria, fortunately for the historian this is explained by Josephus. Thus by him we are told that Terah had been much embittered by the loss of his son Nahor, implying that the cycle of Abram which like the cycle of Nahor had come to an end in B.C. 528,000. And although nothing is said of the other brother Is-cas-h which may be taken to imply the Hebrews who remained in Sumeria as subjects of the Chaldeans who had set up Ishtar at Erech, Josephus explains that eventually Terah, with Abram, Sarai, and Lot who had married Mi-l-chi, implying the mysteries of the Ka-bi-ra which had been established at Ya-ru-siloam by the eponymous Righteous King, M-el-chi-ze-dek, all removed to Haran. And here we must note that if the cycle of Nahor had expired in B.C. 528,000, that of Peleg expired in B.C. 510,000 and that of

Noeas in B.C. 500,000, just at the time when the Old Stone
Age of modern Ethnology is supposed to have ended and that
of the Megolithic, or Middle Stone Age is supposed to have
begun, with the Neanderthal type of man to which the Heidel-
berg giant is traced.

We may safely assume, therefore, that the Second Glacial
Period had come to an end with the passing of the Noachean
cycle, and that by B.C. 483,000 when, according to *Genesis,*
Abram, Sarai, and Lot departed from Haran, the Second Winter, or the Winter of the Wolf described in the Volsunga Saga,
had begun. Certainly anyone familiar with the mountainous
region of Haran at the upper reach of the Euphrates, can readily understand it was not a region in which the Abramites
might hope to expand rapidly in competition with the Ionians
who had established themselves in Ma-zi-ac-ca and in T-ar-sus.[1]

But again there is a hiatus in *Genesis* that was explained by
Josephus who showed that Abram, Sarai, and Lot did not proceed directly to Hebron in Canaan. According to him it appears that Abram was possessed of great sagacity, "for understanding of all things and in persuading others." Moreover he
is described as having notions of virtue higher than others,
and as one determined to change the opinion all men had of
God. "He held that if the gods men were worshipping were
contributing anything to the happiness of men, it was because
they were appointed to do so, not of their own power." This
opinion the Abramites are shown supporting by the argument
that the Transcendent Wisdom ruling the Universe was manifested through the phenomena of nature just as held by the
Wisdom Philosophy.

It will be observed that Haran lies due west of Nineveh
where the Pa-te-si, or Priestly Patriarchs, were ruling the Assyrians, and of course the monotheism ascribed by Josephus to
the Abramites would have made them hateful to both the
Pantheists of Assyria and the Chaldeans as the King of Nations. Accordingly Josephus relates that they raised a tumult

against him. So there was a second good reason for the departure of the Abramites from Haran.

Yet, they had won over many hostiles when, according to Josephus, they proceeded to Damascus where they appeared with a large army.[2] There at another Haran just to the east, still called the habitation of Abram, they remained a long time, apparently proselytizing and recruiting the strength that would enable them eventually to overrun Canaan. And of course in Damascus they would have learned all there was to know about the Medi Terre, Grecaland, Italy, Egypt and Canaan.

If a map be examined it will be seen that from the Waters of Me-ru-m, 'the Melas, the Ru, of Mu,' constituting the source spring of the realm of Dan, the J-o-r-dan trails southward like the root of a lotus to the Dead Sea that eventually came to spread over the area of the great salt pits which had caused the Assyrians to seize the Canaanite cities of Sodom and Gomorrah. By doing so, of course, the Assyrians had embittered the Canaanites who were dependent upon Sodom for their salt. At the North of the plain on which stood the two originally fine cities of Sodom and Gomorrah was the Ridge of Ana-k-i-m with the Jordan at the north, on which undoubtedly at Beth-el the Canaanites had erected a beth or idol, somewhat north of Ya-ru-siloam (31° 30' N. 35° 50' E.). Between Bethel and Hai was the ideal position for the Abramites to occupy as there they could play off the Assyrians against the Canaanites and both against the Philistim.

When eventually the Abramites left Damascus they proceeded southward and crossing the Jordan just beyond the waters of Me-ru-m, came to Se-ch-e-m (32° 25' N. 35° 10' E.) on the plain of Mo-r-e-h between Mount Carmel and Ya-ru-siloam. They must defend themselves, however, against the Canaanites as well as against the Assyrians and the Philistim. Therefore they soon established themselves on the Ridge of Ana-k-im.

Although Abram is shown in *Genesis* as going southward

from Bethel, no explanation of his objective is given. Yet, from subsequent events it seems certain the Abramites were now taken into the fold of the mysteries of the Ka-bi-ra which had been established at the Pool of Siloam, of which the mythical King Mel-chi-ze-dek, 'the Melas, the Chi, the Serpent, the Dekkad of the Zodiac,' called the Righteous King, merely implied the Hierarchy of these mysteries which undoubtedly had been established also at the cave of Mount Ca-r-mel, 'the Canaanites, the Ru, the Melas.'[3]

Enough has been said to eliminate the element of chance about the occupation of the position between Bethel and Hai by the invaders who were at last in position to deal with all their enemies.

[1] It was in Tarsus at which Saul or St. Paul would eventually receive his education at the University there which had been patronized like the one at Sardis by the Emperor Augustus.

[2] In support of this statement Josephus quoted Nicolaus of Damascus.

[3] It was at Carmel that the Prophets Elijah and Elisha eventually appeared.

CHAPTER XXVII

THE ABRAMITES VISIT EGYPT

*Secret Diplomacy And A Secret Alliance Between
The Abramites And Egypt.
The First Assyrian Wars.
Abram Becomes Abraham.*

FAMINES in the old days occurred not alone from the plagues
sprung of shallow wells and the filth of human habitations,
but from unseasonable weather. The Second Winter would
have accounted not only for the famine that came upon Palestine, but the inertia of the Canaanites in the great ports of
Sidon, Joppa, Askelon, of the Philistines in Gaza, and the
Assyrians who had founded Sodom and Gomorrah on the
plain at the east of Bethel.

During the famine it would have been impossible for the
Abramites to do more colonizing in Palestine. Moreover, the
grand scheme of Eber had not conceived of mere static colonies as terrestrial possessions. Inasmuch as Egypt was still the
most advanced country on earth, it was the logical place for
further expansion of the Abramites.

The Righteous King Melchi-ze-dek would have known that
a splendid opportunity existed for diplomacy in dealing with
the Faro's court where a terrific feud was waging among the
different priesthoods, due in part to the Hebrews who had occupied Lake Salah and Lake Serug at the east of the delta.

Inasmuch as S-ara-i represented the Aryans of Samaria, who
were akin to the Cushites in Egypt, the agents of the Abramites who visited the court of the Faro must pose as brother
and sister of the same blood, else the Abramites, as Hebrews,
hostile to the various gods of Egypt, would be killed. So it is
said that before Abram and Sarai departed from Bethel for

Egypt, Sarai was instructed to pose as Abram's blood sister. In a word, already diplomacy had become the high art of dissimulation, more vulgarly declared as professional official lying.

According to *Genesis* and Josephus those despatched by the Abramites to Egypt were welcomed by the Faro who showered gifts upon the visitors, and was so fascinated by Sarai that he contemplated making her his wife, implying the adoption of the Abramite philosophy. Not only this, but Abram was permitted to discuss matters of religion with the priesthoods to whom he delivered mathematics and astronomy. This, of course, implies that the Abramites undertook to proselytize by delivering to the Egyptians dissertations upon the Wisdom Philosophy embodied in the Zodiac.

But although Abram is said to have been very eloquent and persuasive, the best of diplomats are apt to blunder when they touch upon religion. So it was with the Abramites. Soon the priests who had direct contact with Damascus, discovered the ruse of their visitors. Thereupon Abram found himself beset with another tumult. Since the famine had extended to Egypt, even it was charged to the Faro because of the favor he was showing the unmasked Monotheists who were undermining the gods.

The upshot was inevitable. Favor extended the Abramite mission suddenly came to an end. Thereupon Abram and his "beautiful wife" are shown departing the land of the Lotus Eaters.

Yet, the Abramites had not failed to show Faro what was possible. Therefore when they returned to Bethel they were allowed to take all their newly acquired wealth with them. Plainly the Egyptians, as well as the Philistines had seen that the Abramites would be valuable allies in defending Philistia against both the Canaanites and the Assyrians. In other words the eponymous King Belus of Egypt was but another ruler who, though outwardly he must meet the demands of his people, ignored their demands in matters of diplomacy.

As time went on, however, and the Abramites and Lotites

became more numerous, the region which they had settled in would not support their flocks. Frequently discords arose between the Abramites and the Lotites who had fallen victim to the materialism of the Sodomites. To end the friction Lot was allowed by the Lord, implying the Hierarch of the mysteries, to choose the lands they desired. Thereupon they selected the plain of Sodom, while the Abramites removed to the plain of Mamre on which stood at Hebron the sacred Oak of Ogyges, just west of Ya-ru-si-loam. There they reared an altar.[1] Thus came into being the senior group of the ark of Abram which had been set up in that part of the realm of Dan henceforth known as Ju-da, in which appears the Hebraic name Jupiter, coupled with that of Dan. Eventually, therefore, the Abramites who founded the kingdom of Juda with its altar at the Oak of Ogyges, would come to be known as the Sceptre Tribe of Israel.

With Juda established at Hebron, and the Lotites at Sodom and Gomorrah, undermining the Assyrians in those parts, a reckoning was bound to come. This the Faro and his vassal, the King of Philistia, both must have known. At any rate during the next 7,000 years, more Hebrews appeared in the region of Lake Salah and Lake Serug where louder and louder had grown the protests of the Egyptian priests against the Hebrews who were infiltrating Egypt despite the illusion of the isolationists that fortifications could prevent the undermining of their gods.

At the end of this period the threat of both the Hebrews and of Assyrians who meant to recover their cities from the Lotites, became so plain that the Faro at last erected the city of T-an-is (31° N.) on the river Tanais, just east of the Da-mi-e-t-t-a branch of the Nilus, to defend Egypt.

When at last the Pa-te-si of Assyria had come to realize that the Lotites had suborned the Sodomites, the inevitable occurred. An Assyrian host, divided into four armies, was despatched against the intruders. Now the whole of Canaan was to be conquered. Soon they had subjected the Lotites who for 12,000 years were held under tribute. At the end of this time, however, or 19,000 years after the Abramites of Juda had established themselves at Hebron, the Abramites achieved an open alliance with the Egyptians. Associated with King Abimelech of Philistia they now fomented among the Lotites a rebellion against Assyria. Thereupon the Assyrians formed a confederacy with the King of Kings, the Amarites of Sumeria, and the Elamites beyond the Tigris, so that the Lotites were soon assailed by four kings. Quickly the whole of Syria was overrun by the confederates, and not only were the Lotites subdued, but the eponymous Lot was taken prisoner.

In this situation the Abramites must fulfill the terms of their arrangement with the Faro whose vassal, King Abimelech of Philistia, was being seriously threatened. Accordingly it appears in *Genesis* that 318 Abramites, with 300 Philistines, under the Abramites, marched against Sodom while the Assyrians were carousing in a drunken revel and were looting the country of the Lotites. Caught unawares, their vast numbers meant nothing. Fleeing in disorder they were pursued close to Da-ma-s-cus. Thereupon the Abramites who had recovered the eponymous Lot, returned to the great lime pits at Sodom, to receive the honors bestowed upon them not only by the King of Sodom, but Mel-chi-ze-dek, "the Righteous King" of Salem.

The Abramites, however, were not unaware of what would befall them as open allies of the Philistines and the Faro, when the priest kings of the Confederates reorganized their armies. Indeed they were considering fleeing into Egypt when "the Lord" promised them that after their posterity had inhabited Egypt 400 years, they would receive unto themselves the Land of Canaan.[2] From this it is to be gathered that the Abramites had come to be looked upon by the Faro, as well as by King Abimelech as friends and valuable allies.

The constant references to the giants of Canaan at this time indicate that the Gaur of Syria were of immense stature.

Still S-ara-i had borne the Abramites no progeny. This was only natural since the latter who inhabited the region around the oak of Ogyges near Hebron were no longer in touch with the Sumerians whom the Assyrians had cut off from Canaan. But if the Abramites were to evolve into a people capable of possessing themselves of Palestine, they must have progeny. In this situation, according to the scripture, Sa-ra-i induced her Egyptian handmaiden Ha-g-ar, to lie with Abram, with the result that in B.C. 472,000, when the eponymous Abram was 86 years old, the Egyptian peoples in Palestine represented by Hagar, bore Abram a son Is-ma-el, "Isis, the mother of the Elohim," described as Abram's first born son.

Because the Abramites had found it necessary to inbreed with the Egyptians in Palestine, henceforth Abram is designated in the scriptures as Abram-Ham, or Abraham, while S-ara-i is given the name Sa-ra-h. In other words the progeny of the Hebrews represented by Abraham were half Egyptian, as indicated by the letter H introduced into the new eponyms, implying descendants of Ham. This cross, of course, recommended them to the Philistine King A-b-ime-lech who also is shown as the near victim of an attempt to deceive him as to the religious objective of the Abrahamites.[2]

In the course of time the Assyrians had evolved the vile Female Cult associated by them with the Moon Goddess Ashtoreth, involving the sexual perversions for which the fine city of Sodom gradually had become infamous.[3] This horror was, of course, shocking to the spiritual teachers of God's House. So it is said that God destroyed Sodom with a bolt of lightning. The myth that Lot's wife was turned into a pillar of salt, simply implies that in the region of the Lime Pits which had produced the progeny of the Lotites, now appeared the salt of the Dead Sea that made those waters unfruitful. This compelled even the Lotites to remove to Zoar. From them evolved the Ammonites, and the Moabites of Cilicia, said to have been begotten by Lot in his old age out of his two maiden daughters who lay with him as he slept, implying merely that they begot offspring out of the peoples among whom the Lotites settled.

1 The Oak was designated by the Greeks the *Tree of Jove.*

2 Author's note: The Hegira of the Exodus from Egypt in the Mosaic period is generally placed at about B. C. 1,300. Measuring back 400,000 years fixes the time when the Hebrews were allowed to occupy Egypt, as B. C. 400,300.

3 One may well shudder today when it is officially reported that over 3,000 sexual perverts are on the payrolls of the U. S. Government in Washington alone, even after 330 were dismissed from the State Department. Statistics show that sexual perversion is increasing at an appalling rate along with bestiality. See police court records of the United States in any of the big cities.

CHAPTER XXVIII

THE EVOLUTION OF ISRAEL

The New Chaldea.
The Cycle of Joseph in Egypt.
The Biblical Hiatus Between Josephus and
That of Moses Explained.

IN THE ALLEGED friendship between the Abramites and King
Melchi-ze-dek of Salem a complete explanation is found of what
occurred in Canaan following the destruction of Sodom and
Gomorrah. Out of the mysteries of the Kabira by which the
Wisdom Philosophy in its ever evolving form was preserved,
was to evolve the Ark of Is-aa-c in the name of which is seen
that of the Na-ac-als or Nabatheans, coupled with that of the
Naacals, and ever interpreted as the rule with God.' Accordingly it is said that in B.C. 458,000 or 100,000 years after the
Abramites had appeared in Sumeria, and 42,000 years after the
old Cycle of Noeas had expired, Sarah at the age of 87 bore
to Abraham at the age of 100 years, implying ages compiled in
biblical years, Is-aa-c as the brother of Ismael.

In view of the real nature of Is-aac there was no place for
Hagar, representing the Egyptians. Now that the Abramites
had made use of the Egyptians to produce the eponymous Is-
ma-el, and thereby gain a right of occupancy in Palestine
which the Faro would openly recognize, the Egyptians who
were co-operating with the Abramites were to be employed to.
further useful ends.

Representing the Samarians who looked on Isaac as the
rightful heir of the Hebrews, Sarah is shown persuading some
shepherds to carry off Hagar and her son. This simply means
that the Hierophants of the Kabira led the progeny of the
Abramites out of the Egyptians into the realm of the mythical

Queen of Sheba of Rub. There in the realm of Mash, or the Massaneans, between the Euphrates and the Red Sea, the Ismaelites as the agents of the eponymous Melchizedek, would beget the twelve groups called Nabaoth, Kodar, Abdeal, Mabsaro, Idumes, Masmaos, Masaos, Chodad, Themau, Jetur, Naphesus, and Cadmad. Because the Nabaoth represented the Nabatheans, the part in which these groups evolved, was called Nabatene.

More and more peoples were coming to occupy the realm of the Queen of Sheba, when the half-Egyptian Is-ma-elites in fact, thanks to the Righteous King Melchi-ze-dek, had added new territory at the west of the Jordan to the Pharaoh's Spiritual See. Moreover the Ismaelites not only gave the Egyptians better access to Mesopotamia, but constituted a barrier state between Palestine and Assyria. Therefore the Egyptians, the Philistines, the Sheba and the Abrahamites, all may be assumed to have had a part in producing the Ark of Isaac. In a word, Nimrod and Melchizedek had been playing a shrewd game against the King of Kings, the Assyrians, the Elamites and the Aramites.

With the appearance of the Ark of Isaac as the foundation of Israel, a new Planetarium was to begin—that of Israel with the cycles of Abraham, Isaac, Jacob, Joseph, and their successors, while the Hierophants of the Mysteries in each of these cycles, would hand down to those of the next all the history of the past.[1]

When the Cycle of Arphaxad expired in B.C. 445,000, two years after that of Serug, God's House could not have failed to see that the Chaldeans or the so-called King of Kings, who had combined with the Assyrians, Aramites, and Elamites to overrun Palestine, in whose reign had occurred the horrors of Sodom and Gomorrah, were incapable of combatting pantheism, overthrowing the growing idolatry born of it and purging the increasingly foul earth of the moral impurities of men. Therefore, Chaldea must be re-organized and placed under a higher spiritual governance.

At last in B.C. 432,535 the First of the Ten Dynasties of Chald-ea was founded with its capital at Ba-bel, bearing the name Al-o-ru-s, "The Atlantean Circle of Ru in Sumer."[2]

Meantime Nahor II, the putative brother of Abram, who had remained in Haran, had begotten out of M-i-l-chi, the eight Danitic sons—Uz, Damas, Buz, Ke-mu-el, Che-sed, A-z-a-u, Phe-l-d-as, and Ja-del-ph. As Uz represents the Damasceans, in the eponymous Ja-del-ph appears the name of Joran along with that of Delos. The seventh son was Beth-u-el.

The Hittites, however, were a highly mixed peoples. Therefore it is said that by R-e-u-ma, a concubine, representing a Caucasian-Ethiopian cross, Nahor II begot four other sons— Te-ba, Ga-am, T-a-chi-a-s, and Ma-acca. In these eponyms are seen the names applied to the Ionian descendants of Tubal, Gomer, Tira and Meschec, or Mesa, of whom the last had founded Ma-zi-acca. Because the Hebrews in H-ar-an had merged with non-Shemites the cycle of Terah expired in B.C. 423,000.

By B.C. 418,000 B-eth-u-el, a legitimate son of Nahor II, had begotten a daughter Rebecca. With the Abrahamites and Sarahites threatened by the Canaanites, inevitably they would have sought to strengthen themselves through another union with the peoples of Haran. Accordingly, in *Genesis* it is said that Abraham demanded of Nahor the latter's granddaughter Rebecca as the wife of Isaac, and that in B.C. 418,000 Isaac married Rebecca. Thereby the two Hebraic arks of Is-a-acca and Re-be-acca were merged, just five years before the Cycle of T-e-rah expired.

The First Divine Dynasty of Chaldea expired at the end of ten sari, or 36,000 years, in B.C. 396,535 during the cycle of Abraham and Sarah, and was replaced by that of Al-pa-ru-s, with its capital at Sippara, or Sephervaim (33°) which had arisen near Akkad.[3]

The removal of the Chaldean capital from Babylonia to the higher region of Sippara in Shinar, between the Euphrates and the Tigris just east of Akkad, suggests more than the floodings of Babylonia during the second glacial period. At that point the Chaldean spiritual teachers might command the intercourse between Assyria and Sumer. Plainly, as shown by the gradual movement northward of the Chaldean capital, the Chaldeans were determined to bring both Assyria and Armenia under their jurisdiction.

During the Second Divine Dynasty of Chaldea, Sarah, the putative wife of Abraham, passed away because in fact the peoples represented by her had merged with the Egyptians who had produced the Is-ma-el-ites.

After the death of Sarah, Abraham is shown marrying the Egyptian woman K-e-t-u-r-a-h, although it is said that he denied to Isaac nothing that was rightly within his inheritance.

By Keturah he is said to have begotten six sons, all men of courage and sagacity—Za-m-bran, Ja-zar, Ma-dan, Ma-di-an, Jo-sa-ba-k and Sous, and to have placed them all in the land to which the Is-ma-elites had been transferred, to which they gave the name Arabia.

In B.C. 388,000 or 5,000 years before the cycle of Abraham expired, the Ark of Isaac begat out of the mixed peoples represented by Rebecca, two offspring, said to have appeared in her womb, of which the first was E-sau, and the second Jacob.[4]

Because Esau in fact represented a cross between the Hebrews and the Egyptians he is described as red and hairy. But although he was much beloved by the Hebrews of the Ark of Isaac, the people represented by Rebecca were determined that their offspring should inherit the birthrights of the Abrahamites.

Although it is said that Esau was first delivered of his mother, when Jacob was preferred to Esau, as the heir of Isaac, the Egyptian progeny of the Ark of Isaac were greatly embittered. Accordingly Esau is declared to have sworn to kill his younger brother. In this situation Rebecca is shown as greatly alarmed. According to the scriptures she arranged to have Esau carried off by some wandering shepherds, just as Sarah had caused Ismael to be removed from Palestine.

The Chaldean Dynasty of Alparus lasted 3 saros, or 10,800 years, being replaced in B.C. 385,535 by that of A-m-i-l-a-r-u-s, just 2,265 years after the cycle of Jacob began, with the Chaldean capital still at Sippara.[5]

In B.C. 383,000 at last the cycle of Abraham expired just three years before that of Salah.

Whether or not it was because God's House was exercising some special supervision over Chaldea at this time in order to overcome the degradation which had marked the decline of the King of Kings, it is said that in the Third Divine Dynasty of Chaldea, O-an-n-es, the first Annedotus of Chaldea, known to the Assyrians as D-ago-n, "the Divine Ark, Narayana," at last appeared in Mesopotamia. Called the *Fish Man* because of his mitre and vestments depicted in the tablets and by Herodotus, he was in truth the High Priest of Chaldea of his time. When, however, he appeared in the waters of the Euphrates, the Sumerians who first beheld him fled in terror, thinking a fish had arisen from the deep.[6] His appearance indicates that the second glacial period had begun following the end of the Second Winter, and that now more of the mounds radiating over the Earth from the Gobi, were erected.

In B.C. 348,000 the cycle of Shem expired, and that same year, when the cycle of Esau had run 40,000 years, the Arabians represented by Esau formed an alliance with the Hittites in Canaan. With their alleged brothers established at S-e-i-r, still supposed to be determined to destroy the Jacobites, his mother Rebecca is said to have been greatly alarmed.

There was but one way to safeguard the Ark of Isaac in Palestine against this combination. The eponymous Jacob must be sent from Hebron to Haran to form an alliance between the children of the Ark of Isaac and Rebecca's alleged brother Laban. Accordingly Jacob is represented as travelling through Canaan, which he is said like Isaac to have hated, to Haran in search of a daughter of Laban as his wife.

To him great dreams of future greatness are ascribed. As the story has it, he was well received by Laban who insisted that first his older daughter Lea be taken by Jacob before he took Rachel to wife seven years later.

To Jacob Lea bore Reuben, Simeon, Levi, and Judah, while Rachel's hand maiden Bilha, representing dependents of the Labanites, bore him Dan, and Nephtalim. At the end of seven years Jacob married Rachel and out of Lea's hand maiden begat Gad and Asher. Then Rachel yielded Jacob to Lea, who bore him Isaachar and Zabalon, and a daughter Dina. After some time Rachel bore Jacob a son Joseph.

Confusing as all these marriages and births seem, in truth they merely represented the crossing of various Danitic groups with the Jacobites that brought into being eleven of the twelve tribes of Israel.

At the end of 20,000 years Jacob and the two daughters of Laban whom he had married, decided to remove to Palestine clandestinely lest Laban prevent them. With their flocks and all the possessions the Jacobites had acquired while serving under Laban, they made off only to be pursued and overtaken by the Labanites. A conflict was threatening but it is said that God intervened. Thereupon the Jacobites and the Labanites entered into a compact on the Hill of Giliad, and there the formation of the league into which they entered was duly celebrated. In a word the Jacobites had accomplished their original purpose, being now strong enough to meet the threat of the Esauites and the Canaanites.

It appears that on the way southward through the hated Canaan, Jacob was met by an angel whom he is said to have bested in a wrestling match.

It does not take much imagination to see in the angel a Fish-Man representing God's House, and in the besting of the angel, the agreement that was now reached with the Chaldeans. The Jacobites were to be allowed, despite the Assyrians and their allies, to seize Palestine in fulfillment of the alleged promises of God to Abraham.

Certainly God's House would have seen that by allowing the Jacobites to interpose between Chaldea and Egypt, was the best way to insure a union between Chaldea and Egypt that would isolate Canaan and enable the Chaldeans eventually to bring the evil Canaanites into obedience to God. This was to be accomplished by the Jacobites as the champions of the monotheism inherited by them from Abraham.

Pursuant to this arrangement Jacob commanded Rachel to put aside her images of the gods which the Labanites and their Hittite dependents, as Pantheists, had come to cherish. The angel is then shown commanding Jacob to change his name to Is-r-a-el. And this Jacob agreed to do. Accordingly today Israel is deemed to imply "a man seeing God, or ruling with God." The old religion of Yaveygh was doomed.

But God's House had done more than this. It had arranged to end the feud between the twin sons of Isaac.

As the eleven groups born of the Jacobites in Haran moved southward from Gilead, the eponymous Esau appeared in their wake. Although the Israelites believed that the Esauites meant to assail them, in his alleged old age Isaac had persuaded Esau to put aside his Canaanite wives, and to marry the daughter of Ismael whom the Abrahamites had begotten out of the Egyptians represented by Keturah. In a word, a union had been effected between the half-Egyptian Ismaelites, and the half-Egyptian Esauites in Arabia, designed to ally them with Israel against the Canaanites.

The upshot was that instead of a battle between the Israelites and the Esauites, Esau is said to have made his abeyance to Jacob, implying a compact between them. This in addition to the Jacobite-Laban League, had rendered the Canaanites more or less helpless when the Israelites reached the city of Schechen in Canaan, one over which Hamor ruled as King.

There, it appears that Schechen, the son of Hamor, defiled Dina, the one daughter of Jacob, and that following this Hamor sought her hand for his son. It seems evident, therefore, that the Canaanites were now anxious to enter into a league with the Israelites that would secure them against the Ionians at the north and west, the Chaldeans and Assyrians at the east, and the Arabians and Egyptians at the south. But the Israelites having gained the Hittites and Arabians as their allies, had no idea of falling victims to Hamor's diplomacy. Instead of accepting his proposals, the groups of Simeon and Levi, the brothers of Dina fell upon the Schechenites and wiped out the males of Hamor's kingdom.[7]

Following this Rachel bore to Jacob in his old age his last progeny—the tribe of Benjamin. Thus was completed the twelve tribes of Israel, four begotten out of Rachel, four out of Lea, two out of Bilha, and two out of Zilpah. As all but two of these—Judah and Benjamin—had evolved from the Danitics of Samaria, the ten Danitic tribes together constituting the peoples of Dan, were called "the Name Bearers," while the Judah who had begotten Benjamin, were called the Sceptre Tribe.[8]

Meantime the sons who had been begotten by Abraham out of the Egyptians, represented by Keturah, had spread far and wide over Arabia, and from there over Libya beyond Egypt. Accordingly it is said that Apher and Japhren, the brothers of Esau's third wife, gave Ethiopia the name Africa. And to them also is to be ascribed the name Abyssinia.[9]

According to the Hebrew scriptures the life span of Isaac was 185,000 solar years.[10] Inasmuch as his cycle began in B.C. 458,000, it expired in B.C. 273,000 during the Fifth Divine Dynasty of Chaldea, or that of Me-ga-l-a-rus (B.C. 295,435—230,635), with the capital still at Sippara or Sephervaim.

It was high time that God's House should make a special effort to uplift Assyria and Chaldea from the moral degradation into which they had fallen when in B.C. 230,635 the Sixth Divine Dynasty of Chaldea began. In this cycle of 64,800 years the Musaros Oannes, appeared several times as the Assyrian Fish Man Enedocus, Enegamus, Eneabolous, and Anementus.[11]

This indicates that the second glacial age was producing more and more floods upon the earth.

The question naturally arises, just what did the people of the earth look like when the Israelites came to Egypt.

If one should go to the province of Indra La Lois in France, not far from the Magic Pool of Helgoat in Amorica, and peer into the cave of Cro Magnon, he would find in it the skeletons of many men arranged in a circle corresponding to the name C-ro, the Circle of Ro-mu-l-us. While the Ro-mu-lus were not giants, still they were dark colored with large heads, and of the Ethiopian type. A very learned people, on the walls of their caves is depicted a bull of the reindeer type, perfect in its anatomical aspect, and to the art found in this cave the anthropologists assign an age of not less than 200,000 years, bringing it back into the Sixth Divine Dynasty of Chaldea before the cycles of Jacob and Joseph expired.[12] The Cro-Magnon art, of course, identifies those buried in the cave as devotees of the old Cow Worship to which Israel was bitterly opposed.[13]

To be sure the twelve Tribes evolved in their areas in the manner already shown. Nevertheless it was while the Chaldeans were bringing the Assyrians and Sumerians into the Spiritual See of the Divine Dynasties which had found their seat at Sippara or Sephervaim, the various cities of Assyria, Akkad, and Sumer, were evolving from their humble beginning at some sacred tree like Din Tir and the Oak of Ogyges into those whose ruins are now found. The strata of culture found in these ruins disclose their vast antiquity.

Yet, in the nature of things, there is no way to tell just exactly what these centers of civilization had come to be at any one stage of their growth since the material in a city of one age is that of an older one. Consequently it is impossible for archaeologists to unravel the history of the past from the remains available to them, which can only yield the evidence the ruins afford of successive cultures.[14] The same is true with respect to the human remains that have been found.

Nevertheless the scriptures show that the cycle of Joseph in the Planetarium of Abram, emanated from that of Jacob. Exactly when it began is shown by the age of seventeen ascribed to Joseph when the cycle of Isaac expired. That would fix it in B.C. 290,000, and inasmuch as Joseph at the birth of Benjamin, is allowed an age of 110,000 solar years, his cycle would have expired in B.C. 180,000.

Being of the tribe of Benjamin, Joseph was ever deemed the "Little Benjamin" of Jacob. When his cycle began the mission of Israel was not limited to the relatively small task of bringing a part of Canaan into the fold of the Ark of Isaac. While Chaldea was being reformed, the Fish-Man O-da-con appeared during the Seventh Dynasty. Now must Israel fulfill the grand mission envisaged by the eponymous Abram when he had first gone to Egypt. Accordingly, as the story of Joseph unfolds, he of the many-colored coat is shown being spirited off by the Ismaelites to Egypt and sold to Potiphar, the captain of the Pharaoh's guard.[15]

The many colored coat of Joseph, however, merely represents the cardinal colors of the solar spectrum ever associated in the Hebrew Scriptures with the seven spheres of the Kabira, and with the seven mountains of Enoch, in the seventh of which dwelt the Seraphim and the Cherubim, implying the High Place of God's House. Thus the alleged enslavement of Joseph implies actual bondage of Israel to Egypt only in the spiritual sense while fulfilling the mission of liberating the Egyptians from the idolatry of countless Gods by instituting the monotheism which the eponymous Abram had preached ages before the Ark of Isaac had been founded. In a word with the arrival of Joseph in Egypt, began the consummation of a plan which had been in execution for ages. Consequently Joseph is shown as the virtual master at the court of the Faro in the land that had become a part of Africa. Plainly, for this the way had been prepared by Apher and his brother Japhren, the sons of the half-Egyptian Esau.

Already Joseph had become premier of the Faro and Egypt

had waxed strong and mighty under his wise direction when his brothers visited him. Joseph loves his brothers and longs for his father. The brothers return to Judah and fetch Jacob in his old age, and in Egypt where all tribes of Israel settle in the cycle of Joseph. Jacob passed away at the age of 130,-000 years, followed by Joseph in B.C. 180,000. Therefore in Egypt today one is shown the mythical well of Jacob near Memphis where the eponymous Joseph ruled over Egypt, close to the region of Babylon hard by Gaza and Sa-k-ka-ra wherein eventually arose the City of C-a-i-r-o.[16] In the mythical well of Jacob is to be seen, as in the well of the Norse Mimr, but a figurative well of wisdom. This again verified the Ramayana, and also the papyrus in which it is declared that Egypt and Chaldea were Twin Sisters.

The story of Joseph's cycle in Egypt given in Genesis 39-50, showing how the Israelites evolved there, as well as their relations to Syria during that cycle, are so clear against the historical background which has been constructed, it requires no analysis. Unfortunately between the passing of the cycle of Joseph in B.C. 180,000 and the Exodus, an immense gap occurs in *Genesis* of about 179,000 years. The reasons for this hiatus, already have been explained. Yet no Egyptian of the worldwide empire of Rameses the Great, could have imagined that the history of the Egyptians during the biblical hiatus between B.C. 180,000 and the Exodus, could have been so well hidden as it has been since the destruction of the Library of Alexandria during the Dark Age of Europe. Indeed one must marvel at the cleverness with which the Hierophants of the Mysteries succeeded in veiling the story of Israel in *Genesis* so skillfully that modern historians have found themselves utterly at sea while trying to relate the history of civilization to the earth in its present form, and to bring the history of Mesopotamia, India, China, Egypt, Europe, and America down to a late cycle. In the interpretation of the Hebraic Scriptures that has been given, however, will be found the skeleton for the history of the so-called Archaic Age.

It was in the year 1938 that the Episcopal Church officially proclaimed the account of the Creation embodied in *Genesis* a purely mythical one giving rise to the conclusion that it had no real historical basis. This was a strange holding indeed since a myth properly defined is merely a figurative record of fact as distinguished from a fable. Perhaps in view of what has been shown, it went too far, misled by Cheyne and others who have dismissed things they did not understand as unworthy of serious consideration despite the warnings of Montaigne not to reject the seemingly incredible. At any rate, in this chapter the guide has been given for the interpretation against the background of modern scientific findings of the myth in which was embodied the origin and evolution of Israel which it seems evident was known to the compilers of Koran. They knew the extent to which the scribes of the Mosaic Scriptures went to conceal in their esoteric account of the founding of Israel the fact that the Sumerians, Assyrians, Hittites, Syrians, the Ionians with whom the Hittites mingled, the forebears of the Arabs who spread Asia Minor over Misraim and Northern Africa, as well as over Egypt and the realms to the south, all contributed to bring into being the twelve tribes of Israel, yet there was no falsification.

1 So Moses would receive the Decalog or Book of the Israelitic Dekkad.

2 See Appendix "A" for the *Ten Divine Dynasties of Chaldea.*

3 Al-pa-ru-s, "Atlantis, the Papa of Ru, Shinar."

4 E-s-a-u, "Ethiopia's Son, the Arabian Twin."
J-aco-b, "the First, the Ark of Brahma."

5 A-m-i-la-ru-s, "the Light of Mesopotamia, the Spirit of Atlantis, Ru, Shinar."

6 The Nine Muses, Herodotus (B. C. 450).

7 See Josephus. Thus Dina became the putative ancestress of the Phoenicians who eventually founded Carthage with Dinah as their patroness.

8 So is explained the fact that upon the expiration of the cycle of Solomon the Ten Tribes of Samaria seceded from the Kingdom of Judah founded by David with Jerusalem as his capital, and founded the Kingdom of Israel in Samaria.

9 See the works of Cleodemus, the Jewish Prophet-historian. Afr-i-c-a,— "Apher, the Israelitic Chus of Arabia." Aby-sin-ia, "Araby-Sin."

10 See Josephus.

11 See Appendix A.

12 *The History of Civilization,* THORNDIKE, Professor of History, Columbia University (1932). In view of this art it is easy to see the origin of the Span-

ish House of Borgia of which the symbol was the Bull while that of their mortal enemies, the Orsini of Italy, was the Bear. To the Romulus may be traced the sacred rite of bull fighting introduced by the Cid in Spain as a symbol of hostility to the Moors who were descended from the Cro Magnon type of man. Also the hostility of the secret order of the Mithraists of Persia to the Cow Worship as shown by the picturization of Mithra fighting a bull.

13 In the Cro Magnons may be seen the ancestors of the Celtic Druids in whose sacred rites the Bull played so large a part as in the Egyptian mysteries of the Apis Bull associated with the Cult of Cerberus or the Italic Serapis.

14 Per example countless modern houses still possess the cellars and fireplaces of earlier cycles. Thus in colonial America the mansions of the 18th evolved from the log cabins of the 17th century.

15 Genesis 39.

16 C-a-i-r-o, "the Circle of Aegyptus, the Spirit of the Roc or Spiritual Bird."

Chapter XXIX

THE CYCLE OF PELEG-JOKTAN
THE HINDUS AND THE UIGHURS
THE ORIGIN OF THE CELESTIAL EMPIRE

IT IS IMPOSSIBLE to say how many realms the Hebrews brought into the fold of the Tree Cult during the 34,000 years that elapsed before the Cycle of P-el-e-g, 'the Philosophy of the Elohim, the Erythrean Gods,' evolved from that of Eber, 'the Colonizer.' Nevertheless the story of the grand events in the latter cycle are clearly told in *Genesis* 10, or X, comporting in its mathematical symbol with the circumference of the earth, and also with Plato's myth of the Ten Twins.

The physical circumstances to which the peoples of the earth were now subject are clear. More than the imperialism of the mythical King Belus of Egypt was possible. In a word by B.C. 749,000 the winter of J-or-h-o-r-g-u-mund, had abated to the point that despite the cold which had been followed by countless local floodings during the first interglacial period, it was possible for the Chi-chi-en-s and the Chi-el-a-s of God's House to come to the aid of mankind in both hemispheres, and for the Na-ba-the-ans to whom the name The-ba, common to Grecaland and Egypt, is to be traced.

According to *Genesis* 10 the grand task of setting apart the domains of the nations of the various gentes who had appeared in the two land masses of Libya and Atlas that were still connected by the Land of Is, logically was assigned to the Caucasian Danitics to whom King Belus had given Libya and Philistia in which the place name Atalla appears. Accordingly in *Genesis* 10 we read:

"By these were the isles of the Gentiles divided in their lands; every one after his tongue, after their families, in their nations."

All that is necessary to do to find a mathematical verification of this passage is to stick pins in the major centers of civilization of the present Europe including the British Isles, Ireland, and the relics of the Land of Is wherein R-i-g-ja-v-i-k or R-e-y-ja-vik, appears in Is-landa, to see their geodetic relations.

Eventually the great maps in stone called C-ro-m-lichs, 'the Celestial Roc, Moo, the Loti of the Chis,' were located in the ancient Hell all the way from the Rhine to the H-e-b-ri-d-e-s where the grand discussed swastika of C-ala-r-n-is-ch, appears in the ancient realm of the M-ana-x on L-e-w-e-s Island (62° 30′ N. 7° W.), due North of the holy shrine of T-ara in the county of Mona-g-h-ana. In the Irish Kingdom of Ar-ma-g-ha, also eventually the Hebrew Prophet Jeremiah in B.C. 587 would place the *Lia Fail,* or Stone of Destiny, upon which every British King has been crowned since Edward II pursuant to the agreement he reached with David Bruce, the alleged successor in Scotia of David, 'the Lion of Judah,' providing that the survivor of the two should govern both Scotland, and England and for the removal of the Lia Fail from E-din-burg, 'the din, or garden of the burg, or oracle of Scotia.'

Then it will be seen that the Mark, or domain of the Dan-s-k, to-day called Denmark, found the original seat of its culture at Co-p-en-ha-g-en, 'the Serpent of Peleg, the En Zu, Ha, the God of Wisdom' (56° N. 12° E.) marking exactly the meridian passing southward from Sval-bard through the area of O-s-l-o, the former Christianna, (58° N.) at the latitude Got-land in the Baltic (20° E.), Hel-sin-ki (25° E.) in F-in-land, Cronstadt (30° E.), the port of St. Petersburg (Leningrad), and the virtually unknown parts of Siberia. But also this holy shrine near which are the oracles of H-am-burg and Heidel-berg, 'the oracle of Hell,' marks the meridian of Swyz-land, Rome, and Tri-poli-t-ana in Libya where the Greeks erected U-t-i-ca, and the Phoenicians later started Carthage. And if the Temple of J-an-u-s on the Jan-i-cu-l-u-m, one of the Seven Hills of Rome, be examined, it will be seen that this four-way oriented arch which came to be the *Arch Triomphans* of the Romans, contains on its face 32 inches, corresponding to the basic symbol of the Sepher Y-e-t-zi-ra-h, and that it was erected out of the material of an older structure.

Of course G-ra-v-es-end was not sited at 51° 30' N. the basic meridian dividing the Eastern and Western Hemispheres, at the latitude of Newfoundland in the West, B-e-r-l-in, and W-ars-aw in the East, and on the antipodal meridian of W-r-angel Island at the North of Ka-ma-chat-ka, and of the present Midway Island in the Pacific, by mere accident. With the aid of the Italic alphabet it is a simple matter to interpret the original names of all the Irish Kingdoms, the provinces of Franconia, Iberia, Germany, Italy, and the original kingdoms of Grecaland. Moreover it is abundantly plain that to the Danitics among whom the Hebrews introduced the Tree Cult, trace both the Dracontia Cult of the Boreans and Druidism since these Druids whose name traces to Druvyd, 'the Oak,' above all else were noted as a secret order of selected scientists especially devoted to the study of the Zodiac and of geography.[1] Inasmuch as Libya and Atlas were still connected in the cycle of Peleg inevitably the same social concepts existed among the Siouans, Algonquians, Iroquoians, Muskhogeans, Caddo, Shoshoneans, and the various Pueblo groups of Arizona who traced their origin to the Serpent Cult of A-zi-t-land in the North, as among the Boreans of Europe and the Egyptians in the matter of gentes, fratres, clans, and tribes.[2]

Inevitably the Caucasian ancestors of the Hindus who had appeared in the Hindu Kush with which the Pamir at the north of Irania unites, or the Para-mi-shi-ra Range of Afghanistan through which the Pass of Ba-mi-ana near Ka-bul leads into Trans-Oxi-ana, would have inherited from the Kara all the knowledge possessed by those great surveyors of India in the cycle of Adam V.[3] And the same is true of the E-ski-moo descendants of the Kara.[4] In the latter we see the descendants of the mixed peoples who still moved around the Arctic Zone in both Hemispheres and to them are to be traced the Hakka and the Ski-di Pawnees of T-ex-as and their peculiar

knowledge of astronomy which enabled them as the founders of the so-called Pawnee Republic, to site the cities of their
domain with respect to the planets, just as the Muskogi also
located their cities.

Because of the affinity between the Caucasian ancestors of
the Hindus and the Hebrews, who also were Aryans, it is
stated in *Genesis* 10 that Peleg had a brother J-o-k-t-an, 'the
First, Brahma, the Kara, the Taux of Ana.' Also it is stated
that during the cycle of Peleg and Joktan, the whole earth was
divided, clearly indicating that at this time the several spiritual sees of the Danitics, the Chaldeans, the Hindus, and the
Mongoloids of the Sinitic realms in the East, came into being.
Thus, just as we see in the Hindus, the Hierarchs of Indra
whose forebears had brought the Naga and the Parsee of
Irania into the Aryan fold, in the Celestial Empire which
eventually fell under the domination of the Chinese, we see
the relic of the great Uighur Empire which evolved from a
union of the Caucasian Turanians, Mongolians, Manshu.

Before considering the Uighur, however, it is important
to note that Joktan is credited in *Genesis* with the following
progeny — Al-mo-da-d, She-l-e-ph, Ha-z-ar-ma-v-eth, Te-rah,
Ha-d-o-ram, U-z-al, D-i-k-la-h, O-b-al, A-b-i-ma-el, O-ph-i-r, Ha-
vi-la-h, and J-o-ba-b. Their domains were those beginning at
Me-sha, and "going to Se-pher, a Mountain in the East."

While there are two Me-shas, 'Heads of the Melas,' one at
the center of Arabia, and one at the center of the Dek-k-ana
of India, yet there is no Mount Sepher on any graph of Gea,
or mentioned in any gazetteer. The reference to it was made
in the present tense of the Mosaic Scribes, however, who also
knew that in their time God's House had come to be located
at La Ha Sa to which one would come by moving eastward
from Mesha in central Arabia, since Mesopotamia lay in the
Turkish province of El Ha Sa. The conclusion is that *Mount
Sepher* had reference to La Ha Sa where the *Sephervaim* was
enshrined just as at the City of *Sephervaim* in Chaldea near
the city of Si-p-para.

Of the twelve sons of Joktan, some occupied Sumer, and others occupied S-ind, which as a part of Ra-j-p-u-t-ana was included in the delta of the Indus in which Kara Chi appears. Thus again we find a verification of the statement in the *Ramayana* that the cult of the Naacals was conveyed to Chaldea, from which it would have been conveyed to Egypt by the peoples common to the Dek-k-ana of India, Chaldea, and the northern part of Ru-b (Arabia) in which the Philistim had settled. Accordingly the name applied to the land of Havileh referred to in *Genesis* as that of the Head of Pi-son, the red or spiritual sons, implying initiates of the mysteries inherited from the Python, or those established by Rameses II at Delhi, the eastern counterpart of Delphi, is the metathesis of Hel-i-vah implying that the philosophic vehicle of Pison originated in the terrestrial Hell whence had come the Naga ancestors of the Hindus. This was but another clever ruse of the Scribes who produced the scriptures ascribed to Moses to conceal the common origin of the Hebrews and Hindus and the source of their philosophic vehicles.

On the other hand it is obvious that the Hindus were now colonizing in Malaysia where Mount Ophir is found on the Equator in Su-ma-t-ra (100° E.) due south of the Abyss of Learning. Also the Grand Rajah (Mount D-o-e-s-sin), is found on the Equator in Borneo also due south of the Gobi, and on the antipodal meridian of "The Watcher" in Franconia Notch, and of Cuxco in Peru.

It appears that the Celestial Empire of historic times traces back to the Uighurs in whom Spiegel saw the original and only true Aryans. It must be fixed in mind that the vast Uighur Empire gradually extended its sway over Japan, Malaysia, and extending clear across Asia at the north of India, including the present Sin Kiang, Tibet, and Turkeystan, as well as the whole of Siberia, and eventually even into Russia. Thus arose the idea of a Turanian invasion of Europe. But this Empire implied nothing of empire in the political sense. It was a Celestial Empire in the sense of a spiritual see.[5] To the Uighurs and second to the Hindus are to be traced the worldwide system of symbolic mounds spreading over the earth from the center of civilization at the Abyss of Learning, and also the oldest symbol known to man called Swastika which has been shown to have migrated around the earth in both directions. Also it has been shown that its various forms constituted a series embodying the concepts of the Wisdom Philosophy with respect to the evolution of man.[6]

It is manifest, however, that the Tree Cult was imparted to the Uighurs as well as to the Hindus. For just as the Hebraic J appears in Raj-pu-t-ana, other place names in India, and in Java, the Hebraic T appears in the names born by the Tien Shian Range and the grand peaks of T-i-ri-ch Mir, and Khan T-en-g-ri, both symbolizing the Taux of the Rishi, Sh-ga-t-zi in Tibet, Yangtse Kiang, and Tien-sin, as well as in the name of the Sinitic Tzin who became T-i-en, 'The Taux of the Spirit, En Zu.'

So we see that although *Genesis* was designed as a history of the Hebrews, it solves many mysteries of the so-called Archaic Age, by peopling the whole earth with the spiritual teachers of God's House who, it is evident, originated the Tree Cult upon which Hebraism, as a successive advance in the evolution of the Wisdom Philosophy was bred.

---

[1] See the *Gallic Wars* by JULIUS CAESAR whose childhood tutor was the Druid Grypho, and who pointed out that the Druids were a peculiarly learned order and far more advanced in self-government than the Italics.

[2] See Topical Bibliography, the *Consanguinities and Affinities of the Human Race,* MORGAN (1871); *A Study in Parallel Culture,* MALLERY (1877); *The Heterogeneity of Language,* CARL HUMBOLDT (1820).

[3] E-ski-Moo, 'the Earth spirits of the Moon.'
S-k-i, 'the Serpents of the Kara, Indra.'

[4] H-in-d-oo, 'the Hierarchs of Indra, the Diva of Heaven and Earth.'
H-ind-u, 'the Hierarchs of Indra, Uratur.'

[5] U-i-g-h-ur, 'The Universal Spirit of God's House Uratur.'

[6] See Topical Bibliography, "Symbols," particularly the work of Wilson giving the American form of the Swastika which is the reverse of the eastern form.

CHAPTER XXX

HERCULES AND THE DRACONTIA CULT.
DRUIDISM. THE END OF THE CAINITES.
THE COSMIC DELUGE OF B.C. 36,000, AND THE
APPEARANCE OF THE PRESENT TYPE OF MAN.
THE WHITE SUB-RACE APPEARS.

THE GEOLOGIST Lyle was of the opinion that the peoples of
Kamachatka and Alaska were passing freely back and forth
between those parts in B.C. 300,000. Apparently the ancestors
of the Eskimo were still navigating the polar arctic zone, although the hiatus in *Genesis* makes it impossible to find more
guidance in that Ana in tracing the history of the so-called
Archaic Age, already it has furnished the chronology enabling
what followed the end of the cycles of Jacob and Joseph to
be understood.

The cave of Cro Magnon displaying the art of the Negroid
type of man still upon the earth when the picture of the bull
was limned by the denizens of this refuge from the cold, indicates quite plainly the implications of the Greek Hercules who
by the Jewish Prophet Cleodemus, cited by Josephus, declared
that Aphren had given his name to Africa and aided Hercules
to overthrow the giant An-t-e-n-or of Libya.[1] Moreover we
are not dependent upon Cleodemus and Josephus alone. Thus,
the Roman Scholar, Alexander Polyhistor, as the contemporary of Josephus, the younger Pliny, the Greek historian Ar-
rian, and the disciple of the Greek philosopher Epictetus, declared that Hercules married the daughter of Aphren.

If the Greek myths be examined with care it will be seen
that Hercules is merely the mythical eponym that was applied
by the myth-makers of Greece to the Danitics who had founded the Dracontia Cult in Hell during the cycle of Peleg-Joktan. It derives from 'Hera,' and the word *cu-les* implying the

Cusites or Cushites from whom the Danitic Greeks were descended as were all the Punics of the Mediterranean World, and who as a sub-race of the Lion Men produced the Cor or Hor of ancient Greece to whom Hermes-Trismagistus is to be traced. Thus in early Italic Hercules or Hera-clitus implied the glory of Hera,' or the light shed by the Dracontia Cult, and the pre-Celtic Druids in whose mystical rites both the bull and the tree played a large part. So the name of this champion of Hera whose name like Eve was derived from *ebba* implying the earthly mother, is well preserved through Europe.[1]

Because the concept of Hercules went far back to the cycle of the Serpent Cult before it was replaced in the Isles of Israel by the Hebrews with the Tree Cult, originally Hercules as the champion of Athena who was ever his aid, is depicted in ancient art garbed in the pure white gown, implying the reformers in the cycle of the Dahana, or the cycle of the 'ever widening light' associated with Ornyth and Athena, just as were Orphic reformers of a later day. Moreover, he is shown bearing the bow of Athena.

When, however, the alleged marriage of Hercules to Aphren's daughter took place, occurred the union of the Danitics of the present Europe and those of Africa in the realm of Libya which had been given to Danaeus by King Belus. When the Hebraic Tree Cult was introduced into Libya, Hercules discarded the bow and the white gown and replaced them with a great club as the symbol of the Tree Cult, and the skin of the Lion which he is described as having failed to slay, implying the descendants of the Fourth Root Race, or the Chus. Now by the Danitics were brought into the fold of the Aryans. In the same manner, when the Aryans overthrew the Python, and Hermes was replaced by Apollo, who with his twin sister Aphrodite said to have been born at the island of Delos in the Aegean, implying the founding of the Pythean mysteries. They were established at D-el-phi near Mount Parnassus and just north of Mycenae in Greece before the Gulf of Corinth came into being. The *cadaceus,* or two headed serpent wound round the staff of Hermes was replaced by a bough with two branches.

The Danitics of the Dracontia Cult not only fashioned their craft to resemble dragons and serpents but their sacred trees were so pruned as to form the sacred Hebdomad with three branches above four of which the lower ones were oriented to the points of the compass just as were those of the Mayas in Mexico, Yucatan, Guatemala, and Central America when the Spaniards arrived in those parts.[2] So large were they that within their trunks were temples. Thus again we have a suggestion of what was being taught by the Spiritual Twins of Plato in his mythical Kingdom of Atlas. Therefore we may assume that while the Danitics were endeavoring to civilize the smitten peoples of both Libya and the West they were sparing no effort to indoctrinate them with the principles of the Tree Cult which formed the basis of the common cult of Nana-bo-z-ha among the Indians of North America as well as among the peoples of the southern climes. So is accounted for the symbol of the tree cherished by the Oneida as the senior tribe of Iroquois, and the sanctity in which the poplar was held by the Siouans and other plains Indians, and the Y-u-c-ca by the Pueblo groups of Arizona.

Undoubtedly it was the teachers of the Dracontia Cult who applied the name L-ar-is-sa to the region of Thessaly in which stands Mount Olympus (40° N. 22° 30′ E.) just east of the region of Ya-nina or Ja-nina. This same name appears in many parts of Asia Minor, and at last when the Eighth Divine Dynasty of Chaldea was founded in B.C. 130,135, about 50,-000 years after the cycle of Joseph had expired, its capital was established at L-ar-is in Sumer instead of remaining at Si-p-para. Thus the influence which the Danitics of Ya-nina had come to exercise over the Assyrians of Nin-us-s or Nin-e-veh, marking exactly the latitude of An-t-i-och (36° N. 36° E.) just beyond which lay the island of R-ho-de-s on which the Pythean mysteries were established, and also the grand mountain Trinity of Karakorum at the north of India, is explained. Manifestly the Danitics of Libya were now co-operating with their kinsmen among the posterity of Ismael and Esau in Syria, Armenia and Arabia.[4]

Eventually among the descendants of Ismael, or the Osmanli Turks and the descendants of Esau, were united to form Islam, and among the descendants of Apher and Japhren would appear the Shi-ite, Sin-ite, and the Moorish sects of Moslems, to which trace the three Caliphates of Bagdad, the Abassid Caliphate of Mecca, and the Omayad Caliphate of Cordova in Spain. So it was that the Arabs possessed the vast wisdom handed down to them through the mysteries of the Kabira that made Cordova the most enlightened city in the world during its heydey when the Omayad Caliphate produced the great Jewish Kabalists as well as Averroēs, the most enlightened man of his age, and the associate of Saladin and Moses Maimonides who together with Averroēs, the Holy Moor, as the first exponent of universal peace induced Richard Coeur de Lion to enter into a pact with Saladin providing for his withdrawal from Palestine. It was Averroēs who gave to St. Francis of Assisi the inspiration of his effort as founder of the Franciscan order to establish peace in the warring world.

We have already seen the two geodetic Chi which the Uighurs and the Danitics had surveyed. When the Neolithic Age began America, of course, was well known to them both. Thus a study of the terrestrial sphere will show that a great circle passing from X-o-chi in Mexico with a bearing N. 36° E. will pass through Newcastle in England, Prague in Czechoslovakia, Buda-pe-s-t in Hungary, Bu-ch-a-r-e-s-t in Rumania, Ankara in Turkey, Ham-ma-m in Syria, Muskat in Saudi Arabia, Danger Island in the Ch-agos Archipelago, Ma-c-que-r-i-e Island about 300 miles to the southeast, and to O-en-o Island in the Tu-a-mo-t-u Archipelago. Another great circle passing from X-o-chi with a bearing N. 41° W., will pass through Mo-i-oka and Na-ga-sa-ki in Japan, W-en-ch-ow in Japan and Hong Kong in Chi-na, Sa-i-gon in Indo Chi-na, Georgetown in the Malaya

States, and Sin-g-k-ii Meer in Su-ma-t-ra.⁵ So are explained the Ma-n-x, or M-ana-chi, and the Cross of St. Andrew or the X, appearing in the Island of Manx and O-x-ford, as distinguished from the True Cross or the T appearing in Tara, Tree Island in the Irish Sea, and the Irish Cross of Cong.

Inasmuch as the whole world was closely connected by these two circles as well as by the True Cross and the two Chi, inevitably Darwin found that in 100,000 B.C. a civilization of high development existed in the Pacific Continents, and after visiting the Caribbeans, Mexico, Brazil, Peru, and Central Asia, Alexander Humboldt pointed out that a civilization existed in the Galapagos Islands west of Peru, certainly in B.C. 80,000, and probably long before.⁶ Nor is it to be doubted that the Cainites who had been exiled to Daitya had exerted a profound influence on this civilization when in B.C. 94,195 the Eighth Divine Dynasty of Chaldea of Ardates was founded with its capital in La-r-is-sa.⁷

It was during this dynasty, or about B.C. 70,000, according to the Hindus, that at last the island of Daitya, to which the Cainites had been banished near two and a half million years before, vanished beneath the waves with its evil freight, thenceforth being known as the Land of NOD. Nevertheless the blood of Cain would remain in thousands of the Polynesians.

In view of the relatively small number of Israelites in Egypt it was inevitable that the character of these originally hardy peoples should have been profoundly altered by the wealth they had acquired in the lush land of the Nile where no others from abroad have ever retained their moral stamina.⁸ Certain it is that mankind generally had begun to fall into degeneracy again, notwithstanding the efforts of the Danitics when in B.C. 63,035 the Tenth Divine Dynasty, or that of X-i-s-su-t-h-ru-s, was founded at Babel, bearing a name indicating very clearly a great confusion of peoples and ideologies.

In it appears not only that of the Aryan Chi, but that of the Moon God Sin.⁹

The seating of the Tenth Divine Dynasty at Ba-bel which eventually came to be called B-a-b-y-lon, 'Bel, Ark of Brahma, the Ya, the logus of the Nether Serpent,' interpreted by the Greeks as 'the Gate of the God,' indicates far more, however, than Danitic influence. We have seen that the mythical King Belus of Egypt gave to the twin brother of Aegyptus the realm of Arabia. Undoubtedly already had occurred the perversion of the Chaldean Anu and Anuit into the Assyrian Bel, deemed the creator of the earth and man, and his consort Bel-i-t, who was said to be the creator of the great gods. Plainly the posterity of Ismael and Esau in Arabia, as the allies of the Egyptians who had enshrined the god B-u-ba-s-t-e-s in the delta of Misraim, were reasserting the control of the mythical King Bel-us and Nimrod, representing the Chus, over Sumer where still Sin was worshipped at Ur or Mugaya as the Moon God.

"Man, know thyself," was a maxim of the Hindus, hoary with age before it found expression in the Hebrew proverbs. That was exactly what the peoples of the so-called Old World were incapable of doing.

In the situation described a new cosmic deluge was necessary in order to bring into being a new type of man. So it is now agreed that the present type of man sprung from the Caucasians, came into being during a great flood in Chaldea fixed by some scholars at B.C. 36,000.[10]

The names *paleolithic, megolithic* and *neolithic* applied to the successive stages of culture, are purely arbitrary terms, just as are the *Old Middle* and *Stone* Ages; and the *Stone, Copper* and *Iron* Ages of which some scholars conceive. With our reference to periods definable in solar years, they merely imply types of culture. The most science can do is to indicate that in a particular period the characteristic of culture was of one type or an earlier one. Thus to-day there are savages in the Old Stone Age, actually trading and doing business with others of the most advanced culture known to man. It is impossible to illustrate this better than referring to the case of Australia and Ceylon where the Pi-sha-cha from their jungles behold the motor trucks and the airplanes of those who have invaded their realm.

What is taking place today in the Arctic Zone and in the Green Hell of Brazil, has been going on down the ages. Different cultures have existed side by side. In the parts mentioned not only do those we call mere savages suddenly find themselves using such words as *tobacco* and witnessing *the movies* imported to them,[11] but the importers of names to the savages borrow words from the savages. Consequently in the slang of the west a Gook has a special implication.[12] One who visits Oregon, Nevada, and Northern California will find there the relics of numerous once-large boom towns. The ghost towns of the Gold Rush came into being overnight just as did those in Kentucky, and in the Northwest and the Southwest territories following the Revolution. Today sheep and cattle graze among their ruins. Wagon loads of bricks and stones are constantly hauled off to neighboring ranches to build chimneys and foundations. What can an archaeologist tell a thousand years hence about a fine ranch house built of the materials from a Ghost Town, and what remains of the latter?

Obviously, therefore, there are limitations upon archaeology as well as upon cephalic indices. When, however, the symbolism of a structure, its name, and its geodetic symbols all accord, as in the case of the Neolithic ruins tradition ascribes to the Cyclopes, we are on more or less firm ground. We may safely conclude that the site of the structure was originally one of a sacred tree even though we may not say with certainty when the present structure was reared.

But this is certain. The so-called Neolithic Age had begun when the modern type of man was produced by the cosmic deluge described in the Chaldean and Assyrian tablets as the deluge of Ha-si-a-t-ra, and X-is-su-t-h-ru-s, respectively, wherein the hero of these myths was made to employ a role identical with that of Noeas, and of Manu in one of the younger deluge myths. It was at Mount Ni-s-s-ar in the Pa-mir, or Para-shi-mi-ra Range known to the Hindus as the Hindus Kush, that Xisusthans is shown landing in an Ark.

We may assume that it was now that the men and women said to have been produced by Deucalion and Pyr-ra who had landed in an ark at Para-na-s-sus (37° 30′ N. 22° 30′ E.) due south of Mount Olympus in Thessaly, representing the solar cult of Helios, and the old cult of Athena, appeared in Greece. And here is to be noted the magic appearing in the geodetic symbols of Para-na-s-sus yields $3 + 7 + 3 + 0 = 13$, in which appears the Dekkad 10 of the Sepheroth, and 3, implying the Divine Lotus, while 1-3 implies the upper triad of mortality. This suggests that the Pythean Mysteries already had been established at D-el-phi close to Para-na-s-sus.

The Phoenicians insisted that their great Neolithic cities such as Tyre, Sidon and Baal-b-e-c had appeared by B.C. 30,-000. Accordingly Baal-bec has ever been ascribed to the Greek god Helios of this period who derived his name from the Hellenes.

Only recently a Rumanian Archaeological expedition reported finding the evidence of a great conflict that raged there about 25,000 years ago between the Old Stone Age Men and the Sun Men who were identified with the Heliocentric civilization which had appeared by that time in Bharata-sa-va-r-sa at the north of the Dek-k-ana of India, while the Maharajah of Udipoor traces his descent back to B.C. 30,000 in the age of Rama Balarama. Moreover, even the ultra conservative, Hřdlicka, as Curator of the United States National Museum, admitted just before his death (1942), that the present type of man had come into being by B.C. 30,000.

Exactly when the white Hellenes described by Plato as the noblest race that had ever appeared on the earth, evolved from the posterity of Deucalion and Pyr-r-a who had landed in the Ark of the Cross on Mount Para-na-s-sus, can not be said. Nor is it of vital import. Ever said by anthropologists to have evolved originally in the area of the White Sea, eventually the white sub-race of the Fifth Root Race appeared in Ireland.

The Aryan T-u-a-ha-ti-da Daanan are deemed the first of the new sub-race to appear there with a name indicating quite clearly the connection of the Irish with the Scandinavian Danitics. In all probability about the same time the new type of Caucasians who came to be called Brahmans in Bharatasavarsa appeared in that part.

The important thing to note is that from the first Mont Blanc near the Young Frau of the Alps was deemed a natural symbol of the innate right of the White Man to rule Libya, and that from his appearance the Negroid predecessors of the White Hellenes who did not migrate from Libya, or were not absorbed, were doomed. For so enamored was Zeus with the charming nymph Io whose name appears in Io-Sin-Fa Zembla, that Hera is said to have fallen into a fit of jealousy, and to have changed her husband's enamorata into a white heifer. This myth, of course, explains the whitish Ionians who deemed Europa the daughter of Phenix.

The mythical Cyclopes of Greek mythology associated with the Neolithic age implied nothing of blood, merely implying the magic reflected in the type of architecture which appeared on the earth in the Heliocentric age of culture common to India, the South Pacific, Syria, Greece, Libya, as a whole. Of this type monument the characteristic was the circle called *pillar,* or *tello,* and also designated as the co-in 'the serpent of Indra,' to which traces the word coin. To it traces the name *Coremus.*

The vast knowledge preserved in the mysteries is shown by the fact that the circular mounds, or *co-ins,* erected by the initiates all over the world, possessed the form of the fossils found at altitudes of 15,000 feet above the sea level which from the Pyrenees to Japan, called Nummulites today are assigned to the eocene epoch of the Tertiary.

Consisting of two fine tabulated nummulitic lamellae, or discordal shells, they display in their tabulation the spiral principle involved in the earliest form of marine life, to which corresponds exactly the basic concept of the Wisdom Philosophy. While the Numismatic Science, or that of coins, derived its name from the Nummulite also in the medical science, *nummula* is the name applied to the sputum or expectoration which flattens upon the ground like the circular shell. Accordingly it was the spiral principal of life that was taught by the spiritual teachers of the Dra-con-t-ia Cult as well as by the Aryan Uighurs. Thus the science of Numbers owes its name to N-u-ma, 'the Nether of the mother Ana,' of which the nummulite was deemed a symbol. So the L-u-si-t-anna-ia designated their ancient shrine as Nu-m-an-t-ia which is still to be seen on the D-u-ro near the modern S-o-r-i-a originally called Ara-va-ci.[13]

Humboldt was of the opinion that while peoples from the Pacific contributed to the population of South America, the Uighurs were in Portugal in B.C. 22,000. This indicates that some of the Uighurs were passing into Libya as well as into the Pacific Continent, and into the present Western Hemisphere.

The presence of the Uighurs in Portugal, of course, would explain the devotion of the Lusitani to the Wisdom Philosophy, and their early hostility to the Latin Church.[14] To them is to be traced the Neolithic dolmens of Portugal marking exactly the meridians of Britain and Ireland, as did the cities of Cadiz, Lisbon, Numantia, Seville, Toledo, Madrid, and Burgos. Moreover, among the prehistoric works of the Iberian Druids, are found unique subterranean temples, circular in form with an aperture at the summit, and spiral staircases descending into them, symbolizing the Nu-ma.[15]

By B.C. 22,000 the influence which the Mongoloid Uighurs had exerted upon Ru-s-k-o-i, Ru-sa-ya, or Ru-s-sia, had become so marked that in that realm had appeared the Eurasians called Mu-k-o-vi-t-es whose holy man, the T-sa-r, or C-z-ar eventually was symbolized by the two-headed eagle, corresponding to the two heads of Janus facing east and west respectively.[16] Because of the worldwide spiritual influence of the Cross, the Eths who preserved the name of Ethiopia, have been identified with the Ba-ski of the Pyrenees. The presence of the Uighurs west of the Urals shortly gave rise to the erroneous idea of a Turanian invasion of Europe.[17]

In view of the identities between the Iberians, E-t-ru-ska, the Eths, the Rus-koi, and the Sa-b-in-e ancestors of the Romans, it is highly probable that the first temple of Janus already had been erected by the Uighurs from Rumel in Russia in the Italic Rumel on the Janiculum with the material employed to build the present Arch Triomphans displaying above the portals the two-headed Janus. On its face are 32 vacant niches corresponding to the mystical number 32 of the Sepher Yetzira. Undoubtedly those niches represented the vanished peoples of Lemuria.

It is especially significant that eventually in this four-way oriented arch, corresponding to the similar arch upon which the so-called Hanging Garden of Nineveh was planted to symbolize the Garden of Eden, appears the Greek Poseidon, or the Italic Neptune, driving a spike team of Delphin. In addition to this the Janiculum became the Mint of Rome, displaying over its portals a superb tri-reme with full sails set for the golden West.[18] Surely in this there was a reminiscence of the past.

Obviously Humboldt had received historical guidance in Central Asia just as Sir William Jones, Ambassador to India had done, when in 1794 he called attention of the Western World to the ancient symbols in that part, and urged a rewriting of history. Subsequent explorations in Siberia and Mongolia have brought to light many facts about the so-called antediluvians. Thus, even before a mission of Jesuits undertook to explore the Gobi, Kosloff, Idriantseff, and other Russian archaeologists had exhumed at Ka-ra-korum, or Chara Chota just northeast of the Abyss of Learning, Maya symbols including those belonging to the series of the Swastika, long erroneously ascribed to a people of that name in Tibet, and also to the so-called J-an-s of that part, or the red men of the H-i-ma-la-ya. Perhaps the dinosaurian eggs buried with these Maya symbols had been collected by the Uighurs as natural symbols of the origin of man. Be that as it may, they had been so perfectly preserved beneath fifty feet of sand, that it was possible to find in them the unhatched reptilians of the Secondary.

On the other hand the many remains of the so-called Dune Men carried back by common consent to B.C. 20,000 or earlier, were no longer giants. With pygmies still inhabiting the Alps of Libya, as well as Uganda, the Andaman and other islands in the Indian Ocean, Easter Island, or the Grand Rapa, and the Mu-s-quito coast of Ni-ca-ra-gua, Dune Men appear to be like normal man to-day notwithstanding the giants still in Mongolia and northern Japan. It is equally clear from the great complex of mounds, many of which were of mathematical form, spreading over Mongolia and Manchuria, that already the Red-brown M-an-ch-u beyond the Ya-l-u with whom the Ta-t-ars had mixed to form the Tartars of the Uighur Empire, had become the dominant race in Eastern Asia. Nor do the symbols of the mythical Mount Meru of the Hindus, or the Abyss of Learning, leave any doubt as to the philosophy of God's House at this time, and that already the Uighurs had overrun Japan, as well as Malaysia, Melanesia, and Oceanica. Thus included in the series of the S-w-a-s-t-i-ka, in fact tracing back to the septenary philosophy of K-ara, 'Kings of the Aryans,' were the following progressive forms, which, to repeat, like the mounds, radiating from the Gobi have been traced around *the earth in both* directions.[19]

In these are to be seen the evolution of the man from the germ of matter in the ovum to the material man represented by the $+$ symbolizing the cross purposes of the spiritual being or Higher Self, and the material being or Lower Self, combined in every mortal frame.

In addition to these are found the $+$ a characteristic Fifth Root Race symbol of the Egyptians representing the descent of material man from No to the Nether, just as described in the *Rig Veda* and in the Hebraic Kabala of Lucifer.

Also there were two symbols indicating as here shown the

apparent movement of the Sun around the ecliptic as it is viewed from the Northern and Southern Zones, respectively.

The second of these two un-discussed *swastikas* is known to Science as the American form because it appeared first in the southern climes where American civilization first evolved to a high plane.

THE SYMBOL OF THE SWASTIKA

Philosophical Interpretation of its Progressive Forms

I. ○ The Infinitude of Space or the Cosmos.

II. ⊙ The Germ of Cosmic Matter.

III. ⊖ Man on the plane of Uninspirited Matter.

IV. ⦶ Inspirited Matter.

V. ⊕ The Archtype of Inspirited Man.

VI. ✝ The Inspirited, fully sexed Man.

VII. ♀ The Egyptian form symbolizing the present Fifth Root Race with the *ankh* representing the spirit of God upon the waters of the Earth (liberated from the Moon, the Mother of Mortality).

VIII. 卐 Displaying by the undiscussed swastika the apparent movement of the sun as viewed from the north of the ecliptic where man first appeared on the earth.

IX. 卍 Displaying by the undiscussed swastika the apparent movement of the sun as viewed by man from parts of the earth south of the ecliptic, known as the American form.

(See *The Swastika. the Earliest Known Symbol and Its Migrations,* WILSON [1898], United States National Museum. Also the *Secret Doctrine,* BLAVATSKY [1886], for Occult interpretation denying the alleged phallic basis of the symbol.)

Of course it is to the Uighurs that the great triangular mound upon which Na-ga-sa-ki stands is to be traced, and also the triangular mounds in the region of Chung King due south of Cha-ra-Chota or Ka-ru-ko-rum in the Gobi.

In the American Swastika, of course, is found an explanation of the so-called Ha-t-an-Ru-na civilization of Peru which modern research indicates preceded that of the so-called first In-c-a and has been shown to have been of Heliocentic type associated by the Naguals or Serpent people. From them the Zuni and other Pueblo groups claim descent. Symbolized by the serpent bird they called the Nuhuatl to which traces back the concept of the mythical Seven Cities of C-i-bo-la implying the septenary mysteries of the Maya.

In *Nu-huatl,* however, is to be seen a combination of *No,* or the Nether, and of *huatl,* woman, a name appearing all over Ana-huac, together implying 'the Mother of Heaven,' just as *hu-ac* implies 'the Heavenly Twins, the Light,' to which traces the Peruvian concept of Mamma Sin-ya-cu as the mother of the first In-c-a, 'Indra, the Celestial Twin,' to whom the ancestors of the Arya-Maya peoples called *Armaya* still inhabiting the region of Lake Ti-ti-ca-ca, gave the name M-an-c-o C-o-p-ac.[20] In short, the word *huatl* had exactly the same implication as the Greek Atalanta, the alleged beautiful woman of Ho-as Atlanta said to have been the wife of Ares, 'the God of War.'

From all this it seems increasingly obvious what Plato's Twins implied. As we shall see later already had evolved the fifth pair of Twins—Gaderius and Diaprepes, representing the Atlantean mysteries in the cycle of the Neolithic Age, characterized by the philosophy of the Hellenic God Helios.

Knowing that it was the Uighurs together with the Danitics of Libya who had surveyed the geodetic Chi of America, safely we may conclude that without regard to the Neolithic Monuments which appeared in Mexico and Peru. To them is to be ascribed not only the great mound upon which eventually the Hall of Wisdom was reared at Te-o-hu-ana-co on Lake Ti-ti-ca-ca, but the grand Temple of the Sun, or T-e-hu-ana-ta-sa-ya, to be seen at Cu-x-co which makes all the Neolithic Monuments of Europe and Asia, and Africa, sink into insignificance.

It was the mythical Cyclopes who also produced the Co-r-ydean ancestors of the Corinthians, as well as the British who held Corenus, an older God than Pytheas to be the brother of Python. Thus it is manifest that the civilization of the mysterious Manx, or M-ana-chi, who in fact disappeared like the ancestors of the Welsh Cimbrians of Cor-n-w-all, 'Corenus, the Nether Wombman, the Ark of Hell,' by process of evolution, leaving the white Tu-a-ha-t-i Da-ana-n as their successors, just as the white Hellenes evolved out of the progeny of Deu-ca-lion and Pyr-ra, and the whitish Ionians out of the Danitics of Sa-mo-th-ra-x and eventually came to occupy Mo-e-sia where they founded the T-ro-ja with H-is-ar-l-i-k, as center of its culture.[21]

Monuments, to repeat, are expressions of reminiscences. This is manifestly true of the Cromlechs of Scandinavia, Germany, the Netherlands, Britain, and the Hebrides, irrespective of when the stone markers were erected at them.[22]

The most enlightening of these works is found at C-all-e-r-n-is-h (57° 30′ N. 7° W.) on Le-w-is Island marking the meridian of Tara in Ireland, and the Island of the Faro (62° N.), a relic of the Land of Is. Consisting of a huge circle with a Taux formed by the elevated stones marking the axes, the meridian corresponding to its vertical arm passes from the North Pole through Scalp Mountain at the summit, and through Tara and Cork at the south west of Ireland. Leaving Iberia it then passes through the Atlas Range of Morocco to the northern Gold Coast of Africa just to the east of the Ca-na-ra Islands (30° N.), and southward through S-en-a-ga-la to the Ivory Coast on which is the realm of Si-er-ra Leon out of which the present Liberia was formed.

This great stone map also stands at the latitude of the S-ka-g-ge-ra-k beyond which lies Got-borg (12° E.). Inasmuch as Got-borg marks the meridian of Co-p-en-hagen, Rome (42° N. 12° E.), and Tri-poli (31° 30′ N.), the origin of the name Cro Ma-g-n-on applied to the region in the province of Indra in Franconia, where the remains of the Cave Men were found, seems obvious.

On the same circle as Gote-burg stands the Gulf of R-i-g-a in which lies the Island of Go-t-land in the Bal-t-ic from which access to the Atlantic was had by the Hellions of Finland, White Russia, Poland, Prussia, and Copenhagen, through the Ka-t-e-g-a-t.

This same circle, however, passes westward to Novaya Scoti. The route from Dan-t-zi-g to C-ana-da, therefore, is clearly marked by the Cromlech of Ca-el-e-r-n-is-ch just as by the Cromlech at A-v-bury also constituting a stone map of the route both to the Baltic and to the Medi-Terre.[23]

The Cromlech of Stone H-en-g-e stands on Sa-l-is-bury plain in Britain about eight miles from the grand height of Sa-ru-m (51° 4' N., 10° 48' W.). Consisting of two concentric circles formed by upright monolithic shafts or menhirs, it enclosed two elliptical spaces and is, of course, another pillar of Hercules.

Close to it is a race course to which may be traced the traditional love of the British for horseflesh and racing.[24]

Certain too it is that each and every one of the cromlechs was cited pursuant to the geodetic grid as was the Piran Round (50° 10' N. 5° W.) which stood at approximately 5° W. on the meridian of the Pillars of Hercules (5° W. 36° N.) and the circle of Astra-Khan (50° N. 50° E.) near which is S-amar-ra on the Volga.

It is a notable fact, that no one yet has ever advanced the proof whence came the monoliths in the Cromlech of Stonehenge.

To be sure the huge stones in the cromlechs might have been conveyed on barges from the place where they were quarried. Yet, there were but two ways they could have been placed. One was by rollers as in the case of the pyramids of Gizeh to which the huge blocks were conveyed from the quarry east of the Nile. The other was by sledding with the aid of oxen. The fact that the quarries whence came the monoliths have never been located suggests that they were placed before the British Isles assumed their present form in B.C. 10,000.[25]

All this was obviously known to the eponymous **Pytheas** of Ma-sa-l-en-s-is, or the Phoceans who had established the Pythean mysteries in Ma-sa-l-en-s-is 350 years before northern Scotland was accurately surveyed by Pytheas in B.C. 250, and it may well be that the Phoceans constituted one of the original *Two Brothers* to whom the youngest of the 7 Linguist families, and the smallest, or the I-ra-nak hoiw called Iroquois by the French, and "Adders" by their Algonquian neighbors, inasmuch as they had their origin in La-bra-dor and were of the Druidic Tree Cult. Also, inasmuch as red men from the west were visiting Germany at this time, it seems entirely likely that the Greeks knew of "the Watcher" long before the time of Plutarch who declared that the Arcadian Greeks had been maintaining for some time a colony beyond Ogygia (Greenland) at the latitude of the Caspian among some islands, clearly suggesting Newfoundland.

Be that as it may, the Cromlechs of Britain pointed straight to Que-bec and "the Watcher," and to repeat, the fact that the monoliths may not have been set up until later, does not mean that there were no earlier markers at their sites. In the latter we find conclusive evidence that both the Kara and the Uighurs were familiar with the entire earth.

---

[1] *Etruskan*: Hercle   *Old High German*: Herrold
Old French: Heraldt   *Danish*: Harald, Harold, Hurold
Middle English: Herod   *Icelandic*: Huer.

[2] Alexander Humboldt found a Dracontia Tree in the Canary Islands said by him to be 2,000 years old, like some of the Yew trees of the pre-Celtic Druids of Ireland and Scotland, and some of the olive trees in Greece, Italy, and Asia Minor.

[3] La-ri-sa, 'Atlantic, the Rishi, Sa.'

[4] Amen-i-p-si-m-us, 'Armenia, the Spirit of the Phenix, Sin, the Melus, the Chus.' This fully explains the claim eventually laid by the Turks to the Balkans.

[5] As determined by the author by the United States Coast and Geodetic Survey (March, 1953).

[6] See Works of Darwin and Wallace. See evidence collected in *The Lost Continent of Mu*, CHURCHWARD (1932).

[7] Back to this Dynasty traces the empire of Mithradates of the Pomtus in Roman times in which Mithras was represented by the Secret Cult of Mithras as a crusader against the Bull. It was in the secret temples of the Mithraists that prisms were used to cast the Tau before the altars of the sun by day, and

the altars of the moon by night. To Mithraism the army of Pompey succumbed and imported it back to Italy whence it spread all over Gaul. In Rome even before the Christians found a refuge in the catacombs they had been employed by the Mithraists who down to A. D. 250 were the most potent obstacle to Christianity. Nevertheless, Mithraism exerted a profound effect upon the council of Nicaea that formulated the Christian doctrines, and did much to prepare the way for Christianity.

8 The Assyrians, Persians, Shepherds, the People of the Sea, the Greeks, Romans, Vandals, Turkish Mamalukes, Arabs, each in turn would there succumb to weakness. The exposés of the recently deposed King Fuad are but a repetition of what has occurred over and over.

9 X-is-su-t-h-ru-s, "the Chim Ishtar, Sumer, the Taux, Ru-Sin."

10 *Records of the Past,* SAYCE (1888-91). *Races of Men,* HUNTINGTON (1925). *The Origin of the Aryans,* TAYLOR (1880).

11 The psychology factor involved in this is important. Recently the writer spent several evenings conversing with groups of students from Siam, different parts of the Philippines, and Turkey, trying to discover the reactions in their minds from the American movies the masses in their countries are beholding. He concluded that the Westerns and Gang Buster type of picture were having a most unfortunate influence upon such minds.

12 In weaving their fine theories about the evolution of the Anglo-Saxon tongue modern scientists forget that for 1,000 years the British, Scotch, and Irish overran France; that down to the time of Henry VII the nobility employed the Norman tongue. Thousands of soldiers returned to the British Isles speaking French. They forget the invasions of the Jutes, Saxons, and Normans, that the Angles were not in fact a race, but were the spiritual teachers of the Saxons who when they formed the Seven Kingdoms of Great Britain spoke a language similar to the Italics in its symbology, and plainly akin to the ancient Quenban of Scandinavia.

13 To the Druids who brought the science of geography and numbers to a high development also is to be ascribed the name applied to Numentor, the mythical grandfather of Romulus and Remus, and also to Numa Pompilius (715-672 B. C.), the second king of Rome as well as to Marcus Aurelius Numerianus, the great Stoic emperor who in 283 A. D. ruled the Roman Empire with his brother Carinus and like the latter reflected the Wisdom Philosophy of Apollo and the British Corenus in the age when the secret brotherhood of the Persian Mithra were dominating Rome just before Constantinius invaded Britain and fell at York (293 A. D.) leaving his son Constantine as Augustus. To the Numna also traces the name Numidia applied by the early Romans to the Barbary states.

Hence, it is particularly interesting to note that the first coin of the Iberians, or the peso, displayed the pillars of Hercules showing exactly how those important geographical points derived their name. The peso among the British Druids became the A-t-h-aler. Thus bank clerks today are called Tellers. In time the word dollar evolved from the word dol-ma-n, implying a pillar, or T-ello inasmuch as the Druidic dolmens consisted of crude circular co-ins resting upon vertical monoliths called men-hirs, symbolizing the *herrs* or heralds of the Pythean mysteries.

14 In the age of Sulla, Marius, and Caesar they revolted under the Roman Governor Sertorius not alone because they would not accept the stoicism which had been established as the state religion of the Roman Republic under Pontifax Maximus. The Lusitani knew perfectly well of the Western Hemisphere which they called the Land of Antillia. The Lu-si-t-ani traces back to Lud, an Iberite.

15 The name Dol-men, "Dollar Men," or builders of the coins, is synonymous with *Cromlech*. See *Man Before Metals*, JOLY.

16 T-z-a-r, "the Taux, the Ark of Ru."

C-z-a-r, "Cronus, the Z of the Ark of Ru."

Mu-s-ko-v-y, "Mu, Sin, Kronus, Varaha, Ya."

17 Winchell.

18 It was because of the enduring influence of the Uighurs as the champions of the Aryan Ark, upon Russian thought, that the Latin Church was never able, despite the most serious efforts, to bring the Patriarchy of Russia into its fold, even after the Medici undertook to finance the first Tsar, Ivan "the Terrible" (1547).

19 S-w-a-s-t-i-ka, 'Sa, Twins, Ark, Symb, Taux, Spirit of the Kara.'

20 In Ti-ti-ca-ca we see the two Taux symbolizing the mixture of Sinitics and Aryans in the region lying immediately south of Sha-ka-co-n-ia, or Mount Washington, while Manco Copac, ordinarily interpreted as the Ever-widening Circle,' is derived as follows: M-an-c-o, 'Maia, Ana, the Celestial Sphere'; C-o-p-ac, 'the Celestial Sphere, the Philosophy of Light.' Moreover in the O we see the symbol of Ornyth, or the Greek Athena. Thus, C-u-x-c-o where the first Inca is said to have thrust his Golden Wand into the soil, implies 'the Celestial Twins, the Chi, the Celestial Sphere.'

21 At Hisarlick in which is preserved the name of Ha-si-at-ra, the hero of the cosmic deluge that had brought the present type of man into being, Schliemann found seven strata of culture corresponding to the culture of Argos in Greece. It was in Argos that the great civilization of the Danae called Argives by Homer, evolved in the age of the mythical Cyclopes, to whom the The-ba of both Greece and Egypt is clearly traceable.

22 C-rom-l-e-ch, "Corenus, Roma, Itala, the Earth of the Chi."

23 The Piran Round in Devon near Land's End, preserving the name as Pi-sa-no in Peru, Pi-sa-no and Pi-sa in Italy, Pi-sa at the Golden Horn, and Pi-ra-n in the Pa-mir still constituted in the time of Shakespeare and Raleigh the stage on which the Cornish mysteries which had been enshrined in Fingal's Cave, were enacted.

24 Personally examined by the writer in 1926.

25 After studying the Pyramids during five months in Egypt in 1906, the writer demonstrated the manner in which they were erected. When the volume of stone required for the finished structure had been calculated, the tier was laid with rollers from the quarry east of the Nile to the sites of the pyramids. On this another tier was formed requiring each stone to be raised only about 36" before being rolled into place. When the ramp thus formed came to contain all the stones necessary for the finished structure, the tail of the ramp was used up by rolling forward the stones into place. Each stone was numbered at the quarry so as to be properly placed in its ultimate tier. Thus, no stone ever had to be lifted by a derrick more than 36" at one time as the pyramid came into form by consuming the ramp.

Chapter XXXI

THE CIRCLE OF MYCENAE
AND THE PALACE OF KNOSSUS

Gold The True Magnetic North.
The Library Temple of Nippur.
The Glory of Chaldea.

WHAT WAS TAKING PLACE in Egypt and Asia Minor while the Red man was being transferred to North America, and while Gi-t-che Man-i-to was striving to pacify the peoples of the Greek Continent of Atlas, is clearly revealed by Geodesy.

In the Greek realm of Argos presently within the P-el-op-p-o-n-essus in the name of which is preserved that of the mythic Pelops, the god Ops, and the peaceful Euseues in combination, we find just at the south of the Gulf of Corinth which owes its name to the Punic Cor represented by the British Corenus, the alleged brother of Python, from whom the Corydeans, or gigantic ancestors of the Cimbrians of *Insuliae Britannicae* took their name, the city of Mycenae just as we find My-k-en-a in Crete.

There at 37° 36′ N. 22° 30′ E., displaying the magic of Trismagistus in its geodetic symbols, due south of Mount Olympus, Mount P-ar-ana-s-sus, close to D-el-phi in the realm of Ph-o-c-is, and not far from T-he-ba preserving as did Thessa-ly the name of the biblical Tiras and the mythical Theseus, stands the colossal Circle of Mycen with the Lion Gate as its adit displaying the two lions rampant and the inscription relative to Mizr. It was the discoveries of Schliemann in Ilios or the Troja in M-o-e-si and in the Peloponessus that compelled the carrying back of the so-called Mycenaean Age beyond the dates of which Winckelman, the founder of the Science of Archaeology, had conceived. In short he found at H-is-ar-li-k on the D-ar-dan-elles where once the presently submerged Hell-es-pont, or bridge of the Euseues from Hell, connected Thrace with Asia Minor, seven strata of culture.

Ever ascribed to the Cyclopes and erected of huge monolithic blocks the circle measuring 80' in diameter, an obvious symbol of the Moon, and of Ornyth, 'the Bird of Heaven,' not only marks the meridian of Spitz Berge, O-l-y-p-us in Thessaly, and P-ar-ana-s-sus where the mythical Deuca-lion and Pyr-ra, the putative ancestors of the Hellenes had landed in the Ark of the Cross, but the latitudinal circle passing through Ash-ka-b-a-d (58° E.) in the Kara Kum; T-a-b-ri-z (in the Caucasus); and the sacred isle of Chi-o-s presently in the Aegean; and S-e-v-illa (6° E.) in the western Iberia where numerous dolmens of the nummulite type mark the meridians passing through the British isles and Ireland.[1]

A circle described with a radius of 40° with its center at My-cen, will pass through the area of old Merv in the Kara Kum, the Ridge of Ten-e-rif-fe (170° W.) beyond the Ma-d-e-i-ra Islands, and close to the hypothetical Mount Atlas (40° N. 30° W.), at the north through Tu-r-ku and Hel-sin-ki in Finland; and at the south through Nigeria (17° 30' S.). Thus it will include most of Libya, all of Syria, and much of the richest gold field in the world in Africa.[2]

For many years the attempt was made to explain the immense amount of gold possessed by the ancient Irish by ascribing it to the sands of Is-la-y. The Swedish anthropologist Montelius, however, exploded this theory by showing that in the Neolithic age there was more gold of non-native origin in Ireland and Scandinavia than in any other parts of the Eastern Hemisphere, and that in Scandinavia there was also non-native silver, or the *bdellium* mentioned in *Genesis,* in which Plato declared the Kingdom of Atlas to be specially rich as well as in gold and gems, or the so-called onyx stone of *Genesis.* Nor is it difficult to find the proof that gold was already reaching Grecaland by way of the Dan-u-be, and also the Ionians, during the conflict with the invading giants.

At the south of the Peloponessus lies the present island of

Crete, measuring about 160 miles from east to west, 35 to 7½ miles, from north to south, lying between 23° 30′ E. and 20° 20′ E.[3] At its center looms Mount Ida with an elevation of 8,000′, where Zeus is said to have been saved in his infancy.

It is unnecessary to examine all the Cyclopean ruins in the traditional realm of King M-in-o-s whose symbol was a bull. Suffice it to say that through the center of the island passes a grand highway that led, before the Medi Terre was submerged, into the Pelop-po-nessus and to Egypt.

Somewhat to the west in the island at 35° 20′ N. 25° 9′ E. is the site of C-no-sus, marking the meridian of the Sea of Atlantis, A-t-t-i-ca, and E-l-e-u-s-is (38° N.) close to which is the Pe-la-s-gi, port of the Pi-ra-eus near where A-t-h-en-s arose.[4] Also it marks the latitudinal circle of C-y-p-ru-s (34° E.); Ha-ma-t-h, the northern part of Aram (37° E.); Asshur (43° E.) on the Tigris; and the region of Madai south of the Caspian Sea. There in the valley of K-a-i-ra-t-o-s on a knoll which was levelled with vast labor, is a complex of structures covering some six acres, including a rectangle with immense columns, called the Palace of Knossus.

The walls of the interior chambers display huge griffins and also fresco paintings. At the side of the throne room adjoined by the lustrum on a lower plane, there is a huge bathroom with an oval tub of stone, and also a latrine, while the palace is equipped with piping of terra cotta for admitting water from an aqueduct, and with sewage facilities.

In one chamber still stand lines of huge jars, latterly used as oil containers, but originally as the vessels wherein gold was stored. Consequently, in a line of vases with lead linings, are found even now bits of gold.

Not far away from Cnosus are other ruins showing a similar advanced knowledge. Thus, at Khani have been found bronze axes and several score of tripod altars said to identify Khani as a factory for religious equipment and the arms of King Minos.[5]

The mythical Ceryneian Stag of Argos and Arcadia, was

especially dear to Apollo and his twin sister Artemis, or Diana. A creature with golden horns and brass hoofs, its capture was one of the twelve labors assigned to Hercules. For a whole year it raced to the land of the Hyperboreans before returning to Mycenae, and would have been slain by Hercules had it not been for Apollo and Artemis. Plainly gold and bronze had become of too much economic value to the Greeks despite its demoralizing effect, to permit the trade with Hell in the precious metals by way of the Danube, to be destroyed by the reformers.[6]

Archaeologists have shown very clearly that in the age of the mythical King Minos the Syrian mysteries of the Ka-bi-ra were symbolized by the seven headed monster Cerberus, said to be the watch dog of Hell who eventually appeared with three heads. His function was to lure all he could into Hell but to allow none to escape, implying the irrevocable oath exacted of initiates. By B.C. 1,700 the mysteries of the Kabira had become the Ionian mysteries of the Caberi which were enshrined at Sin-o-pe or Sin-ub, (42° N. 35° E.) marking the boundary between Ionia and Armenia, and the meridian of Mount Carmel, and Mount Sin-a-i. For political reasons these mysteries which had been established at Pa-t-ra-s as well as on the islands of Lemnos and Samnos, and were particularly dear to the seamen of the Mediterranean world of old called Pelasgi, were imported to Egypt, and were known to the Italics as the mysteries of Serapis.

The first Temple of Serapis in Egypt was erected at Memphis (about B.C. 1700) but was destroyed either by Assyrian or Persian conquerors of Egypt. In the time of Ptolemy, however, a new temple of Serapis was erected at Alexandria. Above the lower vaults in which the bull rites were conducted, stood the figure of Serapis. Moulded of all the precious metals, and crowned with jewels, this idol with a serpent's tail, symbolized the Cult of Cerberus. The basket held by Serapis was the symbol of material wealth. But the metallic body was slathered over with azure enamel to conceal the true character of the Gilded Man.

However, much gold may have been seeping over to Hell from La-bra-dor in the age of King Minos, and down the Dan-ube to Crete, the Land of the Lotus Eaters, at the south of Crete, was not dependent for its supply on the Western Hemisphere, since it had direct access to both South Africa and to the Golden Land of Ha-vi-lah in Arabia and India, as well as to Mount Ophir and beyond.[7]

In view of the palace of Knossus, it is easy to see the hold that gold had fixed on the mythical King Minos. Well may it be said: "By their works ye shall know them."

Verily, have we found in the Bull of King Minos the origin of the Brazen Calf whelped by the Gilded Man, which suggests another reason for the silence of the Hebrew scriptures about the land of Mizraim following the cycle of Joseph.

In the time of Herodotus when the Phoenicians were looting the Gold Coast and visiting the Faro Islands in mysterious voyages, Egyptian vessels were constantly visiting South Africa. See the Nine Muses, Herodotus (450 B.C.). But if it seems plain that gold had already become "the true magnetic North to which all hearts turn," the palace of Knossus also suggests why, according to Plato, one ally after another abandoned the Hellenes, leaving them alone to resist the invasion of Libya by the giants of the West.

Still, however, God's House was determined to enlighten man while Athena was aiding the Hellenes. Thus within the geodetic circle of Mycenae, is found at Ni-p-p-ur (32° N. 45° E.) in Babylonia, another wonder of the Neolithic Age, ever said to be the oldest of the so-called Towers of Babel.

Marking the latitude of Y-e-z-d in I-r-ana, La-h-o-re and Am-r-i-t-sa-r in K-ash-mir; the region of M-ana-so-ro-wa-ra; N-an-king (120° E.) in the delta of the Yang-tze Kiang; and K-y-o-su (130° E.) in Ni-p-p-on, this Zi-g-g-ur-a-t displays in its geodetic symbols more of magic.[8]

Called the Library Temple, like the Tello it was built of

bituminized brick, virtually non-destructible by frost, forming a cube 300′ × 300′ × 300′. Thus, theoretically, its sides unfolded display a Taux with a vertical arm of 1200′, and a cross of 900′, one with 4 and the other with 3 units 300′ × 300′.

In each face are 600 squares 5′ × 5′, each with an area of 25 square feet, with an area of 90,000 square feet in each face, or 54,000 square feet for its six faces, and a volume of 27,000,-000 cubic feet. The sum of the four measures of each square is 1200′. In each face there are 50 squares 60′ × 60′ each of 3600 square feet, and in the whole cube 500 lesser cubes, each 60′ × 60′ × 60′, each with a volume of 36,000 cubic feet. The square 60′ × 60′, or 3,600 square feet gives the sidereal unit of 3,600 years which is known to the Chaldeans as the lesser saros, while the saros divided by 10 gave 360, or the number of degrees in a circle, or 1 (One) 0 represented by 10.

By further analysis any expert mathematician can resolve the cube into a complete Book of Numbers relating time to lineal and spherical measures, and find in it a complete exposition of the Decimal system upon which the Hexagonic System of Mathematics is based, since there are 4 isosceles triangles in each face each with a base of 300′. Thus the Signs, Co-signs and Tangents of Trigonometry are reflected in the Cube, giving the factors of Integral and Differential Calculus, all involving the mathematical constant, or the Spiritual Factor, Pi (3.141596 +).

In this grand monument Chaldea reached the heights of its glory. No wonder the Sumerians preserved the tradition of the great magician El lil, said to have dwelt in a mountain at Nippur.

Verily, the picture which mathematics has been made to yield of the so-called Archaic Age, is different from the one with which modern times have been regaled by self-styled historians. Certainly in it there is much to indicate that a vast amount of wisdom has been lost to man.

Whether the so-called wise men of to-day are as wise as they are prone to imagine is a serious question. Certainly it is not wise of them to conceal from the view of youth, the evidence of a wisdom transcending that of mere mortals.

1 Ar-go-s, "the Aryan God, Sin."
M-y-c-en, "Maia, Ya, Chi, Enyalius."
37° 36′ N. 22° 30′ E.: $3+7=10$; $3+6=9=3\times3$; $2+2+3=7$.
2 M-e-r-v, 'Maia, Enyalius, Ru, Varuna.'
3 C-r-e-t-a, "the Cyclopes, Rama, Enyalius, the Taux of Atlantis."
4 Sir Arthur Evans demonstrated that this great monument was necessarily erected before B. C. 10,000.
5 Sir Arthur Evans has fixed the building of the Treasury of King Minos prior to B. C. 12,000. See *Palace of Knossus* (1911).
6 In the myth of Ceryneian stag we find the clue to the source of the vast wealth of Croesus of Lydia, the contemporary of Solon, who was warned by the latter that one with a stronger sword would seize his wealth.
7 For Solomon's Supply of Gold, see Kings II.
8 Zi-g-gur-a-t, "The 7 Gods, the Gaur, the Aryan Taux, or At-ma, the Atlantis, the Motherland."
$3\times2=6$; $4\times5=20$; $3+2=5$; $4+5=9=3\times3$; $3+2+4+5=14=2\times7$; $32+45=77$; $7+7=14=2\times7$.
9 Author's note: It is the oldest of all the zi-g-g-u-ra-t-s in Babylonia called Towers of Babel. See *The Library of Nippur*, HILPRECHT; *Nippur*, PETERS.

CHAPTER XXXII

THE MOUNTAIN OF THE PRAIRIE
GITCHE MANITO AND E-E-OPS-I-CHI-P-E
THE ORACLE OF WINNEWASSA AND
THE SACRED PIPESTONE QUARRY.

WHILE IT IS PLAIN what considerations dictated the transfer
of the Red Man of Asia to America by way of Alaska, it would
not have been humane to allow the migrants to be massacred
by the savage survivors in the region north of the Rio Grande
who, as shown by Plato, had lost all their knowledge of the
arts and sciences when their civilization was wiped out by the
Ice Cap and the climate of the First Winter of the Great Ice
Age. True humanity, of course, demanded that resort be had
to every possible safeguard against a repetition of the trage-
dies of Cain and Abel, and the strife between the Lion men
and the Ru, such as had begun all over again between the
Ma-t-chi-mu and the White Race in Libya. So is to be explained the second grand monument in North America according
in all respects with the symbolism of "the Watcher."

Moving straight west, as the crow flies, from "the Watcher"
(44° N.) through O-n-ta-ri-o in which, as in Ohio, appear the
symbols for the two spheres, one comes to O-t-t-a-wa (45° 21'
N. 75° 42' W.) standing almost exactly on the meridian of
Sha-ka-max-on (75° 9' W.). From this region the Sioux migrated to Western Virginia where the peaks of Otter are found
in Bedford County overlooking the head waters of the James.

Leaving Ni-a-ga-ra Falls (43° N. 79° W.) at the south, we
pass through W-is-con-sin in which emblematic mounds displaying the avars of the Kasapa, 'the eagle,' as well as the
Bear Mound, are to be seen. Thence we come to the Mountain
of the Prairie (44° N. 96° W.), in Rock County, Minnesota,
'the Land of Sky Tinted Water.'[1]

Consisting of a small circular hillock rising sheer out of the

surrounding prairie, about a mile in circumference, with per-
pendicular walls of red granite, out of the forest crossing the
summit flows a stream that falls by a beautiful cascade to the
prairie below. Near the base of the elevation is the only vein
of red pipestone known in the world, bearing the name Cat-
linite in honor of the antiquarian Freemason Catlin who,
thanks to information given him by the Iroquois in New York,
visited the Siouan Ma-n-dan of the Missouri and guided by
them, found his way to this sacrosanct area. As far as known
he was the first white man ever permitted to view what wonders he there beheld, marking the antipodal meridian of the
area of Gaura-sin in Tibet, Nepal, and the Holy City of Kashi
or Benares on the Ganges, and Ceylon.[2]

It marks the meridian of Omaha, Nebraska, To-pe-ka in
Kansas, Tulsa, Oklahoma, the area of Dallas and Houston in
Texas, and Vera Cruz, in Mexico, all of which manifestly
were located with regard to it.[3]

Beside the cascade and jutting out of a ledge of the red
granite cliff still stands a huge sphinx-like figure 30' high, displaying the head and torso of the red man called by the Sioux
E-e-ops-i-chi-p-e, in which we recognize at once the name of
the god Ops of the Italics.[4]

Not until after Fremont, the Pathfinder who following Catlin's report, visited the shrine in 1832, did Eastman as Sachem
of the Yankton Sioux, the half-blood son of an American
General, by many believed to have been George Rogers Clark,
reveal to Longfellow the facts about this mystic shrine, given
by the poet in that part of the *Song of Hi-a-wa-tha* called the
Peace Pipe, as a plea in behalf of the Red Man whose shrine,
despite the Sioux Treaty of 1820, the Missionaries were determined to destroy as a den of idolatry.[5]

It appears that down the ages pilgrims had gathered from
every quarter of America, a fact shown by the pipe stone bowls
found in the mortuary mounds of remote regions, to hear the
voice of the Prophet Gi-t-ch-e M-an-i-t-o at the far-famed oracle of W-inne-wa-s-sa, counsel the tribes that had been involved

in a bitter strife to return to the peace commanded by the Great Spirit.[6] Back to their domains they carried the pipestone held by them to have been stained with the blood of the perished races of men, from which to carve not the common pipe bowls of the Indians, but the sacred Calumet.[7]

In the smoke that arose from the calumet the tribes were taught to see the all-pervading spirit of the Great Father of whom a likeness was seen in "the Watcher" at Franconia.

Nearby the open vein of the quarry three immense boulders of foreign igneous rock, either conveyed by the glaciers of the Secondary from afar, or of meteoric origin, lie upon the meadow where now graze peacefully the cattle of the Indian school established on the reservation which, by the decision of the Supreme Court obtained by the writer, in 1927, has been set apart in perpetuity, as originally agreed in 1820, to the enjoyment of the Sioux. Called the "Three Maidens," by the Sioux, these boulders are said by them to be the petrified bodies of three wicked maidens representing the first three races, destroyed by the Great Spirit for their sins. They call to mind the three Hesperides guarded by a Serpent, which Hercules was called upon to find as one of the 12 labors assigned him.

Countless petroglyphs were found at the Oracle which the Missionaries subsequently tried to destroy. Of these the shattered fragments, displaying hieroglyphics so ancient that no ethnologist has been able to decipher them, have been collected.

The legends with respect to Gi-t-che M-ana-i-to, whose name is preserved in M-ana-i-to-ba, plainly relate to very early efforts to pacify the peoples of America, the product of the Da-ko-ta, "Seven Brothers," or "Seven Serpents," in whose name appears that of the Danitics.[8] Their mystical brotherhood originated in a relatively late day. Long before the Da-ko-ta arrived in W-is-con-sin and Minne-so-ta, "the Land of Sky Tinted Water," also known as the realm of Minne-ha-ha, "Dancing Waters," the region of Man-i-to-ba, had been occupied by the peculiar yellowish Ch-e-yenne who, we have seen, cherish the crucifix as their symbol. Thus it is to these ancient surveyors of the North to whom E-e-ops-i-chi-pe and the oracle of W-inne-w-a-s-sa must be ascribed.[9]

In viewing the Mountain of the Prairie one cannot but see in it an extraordinary symbol of the Garden of Eden which eventually the Assyrians would symbolize in the Garden of S-e-m-i-ra-m-is by the Hanging Garden of Ni-nu-s, or Nine-ve-h.[11]

We see now the implication of the peaceful city of the Euseues to which Theopompus of Chios referred. Surely E-e-ops-i-chi-pe, the symbol of Gi-t-che Manito the Mighty, implying the Grand Khan of Asia, or the Chichen of God's House, who manifestly employed the Che-yenne as wielders of the Che-ru-b, cannot be put down as a mere savage idol, any more than "The Watcher." Here it would be idle to attempt to rival the eloquence with which Longfellow made Gitche Manito promise to the Red Man through the oracle of Winnewassa a Prophet who would counsel and guide them to the ways of peace. Yet, sad indeed it is that in these days of the Economic Man, those who have appropriated the Red Man's Continent, should be taught so little about the Red Man's original way of life, his hopes and his aspirations, his simple faith in the Great Spirit whom he sought to symbolize on his native rocks with the avars of the Eagle, the King of the Air, the Kasapa ever deemed by him the symbol of Wambda, 'the Great Wisdom,' just as the Hindu K-ya-pa-ya-pa in the *Rig Veda* represented the Seven Sages.

To be sure in the Columbian Age the erudite would know, just as did Plato, how the Red Man of Azitlan migrated to America. But although many of them besides Columbus, and John Cabot, and Hylacomulus, saw in America a realm within the Spiritual See of the Grand Khan of Asia, none would explain a fact upon which all Ethnologists agree.

Instead of being the intractable, war loving savages depicted by the Colonials whose object was to rob the Indian of his lands, by nature the Red Race was the most highly spiritual and the most peace loving disclosed by the history of civilization.[13]

Also for the same reasons which will be shown they looked upon the domains which were set apart to them as "god-given," and of their race as born of a Giant whose blood had deluged the earth. Thus their psychology, never understood by the colonials, was that it was their moral duty to the Great Spirit of whom they saw the symbol in "The Watcher," and in the great Ana-con-das of the Mountain ranges, to defend their domains against intruders, gifts from the Great Spirit that mortals could not alienate if they would, since this would leave the landless at the mercy of others and also certainly prove provocative of strife. In a word, their racial concept of land as a communal possession, tracing back to the allocation of the domains of the earth by the biblical sons of Japheth, was in direct conflict with the imperialism represented by the mythical Nimrod, and that to which the posterity of the Five Twins of Plato eventually gave over.

Columbus in his first report to Ferdinand and Isabella (February 1493), written while in the Azores on his way back to Spain, described the Caribbs as a kind, peace-loving people whose one desire was to befriend the Spaniards in every way possible, thereby testifying to their true character before they had been outraged by the wastrels of Europe. When they saw in them, as did the Puritans, only red demons without the scope of God's charity, their ultimate fate was certain. For the European Colonials could never envisage the fact that the necessities of the Red Man could not be met by allowing him acres sufficient for those who had attained to a stage of development beyond that of a Stone Age people who must have domains of a size depending upon the wild life they would support. Nor would they recognize that their settlement in the native domains necessarily diminished the old reservations within which a sufficiently abundant game could exist. The very existence of these Stone Age people was threatened not merely by seizing a site, here and there, but by the white man's system of life, especially by his greed for the gold which the meat and the furs and hides of the game yielded him, whereas the Indian only killed game necessary for his existence and even then in accord with conservative methods.

"The Watcher" and the Oracle of Winnewassa together, however, fully explain the psychology of the Red Race.

1 Near here in Douglas County have been found petroglyphs ascribed to the Vikings.

2 Coronado had searched in vain for this alleged sacred shrine of the mythical Seven Cities, of Ci-bo-la, implying the mysteries of Nana-bo-za-ha, and had been led away from it by native guides faithful to their race, until he had come from Mexico to the Mississippi in Arkansas near Na-t-che-z, and returned to Mexico. DeSoto scoured Florida, South Carolina, Alabama and T-ana-sa, also in vain looking for the Seven Cities just as Ponce de Leon had done before him, just as Cortez tried to locate them in Mexico. Lewis and Clark were led past the shrine and never beheld it. Yet, the Iroquois in New York had informed Catlin about it just as they disclosed to his contemporary, the Freemason Joseph Smith, the location of *Bright Angel's Pass,* revealing to him the history of the past upon which he based the history embodied by him in the *Book of Mormoni.* Possibly the golden tablets Smith saw were revealed to him in a dream by an angel corresponding to the Mosaic revelation on Mount Sin-ai.

By this the writer suggests only what is known to all psychologists. No one can say when the human mind rests. All scholars who apply themselves intensely to studies know how upon arising it seems to them that they have never slept. Hence for the benefit of psychologists the writer records two incidents of personal experience.

In 1932-33 while working intently in the Congressional Library preparatory to visiting the wilds of the Northwest and exploring the Valley of Wisdom and other parts, the writer occupied a chamber at the Metropolitan Club in Washington between the ones occupied by Gen. Pershing and Gutzon Borglum who frequently came to his room late at night before retiring. One night we had been discussing the visit of William of Hohenzollen to Jerusalem, and comparing his spectacular entrance to that of Allenby. We all agreed that William had dreams of emulating Alexander the Great, and discussed the miserable end of the latter at Babylon. We then discussed the Tower of Babel. Borglum recently had seen the fallen tower at Borsippa near Babylon which Nebuchadnezzar had repaired. When they departed, the writer retired. The tower of Borsippa was on his mind. Over and over he dreamed of its measures. Loftus had given those of the slanting and fallen part. Apparently while sleeping the writer's mind added the two, divided the base by twice the reconstituted altitude, and obtained the factor Pi, $3.14159 + 6$. Springing out of bed he made the calculation on paper so that the apparent dream would not fade.

A year later after returning from the Northwest where stands Mount Pi in the Valley of Wisdom, still the writer, misled by western scholars, was laboring to work out the meaning of certain passages in *Genesis.* Four nights in succession after long labors, in his dreams a great white face formed itself against a disc of light. Each time the lips of the apparition would utter the single sentence, "I am Nordern." Thereupon it would vanish. The writer wondered if he were working too intensely. Consulting ancient works, there was no trace of Nordern. He soon dined with his friend Grant, an invalid who had written the *Passing of the Great Race.* They agreed that Nordern was the name applied by the great Swedish explorer de Nordenskjiold to the people of Spitzbergen, called Nordics by Grant in his work. From then on the seeming mystery of the evolution of civilization resolved itself. No longer was the writer misled by what had been written. Following de Quatrafrages to the Arctic Circle, the original site of civilization Mount Meru, that latterly had been transferred by the Hindus to the East, the northern sign of civilization became plain to him.

3 At Vera Cruz eventually would be erected several te-o-calli.

4 E-e-o-p-si-chi-p-e, "Euseues, the Serpent, Python, Sin, the Chi, the Papa of the Earth."

5 Eastman would never admit that Lewis and Clarke had visited the shrine, and it was not published in their report. Nor did Father Hennepin, who visited the Sioux from Canada about 1660 and was made a prisoner by them, ever admit knowledge of it.

6 G-i-t-ch-e, "C-alumet, 'the Celestial Light,' Taux, Chi, Enyalius."

M-ana-i-t-o, "the Mother, Ana, the Spirit of the Cross, Python."

W-en-ni-e-w-a-s-sa, "Wambda (eagle) of Indra, Nu, Enyalius, the Wambda of the Ark, the Serpents, Sa."

7 In the writer's possession is the Calumet of Sitting Bull, the head sachem of the Sioux nation, given to the writer by Standing Bull. A thing of superb workmanship, the bowl is formed of pipestone inlaid with iron, and encircled by two parallel inlaid silver hands with 7 x's included between them. At the initiation when the calumet was presented to the writer in the presence of Red Bird, Sitting Bull's granddaughter, the wife of the writer's half-blood law clerk, Capt. Raymond T. Bonnin, A.E.F., 1917, it was explained that the down taken from a mallard's throat, with which the stem was bound, represented the spiritual bird of heaven. At the same time the writer was given a staff of poplar wood entwined by a Serpent and surmounted by a sphere of pipestone which, he was told, represented the Red Man World. Plainly it corresponds to the monde of the medieval royal regalia.

8 The Da-ko-ta were descended from the Na-da-w-esseus and also were called the It-a-sa, and like the older Hi-da-t-sa Siouans of the southern A-pa-la-chi traced back to Itza-land. They came to include the Sioux of the Mississippi or the four tribes of Yankton, Yanktonais, Wahpeton, and Medawankaton. The other three Brothers were the Teton, Oglala, and Bruli of the Missouri, to whom the Ma-n-den and M-in-a-ta-ree, of the upper Missouri, and the Mo-d-ock of the Klamath River in Oregon, are related. The movement of the Sioux up the Missouri and to the Klamath occurred in a relatively late period. It was during this movement that the Wahpetons became the Levites of the shrine, eventually to be succeeded by the Yanktons.

9 Eventually some of the Cheyenne were absorbed by the Sioux and others by the Cho-cho-es of U-t-a-h who, as a mixture of the Punics, and Negroids were designated as Serpents in the sense of a slovenly, dirty, low type of man despised by all their red neighbors.

10 For the later history of the Shrine of Winnewassa see Appendix "B."

11 K-la-ma-t-h, "the King of the Bears of the Motherland, the Taux, Ha."

Ka-l-i-fa, "the Kara, the Bear, the Spirit of the Father." So California is called today the Bear State.

12 It is only logical that the name Pi should appear in the region of Kla-math in view of the meaning of the Trismagistus.

13 See *Handbook of American Indians,* Bureau Am. Eth. (1907).

[279]

Chapter XXXIII

THE REVOLT OF POSEIDON AGAINST ZEUS
THE MIGRATION OF THE RED RACE
FROM ASIA TO AMERICA

By B. C. 14,000 when the great Uighur Empire is said to have reached its maximum development, and had come to include Mu-s-ko-vi, the peoples of Egypt as well as the Zuni and other Pueblo groups were giving expression to the Tree Cult through the art displayed on their pottery.

The picture of the earth revealed by Plato in one of the greatest scriptures ever penned by man, leaves no doubt as to what happened as the Tenth Divine Dynasty of Chaldea wore on. By the wisest man of his age we are told how the blue-eyed and golden-haired Hellenes, guided by Athena, gradually came to take the lead in the struggle which the mythical Hercules had been waging down the ages, against the forces of Sin.

Being rich in gold, and a gray metal, as well as in precious stones, for ages the Ten Mythical Kingdoms of Atlantis had enjoyed a prosperous and peaceful trade and commerce, with justice and satisfaction to all. In the end, however, the inevitable occurred. Having lost their spirituality, the Atlanteans set out to conquer the earth.

Plato did not manufacture this upsurge of imperialism. In the Theogony written long before his time, is depicted the rebellion of Poseidon against Zeus during which his alleged son Triton, aided a host of lesser Tritons, implying the mysterious Pe-la-s-gi, or dark predecessors of the White Race in Libya whose name implies 'seaman.' Obviously it was applied to the Punic descendants of the Danitics in the cycle of Peleg, or the people of the Phenix back to whom traced all the descendants of the biblical Tiras who had conveyed the Tree Cult to the various original Greek Kingdoms and to Albanians,

Etruscans, Bas-ski of Iberia, and the Berbers of Tripoli-t-ana.

No more did he manufacture the dark Carians of Asia Minor who produced Herodotus before Plato was born. The latter placed the Atlantides in Tripoli-t-ana wherein had appeared the Atlas Mountains. Also the beautiful Atalanta of the Homeric myths who eventually gave her name to the Sea of Atlantis which was to appear at the north of Attica, and to her Ionian city of Atalla is to be traced with a name identical with that of Atalla in Alabama, while Atala is to be found in both Illinois and Alabama, Atlanta in Georgia, and T-ala-ha-ssee in Florida, near the S-e-w-an-ee River.

Theopompina, was a Hierophant of the mysteries of the Caberi which the Greeks had based on the Hebraic Ka-bi-ra, and which had been established at Chios, just as in the labyrinths of Samnos and Lemnos, and at Sin-o-pe, or Sin-u-b, (42° N. 35° E.), marking the head of Moesia and the boundary between Armenia and Ionia, and at Pa-t-ras in the Peloponessus when they were imported to Egypt for political reasons in B.C. 1,700, and the older contemporary of Plato, left a complete explanation of the myth of Poseidon's revolt.

According to him, there arrived in Libya, which had come to be called Europe in his time, a host of giants from a vast continent beyond Europe to the number of 10,000,000 possessing two great cities, in the sense of civilizations, they were of two sorts. The Euseues were of a peaceful type, implying the adherents of God's House. The Ma-t-chi-mu, however were fierce and warlike who, upon coming to the land of the Hyperboreans, despised them for their sanctity, ridiculed the smallness of their realm. Their own land of whose many wonders and huge animals they told, was the only true continent. Accordingly they withdrew from it for reasons not otherwise explained by Theopompus.

The Ma-t-chi-mu, he declared, were twice as large as the Europeans although they only lived half as long, and because they called their city Merop-es their land was called by the Greeks *Meropia.*

Here Theopompus gave the clue to the identity of the Ma-t-chi-mu inasmuch as Merope was the name applied to one of the Ten Pleiades said to be the daughters of Atlas. Inasmuch as Maia was the sister of Merope we see in Ma-t-chi-mu, 'the Maya, the Taux, the Chi of Mu.' Plainly Theopompus was dealing in esoteric terms. Nevertheless it was appropriate that he should have used the name Merope applied to the dimmest and reddest of all the astronomical Pleiades inasmuch as the land of the Meropes had vanished from the earth. But although the name of Merope was eventually applied to the disease of the eye involving obstruction of sight, we are able to understand the implications of what Theopompina and Plato wrote.

The truth is Theopompus was merely confirming what Plato wrote about the vanished Atlantean world in which the Melas, or the aborigines of the present race overran the Euseues or spiritual taches in the Hyperborea or land of the Gods and the whole land mass known to the Greeks as Atlas which included the present North America as well as the Land of Is and the present Europe. Mixing with the Ru to produce the red brown Punics, the Melas who did not so merge were gradually driven, as already explained, into the southern climes.

The history of many other peoples besides those in Libya shows them unable to govern themselves according to the principles of pure philosophy, still the peoples of the earth must have a god in their own image. Anthropomorphizing the Wisdom Philosophy in order to bring Divinity down to their own plane of understanding, they had confused the Erebus, or the dark nether world over which Hades was said to rule, peopling it with red devils. Thus they had created an Inferno of which Sat-an, instead of Hades or Pluto, was deemed the major-domo under the direction of an avenging God in their own likeness.

Nor had the various priesthoods failed to contribute to this fancy since the disobedient could be intimidated with warnings that the hot coal holes the hellions of the all-seeing Satan had stoked for the disobedient, were awaiting them. In this imaginary Hell the lesser devils with their tridents would inflict terrible tortures upon wrong-doers.[1]

This was the sorry pass to which conflicting religions had led. Naturally the priesthood found in a philosophy that challenged their control over a man a detestable thing. The idea that pursuant to the law of Karma a man might save his own soul without the interposition of priests, was not to be tolerated. So a bitter conflict between the teachers of God's House and the degenerate priesthoods, was inevitable. Then too there were the Black Magicians who in time had perverted the concept of reincarnation into the doctrine of Metempsychosis found among the early Druids, holding that unworthy beings would reincarnate in the form of lower animals.

In one thing the various priesthoods, each at war with the others, were agreed. None of them were willing to submit to the dictates of the Seraphim and Cherubim who had wielded the Flaming Sword to guard "all ways the way of the Tree of Life." Each meant to wield the sword in its own interest. Accordingly, the idea was fostered that organized murder could be perpetrated by a nation with impunity so long as it had the sanction of its own priesthood. Along with such abuses as scalping, crucifixion, burning at the stake, and the taking of virgins with chattels as tithes, also evolved the concept of slavery as having the sanction of God for the punishment of enemies. Therefore, as shown by ancient scriptures, already the weak were being enslaved by the strong pursuant to the doctrine eventually proclaimed that men were as fishes, the little ones created as the food of the mighty.[2] Of this concept the Za-l-ma-t-s were to be the major victims. Indeed the dark Sudaens were held in such contempt by the Boreans and especially by the White Sarku, that it was deemed the right of enlightened peoples to subject the Negroids to servitude.[3] Undoubtedly the Punics in Egypt were subjecting the Negroids of Africa, and selling off their surplus to others.

Lotus Eaters! How well the name has been employed to conceal another abuse by no means limited to Egypt. The finest poppies in the world are the dark Nilus that still grow around the Black Sea and along the Shat-en-Nil, far excelling in the quality of the opium they produce, the product of northern India, Burma, China, and Egypt. Lotus Eating in fact implied all the vices that go with addiction to the distillate of both the poppy and the Egyptian Lotus, that has ever been deemed an antidote for bodily ills.

Narcotics would have helped to make men generally forget God along with other things, in the time of Athena, the champion of virtue, just as presently.[4]

The character ascribed to the Ma-t-chi-mu by Theo-pompina accords exactly with Plato's story of the eventual decline of the posterity of Atlas. The name of the peaceful Euseues is well preserved in that of many peoples of the old Libya. Also we find it in the names M-euse in Franconia in the N-euse of North Carolina and in one of the names of the older Siouans of North America who called themselves the Na-da-w-euseues, corrupted by the French into Sioux, and who, known to all their neighbors as Serpent People, also are known to have swept down out of the far North into Quebec and Ontario before spreading southward as the H-i-da-t-sa along the Appalachians, and westward from Ontario and Minnesota as the Da-ko-ta, 'Seven Brothers.'

Against such an invasion as that described by Theo-pompina naturally the mythical Zeus would have called upon Vulcan to forge for him the thunderbolts with which he proposed to reduce the rebellious Poseidon and the Tritons who are described as possessing a navy with vessels capable of transporting war elephants, to submission. In other word the Hellenes and other white peoples of Libya did not mean to permit intruders to overrun them. So, according to Plato the Hellenes with the aid of Athena, as shown by Plato in complete accord with the Volsunga Saga, joined in the resistance to the gigantic Ma-t-chi-mu whose descendants are to be seen in the red-brown peoples akin to the Lapps who, according to Bowers eventually came to the Himalaya from the Northwest. Certainly by

14,000 already undoubtedly had appeared signs that the Winter of the Sword during which, as shown by the *Heldensage,* the ancestors of the Germans, made common cause with their Teutonic kinsmen, against the Giants, was drawing to a close.

What now occurred, however, was not a matter of accident. North America was an immense world in itself where the fresh grasslands which would come into being during the next glacial advance would provide for many people and save the red man of Northern Ana from destruction by the Tartars and Mongolians of Siberia.

Bowers showed that while many of these people continued to find a refuge in the Himalaya, others migrated to America, just as held by Matthew, Huntington, and others, before the last glacial advance which until recently fixed by the Radio Clock at B.C. 10,000, was commonly deemed to have begun between B.C. 14,000 and B.C. 12,000.

The migration, however, did not occur as a mass movement, but in successive waves made up of small swarms each led by a chela furnished by the Uighurs just as in the case of the migrants of the European Colonies of a later age.

Popular concept of a vast number of migrants is but another fallacy. The most careful scientific analysis indicates that at no time down to the coming of the White Man, were there ever in excess of 2,500,000 Red Men in North America above the Rio Grande.[5] Nevertheless the migrants fully explained many of the dual names of the 70 tribes that eventually appeared among the 7 Linguistic families which the European colonists would find in America, varying in color and tongue because of the varying mixtures in the Red Man's ancestors. For the migrants in Alaska, still a harsh, barren land of cold and ice, under pressure of both climate and the following wave, the migrants fanned out southward at such widely separated times that different dialects evolved through admixture with the few inhabitants of the northern continent.

On the other hand it is plain from the mongoloid skulls and light complexion of the Ath-a-pa-s-c-an linguistic family, some of whom gradually flowed down the Coast of California and along the Rio Grande, producing the A-pa-che and the Na-va-x-o, or Na-ca-jo that they had yellow blood in their veins. To them is to be traced the highly developed Secret Societies of the Bella Coola in the original O-re-gon where the Tian Shiana also with highly developed mysteries, preserved the name of the Celestial Mountains. Just as the name of Mount E-l-i-as (McKinley, 60° N. 150° W.) is to be ascribed to the Atha-pa-s-ls, so is that of Mount Pi in the Valley of Wisdom in the K-la-ma-t-h Range of O-re-gon, upon the cliffs of which are inscribed hieroglyphics so ancient that no ethnologist has ever been able to translate them.

So was introduced among the older peoples of North America one stream of fresh red blood by the migrants from Asia who in course of time had become redder and redder as did the Hakka of Ana and the red ancestors of the Rajputs of Raj-pu-t-ana in India. Accordingly Hřdlicka, eventually traced the Athapasca whom he distinguished from their red-brown predecessors, to the mounds in Mongolia which they had erected before their migration.

In the nature of things there were conflicts between the on-coming hordes and their predecessors during the process of absorption. Nor do the remains of the elephants found in Nevada and Arizona along with human artifacts fail to suggest the nature of the strife was similar to that ascribed to the Winter of the Sword.

---

[1] In the *Divina Commedia* the whole concept was ridiculed by DANTE (1310) who brought down upon himself terrible penalties for daring to satirize standard Christian ideas just as did ANDREA by his *Mythologia Christiana* (1586-1654).

[2] Such was the doctrine drummed into the heads of the Germans by a host of madmen under the lead of Nietzsche to prepare the Germans for the First World War. This perverted, un-Christian doctrine was applied to politics not only by Nietzsche but by Trietsche with the approval of William II of Hohenzollern and, of course, led straight to Na-zi-ism which ascribed to the German Race the rightful rule of the earth. From the same idea evolved the anarchism of William Godwin of England, the Socialism of Louis Blanc and Mazzini of France and Italy, the Communism of Karl Marx, Proudhon, Bakunin, Lenin, Trotsky and Stalin, as well as the Nihilism of Kropotkin.

3 In the Hebrew Scriptures Abram's Egyptian concubines are described as the servants of Sarai, but it is plain that the Abramites had enslaved the Egyptians who constituted the mothers of both the eponymous Is-ma-el and E-sau.

4 This fact, like that of slavery, the sexual perversions of the Female cults, and other vices have been so well concealed along with the curse that gold had brought, notwithstanding the blessings it might yield the wise, that one who dares expose the facts, runs a great risk indeed. Yet, why attempt to write history merely to flatter its readers? If its true purpose be not to help man know himself, why write it at all? Yet, the grand old Hebrew Prophets would hesitate to brand gold along with the Moon Goddesses as anti-Christ. Neither did Socrates, Appollonius of Tyana, Seneca fear to speak the truth though it spelled their dooms. Lorenzo the Magnificent, Giovanni de Medici (Leo X); Savonarola, John Huss, Sir Thomas More, William the Silent, Coligny, Jerome of Prague, Xavier, Pocahontas, Sir Walter Raleigh, William Penn, Roger Williams, Tecumseh, Lincoln, and Lee make up a glorious company of martyrs.

5 See *Handbook of American Indians* (1907). Yet, by 1200 A. D. it is said there were 50,000,000 inhabitants south of the Rio Grande including the Caribbeans.

CHAPTER XXXIV

THE REMOVAL OF GOD'S HOUSE FROM THE GOBI TO LA HA SA
THE MAGNETIC CATACLYSM OF B. C. 10,000
THE FIFTH WORLD CONTINENT OF AMERICA.

As THE WINTER of the Sword wore on towards the last glacial advance, now fixed at B.C. 10,000, the signs of a rise in temperature would have multiplied. Inevitably the wise men at the Abyss of Learning would have seen what this portended. Again the low places of the earth, just as during the Noachean flood, would be inundated when a new glacial advance began.

The Seraphim and the Cherubim, or the Chichen and the Chelas at the Abyss of Learning, would have known that the gas pockets beneath the extinct volcanoes of the Himalaya had been discharged, and that the earth crust in that part was especially thick. This being so, T-i-b-e-t, which had derived its name from Ti-bet, 'the Covenant of Tien,' because the intersection of the World Cross in Burma was at 30° N. 30° E., offered the best asylum for the teachers of God's House. Here, among the peaks still clad with snow, with compassion the Spiritual teachers of men might continue to look down upon the earth below, while the earth again was being washed of some of its evil, nor is there room to doubt that God's House was not shifted to the forbidden area of La Ha Sa, 'God's House,' which had given its name to the region of El Ha Sa in Mesopotamia.

Despite their heroic resistance, to the invaders from the West the Hellenes seemed doomed since the Ma-t-chi-mu of Theopompina, in course of time, as shown by Plato, extended their conquests as far as the Tyrrhenian Gateway in the Medi Terre while also overrunning the Iberian peninsula and parts to the North. What at last occurred, however, explains the withdrawal ascribed by Theopompina to the Giants.

[288]

The *Volsunga Saga,* erroneously accredited to Saemond the Wise of Norway, who in truth merely derived his knowledge from the record handed down to the Freemasons who had founded the Grand Lodge at York in Britain before the age of Saemond, (A.D. 823), and even before the pagan Island-ingas founded their Republic about 930 and declared their independence of Norway whose King Hakon had been brought into the fold of Rome, is in complete accord with the Maya Glyphs. That record, of course, was known to the Freemasons of France, including Fabre d'Olivet, the foremost esotericist of the Napoleonic Age who eventually was exiled from France by the Emperor Napoleon upon the demand of the Protestants and the Bourbon Catholics of ancient Franconia.

"Bacon believed, as I do," wrote d'Olivet, referring to the *Atlantida Nova* (1611) of Francis Bacon, head of the secret order of Utopians in England, or the inner circle of Freemasons of which Fleming was the Grand Master in the time of Raleigh and Bacon, "that America had been part of the ancient Atlantis. He makes it quite plain in his *Atlantida Nova."* He then went on to say: "The frightful cataclysm that submerged Atlantis was caused by a sudden movement of the terrestrial globe, which, suddenly raising the Boreal pole, which had become lowered, caused it to take a contrary position to what it had formerly. In this movement, which perhaps had many oscillations, the mass of waters which had been upon this pole, rolled with violence towards the Austral pole, returned to the Boreal pole, and back again many times toward the opposite pole, where it finally became fixed, over-powered with its weight. The earth-work gave way in many places, particularly where it covered caverns and deep anfractuosities and, in falling opened immense abysses where waves rushed furiously, engulfing the debris which they had drawn after them and the multitudes of victims whom they had deprived of life.

"The Eastern Hemisphere resisted longer and was only washed, so to speak, by the waves which crossed over it without stopping; but the other was everywhere sunk and covered with stagnant waters which remained there a long time. All the austral lands, where Atlantis properly so-called was, disappeared. At the opposite pole, the Borean lands emerged from the depths of the waters and became the cradle of the White or Borean Race, whence we issued. Thus it was to the disaster of Atlantis that we owe in a way our existence. The Black Race, being born, as I have said, in the neighborhood of the equinoctial line, suffered much from this catastrophe, but infinitely less than the Red or Austral Race which perished almost entirely. Only a few men, whom a fortunate destiny found upon the Appalachian Mountains, the Cordillera, or the Tapayas were able to escape from destruction. The Mexicans, Peruvians, and Brazilians have a special veneration for these mountains. They had a vague memory that they had been a refuge for their ancestors. It is said that still in our day the savages of Florida make a pilgrimage four times a year to Mount Olaymi, one of the highest of the Appalachians, to offer a sacrifice to the sun, in memory of this event."

Here the influence of the sudden lowering of temperature that ushered in the Great Ice Age concurrently with the beginning of the Post-Tertiary and caused the formation of the ice caps, is entirely ignored.

Again referring to Bacon, d'Olivet wrote: "He said that the inhabitants of this part of the world were once very powerful and that they tried to subjugate the ancient continent. After the submersion of their empire a few scattered men saved themselves upon summits of the mountains. These men, he adds, rapidly degenerating, forgot all the arts and became savages. They lived for a long time isolated and without laws and were only united when the plains were uncovered and they were able to inhabit them. Boulanger, who has made great researches in this regard, thinks with just reason that after the loss of Atlantis the people of this hemisphere who survived fell into a stupor and wandered for a long time without daring to found a settlement; he believes that the savage life was the result of the terror imprinted by this event and was the fruit of isolation and ignorance. Many of the savants have since expanded and commented upon these ideas which are only a renewing of those Plato had received from the Egyptians and which he admirably described in his Book of Laws. The men, said this philosopher, who escaped from the universal desolation were for the most part herdsmen, inhabiting the mountains, deprived of education, where all the discoveries in art, politics, and sciences were unknown; they were lost and not the slightest vestige remained of them. The most flourishing cities situated in the plains and on the borders of the sea had been carried away with their inhabitants. Everywhere was a picture of vast solitude. The immense country was without inhabitants. When two men encountered each other upon the gloomy ruins, they wept with emotion and with joy."

The geophysical views of d'Olivet are fully supported by the fact that the present magnetic pole is not at the North Pole of the spheroid but at a point about 98° 30' W. in the island of New South Wales (70°-75° N.) whereas undoubtedly it had been at 99° W. when Mexico City and X-o-chi were located on that meridian. Moreover it seems certain that much the same thing had happened during the so-called Biblical Deluge of Noeas and that d'Olivet did not dare explain that much of what Plato had written about America referred to the early Deluge when the ice cap again caused the wobbling of the earth. For certain it is no such denudation of civilization in America as that described by him occurred during the Magnetic Cataclysm which occurred in B.C. 10,000.

The Maya Glyphs of Yucatan record that as the signs of an impending cataclysm multiplied, the peoples inhabiting the "Lands in the West," implying the Pacific Continent, and the Land of K-ui, or the Uighur Empire in which Shang Hai bore the name Kui, also designated as the "Land of the Gods" since the Abyss of Learning was located in the Gobi, received warning from the Aryan priesthood designated as Ra Mu, implying Rama Balarama. Also this is shown by the inscriptions to be seen in the temples eventually erected by the Maya-x and Qui-chi-es in Ana-huac, and other inscriptions, in which it is recorded that many people of the Pacific Continent sought refuge in America and elsewhere. In addition to what appears in the Troana Manuscript or the *Codex Tro,* and in the *Codex Cortesianus,* and the *Codex Berlin,* in the so-called La Ha Sa Record which Scliemann brought to light, and which apparently was discovered by him during his researches in Japan and China, or in the Mesopotamian La Ha Sa, since he never visited "God's House" in the sacrosanct area of Ti-bet, is given a graphic picture of the terror in which the so-called *Lost Continent of Mu* was involved. In that record Ra Mu is described as Bal, and in it is disclosed the fact that when the remnant of the Pacific Continent was torn to pieces and the temples of a sinful people were cast down upon them, there were already White as well as Yellow, Brown, Black and Red people inhabiting the land in which dwelt the posterity of Cain. Also it is shown that the inhabitants had given over to slavery and polygamy as well as to the adoration of Gold and material wealth, and that Black Magic had succeeded to the Philosophy of God's House. So is explained the presence of both yellow and white blood in the present relics of the Pacific Continent found in Polynesia and Oceanica.

But if the Gobi was emptied of its waters that swept over the present China which for many millenniums would be uninhabitable with the exception of the mountains wherein survived the red Hakka, also the waters of the Caspian Sea washed over the Kara Kum while those of the Indian Ocean washed over Arabia bringing into being the present great desert of Ru-b as well as the deserts in I-r-ana. Now the Red Sea came into being separating Ru-b from Egypt. There Brusch Bey showed thousands of migrants had found an asylum by B.C. 9,500, or the date when, according to Plato, suddenly the great island of Posidonis was torn to pieces by volcanic eruptions and vanished beneath the Atlantic almost overnight, leaving only the Azores and Bermudas as the relics, and ending the invasion of Libya by the peoples of the West designated by Theopompina as the Ma-t-chi-mu.

This catastrophe is readily explained. While it seems certain that long ago the Gulf Stream had broken through the Land Bridge that had connected the Continent of Atlas with the Continent of Libya, there is little room to doubt that now the waters of the Arctic Zone broke through the Land of Is separating Britain from Britanny which formerly together had constituted the realm of America. Now too Ireland was torn from Britain, leaving the Giant's Causeway, ever ascribed by the early peoples of Ireland to Fin Mac Dougal whose name survives in the Cave of Fin-ga-la on the Island of Islay in the Irish Sea. And here it is to be noted that just above Londonderry stands Scalp Mountain at 7° N. marking the meridian of the Faro Islands on which also stands the holy shrine of T-ara to which eventually Jeremiah would bring the Lia Fail, or Stone of Destiny from the Temple of Jerusalem and undoubtedly with it the Freemasonry which had been established in the mythical Temple of Solomon. From Scalp Mountain the Giant's Causeway leads straight toward Scalp or Scalpa Flow at the head of Scotland which eventually would be surveyed in B.C. 250 by the mythical Pytheas of Massilensis, implying the Phocians who had founded Massilensis or Marseilles in B.C. 600 just before Jeremiah's arrival in Ireland by way of Sa-ra-go-s-sa in Spain.[1]

The bursting of the northern waters through the Land of Is, of course, fully accounts for the vanishing of the inhabitants from the present England and an end to the Manx and Cornish civilizations. Undoubtedly many of the Corydean giants fled into the mountains of Scotland and into Brittany, thus explaining the relation of the Cimbrians who eventually reappeared in England and the Cimbri of Bel-gi-um.

As the waters from the north rushed southward they would have subjected the earth crust above the gas pockets which had produced the Ridge of Ten-e-ri-f-fe to great pressure and caused volcanic explosions which destroyed Posidonis in the cycle of the youngest of Plato's Twins—Diaprepos and Gaderius of whom the latter's name is preserved by Gades or Ca-d-is and by Ga-d-e-mi in the present Libya. The fact that the giants of the island had already extended their conquests as far as the Tyrrhenian Gateway in the Medi Terre through which the stream from the Aegean passed to the Atlantic, fully explains the placing by Herodotus of the Atlantides in the Tripolitana. There eventually appeared the three Barbary States which derived their name from the Berbers who were an obvious mixture of Punics with the peculiar Gooms of the Atlas Mountains in Morocco whose kinsmen are found in the Madeira Islands, the Canaries, the Cape Verde Islands, and the Azores.

The cave in of Posidonis, of course, would have caused the vast eddy of waters in the Atlantic described by Plutarch as an impassable mass of muddy sea, and which eventually came to be called the Sea of Sa-ra-go-s-sa around which all manner of myths would gather.[2] As part of the general propaganda designed to keep the veil drawn over America, it would continue down the centuries to be represented as impassable. Around this great eddy in which an immense mass of sea growth still is found, the larger Gulf Stream would circulate carrying the warm waters of the South so close to America that civilization on the Atlantic Seaboard would be able to prosper more than before.

The cataclysm, however, did not end with the destruction of Posidonis. With the melting of the glaciers in the Urals and Balkans, just as Mesopotamia was flooded by the waters from the Ararat, and Irania by those from the Pamir, so also was Samothrax or the old plain of As-ke-na-z, bringing into being the Black Sea and separating Russia from Asia Minor. Tearing their way through the Dardanelles they submerged the Hellespont and forming the Ionian Sea separated Thrace from Asia Minor and brought into being the sea of Atlantis at the North of At-t-i-ca, the Dodecanese and Aeolian Islands, or the Cyclades as well as the island of Rhodes and Crete, converting Lower Egypt into a virtual morass. The immense pressure upon the Medi Terre, as shown by Plato, caused the cave in which occurred in B.C. 9,000, leaving Crete, Malta, Sicily, Sardinia, Corsica, and the Balearic islands as relics of Rumel, and carrying into the depths twelve cities of Rome along with all the Olympii save the three in the new island of Euboea, Thessaly, and Moesi, respectively. In token of the thunderbolts which Vulcan had forged that Zeus might end the rebellion of Poseidon, the smoking Etna and Vesuvius remained as if in warning to the survivors of the vanished world commemorated henceforth by the Italic festival of the Lemuria.

But the waters of the Atlantic and those of the Tyrrhenian Sea must seek a level so that now the waters of the former broke through the so-called Pillars of Hercules and the Medi Terre eventually separating the present Libya from Gaderius, or the Gallia and Gaul of the Hebrews and Italics, respectively. So "All Gaul," as pointed out by Caesar came to be, "in tres partem divisa," beginning at the Rubicon with Cis-Alpine Gaul, with Franconia constituting Ligurian Gaul and the Iberian peninsula a third part, with *Insuliae Britanniae,* and *Irlandiae* beyond.

Inevitably, of course, the utmost confusion reigned for many years in Egypt by reason of the migrations into the Nilus from Nubea and the Sudan, and the mixtures which took place between the Ethiopians of the south, Punics, and the Caucasians from Arabia.

With Brazil converted into a virtual morass of which the present "Green Hell" that was flooded by the waters from the Andes is the evidence, because of the immense mass of water that flowed in to the Pacific vortex before the waters of the Atlantic and Pacific reached a level, the great plateau of the Puna in Peru appears to have been elevated, and we may be sure that great floodings also took place in Mexico and all along the Cordillera from Alaska to the Fa-l-k Land below

Cape Ho-r-n. Also the mid continent would have been flooded although eventually it would be drained by the Mississippi and its great branches including the Missouri, the Ohio, and the Red Rivers.

Of course it would take years after the terrestrial sphere regained its balance for the Yalu, the great rivers of China, the Irrawaddy, the Indus, the Oxus, the Euphrates and the Tigris, the Nile, the rivers of Gallia, the Congo, the Mississippi, the Amazon to drain their respective regions. Fortunately for India, however, the Indus, Ganges, Brahmapootra, and Irrawaddy saved Bhara-ta-va-sa, from submersion while the Hindus also found security in the Vidya Range of the Dekkan below which eventually came into being the vast deserts of Ma-d-ra-s. For a thousand years the Pi-sha-cha in Sin-ga-la would cling to Adam's Peak just as declared in the Koran. With the Uighur Empire wiped out it would be a very different earth the survivors of the awful climatic transformation which has been described, would inherit, as shown by the *Volsunga Saga.*

Very beautiful it is how all the sacred scriptures conspire to show how at last the Fifth World Continent of Occult Science, known to it as America, came into being, so called in fact because down the ages the Goddess of Amaraka who had been worshipped by the Nagas at Mount Amara-ka-n-t-aka was none other than the impersonation of the Amara, or immortals whose names have been preserved all over the earth. Now it was that advised by the one-eyed giant Mimr, 'the well of Wisdom,' from the great central mountain of the earth, O-d-in, 'Ornyth, the Diva of Indra,' corresponding to the Germanic W-o-dan, W-o-t-an, or Wo-din, was advised to summon the champions of God's House in the terrestrial Hell, from their castles, or caves, and overthrow the savage giants. This having been done, the *Volsunga Saga* shows how the younger gods, praying for the resurrection of Baldur, the Son of Light and Love, gathered on the mountain of the earth to contemplate the past, and watch the new races of men take up the fresh grasslands of the post-cataclysmic age following the Winter of the Sword. Yet,

the Sibyl of the Ru would down the ages continue to tell of
them. In their runes the bards would find the tunes for countless lyres. In the eddas of Odin's antique realm as in those of
Hindustan would be found the lyrics for the *Ni-bel- lung-gen-
leid* born of the *Volsunga,* and in time would wake the lyre of
Wagner and the world would hear again the surging anthems
of the past, and out of V-al-halla would come the V-al-kyrs'
shrilly wail. Even the Christians in the catacombs of Rome's
old labyrinth, on the festivals of Odin's giants would chant the
praises of the Son of Light and Love while the Three Brothers
of the North hopefully prayed for Bal-dur's soon return,
while the Egyptians told of how Osiris was resurrected despite his crucifixion by the cruel Set.

In view of what has been shown very definite conclusions
are possible as to the manner in which the successive mixtures
of Ru, Melas, and the later red migrants from Mongolia and
Itzaland, produced the mixtures of the tribes and the heptarchy
of the Seven Linguistic families of North America above the
Rio Grande. Naturally the darker tribes were found in the
South where the late migrants pressed them just as they were
pressed southward in the Eastern Hemisphere. Also we must
remember the antique connection between South America and
Africa, and the migrations to the Andes of Melanesians from
the vanished land of Mu in the Pacific indicated by Humboldt.

What really produced the highly mixed and varying tribes
of North America as distinguished from the linguistic families
that included different peoples, is plain. The original Ru as
red people expanded southward as the continent expanded.
Their mixture with the brown fourth root race produced peoples similar to the Punics. As the Negroids pushed up from
South America after the two continents were joined they naturally infused more of their blood at the south than at the North.
Then came the new red migrations from the Northeast and
Northwest following in general the lines of the Western Chi,
meeting their mixed darker predecessors who surged back

northward to claim the fresh grasslands after the successive winters had pressed most of them southward, and producing still further mixtures. In this collision between the red migrants which took place in the present glacial period following the third winter described in the Volsunga Saga, inevitably there were bitter local conflicts until finally through such teachings as those ascribed to the Oracle of Winnewassa the contestants settled down in the domains they were found inhabiting by the European colonists.

Exactly the same thing occurred in Europe with this exception. There the factor of the white sub-race produced by a successive merger of red, brown, black, and Caucasian mongoloids, appeared, with the whites less white to the south. In Asia, however, the expansion of the yellow sub-race of the Fourth Root Race made impossible the southward expansion of the whites to the point of altering the color of their mixed predecessors. With the black peoples of Africa and Melanesia we have already dealt.

The civilization in North America will be dealt with further in Appendix "D", just as in Europe it will be elaborated in Appendix "B".

We must conceive, therefore, of varying mixtures taking place all over the earth just as the whites are mixing with Eskimo in the Arctic Zone today with their ideas being absorbed by one of the most backward groups on the earth until lately, prizing the television sets familiarizing them with things they never dreamed of until the most advanced sciences suddenly invaded their realm.

But in all ages there have been corresponding ventures, among others the far-flung trade of Carthage and Egypt in the Black Continent, of which the Portuguese slave trade of the Middle Ages was merely an inheritance. Thus it is useless to dogmatize about when ideas are mixed. Who shall say, for instance, when the Tuaregs of the Sahara overran Nigeria driving the pure Negroids to the Guinea Coast? A million years hence will ethnologists be able to envisage such social revolutions as are taking place in the Arctics and in Nigeria to-day, and the enormous flow of goods into those parts from American ports?

Yet, the manner in which the more advanced peoples of ancient times dealt with savages, without leaving any skulls among them, is fully shown by the highly standardized system of barter common to the Negroids of Africa, the Egyptians, and the Phoenicians that required no contact between the parties to the trade by successive pilings of goods on the beaches until bargain was reached. In all probability it was exactly in the same way that the Pirati would deal with the Indians of America. In a word the goods flowed to trading points as to magnets of demand, from parts the crews of the ships never visited.

[1] See *The Early History of the English People,* TURNER (1802).

[2] See the *History of Africa,* IBN BATUTA and also the works of Yehudi. Also the *Brendianna myths of 570 A. D.* and *Legendary Islands of the Atlantic,* BABCOCK, (Am. Geo. Asso., 1922).

According to modern scientists all the eels in the world are bred in the present Sea of Sargasso and spread from there over the earth which is only to be explained by the droppings of sea birds carrying the unhatched eggs.

CHAPTER XXXV

THE NEXUS OF THE POST-CATACLYSMIC CIVILIZATIONS

The Hellenes Occupy The Delta of Egypt and Found The Mysteries of Athena or Neith, The Cult of the West, at Sais.

The Sixth Hindu Avatar, Rama, Lunus, or Chandra.
The Unification of The Mesraites.

  The Ismaelites, The Israelites, and The Hindus in Egypt Under Mena, The King of Egypt and The Prince of Kash.

As POINTED OUT in the preface it is not intended that this work should do more than establish the nexus between the Atlantean and the present world, and this will be done only in the most general way. For once the evolution of the latter has been shown and a sound chronology has been furnished, there is no room left for the old arbitrary Archaic World of modern historians.

Let it not be imagined, however, that the Pirati and the peoples of Ireland, Britain, and the Hebrides, known to the new world of the post-Atlantean Age, had lost contact with America. For it would not be until about 1400 A.D. that the relics of the Land of Is would be brought to their present form by new seismic disturbances. Thus it would be possible for the so-called Pretensi of Ireland, Britain, the Hebrides, symbolized by the mythical Irish Sha-ma-roc, 'the head of the Mother Bird,' or the green trifoil symbol, a sham in fact, having no reality in the vegetable kingdom, to reach the "Western Ireland" just as the Pi-ra-ti, or the Three Brothers of Scandinavia would do, with the knowledge of the lands beyond embodied in their great stone maps called cromlechs based on the runes.

Inasmuch as for the reasons shown neither *Genesis* nor Josephus furnish a guide beyond the cycle of Joseph until the cycle of Moses is reached, and following the Cataclysm of B.C. 10,000 the Greeks were to assume the intellectual leadership of the Western World and retain it even after they had been subjected by the Romans, we must depend upon Greek Mythology to an increasing extent down to the time when the new civilizations of India, Egypt, America, China, Mesopotamia and Europe appeared.[1]

Necessarily the ordeal to which mankind had been subjected during the transformation of the earth to its approximate present form could not have failed to have had a demoralizing effect upon all the peoples of the earth. The amazing thing is, how quickly, thanks to God's House amid the snow peaks of the Himalaya, the Hellenes who rightly are entitled to the encomium of Plato, were able to recover.

Here it is to be noted that the Athens (37° 58′ N. 23° 44′ E.) which they founded in At-ti-ca directly west of Mi-l-e-tus on the coast of Asia Minor where grand temples are found, according to *Timaeus* was not the original capital of the Hellenes. Therefore, on the Ac-ro-polis, 'Arc of the Roc City,' above which towers the L-y-ka-b-e-t-t-o-s with a name indicating two peoples, is to be found the Erech-theus, ever ascribed to the Danitic P-el-as-gi, or the 'seamen' of the cycle of Peleg, and that the present Pira-eus, or the present port of Athens preserved in the island of Piros the name of Roc. Also it is to be noted that at the northern end of Attica which preserves the name of Atlantis, is the port of Colon-na, 'the Colonizer of the Nether Ark,' just as the island of Colon-sa-ya appears in the Irish Sea (56° N. 6° 5′ W.). Undoubtedly it was from the Erechtheus that the Danitic Pelasgi had colonized much of Grecaland and the adjoining regions before the destruction of the original Athens.

Bearing the name of Erech the Erechtheus on the Acropolis consisted of a simple structure with columns to which admission was had by two main propylaea or entrances, while ornate columns displaying in their capitals the symbols of the lotus, stood before the lesser propylaea. The site of Eleusis beyond Athens was merely a deme, or locality, subject to the central temple of the Erechtheus.

There the Sinitic mysteries had been enshrined even before the Pythean mysteries had been enshrined by the Phocians at D-e-l-os and at D-el-phi following the mythical slaying of the Python by Apollo.[2]

Eventually on the Acropolis the Hellenic Athenians would erect the P-ar-t-h-en-on, preserving the name of the mythical Partheno-p-a-eus, the alleged son of Ares, the God of War, out of the beautiful nymph Atalanta, making of it one of the architectural wonders of the world, as well as a monument to Atlantis. At the foot of the P-nix on the Acropolis preserving the name of Phenix, on which a colossal statue of Athena was reared, would be erected the Temple of Apollo. In the frieze of the Parthenon would appear sculptures embodying the history of the past. On the other hand, as shown by Gardiner in a superb mathematical analysis of the Parthenon, the technical knowledge of architecture involving the use of a vanishing point to produce the illusion of greater symmetry was employed, exceeding any knowledge in that respect today.

Aside from their agency of God's House, the Hellenes could not have failed to know the situation in Egypt and the importance to the White Race of re-establishing civilization in Egypt. The alleged crucifixion of Osiris and the efforts of his twin sister to save their son Horus from the evil machinations of Set, may be taken to imply that the Ethiopian Khans who had set up the God Khunsu at Karnack had put an end to the Solar Cult of Osiris.[3]

The Hellenes conveyed to the land of Mizraim the Cult of Athena which was enshrined by them as the Cult of N-e-ith, 'the Nilus, Egypt, the Spirit of Athena,' at Säis, the first Neolithic city to be reared in the delta, being located at 31° 30′ N. at the exact latitude of Ya-ru-siloam and Lake M-ana-so-ro-w-ara. Knowing this Herodotus, who as a Carian of Ethiopian descent, and an initiate of the mysteries, explained that the site of the Temple of Neith at which eventually the Hierophant Sa-n-chi-s would instruct Solon, stood at the center of the area of Säis which constituted a vast sun dial just as in the case of the high plain on which eventually the Sphinx of Giza was carved out of the Libyan stone before the pyramidal Trinity of Giza was reared beside it.

In B.C. 8,500, the Delta was a virtual morass through which coursed the two main branches of the Nile, the Da-mi-e-t-t-a at the east, and the Ro-set-ta at the west, with countless smaller branches between hillocks. Of these hillocks the group of ten, with the Temple of Neith at the center, constituted a terrestrial zodiac. Accordingly the isles, called nomes, were given animistic names corresponding exactly to the names of the clans of the American Indians. In course of time each of these names would come to possess local gods so that they would add to the confusion ultimately produced by the three kingdoms of Lower, Middle, and upper Egypt, each with its own pantheon of gods. Meantime, however, the Hellenes established in the delta the so-called Cult of the West in which the Israelites and Ismaelites found a haven under the protection of the white Hellenes, so is explained the fact that the original hierophants of the cult of Neith were white. At this same time was founded the Kingdom of Cyrenaica just east of the delta, ever dominated by the Greeks, who had seized possession of the Island of the Pi-ros, 'the Red Bird,' on which eventually Alexandria was to be founded. Concurrently the Phoenecians established themselves along the coast of Italy which came to be called *Graeca Minores,* and eventually in La-t-i-u-m, or *Graeca Majores.*

From now on the history of Egypt was to revolve around the struggle between the Cult of the West and the Cult of the East.

The occupation of the Delta by the Hellenes fully explains why Lower Egypt, or *Chemi,* 'the Red Land,' in distinction to the part of the Nilus beyond Giza at the apex of the delta, which was called T-o-s-ri, 'the Black Land,' implying the region where dwelt the Ethiopians, also was called the Land of the Ten Archers, according with the ten names of the Zodiac of Säis.

It was an amazing figure that revealed itself to the surveyors of God's House who first outlined on the graphs of Gea the configuration of Italy. Just as Dan's Mark now appeared at the head of the Southern part of Scandinavia, resembling a human head, with Helvetia and Cisalpine Gaul forming the torso, and the Low Countries at the West and Poland and East Prussia at the East, the outspread arms of a mortal, lower Italy formed a perfect leg with Apulia and Calabria in the booted foot. And as Mont Blanc and the Yung Frau lay in the body, the toe pointed to the Greek Ogygia and the Italic Sicily as if the whole figure had been deliberately designed as the symbol of the White Man's undoubted purpose to rule Gaderius despite the mythical giant An-t-e-a-e-us, implying the Ethiopians of the Mediterranean World. This is indicated by the myth of the *Twelfth Labor* assigned to Hercules of destroying the antediluvian Giant with the aid of the sons of Aphren, or the Danitics who as the posterity of Ja-pheth, the Caucasian flower, produced the Sa-b-in-es of Italy while the Lud, or sons of Shem had produced the E-t-ru-ska.

As the thoughtful behold this natural symbol surely they cannot fail to see why the Teutonic Germans eventually insisted upon dominating Italy in order to control the Church of Christ, just as the Russians undertook to assert their control over the Bear of Ala-ska.

Verily do the peoples of the earth have long memories.

It is not to be imagined, however, that God's House was concerned with succoring the peoples of Greece, Egypt and Gaderius alone. The Hindu scriptures show that about B.C. 7,500 the sixth avatar, Rama Lunus, or Chandra, whose symbol was that of a normal man, appeared in India as a teacher of undoubted historical character. As the record has it, with difficulty he was persuaded by the mythical King Bharata of

Bharata-varsa at the north of the Dek-k-ana to assume temporal functions as well as those of a spiritual teacher. Great things are ascribed to him. By this time there were peoples of four colors in India as a whole in addition to the non-Aryan Pi-sha-cha, and only harm could result from allowing them to compete with each other. Until civilization had been thoroughly restored the red descendants of the Caucasian Kara as the seniors were to constitute the Kshittriya, or warrior caste; the white element at the Northwest the Brahmin or Priest caste, the Yellow peoples at the Northeast the Viasya, or caste of farmers and merchants, and the dark Dravidians, or Tamils of the South the Su-d-ra, or laborers. Only the Kshittriya who had the red blood of the Ru in their veins, of the three other castes, could be admitted to the Brahmin, or priest caste, although eventually this limitation was ignored and even Sudra became priests. For many centuries, however, the Maha Bharattas, or great men of Bharatavarsa alone were to furnish the Raja-puts with their capital at Indra-phrasthra, 'the Flower of India.'

With the yellow para-sol, as his royal symbol of 'the philosophy of the Sun,' Chandra as the putative son of the Moon, and the reincarnation of Rama Balarama, was to bring order out of chaos, by driving all the non-Aryan Ru into Ceylon where in the remnant of Sin-ga-la known to his subjects as L-an-ka, the land of the Aryan King of the Ark, even these 'red devils' were eventually reduced to a state of harmlessness. Tradition has it that in and about the conquest of "the red devils" generally, Rama employed an aerial craft which may well have been one of the glider type rather than a balloon.

Whatever the truth about Chandra's airplane, his conquest of L-ana-n-ka explains what has ever seemed a very great mystery.

We have seen that the latitudinal arm of the geodetic *Tau* was marked by Persepolis (30° N.) about 35 miles northeast of the modern Shiraz (25° 36' N. 52° 35' E.) in the modern Persia. Also we have seen the grand Neolithic pillar there, and other ancient mathematical symbols in Persia. We have also seen that the holy cave on Mount Carmel marking exactly the latitude of Babylon, the sacrosanct region of Manasorowar in western Tibet, also marks the site of Nagasaki in Japan, and the head of the Gulf of California where ancient inscriptions were said to have been found at Tex-u-ana.

At Nagasaki just as at Chung King (30° N. 107° E.), also marking the lateral arm of the Tau and the meridian passing through the Abyss of Learning in the Gobi, are to be seen great triangular mounds.

Knowing these things we gaze with amazement as the peoples of the so-called Archaic Age, must have done at the natural Lotus formed by the Indus, Ganges, and Brahmapootra, trailing root-like from Lake Manasorowar into the ancient real of Bharatasavasa, or the present Northern India to which as to the Dekkana they furnished the life blood. No less wondrous is it than the natural lotus formed by the Nile and from the Euphrates and Tigris in Mesopotamia. At times we feel almost apologetic for the so-called historians of civilization who have failed to include these things along with the head of Dan, the leg and foot of Dan, and the Bear of Alaska, among the wonders of the world.

But what is this?

From Lake Manasorowaro (31° 30′ N. 81° 30′ E.) we pass due southward to Mount Amarakantaka (19° N.) in the Vidya Range almost due east of Bombay (18° 56′ N. 72° 56′ E.) where for ages the Goddess Amaraka has been enshrined by the Lota and other Nagas. Keeping on along the same meridian we pass from the Point of Divi near Masulipatam close to Hyderrabad in Northern Circa, eastward of the Coromandel Coast through the Indian Ocean to the Island of Sin-ga-la, the present Ceylon. From it at the north a chain of fragmentary islands constituting Adam's or Rama's Bridge, leads to the mainland of Southern Madras across the Gulf of Manar. Keeping on through the northern jungles we come to Anajapoora where we are shown a great stone demi-lune called the Moon

Stone, one of the most ancient petroglyphs known to man. Around the arc of it trails a procession of aquatic fowl. They, we are told by the priestly guardians, represent the successive lunar races also shown on moonstones in Burma. We wonder why the Portuguese who founded the present city of Colombo (6° 54' N. 79° 51' E.) on the west coast of Ceylon, marking the meridian of Madras and the region of Manasorowar, made no mention of the Moon Stone. Or do we?

The whole of Sin-ga-la, the only vestige of the vanished land known to the Hindus as Lanka, is dominated by Adam's Peak, to the natives known as Pidu-ruta-sa-ga-la, rising on the meridian of Mount Amarakantaka and Lake Manasorowar at 7° N. to an elevation of 7,352' and we note that 7, 3, 5, 2 together give 17, or 10 + 7, and that in 17 also appears 1 and 7. And if the latitude of this peak is 7° N. the numerals in its longitudinal symbol give 8, 1, 3, 0, or a total of 12 corresponding to the 12 signs of the Zodiac. In addition to this there are seven words combined to form Pi-du-ru-ta-sa-ga-la, together giving the meaning of the name implying a relic of the vanished land of Ruta and indicating that it was deemed the spiritual realm of Sa, the God-Land also called Gond-wana-land.

Intrigued by all this with official guards we ascend the glorious mount that by day looms against the azure sky like a huge cone of emerald, by night casts its triangular shadow against the celestial dome in which its lofty apex seems to merge. At last we come to the summit where we rest upon a rectangular platform seemingly formed by volcanic stone, exactly 74' × 24,' oriented to the points of the compass with its longer axis E-W.

Even more amazed we behold at the exact center of the rectangle a gigantic footprint 5'4" × 2'6".

Pointing to the footprint our Brahmin guide declares: "It is the sign of Shiva, the Destroyer," and on our map we note the region of Shiva close to Lake Manasorowar and the grand

mountain Trinity of Karakorum—K², Gushabrun, and Masha-
bruin.

Hasty calculations show that together the measures of the
rectangle give 7, 4, 2, 4, totalling 17, just as do the numerals
in the height of the peak. Knowing the geological history of
the earth who can doubt that the rectangle represents the
measure in degrees of the geodetic rectangle within which the
sages of India deemed the vanished Singala to have been included? Research along this line we must leave to the Geologists and historians of the future. Yet, as we mark such a
rectangle on our map we note that eastward from the peak it
would extend 37° bringing within it the delta of the Yangtze
Kiang. On the other hand the western side would be 44° East,
or the meridian on which stands Nineveh (36° N.), Bag-dad-
da, 'the Gift of God,' (33° 20′ N.) with its ancient inscriptions,
and the sacred region of A-den (13° N.). While the northern
side of the rectangle is at 19° N. marked by Mount Amarakantaka in India, the Island of Hainan in China (110° E.), and
by the Desert of Rub in Eastern Arabia, within the lower
half of the rectangle lie parts of Somaliland and Madagascar
at the west, and of Sumatra, Java, and Borneo at the east.

The axes of the foot, however, give a perfect *tau, ankh,* or
cruciform, with a vertical arm of 64″ and a horizontal arm
of 30″. We note that 6 and 4 together give 10, or one complete
cycle, and that 30 gives 3 × 10, or three complete cycles, corresponding to those of the first three root races shown on the
Moon Stone.

After all is the foot but a symbol of the vanished races that
inhabited the earth before Gondwanaland was destroyed?

Was this extraordinary symbol designed to give to the surviving Red Devils said to have been driven by Rama into Lanka
across Adam's Bridge, a warning through the sign of the cross
of what had befallen the non-Aryan peoples of the earth? Certainly it is most intriguing to read in the Koran that here on
Adam's Peak, Father Adam was required to spend a penance
of a thousand years.

Looking down from the summit of Adam's Peak on the surrounding jungles wherein still a few of the so-called pre-Adamites of the Third Root Race survive, along with their kindred Flat-heads in the Land of the Southern Cross, we do not fail to marvel at another Wonder of the World with which modern historians have failed to deal. What, we ask ourselves, as we descend from the glorious height of Pi-du-ruta-sa-ga-la, will Science eventually make its symbols yield of human history? Surely in the ancient realm of Indra are those to whom have been passed down the knowledge they were designed to preserve for man.

Meantime let us note that the two measures of the rectangle bear the ratio of 3 to 1 $+$, and that the sum in inches of the two arms of the cross, or 94″, yields 9 and 4, and that 9 $+$ 4 gives the mystical number 13 of which 1 and 3 total 4. Also it is to be noted that the ratio of 24′ and 74′ approaches that between the polar axis of the earth and its circumference. All this being so it is possible the axis of the rectangle may indicate the area deemed to lie within the terrestrial realm of Asia as well as the former area of Singala.

Of course it was not an accident that the name Mai-oo appeared on the coast of the Red Sea near the present Sua-k-in not far west of Karnack. Therein truth was the entrepot of the trade between the India of Rama Lunus and upper Egypt. The relations that existed between Kara Chi in the Delta of the Indus, B-o-m-bay, Cal-i-cut, Ur, Mu-ga-ya, and with Mu-s-cat Y-e-men, and A-den in Arabia, are well established. The geographers of the Hindus, Arabs, and Egyptians were constantly visiting the Mountains of the Moon to observe the Zodiacal poles, just as A-za-es, the elder of Plato's Fifth Twin had visited Chi-m-bo-ra-zo on the Equator near Qui-t-o for that purpose.

The fact that thousands of Chaldeans, or yellowish Caucasians had found a refuge in Middle Egypt fully explains the yellowish complexion ascribed to the peoples in the Middle

Kingdom of Kash or Cash which bore the same name as the original Benares—or Ka-shi, 'the Kara, the Son, the Holy Spirit.' Therefore the implications of the mysterious Manetho, contemporary of Herodotus, and an author of many periods to whom the first lighthouse erected at Piros Island in B.C. 315 is ascribed. The Hierophants of the mysteries in the super-structure that appeared at the Labyrinth of Fa-y-oo-mu (30° N. 30° E.) well knew it was in the age of Chandra that M-en-a, the alleged first Pharaoh, united Lower and Middle Egypt, or the Kingdom of Chemi and Kash in which had merged the Israelites and the Caucasian Ishmaelites and other descendants of Esau. Accordingly in B.C. 7,500, just as declared by Manetho in the *Synthesis* (B.C. 300?) M-en-a, 'Mi, the First, the Ark,' held himself to be the King of Egypt and the Prince of Kash, and made his seat at Memphis.[6] They in fact erected the Sphinx at Gi-za during the reign of the mythical S-e-s-o-s-tr-is, an eponym in which appears Tris-ma-gistus, which was applied to the Pharaohs of numerous cycles, being a title im-plying the Twinship between Egypt wherein the name Babylon was applied to the original site of Cairo, or C-aké, 'the Celes-tial Ark,' and fully explaining the claim that the Pharaoh was the King of Egypt and that Egypt and Chaldea were Twin Sisters. In a word Sesostris was but a designation of the Pha-raoh in the aspect of the post-diluvian Nimrod. Thus the whole history of Egypt from now on shows that the Egyptians of the two lower kingdoms including the Israelites and the Hindu element, meant to unite all three kingdoms, drive the Ethiopians into Nubea and the Sudan and recover Palestine as the base from which to subject Syria and Assyria. In a word, the Naacals had united Chaldea and Mizraim, of which the Serpent Bird called the Sphinx was to be the symbol of Sesos-tris as the champion of Osiris-Isis, and the Babylonian Ishtar.

In all such names as Me-so-po-tamia, Medi Terre, Mena, Ar-men-ia, and Me-x-atla, and Me-x-i-ci, one does not fail to see the influence of the Melas. For it was the Greeks, as already shown, who placed many of these names on the graph of Gea.

THE PHILOSOPHIC HISTORY OF CIVILIZATION

1 To no one, perhaps, is the historian more indebted than to Alexander S. Murray of the British Museum, because of his monumental *Analysis of Mythology* to which other great scholars have added. Nevertheless, all myths are subject to more than one interpretation. However rightly or wrongly Murray and the scholars who have enlarged his work may have been in their special interpretation of the Greek myths, their relation of them to astronomical and other phenomena, did not make them yield the vast amount of history embodied in them.

This is particularly true with respect to the *Twelve Labors* said to have been assigned to Hercules, having reference to cycles following the destruction of the Medi-Terre, Posidonis and the separation of Britain from Brittany, of which the *Twelfth Labor* shows why the Jewish Prophet Cleodemus cited by Josephus declared that Aphren, the brother-in-law of Esau, helped Hercules destroy the Giant, having reference to the ultimate conquest by the White Race of its dark predecessors in Libya, and in fact implying the ultimate absorption of the Danitics who were either destroyed, or driven into Tripolitania where the Berbers evolved, from a mixture of Atlantides and Punics, as shown by Herodotus and Voltaire. In Appendix "B" the *Twelve Labors* will be interpreted with respect to their historical significance so that the student of civilization can see how the Greeks undertook to reestablish the civilization in the relic of Libya, or the present Europe and also in Egypt.

2 To this temple traces the name of the grove called Aca-deme, said to have derived its name from Academus, a mythical hero of the Trojan War. Near this grove Plato first had his lyceum, was to be found the *Academie* where Aristotle, a native of Chersonesus in the kingdom of Philip I of Macedon, was sent by his father to be schooled by Plato and Lysikrates. In truth it was a public gymnasium so planted as to symbolize the Garden of Eden, while the school founded by Plato was to furnish the model for the universities that evolved all over the world. It was after this Academie that the Medici modeled the Academy of Florence, and that Jefferson modeled the University of Virginia, designed by him to liberate American youth from sectarianism. So Jefferson was to suffer the brand of *atheist*. About 500 B. C. the Erechtheus was remodeled. In 500 A. D. the Neoplatonian Proclus became its head. Soon it was closed by fiat of the Pope.

3 The story of the crucifixion of Osiris, and his resurrection was unearthed by Mariette in 1852. It was not until the Third Dynasty of United Egypt, that at last Trismagistus, or Thoth, the God of History, ruled after a great litigation in Memphis that Hor-us, the alleged son of Isis by Osiris, implying the descendants of the She-zoo Hor, or the Ru, was held to be the rightful successor to his father Osiris, who after being relegated to Hades had been resurrected and come to the aid of Isis and Horus. See *Of Isis and Osiris,* PLUTARCH. Manifestly the Hellenes must seize the Delta of the Nile in order to dominate Egypt by cutting the Ethiopians off from the Mediterranean Sea as the Ishmaelites and posterity of Esau in Arabia could cut them off from the Erythrean Sea. Accordingly, as pointed out by Plato, in B. C. 8,500, or just 500 years after the Medi Terre had been destroyed, they seized the delta.

5 Now do we begin to understand why the Portuguese knights of the Order of Christ who accompanied de Gama, reached the conclusion that the Hindus were mere unbaptized Christians; why it was said by them that the Hindu epics were a mere plagiarism upon the Iliad.

6 Because the Ethiopians of Upper Egypt still held out in the Land of T-o-s-ri, it was not until about B. C. 3,200 that the eponymous Mena succeeded in uniting the three kingdoms. Confused by this, the Egyptologists have cast the Syntesis of Manethe aside, and still are not in accord as to the date when the First Dynasty of United Egypt embracing the Three Kingdoms began, varying from Boekh's date of 5,702 to Sharp's 2,000, with the consensus around B. C. 3,200 after varying changes by them, such as those of Petrie and Meyer.

CHAPTER XXXVI

PRINCE MAYA VISITS PATALA, OR THE ANTIPODES OF INDIA

GOD'S HOUSE at La Ha Sa which had been helping the Greeks, Hindus and Egyptians simultaneously to upbuild their antediluvian civilizations inevitably would have undertaken to succor the smitten peoples of America while the mythical Hercules was endeavoring to bring order out of chaos in the relic of Libya.

It appears from the Ramayana in which is embodied the history of Rama Lunus, or Chandra, that Prince Maya had paid a lengthy visit to Patala, or the Western antipodes, just as Hercules is shown doing, before he appeared back in India. This is fully explained by the French esotericist d'Olivet who pointed out that several thousand years after the Magnetic Cataclysm of B.C. 10,000, the red Itzas who had survived the trial of this awful ordeal in the relics of the Land of Is, migrated to North America by the way of Islanda, and from Labrador found their way through the Gulf States to Louisiana and thence to Mexico.

There can be no doubt about the veracity of this. Thus the alternate name of the Siouans was Itasa, while the name of the Itzaes also is preserved in countless place names and tribal names among the aborigines of America.

Inevitably the migrants would have known of both " 'the Watcher,' and the oracle of W-inne-wa-s-sa." To them are to be ascribed the older effigy mounds of North America, which are especially numerous in the region from New York along the Ohio, and down the Mississippi to Louisiana, as well as in Wisconsin, Georgia and Alabama, and which are not to be confused with the geometric mounds of the Christian Era. Among them is the Bear Mound in Wisconsin, the Serpent

Mound in North Dakota, and the Great Serpent Mound in Adam's County, Ohio. Located at 83° 30' W. at 38° 45' N. the latter marks the meridian passing from El-s-mere Island in the Arctic Zone, through Hudson Bay, Ontario whence the Sioux are known to have hailed, Lake Huron, Mi-chi-g-ana, Toledo, Ohio, Kentucky, the Big Smoky Mountains in Tennessee (T-ana-sa), Mount Mitchell in the Black Mountains of North Carolina, Athens and Ma-con in Georgia, North-Central Florida near T-ala-ha-see, on through Ha-v-anna-h in Cuba, and Pa-na-ma. Also it marks the latitude of St. Louis at the west, Washington and Ana-polis at the east, and the antipodal meridian passing through S-eve-r-n Novaya Zembla, the Gobi, China, and Burma.

Examining a globe we find that the latitudinal circle 7° N. passes eastward from Adam's Peak through the head of Borneo; the Pacific Continent just north of the Grand Ra-pa through Ca-ja-mar-ra in Peru, and Zu-e-la, where the river Americao is found.[1] Thence across the South Atlantic it passes through the Con-go, Ni-g-e-r-i-a, the Su-dan, A-b-y-sin-n-ia, and back to Sin-ga-la, making a grand sweep through the relics of Gond-w-ana-land which remain in the Indian Ocean, the Atlantic, and Oceanica.[2]

If in an aeroplane we should sail that course we would find not only the great water falls in Brazil that make those of Niagara seem small in the matter of altitude, and also those of the N-y-ana-za in Africa in which the Negroes of Nigeria have ever seen a symbol of the Divine Spirit, just as the aborigines of North America and Brazil held N-i-a-ga-ra and the Falls of Bra-zi-land to be.

If, however, we should sail in an aeroplane from Adam's Peak northward past Mount Amaraka-n-ta-ka and Lake M-ana-so-ro-wa-ra, around the North Pole, and southward through Omaha, Topeka, and Tulsa, to Dallas, and then turn westward, upon reaching the Rio Grande and the realm of the Zuni and other Pueblo groups in Arizona and New Mexico, we would find what aerial photography has disclosed. The Serpent People of these parts in the cycle of Azaes had converted areas even larger than that of the Pawnee Republic, into the great circular domains resembling zodiacs, that were claimed by them.[3]

When at last is reached X-och-i, just south of Mexico City, we would find that not only the great oval mound begun ages before had been brought to an elevation of 450', with a periphery of 3½ miles, but that it was crowned with a Neolithic Temple, the oldest in Mexico, bringing the whole to a height of 500', and that in the frieze of this temple of circular form is the grandest Moon Stone known, wherein not aquatic fowl are shown, but the giants of the five successive Root Races. Moreover, the temple, called the Calco, 'Castle of Flowers,' implying both the human flowers and those raised from the sacred seeds planted on the huge spiral terrace, bears an inscription declaring that the temple had been raised as a memorial to Atlantis.

As we gaze at the stupendous work we marvel at the labor its erection must have entailed. Nor do we fail to see that through that travail thousands of the aborigines of M-e-x-at-la, as part of Plato's the Kingdom of Atlas, were trained in the mechanic arts before the te-o-calli, or so-called pyramids of Mexico and Central America, and Peru, were reared.

While the colossal monoliths in the temples are of the same type as those in the revetments of the spiral terrace that is guttered with wondrous skill to carry over the drainage from the terraces, within the great mound at different elevations are chambers with passageways leading to them, corresponding to the degree to which the initiates of the mysteries of the Ka-bi-ra were admitted as they were advanced upward in spiritual enlightenment by the Che-la, or Cherubim of Atlantis, who presided over the Mysteries of the Maya-x and the Qui-ch-es.[4]

On the accompanying map are shown the locations of the t-e-o-calli, 'houses of God,' erroneously called pyr-a-mids to the older of which Bancroft allowed an age of 6,000 years.[5]

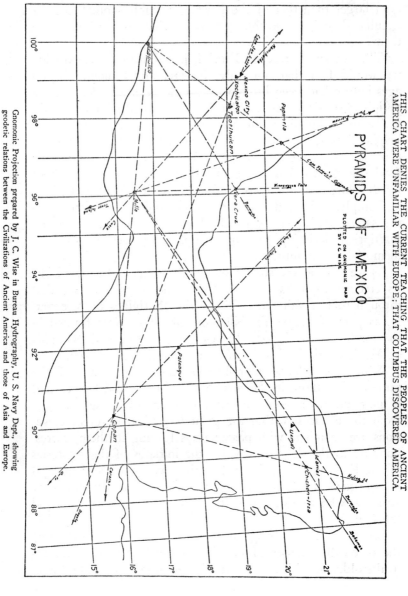

Gnomonic Projection prepared by J. C. Wise in Bureau Hydrography, U. S. Navy Dept., showing geodetic relations between the Civilizations of Ancient America and those of Asia and Europe.

The student of history will have no difficulty, by reference to the other maps in this work, in determining the geodetic relations of the teocalli at Mexico City, Cho-l-u-la, Te-o-t-i-hu-i-can, P-al-en-que, Pa-pa-n-t-la, Mi-t-la, Co-p-ana, and at T-ru-x-illo in Peru. Manifestly they were designed like the cromlechs as maps in stone. Thus they give the bearings from the major cities in South America to the major points including the harbors, of that part of America north of the Rio Grande.

Although Bancroft pointed out the texture of these monuments, showing the art employed to insure against erosion, he did not explain what to the writer seemed evident. It was Raleigh who brought on himself the charge of lying when he told of the lakes of asphalt which he had found in Gui-ana. It is the opinion of the writer that this material, as well as cement, was well known to the builders of the teocalli. At any rate the writer has shown that the factor 3.141596 found in the "Thunderer," the seven-stage tower at Pa-pa-n-t-la, 'the Papa of the Nether Taux, the Bear,' symbolizing the Chichen of God's House in the realm of A-zi-t-land, was known to the Maya in Mexico as well as to the builders of the Planet Tower of E-zi-da at B-o-r-s-i-ppa in Babylon, and to Rameses the Great when he built the Pyramid of Lidzt in Egypt. For the walls of D-el-hi (Delphi), near Indra-phrasthra, (28° N. 76° E.) the ancient capital of Rajputana, stand on the meridian of the mountain Trinity in Karakorum, and the latitudinal circle of Everest, Mount Sin-ai, the Tripolitana, the Canary Islands, Corpus Christi and, also the great circle passing through the area of D-en-ver and the Ana-con-da of Pikes Peak. Moreover an analysis of the walls erected by Rameses II will yield 3.141596 +.

When the writer visited some of the teocalli in 1951, he saw at once the so-called Pyramid of the Sun and the Pyramid of the Moon, at Te-o-ti-huican, where a line of sphinxes eventually arose, had been reared as seed beds, just as the Mound of X-o-chi had been. Therefore, they started at the edge of the former lake bed in which Mexico City had been sited because of its fertility where also there is a teocalli. Even today, the surrounding areas are drained by a system of canals just as were the deltas of the Euphrates, Nile, Ganges, Yangtze Kiang, Mississippi, and Amazon. Plainly the vast engineering knowledge of Prince Mava traces back to the cycle of Plato's Twin Azaes when the remains of the giants were interred in the Andes. He also found a huge Cave close to the two teocalli that would have housed scores of chelas.

Let it also be noted that all over Mexico appears the name *huatl*, 'the Heavenly Twins of Atlantis,' implying a beautiful woman, corresponding exactly to the beautiful Atalanta of Greece, who is described, in the Greek myths, as the mother of Ares, the God of War, of P-ar-thena-pa-eus, one of the Seven who assailed Thebes, during the conflict between Hellenes and the Danitics for the mastery of Greece.

The N-a-huatl, 'the Nether Ark of Ornyth' or the Serpent bird carried into battle by the Aztecs against the Spaniards under Cortez, were identical in their symbolism with the huge spheres mounted on poles as symbols of Ornyth carried by the pre-Celtic Cimbrians, as symbols of the Moon God Dis when Caesar visited these peoples in B.C. 54 after which he planted a group of Miletan Pytheans who evolved into the pagan Mileseans, or Serpent people assailed by St. Patrick (in A.D. 415) following which Colnich, the mythical King Arthur, implying the Augustinians, appeared in Britain. Today as one visits Me-x-atia, 'the Melas, the Chi or Cross, of Atlas,' he finds at 105° W., due south of D-en-ver and the Ana-con-da called Pikes Peak, marking the arm of the geodetic cross at the intersection of which the Abyss of Learning was sited, the city of M-azatian in the ancient realm of Sin-a-loa, located on the Tropic of Cancer due east of M-a-u-ana Loa in the Isle of Ho-no-lu-lo. And in its name is preserved that of both Atlas and of Azitian whence came the Aztecs to Ana-nuac.

Are we then to put the Greek myths of Atlas down to sheer fable?

[1] Z-u-el-a, "the Zi, Ru, the Gods of Ana."

[2] Con-g-o, "the Chon, the Gods of the Serpent."

[3] See *Ancient Civilizations in Southwest America,* VERRILL.

[4] Similar chambers known as the King's Chamber and the Chamber of the Queen are found in the Pyramid of Cheops wherein, according to tradition, Jesus of Nazareth was advanced to kingship in the Mysteries during his alleged ordeal of ten years in the Wilderness.

[5] Those in Yucatan are of a later cycle.

Chapter XXXVII

THE MAHABHARATA AGE OF INDIA
THE AGE OF PIRATI NAVIGATION
THE IMPLICATIONS OF THE TROJAN WAR
THE APPEARANCE OF RAMA CHRISNA OR KRISHNA,
THE SEVENTH HINDU AVATAR
FU SI OF CHINA
SARGON OF ASSYRIA
THE ULTIMATE UNIFICATION OF EGYPT
ITZAMA UNIFIES THE ITZAES AND
MAYA OF MEXICO AND FOUNDS
THE CIVILIZATION OF YUCATAN

WHEN THE MAHABHARATA AGE of Hindu culture began, as commonly supposed about B.C. 5,000, with the Gymnosophs of India compiling the Sanscrit texts, including the *Veda,* inevitably by reason of the presence of the Borean Itzaes in North America, there was more gold in Ireland than in any country in Europe save Denmark, while in Scandinavia not only had silver also of non-native origin appeared, but also great mounds identical with the effigy mounds of North America. Manifestly it was coming from the old realm of Atlas, as indicated by the *Popul Vuh* wherein the ancient relations between the Quiches of Guatemala and Northern Europe as well as with Egypt are shown. Accordingly it was recently held by Brogger of Harvard that this was also the age of a worldwide navigation by the incomparable seamen of Scandinavia who were known to the peoples of other parts as the Pi-ra-t-i, 'the Spiritual Sons, the Taux, of the Spirit.' Undoubtedly it is to their clandestine trade with America beyond Ultima Thule, or Islanda, which eventually their Vi-king posterity would seize shortly after the death of Charlemagne, and founding the Islandinga Republic including Iceland,

Greenland, and Vinland beyond the latter, declare their independence of Norway and Rome.

Nor is there any doubt that now the Egyptians were entirely familiar as were the Hindus with America. Thus great deep-seagoing vessels were plying the Nile and also the Erythrean Sea at the east of Arabia. Moreover in a papyrus brought to light by Scliemann in St. Petersburg it is recorded at about this time, an Egyptian expedition put to sea in search of the vanished Atlantis and remaining abroad four years upon returning reported no trace of the vanished world.

In this report appears only a bit of logic. Naturally there was no trace found of what did not exist. Naturally too the explorers did not disclose the fishing hole they had found.

By this time Rama Lunus had passed and taken his place as K-ya-pa-ya-pa among the Seven Sages of the *Veda.* Since his passing, however, the Brahmins despite the older Hinduism based on the Wisdom Philosophy, had perverted the *Lesser Vehicle of Arhat* enshrined at La Ha Sa into Brahmanism with its pantheon of gods just as the gods of Egypt were multiplying among the various elements of that country and evolving into new types with new names. Such was the situation when Rama Chrisna, or Krishna appeared as the Seventh Hindu avatar and undertook to restore Hinduism to its pristine purity.

While he was engaged in this great reform as the alleged reincarnation of Rama in his third aspect, the Egyptians were waxing ever more rich and powerful. Undoubtedly already they had erected the Sphinx as the symbol of the unity of the Punic world, and had allied themselves with their Danitic kinsmen in Ilios when the Greeks generally saw that Sesostris meant to assert control over the Golden Horn, so called because of the bounty from the East which poured through it to the Mediterranean World. Such was the situation when the D-o-r-ians from the North occupied the Poloponessus of Greece and furnished the ancestors of the L-ac-ae-d-e-mon-i-an-s.

With the Scythians of the Balkans established at Pira (41°

N. 28° 59′ E.) on the north shore of the Bosporus, it was impossible for Sesostris to seize the Golden Horn itself. Nevertheless the Danitics of Syria were able to occupy Ilium, or the Troja across the Hellespont from Galli-poli in Gallia. With them as the allies of Egypt and the mythical Nestor, implying the old imperialism of Nimrod, as their king, the Sini-t-i-c mysteries enshrined at Sin-o-pe became the rival of the Pythean mysteries of Athens.

Because the Hellenes had colonized Hellas and the Dorian as their allies, had brought the Poloponessus within the fold of the Pytheans, Homer substituted the name *Argive* for that of *Dania,* implying the united Aryans of Greece. Accordingly Agamemnon, the King of Attica, and Menelaus, the King of the Lacadaemonia in the Poloponessus, were said to be brothers. Likewise the mythical Helen was said to be the wife of Menelaus. For the same reason A-chi-lles was deemed the champion of Athena. The abduction of Helen by Pa-ris, the son of Nestor, simply implied that the Punics had seduced the Ionians.[1] In a word the story of the Trojan War embodied in the Iliad, is simply a mythical account of the economic struggle begun between the Greeks and Sesostris over the control of the Dardanelles, which began centuries before the actual invasion of Ilium by the Greeks and the destruction of Troy.

With this great conflict in progress Rama Chrisna had passed away in B.C. 4,002, having failed to achieve lasting reforms in India. With civilization growing ever more materialistic and gods representing no more than local political ambitions, already the Babylonians had begun to recover in the so-called realm of Nin-gursu, and the Chaldeans had fallen into utter decline, when there occurred that which could not have been due to mere accident.

Now, at last Egypt was unified under Mena, the alleged first Pharaoh of the First Dynasty, to whom the three kingdoms were subject, with its spiritual seat at Memphis and its southern boundary at 20° N. marked by the Second Cataract of the

Nile and the Ja-bel Tellum. Consequently the eponymous F-u Si appeared in Chi-na. With an amazing knowledge of Engineering the latter set out to construct the system of canals through which Chi-na was converted into a land capable of supporting a new civilization and of inheriting that part of the old Celestial Empire of the Uighurs at the north of Burma and Tibet, extending as far west as Syr where were the Tartars, or ancestors of the Turanians from whom evolved the Turks. Concurrently Sargon I appeared in Assyria and undertook the reforms that were to place Ilium between the pincers of the new Assyria and Greece.

While all this was taking place in Greece, Egypt, Asia Minor, India and Chi-na, there appeared in Mexico the great reformer Que-t-z-al Coatl, 'the Serpent of the Queenland,' whose bearded likenesses indicate that he was in fact a Borean ally of the Pharaoh of Egypt. Uniting the Itzaes and Maya in Mexico who had already received a system of common Hieroglyphics and advanced mechanical training while building the teocalli in Mexico, he led them to Y-u-ca-t-ana where he restored the ancient city of U-x-ma-la, and built the two cities of Itza-ma-l and Chi-chen-itza said to have been named after him. In fact, however, the great Chichen of God's House merely took the name of the composite peoples over whom he ruled as *Itzama,* the greatest figure of historical reality yet to appear in America and who as such would ever be so revealed by the Yucatecs. Moreover by B.C. 3,100 when the Itza-Maya Cycle began, he had given to them the peculiar monotheistic religion still possessed by the Maya-x.

From the bearings of the three cities ascribed to the Chichen Itzama, it seems plain that he was of Borean origin and did in fact hail from the Queen land of Scandinavia as indicated by his alternate name Que-t-za-l-coatl, that he was of the Borean Dracontia Cult. We note the new type of teocalli erected at the Yucatec cities and also at Ce Aké at the north of U-x-ma-la, which is today called Merida although originally it bore the name applied to Cairo. This suggests that Sesos-

tris had much to do with the erection of the truncated pyramids of Yucatan similar to the mastaba of Egypt which appeared at Giza before the True Pyramids of the Third and
Fourth Dynasties (B.C. 3,000-2,500) were erected beside the
Sphinx.² Certainly it is not difficult to see why Yucatan came
to be called the Western Egypt. Moreover, Itzama fully explains why the priests of Egypt had claimed for Rameses the
Great (B.C. 1350-1300) the world empire of which the
Sphinx and the Trinity of Giza, or the Barns of Joseph, had
been erected as the symbols, even before the Egyptians set out
from their eastern base at D-el-hi to conquer China and Poly-
nesia.²

Surely enough has been said to show that the so-called *Lost
Empire of the Itzaes* and *Mayas* implied the spiritual empire
of the composite people who in course of time were absorbed
by evolution, just as were the Lion Men of old, and the Manx.

Recently there have been exhumed in Mexico five colossal
Moon Stones of basalt of which the largest is here shown.

"Many intriguing questions remain to be answered concerning this mutilated sculpture and five other colossal heads
excavated by the same National Geographic-Smithsonian Institute Expeditions to Mexico which discovered the oldest
work of man in the Americas for which we have a date."

The truth is, however, there is no definite date for the fash-
ioning of the moon stones.

But if X-o-chi-calco, 'the Castle of Flowers,' still the most
stupendous work of man to be seen on the earth, had
furnished the model for the Pyramids of Che-ops, suggesting
what the original Tower of Babel might have resembled, and
the older teocalli of Mexico had furnished the pattern for the
ziggurats of Sargon I and his successors in Assyria and Babylon and for the stage towers of Egypt, and among other things
maps in stone, two other things must be noticed here. With the
vertical arm of the True Cross passing through Yucatan there
is no mystery about the Temple of the Cross at Pa-l-en-que.

The Moon Stones recently found in Yucatan as well as

countless small cubes corresponding to the Cube of Nippur, furnished the model for the five colossi carved out of the cliff in the Pass of Bamian (34° 54′ N. 67° 40′ E.) and for the five colossi displayed in the Temple erected by Rameses the Great in Nubea.

Of the five colossi of Bamian the tallest is 172′6″, the exact length of the Sphinx from tail to paws, while the other four taper down to give the relative sizes of the 5 Root Races. The second is 120′ high and like the first contains a spiral staircase. It furnished the model for the Statue of Liberty, and the first that for the Colossus of Rhodes. Note that the geodetic symbols of Bamian yield $3 + 4 = 7$; $5 + 4 = 9 = 3 \times 3$; $6 + 7 = 13$, the mystical number; $3 + 4 + 5 + 4 + 6 + 7 + 4 + 0 = 33 = 11 \times 3$.

Undoubtedly Alexander the Great beheld these colossi while passing into O-x-i-ana to the North. The first scholar to mention them was a Chinese explorer about 800 A.D. During the reign of Genghis Khan the two larger ones were occupied by Buddhist monks. Almost on the antipodal meridian, undoubtedly during the reign of Rameses the Great, whose eastern capital was Indraprasthra (28° N. 76° E.), was erected the great colossus now standing on Easter Island (20° S. 120°W.) on the antipodal meridian of Bamian; an immense colossus is also found in southern India like those reared by Rameses the Great at Tanais in the Delta of the Nile. Whether or not the colossi of Bamian trace to Rameses the Great, or to an earlier cycle, is a moot question.

Bamian stands on the Polar Circle with the "Grand Rapa," or Easter Island (27° 30′ S. 109° 30′ W.) where eventually other colossi arose probably concurrently with those of Rameses the Great, while the Egyptians were overrunning the Austral Seas.

The eponymous Mu-sha, or Moses, implying the Philosophic Ark of the New Israel, which appeared in the cycle of Rameses II, is said to have been found in an Ark by the Pharaoh's sister in the bullrushes of the Nile. This implied that the Mosaic cult was founded in the waste area ever beyond the control of the police.

According to Josephus Moses married an Ethiopian Princess taking as his second wife the daughter of the eponymous Jettiro the first Ethiopian ark of the Roc in Palestine. The Rebekka who Moses was said to have met at the well in Jethro's realm, was merely the same Rebekka said to have been the wife of Jacob. For this reason it was that Jethro helped Moses organize the Israelitic refugees from Egypt following the mythical heroics of the Exodus.

The conquest of the Philistines would have been impossible had the Hittites who had produced the Ten Danitic Tribes of Israel, not aided the refugees gathered in the Desert of Tin by Moses and Aaron. The Hittites had no idea of allowing the Israelites to replace the Mysteries of the Ka-bi-ra represented by Jethro. Therefore Moses was never allowed to enter the Promised Land, before his alleged death on Mount P-is-ga, although no explanation of this is given in *Genesis*. Yet, in the Ark of Israel entrusted by Moses to the Levites, or the Tribe of Levi, as the guardians of the New Ark Israel, is to be seen the Wisdom Philosophy that was embodied in the so-called *Lost Book of Numbers,* corresponding to that embodied in the Cube of Nippur, upon which the Apocrypha were based, and also in the Kaballa of the Jews who eventually replaced Yahveyh with Jehovah.

---

1 P-a-ris "the Punic Ark of the Rishi." Ili-a-d, "Ilium, the Ark of Danaeus." "T-r-o-y "the Tau, the Rishi, Brahma, Ya." T-r-o-ja, the same. In the Odyssey is found a veracious record of how the Danitic Arcadians, represented by O-d-esseus, following the overthrow of the Trojans, were to colonize the western world in the Mosaic Age. Manifestly no one individual could have written both the Iliad and the Odyssey. H-o-m-e-r, therefore implies the Hellenes, Pytheas, Maia, Europa Reincarnated.

2 Among the Appendices will be found a chronological table for the convenience of the reader.

Chapter XXXVIII

THE POLITICAL IDEALS OF THE ANCIENTS

HOWEVER MUCH guidance the Hindu, Assyrian, Syrian, Chaldean, Egyptian, Chinese, Greek, Scandinavian, Finnish, and Maya scriptures of Yucatan, and those embodied in the Easter Island Tablets, may yield the student of history, it is not to be imagined that all wisdom was embodied in them. Eventually Longfellow, adopting the metre of the Kalevala to which he had been introduced by the German scholar Friedligrath would record in poesy as exalted as any ever penned by him, the knowledge imparted to him by a Yankton Sioux sachem. Before reading what he wrote of the Red Men's oracle, it is well for those inhabiting the present tortured world, to ponder his introduction to the *Song of Hiawatha.*

Ye who love a nation's legends,
Love the ballads of a people,
That like voices from afar off
Call to us to pause and listen,
Speak in tones so plain and childlike,
Scarcely can the ear distinguish
Whether they are sung or spoken;—
Listen to this Indian Legend,
To this Song of Hiawatha!

Ye whose hearts are fresh and simple,
Who have faith in God and Nature,
Who believe that in all ages
Every human heart is human,
That in even savage bosoms
There are longings, yearnings, strivings
For the good they comprehend not,
That the feeble hands and helpless,
Groping blindly in the darkness,
Touch God's right hand in that darkness
And are lifted up and strengthened;—
Listen to this simple story,
To this Song of Hiawatha!

Ye, who sometimes, in your rambles
Through the green lanes of the country,
Where the tangled barberry-bushes
Hang their tufts of crimson berries
Over stone walls gray with mosses,
Pause by some neglected graveyard,
For a while to muse, and ponder
On a half-effaced inscription,
Written with little skill of song-craft,
Homely phrases but each letter
Full of hope and yet of heart-break,
Full of all the tender pathos
Of the Here and the Hereafter;—
Stay and read this rude inscription,
Read this Song of Hiawatha!

Following these intriguing passages dealing with the region between the pictured rocks, or effigy mounds at the south of Lake Superior in the domain of the Ojibway near the Great Sable, the poet, inspired by the appeals of the helpless Sioux, proceeds to set forth what Gitche Manito, 'the Mighty,' had been teaching the Red Man down the ages at the so-called heathen shrine where the Cheyenne, bearing the cross as their symbol, had carved E-e-ops-i-chi-pe out of the red granite cliff of the *Mountain of the Prairie.*

The Peace-Pipe

On the Mountains of the Prairie,
'On the great Red Pipe-stone Quarry
Gitche Manito, the mighty
He the Master of Life, descending,
On the red crags of the quarry
Stood erect, and called the nations,
Called the tribes of men together.
From his footprints flowed a river,
Leaped into the light of morning,
O'er the precipice plunging downward
Gleamed like Ishkoodah, the comet.
And the Spirit, stooping earthward,
With his finger on the meadow
Traced a winding pathway for it,
Saying to it, 'Run in this way!'

From the red stone of the quarry
With his hand he broke a fragment,
Moulded it into a pipe-head
Shaped and fashioned it with figures;
From the margin of the river
Took a long reed for a pipe-stem,
With its dark green leaves upon it;
Filled the pipe with bark of willow,
With the bark of the red willow,
Breathed upon the neighboring forest,
Made its great boughs chafe together,
Till in flame they burst and kindled;
And erect upon the mountains,
Gitche Manito, the mighty
Smoked the calumet, the Peace-Pipe,
As a signal to the nations.

And the smoke rose slowly, slowly,
Through the tranquil air of morning,
First a single line of darkness,
Then a denser, bluer vapor,
Then a snow-white cloud unfolding,
Like the tree-tops of the forest,
Ever rising, rising, rising,
Till it touched the top of heaven,
Till it broke against the heaven,
And rolled outward all around it.

From the Vale of Tawasentha,
From the Valley of Wyoming,
From the groves of Tuscaloosa,
From the far-off Rocky Mountains,
From the Northern lakes and rivers
All the tribes beheld the signal,
Saw the distant smoke ascending,
The Pukwana of the Peace-Pipe.

And the Prophets of the nations
Said: 'Behold it, the Pukwana!
By this signal from afar off
Bending like a wand of willow,
Waving like a hand that beckons,
Gitche Manito, the mighty,
Calls the tribes of men together
Calls the warriors to his council!'
Down the rivers, o'er the prairies,

Came the warriors of the nations,
Came the Delawares and Mohawks,
Came the Choctaws and Comanches,
Came the Shoshonies and Blackfeet,
Came the Pawnees and Omahas,
Came the Mandans and Dacotahs,
Came the Hurons and Ojibways,
All the warriors drawn together
By the signal of the Peace-Pipe,
To the Mountains of the Prairie,
To the great Red Pipe-stone Quarry.

And they stood there on the meadow
With their weapons and their war-gear,
Painted like the leaves of Autumn
Painted like the sky of morning,
Wildly glaring at each other;
In their faces stern defiance,
In their hearts the feuds of ages,
The hereditary hatred,
The ancestral thirst of vengeance.

Gitche Manito, the mighty,
The creator of the nations,
Looked upon them with compassion,
With paternal love and pity;
Looked upon their wrath and wrangling
But as quarrels among children,
But as feuds and fights of children!

Over them he stretched his right hand,
To subdue their stubborn natures,
To allay their thirst and fever,
By the shadow of his right hand;
Spake to them with voice majestic
As the sound of far-off waters,
Falling into deep abysses,
Warning, chiding, spake in this wise:—

'O my children! my poor children!
Listen to the words of wisdom,
Listen to the words of warning,
From the lips of the Great Spirit,
From the Master of Life, who made you!

'I have given you lands to hunt in,
I have given you streams to fish in,
I have given you bear and bison,

I have given you roe and reindeer,
I have given you brant and beaver,
Filled the marshes full of wild-fowl,
Filled the rivers full of fishes;
Why then are you not contented?
Why then will you hunt each other?

'I am weary of your quarrels,
Weary of your wars and bloodshed,
Weary of your prayers for vengeance,
Of your wranglings and dissensions;
All your strength is in your union,
All your danger is in discord;
Therefore be at peace henceforward,
And as brothers live together.

'I will send a Prophet to you,
A Deliverer of the nations,
Who shall guide you and shall teach you,
Who shall toil and suffer with you.
If you listen to his counsels,
You will multiply and prosper;
If his warnings pass unheeded,
You will fade away and perish!

'Bathe now in the stream before you,
Wash the war-paint from your faces,
Wash the blood-stains from your fingers,
Bury your war-clubs and your weapons,
Break the red stone from this quarry
Mould and make it into Peace-Pipes,
Take the reeds that grow beside you,
Deck them with your brightest feathers,
Smoke the calumet together,
And as brothers live henceforward!'

Then upon the ground the warriors
Threw their cloaks and shirts of deer-skin
Threw their weapons and their war-gear,
Leaped into the rushing river,
Washed the war-paint from their faces.
Clear above them flowed the water,
Clear and limpid from the footprints
Of the Master of Life descending;
Dark below them flowed the water,
Soiled and stained with streaks of crimson,
As if blood were mingled with it!

[*331*]

From the river came the warriors,
Clean and washed from all their war-paint
'On the banks their clubs they buried,
Buried all their warlike weapons.
Gitche Manito, the mighty
The Great Spirit, the creator,
Smiled upon his helpless children!
 And in silence all the warriors
Broke the red stone of the quarry,
Smoothed and formed it into Peace-Pipes,
Broke the long reeds by the river,
Decked them with their brightest feathers,
And departed each one homeward,
While the Master of Life, ascending,
Through the opening of cloud-curtains,
Through the doorways of the heaven,
Vanished from before their faces,
In the smoke that rolled around him,
The Pukwana of the Peace-Pipe!

These indeed are exalting words constituting a scripture with which as with "the Watcher" every thoughtful person to-day should be familiar.

Did the Mosaic scribes and the Prophets Eli, Elias, Isaiah, and Micah know of "the Watcher" and of the 'Oracle of Winnewassa?'

We only know that when Jeremiah, according to a great English historian, was establishing the Lia Fail, or Stone of Destiny, at the sacred tree of T-ara (7° W.) in Ireland on the meridian of Scalp Mountain and the Faro Islands, more than a century before Micah as the contemporary of Isaiah (c.B.C. 750), of Lycurgus, founder of Sparta, of the mythical Romulus and Remus said by Virgil to have founded Rome, and of the eponymous Hesiod to whom the Greek Theogony is ascribed, had written:

"But in the last days it shall come to pass, that the mountain of the house of the Lord shall be established in the top of the mountains, and it shall be exalted above the hills; and people shall flow into it.

"2 And many nations shall come, and say, Come, and let us go up to the mountain of the Lord, and to the house of the God of Jacob: and he will teach us his ways, and we will walk in his paths; for the law shall go forth of Zion, and the word of the Lord from Je-ru-sa-lem.

"3 And he shall judge among many people, and rebuke strong nations afar off; and they shall beat their swords into plowshares, and their spears into pruninghooks: nation shall not lift up a sword against nation, neither shall they learn war any more.

"4 But they shall sit every man under his vine and under his fig tree; and none shall make them afraid: for the mouth of the Lord of hosts hath spoken it.

"5 For all people will walk every one in the name of his god, and we will walk in the way of the Lord our God for ever and ever."

The time came, it is true, when the Irish bard, Thomas More, standing in the solitude of Tara whence long since St. Columba had removed the Lia Fail to Ionia before its successive removals to Edinburgh and thence to Westminster Abbey by Edward II, would pen the lament:

> "The harp that once through Tara's halls
> The Soul of Music shed,
> Now hangs as mute on Tara's walls
> As if that Soul were fled,
> So sleeps the pride of former days,
> So glory's thrill is o'er;
> And hearts that once beat high for praise
> Now feel that pulse no more."[1]

"The Watcher" and E-e-ops-i-chi-pe, like the red city of Petra, however, no more than the Castle of Flowers at X-o-ch-calco, and "the Thunderer," or seven-stage tower at Pa-p-anas-t-la in Mexico, and the Barns of Joseph at Gizeh could be removed.

Already it has been pointed out that they were in fact the man-reared symbols of the Sacred Hepdomad. And here it is to be noted that this primordial symbol which had been found carved on the crags of the Alps and on bones found in the lakes of Switzerland, had political as well as religious implications.

To repeat in the base of the square, or the Quaternary of Septenary Man, to which was ascribed the color of highest vibration, the Ancients saw the mortal embryo; in the orange of the left side, the period of infancy; in the red, or right side, that of maturity and the procreative period of men, with the green upper side as the period of a cooler, old age.

As men attain to old age, however, they begin to contemplate more and more the meaning of life and the future. In the yellow left side of the triangle they saw the factor of respect for authority, and in the blue right side the intuitive faculty of men and their longing for freedom of action.

If, however, men give over to an inordinate respect for authority, government passes from monarchy to despotism, even though at times a benevolent one, perhaps, which is the most desired because the most efficient. Yet, soon or late despotism passes into tyranny that leads to anarchy and chaos.

On the other hand, excessive indulgence in liberty of action, or democracy, as surely leads to tyranny, to anarchy, and to chaos.

Therefore the ideal was held to be the balance between authority and popular liberties represented by the equilateral triangle along whose medium man was most apt to attain the ideal of happiness associated with the azure of the great beyond. To attain the ideal required not only a sacrifice by the *Haves* but one by the *Have Nots*.

Yet, they conceived of no such thing as a government that would be ideal for all peoples. Manifestly a government that for some might possess excessive authority, for others would be so weak as to be but a license for all manner of popular tyrannies. What was the best government for any particular people depended on their capacity to enjoy freedom without abusing it.

The ancients could not have imagined a wise man teaching,

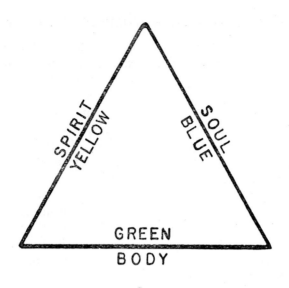

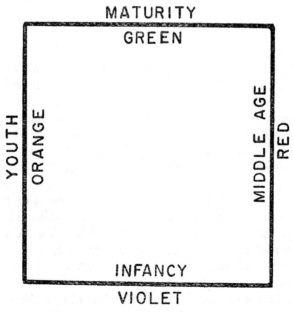

THE SACRED HEBDOMAD

[335]

as some are now doing, that all peoples, irrespective of their intellectual and moral development, are entitled to govern themselves as they see fit, without regard to others. But if they conceived not of the Divine Right of Kings, neither did they sanction the basic principle of Communism. For in truth the latter is but a scheme to place men at the mercy of tyrannical dictators who not only deny them the right of self-government, but make it impossible for them to develop the capacity to administer it.

Such in truth was the philosophy upon which Solon had based the Athenian Republic when Confucius as the pupil of Lao Tze taught: "Government is justifiable only to the extent it serves the governed." Per contra, if it does not serve the governed as distinguished from the governors, it is not justifiable.

This was the idea of the mythical Cincinnatus who undertook to save the Roman Republic in its infancy. Also it was the idea of Plato who wrote the dialogues of the *Timaeus* and *Critias* dealing with the mythical kingdom of Atlas, as mere preludes to his *Republic*.

It was the idea of the pagan Islandingas who about 930 declared their independence of Norway, and certainly aware of "the Watcher," founded the Republic of which Iceland and Labrador which then included Greenland and the Western Ireland, were the domains. Also it was the idea of the mythical William Tell who in 1308, or 48 years after the Islandingas had been compelled to surrender their constitution, founded the Swiss Republic. Moreover, one who studies the *Divine Comedy* of Dante against the background of historical events in his age will see in it but a shaft of ridicule loosed by him against the political materialism of his time. Also it will be seen that the mysterious Beatrice upon whom he expended his devotion in the *Vita Nova* was in fact his ideal of human freedom.

No. The ideas taught by Gitche Manito at the shrine of Winnewassa did not originate in Europe.[2] They were being taught there long before the age of Dante, Wycliff, Cosmo Medici, Prince Henry the Navigator, Edward IV, Lorenzo the Magnificent, Leo X, Leonardo da Vinci, Toscanelli, Columbus, Martin Behaim, Sir Thomas More, Coligny, William the Silent, Edmund Spenser, Elizabeth, Raleigh, Bacon, Drake, Sir Philip Sidney, Sir Humphrey Gilbert, Amidas Waad 'the British Columbus,' and the mysterious magician, John Dee, the tutor of Elizabeth. How the republican ideal, to propagate which Cosmo de Medici founded the Platonian Academy in 1340, was transmitted to Edward IV, to Sir Thomas More who gave expression to it in his *Utopia,* to Coligny who attempted to found two republics in America, to the seamen of Elizabeth who under the lead of Drake demanded a charter of Elizabeth for Sir Humphrey Gilbert (1578) lest they found a republic in America independent, of England, constitutes the epic of Virginia, and is no part of this work. It must here be noted, however, that in 1542, just 20 years after Giovanni de Medici who had launched Columbus, was poisoned, and 7 years after his friend Sir Thomas More was sent to the block, the Great Mogul Akbar was born in India; that he was devoting his life to the ideal of peace when William the Silent in 1582 proclaimed the independence of the Dutch Republic; that he died in 1602, the very year that the Dutch East India Company was established with Grotius as its secretary.

Vast ethnological researches show that the youngest and smallest of the seven Linguistic Families of North America, the *Ira-k-na-hoïw,* 'Adders, known to the French as Iroquois, first appeared as the Two Brothers in the region of the lower St. Lawrence, *with* institutions of a distinctly Druidic type. Eventually they spread into the region of Northern New York at the south of Lake Ontario between the Adi-rond-ac and Ni-a-ga-ra. At some time these peculiarly whitish, round head peoples took into their brotherhood the dark Mohawks who had originally inhabited the region of Montreal from which they appear to have been driven by the French about 1520. Inasmuch as the Mohawks were scalpers by nature, like the Siouans, the

Third Brother was probably a mixture of Siouans and Algooa-makin of the older type. For here it is to be noted that no other aborigines of America practice scalping save the Sioux and those with whom they came in contact, though it was common to the man Pirite of Scandinavan, the Lapps, and the Scytheans in the ancient realm of Hell.

Of the three brothers the O-ne-ida with the Tree as their symbol, were the seniors. Therefore, at the Round Table of their councils, the sachems of the Oneida sat at the North in what erroneously is called the Long House, but more correctly interpreted as the Extended Lodge, implying that the mysteries of N-ana-bo-za had been extended to the Three Brothers. At the East sat the Mohawks, and at the South the O-n-an-da-i-qua.

It was with a fine eye for strategy that these people occupied the Mohawk Valley and seized the salt beds around Syracuse with the O-n-e-i-da seated at Oneida Castle, which took its name from a great stone to be seen there. This stone in all probability was one of the magic stones of antiquity. From the offspring of the Three Brothers evolved the Seneca, as the Fourth Brother who, with their center at Seneca Falls, became the guardian of the western marches, and of them the Ca-yu-ga evolved as the Fifth Brother.

Possibly in course of time it will be shown that the Five Brothers of whom the Seneca were to be the dominant warriors traced back to the age of Seneca who in the *Medea* (40 A.D.) pointed out that eventually another Jason would show that the world beyond Ultima Thule was inhabited. However that may be it is plain that those who had come to occupy the region of the Sha-ta-mu, or the Ta-s-wa-sin-tha were subject to the teachings of Gitche Manito, as pointed out in the *Peace-Pipe* of Longfellow. Surely too, "the Watcher" was well known to them. To be sure they were not to adopt the constitution given to the League of the Extended Lodge, popularly known as the League of the Long House, until 1577. Nevertheless it is certain that they were endeavoring to enforce peace upon their neighbors when Francis Bacon published his *Atlan-*

tida Nova (1611) expressing the ideal of universal peace dealt with by Sir Thomas More in *Utopia.*

Were those who were endeavoring to pacify the 7 linguistic families of America through the oracle of Winnewassa, more practical than those who founded the various leagues of peace that appeared throughout Medieval times?

We only know that they did not limit their efforts to indulging in futile debate with Maliks and Vishinskys. They did not expect their sons to perish in a war with avowed enemies of God and Man while they were furnishing the latter with the means to destroy their youth, either directly or indirectly. Neither did these pupils of 'the Watcher' and Gitche Manito hold that the Economic Man of modern times was the rightful ruler of the universe, and that the spiritual factor of life was a matter to be left to the nursery. From the *Peace-pipe* and the grand septenary monuments of aboriginal America it is to be gathered that their ideal was one expressed by Tennyson, the contemporary of Longfellow, in Locksley Hall:

"For I dipt into the future, far as human eye could see,
Saw the Vision of the world, and all the wonder that would be;
Saw the heavens fill with commerce, argosies of magic sails,
Pilots of the purple twilight, dropping down with costly bales;
Heard the heavens fill with shouting, and there rain'd a ghastly dew
From the nations' airy navies grappling in the central blue;
Far along the world-wide whisper of the south-wind rushing warm,
With the standards of the peoples plunging thro' the thunder-storm;
Till the war-drum throbb'd no longer, and the battle-flags were furl'd
In the Parliament of man, the Federation of the world.
There the common sense of most shall hold a fretful realm in awe,
And the kindly earth shall slumber, lapt in universal law.
So I triumph'd ere my passion sweeping thro' me left me dry,
Left me with the palsied heart, and left me with the jaundiced eye;
Eye, to which all order festers, all things here are out of joint:
Science moves, but slowly slowly, creeping on from point to point:
Slowly comes a hungry people, as a lion creeping nigher,
Glares at one that nods and winks behind a slowly-dying fire.
Yet I doubt not thro' the ages one increasing purpose runs,
And the thoughts of men are widen'd with the process of the suns."

With many of the mysteries of the so-called Archaic Age solved in a rational way, possibly something in the nature of a more detailed history of civilization than this study will be written. For if in truth Eternity and History alone have triumphed over time, as declared by Raleigh, thanks to the revelations of science it is plain, as declared by Bacon, that history lies at the base of the Pyramids, and that Shakespeare spoke truthfully when he declared that the sons of Edward II lay in the breast of Abraham. So, the student of history is prepared at last to understand why both the spread eagle representing the great spirit, the symbol carved on countless rocks in America during ancient times, and the Pyramid both appear in the great seal of the United States, the Republic which, according to both John Adams and Benjamin Franklin was based upon the Iroquois League of the Extended Lodge with the membership enlarged to Six Nations by the addition of the Tuscarora of the Carolinas who migrated to New York in 1716. That year, it must be noted, was the year that Governor Spotswood of Virginia led the Anglican Aristocrats of the old dominion to the summit of the Blue Ridge, and pointing to the serried ridges of Appalachia, formed the brotherhood of the Knights of the Golden Horseshoe to ensure that the British posterity of Abraham would rule the ancient realm of Atlas.

With this work brought to a conclusion the author must leave it to the solemn judgment of the historians of the future how much of the material presented in it is worthy of their consideration. Certainly the reader must wonder if the Church of England was entirely right when it formally declared that the creation narrative in *Genesis* was merely mythologically symbolic and without historical value. Certainly too the pundits of Political Science must wonder just how far modern philosophic thought has improved upon the moral concepts of the so-called Archaic Age into which the author has sought to penetrate with the aid of modern Science.

Surely has it been shown that the alleged prophecy of Jeremiah of the great nation destined to appear in the West giving rise to the dreams of Solon, Plato, Cincinnatus, Vergil, Seneca, Dante and William Tell, the Medici, Columbus, Vitoria, Sir Thomas More and Erasmus, of Leo X, Coligny, William the Silent, the Prophets Dekanawida and Hiawatha who founded the Iroquois League of the Extended Lodge upon which the Articles of Confederation were based, of Amidas Waad, the British Columbus, of Raleigh, Delaware, Henry of Navarre, Grotius, Roger Williams, William Penn, Washington and Lincoln, was based on the Divine Logic that produced each and all of the Hebrew Prophets whose inspired wisdom to-day is so little heeded.

In this work let the thoughtful see but a plea to reason rather than to the Economic Man as the alleged sufficient and rightful ruler of the earth. Let the United Nations Educational, Scientific and Cultural Organization abandon its godless teachings. Let the Parent Teacher Association repudiate the atheistic cult of the cabal that has dared to raise its hand as Nimrod did against both God and Man. Let it remember what the martyred Parson of Ipswich penned in the Text Book of American Liberty—the only practical democracy is a government ruled by the Spirit of God. Let it see that this was but a repetition of the words of the Prophet—only where the Spirit of God is may liberty be found. The writer who closes his work with these words, cares not if he be branded by the blind, as an "Illegitimate historian." For he has let all the sciences combined reveal the pattern of the civilization that finds its true symbols in the pyramid and the spread eagle appearing twin-like on the obverses of the material disc corresponding to the Sea of Time, constituting the Great Seal of the United States of America, the Republic that owes its name not to the Italian banker, Amerige Vespucci, but as shown in this work to the Immortals. His faith in God is such he cannot believe the Amara of the human race now in the forming will let that Republic and its professed faith in God, perish from the earth.   *Finis*

THE PHILOSOPHIC HISTORY OF CIVILIZATION

[1] If, however, More had served with the Irish, Scottish, Welsh, and English divisions along the Somme in 1918, as it fell to the writer to do, and had seen how the skirling pibrochs stirred the army that drenched Ypres, Thiepval Ridge and other battlefields with its blood, with sincerity he could not have written these lines. The writer looks back on the days when he marched to the pipes of his Douglas and Devon ancestors as the most glorious of his long life. See his *Great Crusade* (Dial Press, 1931). The facts behind the shrine of Tara explain the recent attempt of the Scots to recapture the stone removed from the holy shrine of Snowden (Edinburgh) from which Edward II had removed it to Westminster under his arrangement with David Bruce that the survivor was to rule Great Britain.

[2] See Appendix "E".

APPENDIX "A"

The Ten Divine Dynasties of Chaldea according to the *Chronology* of Berossus (B.C. 250).*

1. Alorus of Babylonia.................B.C. 432,535, lasted 10 sari, 36,000 solar years
2. Alparus of Sippara.................B.C. 396,735, lasted 3 sari, 10,800 solar years
3. Amilarus of Sippara.................B.C. 385,935, lasted 13 sari, 46,800 solar years
4. Ammennon of Sippara.................B.C. 339,135, lasted 12 sari, 43,200 solar years
5. Megalorus of Sippara.................B.C. 295,935, lasted 18 sari, 64,800 solar years
6. Daonas of Sippara.................B.C. 231,135, lasted 10 sari, 36,000 solar years
7. Eurodereschus of Sippara.................B.C. 195,135, lasted 18 sari, 64,800 solar years
8. Amenipsimus of Larissa.................B.C. 130,335, lasted 10 sari, 36,000 solar years
9. Ardates of Larissa.................B.C. 94,335, lasted 8 sari, 28,800 solar years
10. Xisusthrus of Babylon.................B.C. 65,535, lasted 18 sari, 64,800 solar years

* *Beros Chalderum Historiaeque Superssiicum Commentationi*, RICHTER (1827). *Ancient Fragments*, CORY (1st Ed. 1832; 2nd Ed. 1876).

HISTORICAL ANALYSIS OF THE TWELVE LABORS OF HERCULES SHOWING THE EVOLUTION OF THE POST-CATACLYSMIC CIVILIZATION OF EUROPE FROM B. C. 10,000 TO THE FIRST OLYMPIAD, B. C. 776

While the Aryan mysteries of the Kabira originally had been symbolized among the Greeks by the seven headed dog Cerberus, in course of time, because of the influence of the Greek mysteries, Cerberus, had come to have but three heads corresponding to the trinitic concept of the elements of fire, water, and earth, and the spirit, soul, and body of man, more compatible with the anthropic concept of Zeus, Poseidon and Hades, than with the old Serpent Cult, and the Tree Cult of the Hebrews, both of which conceive of the philosophic syntheisi symbolized by Naragana, Yaveygh, En Zu, and Enyalius. The first task assigned Hercules, said to have been the most difficult of all, was to bring back to the earth Cerberus in the philosophic sense which had all but vanished from Greece and, therefore, was said to have fallen into Erebus, or the dark realm of Hades.

Because the Sinitic mysteries to which traced the anthropic concepts of the Greeks had been enshrined in a cave near Ta-e-na-ru-m, the promontory of Cape Ma-t-a-p-ana in A-t-t-i-ca by the Ru and the Enix, Hercules is shown entering Hades at that point. The shades implying the priesthood fled in terror. Near the gate of Attica, however, Hercules found his old friends Theuseus, the King of Athens, and Peiri-thous, sitting on a rock, implying the Piraeus, so firmly attached to it that they seemed part of the rock, and in great trouble as the Attican priesthood of the Sinitic mysteries naturally would have been by reason of what had befallen Greece. Although Hercules freed Theuseus in the sense that the Hellenes who estab-

lished the Pythian mysteries at Colonnay in Attica helped
Theuseus upbuild the new Athens and become the Colonizers
of Attica, it was difficult to restore the old city of Athens near
which on the Gulf of Eleusis the Sinitic mysteries had been
established. For when the attempt was made the earth shook,
implying the earthquake that wrecked the old capital of Attica. Nevertheless it was done, and to impart life to the shades
of his friends whom he freed, he obtained the blood from the
cows of Hades which he killed after a severe fight with their
herdsman. In other words the Hellenes slew the cow-worship-
pers who had perverted the Wisdom Philosophy.

At last he reached Pluto who agreed that he might take
Cerberus provided he could do so without a conflict of arms.
This he succeeded in doing, leading the much hated dog to
Eurytheus, implying a reform of the Sinitic mysteries.

2. Hercules next was sent to destroy with the aid of Athena
the cult which the Chus, or descendants of the Lion Men, had
instituted at Nemea which was sacred to Zeus because he
represented the demiurge of the Fourth Root Race. Entering
the cave, or the lair of the Nemean Lion, he strangled the
beast, whose smell made the region of Nemea a foul one.
Knowing the skin of the lion was impenetrable in the sense
that the blood of the Fourth Root Race could not be destroyed,
he skinned the lion and henceforth wore the hide as the symbol
that he was the champion of all the Greeks. In other words
the peoples of the posterity of the Chus had been converted.
So they were allowed in the years to come to hold their own
games just as the Olympiad later was held at Delphi.

3. Next Hercules was sent to destroy the vile smelling
Learnean Hydra, a monster with nine heads, one immortal,
corresponding to the nine muses, who inhabited the noisome
marshlands of Amymone, said to be the daughter of Danaus,
and in whose name we recognize that applied to the eponymous King Lear, Lir, or Leyr, representing the Druids of
Wales who eventually produced King Lud, the founder of
London.

With his unerring shafts of light from the bow of Athena he drove the evil monster out of his lairs into the open, but for every one of the heads he cut off, two others grew in its place. In other words the hydra had many allies among the Druids who still clung to the perversions of the Python. However, he caused his charioteer to set fire to the forest lands of Amymone and burned the heads that he then cut off while the immortal one was placed under a stone. In other words at last the survivors were converted and were allowed to enshrine the Pythian mysteries.

4. The Erymanthean boar in the wild haunt of Mount Erymantheus at the north of Arabia was also a menace. When the hero went in search of the barbarians represented by it, they assailed him. But Hercules had poisoned his arrows with the venom of the hydra and destroyed Erymantheus. So this kingdom tracing to the third Root Race, the Boars, also collapsed.

5. The Ceryneian stag with antlers of gold and hoofs of brass was sacred to Artemis to whom it had been dedicated by one of the Pleiades, or daughters of Atlas. A very elusive creature implying the increasing materialism of the age when gold and metals were coming into common use, it was to be captured and brought to Mycenae. The stag, however, dashed off and ran a whole year, going to the land of the Hyperboreans before returning. This myth indicates very plainly that gold and copper were coming to Greece by way of the Danube from Hell. At last the stag was overtaken by Hercules at the river Ladon, and would have been slain by him had Apollo and Artemis not intervened. In other words gold and copper, as shown by the Palace of Knossus, had come to have an economic value, so that the trade in it was not to be destroyed despite the abuses of wealth.

6. The Vale of Stymphalis lay in the mountains near Mount Cyllene in Arcadia. In those days as now, the world was full of harpies like the vile Bacchante, ever symbolized by birds of prey with sharp beaks and talons. Representing the female

cult, these foul birds looked to the goddess of love as their patron. To get rid of them Hercules rang a bell to bring them out of their evil nests. Although he shot many of them down, others flew away.

The ringing of bells was one of the oldest methods employed to scare off thieves and other criminals. To it trace the chimes of the Christian churches.[1]

7. Augeas, the rich prince of Elis, and his daughter Agamede, a sorceress who knew the potency of all herbs, dwelt at Ephyra. Augeas was supposed to be the son of Helios who kept twelve white bulls which identify him as of the Druidic bull cult. Naturally his realm was a foul, morally filthy stable. Hercules must clean it out. When he attempted to do this, at once war began between Hercules and the peoples of Elis.

8. The Cretan bull had been presented to the mythical King Minos of Crete by Zeus. Eventually it had become wild, implying the debasement of the solar cult. Hercules brought it back to Mycenae just as Zeus in the shape of a bull had brought Europa to the Medi Terre. It escaped so that the worship of the bull in the Poloponessus continued.

9. King Diomedes was noted like his Thracian subjects for fierceness in war because in fact the peoples of these parts were Scythians. Even his horses, implying the mounted kinsmen of the Circassian Cossacks, fed on flesh. Overpowering the guards, he led the horses to the shore, implying the capture of the cavalry. There he was overtaken by a crowd of Thracians and a terrible fight ensued in which Hercules slew Diomedes. The horses were carried back to Mycenae where they escaped to the Arcadian hills. There the captives appear to have been destroyed by wolves.

10.The girdle of Hippolyte, the queen of the Scythian Amazons, the priestess of the Danae who had been given Hera by Ares, the God of War, must be obtained. This evil competitor of Pythias was slain by Hercules. Here it should be noted that among the Indians of Brazil, just as among the Scythians, there were women warriors called Amazons who removed one breast so as to handle huge bows more expertly.[2]

11. Gergoneus, or Geryon, was the son of Chrysaoe and the Oceanic nymph Callarrhoe. In one person he had three bodies, three heads, three pair of legs, and six arms. Gigantic in size and heavily armed as were the British and Irish, he was powerful and provided with wings, implying the Dracontia Cult. Thus he was the owner of immense herds of cattle, and was associated with Apollo and Helios. In a word he represented the Irish, British, and Scotch Corydeans among whom the Dragon Cult of Dis had evolved. In Callarrhoe we recognize Callernish on Lewis Island in the Hebrides. Thus the cattle, representing the people wearing horns, lived in caves. The realm of Geryon, therefore, was called Erythia, implying a land of red people, said to lie in the remote west beyond the Pillars of Hercules. Thither went Hercules in a vessel obtained from Helios, implying the people of the solar cult in Hull. Hercules had to kill Geryon while driving off the cattle. But although he shipped his captives, implying peoples of the bull worship, to Italy, he himself proceeded on foot through Iberia, Gaul, and over the Alps, down through Italy. Thus the Hellenes who invaded the British Isles were the precursors of Wagner's Parsifal.

At Rome he had adventures with a robber, implying the Pirates of the Po. At Cumae he fought the Giants. In the south of Italy one of the bulls escaped across the sea to Sicily. Since it was necessary to follow it, holding on by the horns of another bull he crossed with his herd to that island. There again he fought with giants. Thence he passed up the shores of Illyria and Epirus, to Ambracia where a gad-fly sent by Hera, implying Druidic allies of his captives, caused his cattle to run off in great numbers to the mountains. With those still held by him he reached the Hellespont, and thence proceeded to Mycenae where Eurytheus sacrificed his remaining cattle to the goddess Hera.

From this myth the far-flung activities of the Pytheans in

their efforts to suppress the bull rights of the Druids, seem plain. Plainly the captives were brought to Mycenae for instruction in the Pythian mysteries.

12. The last of the twelve labors is particularly rich in history.

Apparently the Hellenes had learned in the land of Geryon of the three maidens called Hesperides, who represented the old cult of Python, lived in the garden set apart to them. In it a dragon guarded a tree on which grew golden apples, to see that his charges did not eat of them as Eve is said to have eaten of the forbidden fruit in the garden of Eden.

The golden apples undoubtedly represented the gold of nonnative origin which in B.C. 5,000 was more plentiful in Ireland than in any other part of Europe save Scandinavia where there was also silver of non-European origin.* Of course the attempt was made by earlier historians to make it appear the immense wealth in Ireland came of the sands of Islay in Eire, but now it is generally recognized that in B.C. 500,000 the Pira-ti had found their way to the western world and were navigating the seven seas at will. Thus, according to the Hindus, Prince Maya visited the western antipodes at this time, which fully explains the Dragon trees in those parts. Accordingly the Phoenicians, who by B.C. 1700 were constantly visiting the Pharaoh Islands, located the Garden of the Hesperides in the remote west, while Aeschylus placed it in the Land of the Hyperboreans.

Because in fact it lay in America, Hercules proceeded to the Rhine in Ligurian Gaul where with great difficulty he compelled the sun god Nereus to disclose the secret of the garden's whereabouts. Gold in great quantities lay on the Gold Coast of Africa as well as in the west.

But alas! The giant Ant-a-eus, whose name implies peoples akin to those in Antillia, or the Antipodes, inhabited the part of the old Libya remaining in northern Africa where Herodotus placed the Atlantide ancestors of the Berbers of Tri-poli-

* Montelius.

t-ana. Inasmuch as the Atlantides killed any one who ventured into the waste later called the Sea of Sa-ra-go-s-sa and described as impassable down to the time of Columbus, the Hellenes dared not risk going even to Calypso, or the Madeira Islands, where eventually Ulysses would be captured and held by Circe. Nor could they reach Guinea until Ant-a-eus had been destroyed. In the wrestle which ensued between them he came out victor but a very weary one. According to the Jewish prophet-historian Cleo-de-mus it was only with the aid of the eponymous Aphren, the posterity of Ishmael, that Hercules, who had married the daughter of Aphren, succeeded in doing this. While he was resting from the struggle he was assailed by a host of pygmies. These he wrapped in the lion skin and smothered them. According to the same authority, however, Hercules now founded the Sophacians in the Tri-pol-i-t-ana among whom Ulysses would eventually found Utica (12° E.) on the meridian of Rome, and Copenhagen in Dan's Mark and Gote-berg in Norway, giving the Greeks direct access to the Gold Coast.

With Egypt thus cut off by the Sophacians from the Atlantic, it was far more important in the view of the Ishmaelites for the Greeks to go to the aid of the Israelites in Misraim than to find the gold in the west since they now had direct access to the Gold Coast of Guinea.

The Twelfth Labor of Hercules would be difficult to understand had not Plato shown that in B.C. 8,500, or just 500 years after the Medi Terre had been submerged, by way of Libya Hercules proceeded to Egypt.

Although the Ishmaelites had possessed themselves of the important port of Ismailia at the head of the Red Sea, thus giving them complete control of Suez as the gateway from Ru-ten-na, or Palestine, into the land of Chemi, or the realm of the Ten Archers, by this time the Ethiopian element of Egypt were bitterly hostile to the red element represented by the Ishmaelites, the posterity of Esau, and the Israelites alike. Accordingly when Hercules reached Egypt he was seized under orders of B-u-si-r-is, in whom we see the Sinitic mysteries. Although he was to be sacrificed he burst his bonds, and offered up instead B-u-si-ris, his son, and retinue.

Because of the tremendous effort the Hellenes as champions of the Pythian mysteries at once put forth to capitalize the situation, it is said in the Iliad that Hera, implying the Earth, was annoyed by the fast rising fame of the young hero Hercules. The word annoyed as here implied does not mean that the mythical wife of Zeus was hostile to her champion even if others were. Thus it appears that she called upon Eurytheus, plainly implying the priesthood of Pythian Mysteries which had been enshrined at Delphi, to exercise the authority given him at his birth by Zeus, to call on Hercules to enter his service. Although Hercules enquired at the Delphic oracle whether it was possible to escape the summons, he was told that he must carry out successfully the twelve tasks that were imposed upon him by Eurytheus at the instance of Hera, and that when he had done so, he would be reckoned among the immortals. Thereupon Hercules, leaving Thebes, presented himself with his club, implying the Tree Cult, to Eurytheus at Mycenae, and undertook the tasks assigned him.

From Egypt, according to the myth dealing with the twelfth labor of Hercules, he proceeded to India. This does not mean, of course, that the white Hellenes now occupied the whole of India. It does, however, explain the name Del-hi, applied to Indra-phrasthra, the capital of Rajput-ana, by the white Caucasians who were to furnish the Brahmin caste of the Hindus.

Why had Hercules gone to India? The answer is plain. Already, as shown, the Grand Khan of Tartary had made his seat La Ha Sa, or God's House, in the mythical realm of Panchia which included Tibet at the North of Bharatasavarsa.

The remainder of the twelfth labor leaves not the slightest room to doubt what followed the alleged visit of Hercules to India. Plainly it was now arranged that the Hellenes as the champions of the Dhahana in the West were to have the task of re-enlightening the Druidic world, and of re-civilizing the Libyans generally as well as the Caucasians of the Urals, Russia, Circassia, and the Caucasus. Thus we are told that from India Hercules returned to Greece in a northwesterly direction by way of the Caucasus, where he liberated Prometheus from his bonds.

The act implied simply that the non-Caucasian peoples of the Caucasus, descended from the Ru, were brought into the fold of Pythias along with the Turkomen Scythians of Syr, whose civilization had been all but wiped out, as shown by the great dunes in the Kara Kum and the ruins of Old Merv tracing back to the Uighurs.

In the myth it is said that in return for this act of kindness, Hercules was informed how to find the Golden Apples of the Hesperides. Part of the arrangement he made was that Atlas, implying the ancestors of the Pirati in the Queenland, should pluck the apples for him. The implication of this is that while the Pirati who were the kinsmen of the peoples in the Western Hemisphere beyond Ultima Thule, or Islanda and Greenland, or the Ogygia of the Greeks, might traffic with the Indians, still the Gauls were debarred from direct dealings with them. To enable Atlas to do this Hercules agreed to relieve him from the punishment which had been imposed upon him for engaging in the rebellion against Zeus.

Atlas returned with the three apples and naively suggested that he himself deliver them to Eurytheus. Hercules, however, wanted none of this. Pretending to appreciate the offer, he declared he must have a pad for his head to bear the weight of his burden. In a word the people of the Queenland must stand as a buffer state between the Western World and Gallia lest the Druids of the British Isles and those in the relics of the Land of Is undertake to punish the white race for its intrusions.

According to one version of the myth, however, Hercules himself entered the garden of Hesperides, slew the Dragon, and carried the apples back to Eurytheus. This is not in conflict with the other version, merely implying that the white

Aryans called Tuahati de Danaan, who had appeared in Ireland, overthrew the old Dracontia Cult which had evolved from the Python and substituted for it the cult of D-is which Caesar in B.C. 52 found enshrined on the isle of Mona in the Irish Sea as guardians under the sanction of God's House of the seaway to Islanda or the Greek Ultima Thule. The twelve labors of Hercules so interpreted give a very accurate record of the conflicts between the peoples of Europe and Northern Africa who survived the Cataclysm of B.C. 10,-000 some of whom traced their descent back to the mythical Atlas who according to Greek mythology, following the submission of his alleged father Poseidon to Zeus, was punished for his rebellious course although ultimately pardoned. Inasmuch as some of them traced their descent back to Danaeus, the putative son of Belus, and others to Deucalion and Pyrra, with varying admixtures of red, brown, and white blood in their veins, naturally they cherished varying traditions that had to be harmonized by the alleged labors of Hercules to bring into being the Greek nation they ultimately produced. Nor is it difficult to see the origin of the concept of the Pillars of Hercules constituting the gateway from the Mediterranean to the Atlantic. For Atlas is shown not only upholding with his arms the universal sphere, but also bearing the burden of it upon his shoulders, symbolizing the periods of his sway and punishment. During the latter the mythical Hercules was called upon to reestablish the rule of Zeus, or the philosophy symbolized by the pillars of which the present Gibr el Tarik was deemed by the post cataclysmic peoples inhabiting the relics of Libya on either side of the Strait leading into the old realm of Atlas, to be a natural symbol.

[1] When the Irish monks under Dicuil first went to Iceland in the eighth century they reported that they found only the bells of the Milesians whom they probably destroyed.

[2] The Spanish Conquistadore Oveido fought with Indian Amazons while overrunning Brazil from Peru in 1542. See his *Historia natural general de las Indias* (Seville).

APPENDIX "C"

THE SACRED RED PIPESTONE QUARRY AND THE RECOVERY OF THE RIGHTS OF ITS GUARDIANS, THE YANKTON SIOUX.

Originally the Wah-p-e-t-on of the Seven Brothers constituting the Da-ko-ta, had been the Levites of the Oracle. In 1812 the Sioux had been the allies of the United States against the British. Their treaty of 1820 was replaced by that of 1851, recognizing the rights of the Yanktons, Yanktonais, Wahpetons, and Medawankaton in the Pipestone Quarry. However, this treaty was ignored. After the so-called Sioux Massacre of 1862 in Minnesota, in fact a contrived affair to justify the seizure of the Quarry, the Wahpetons like the Medawankatons, were powerless because of the terrible punishment they received for a provoked defense of their treaty rights. Of all the Dakota Yanktons, and the Yanktonais were by far the most enlightened. Driven into South Dakota and placed on the Lake Andes Reservation beyond Sioux Falls, they continued to fight for their rights in a legal way. The other three tribes of the Dakota including the Brule, Oglala, and Teton, were herded upon the Rosebud Reservation in the Black Hills under a treaty of 1857. It, too, was utterly ignored after a drunken Indian appeared in a bar with a huge gold nugget, leading to the Sioux war of 1876 wherein the Custer Massacre occurred.

By 1890 when the Northern Pacific Railroad was built through the Pipestone tract the Missionaries attempted to destroy the cascades and the alleged idol with dynamite. All this led to the Messiah Dances of 1891 during which an Indian Scout was employed to kill Sitting Bull, the head Sachem of the Sioux, by shooting him in the back. Eventually an Indian school was erected by the Federal Government upon the Quarry Tract in which the writer established the rights of the Sioux in Yankton Sioux vs. the United States (1927).[1]

In 1792 Aaron Burr and Tammany Hall, dispatched agents to Georgia to suborn Chief McIntosh, the half-Scotch sachem of the Greek tribe, to sell a group of Tammanyites in New York the gold fields they possessed, despite the tribal laws imposing death upon any chief for alienating tribal property. A scheme was worked out to bring all the chieftains to New York, get them drunk and obtain the treaty from the whole group. The Tammany braves received them in Indian costume and went into camp with them on Brooklyn heights. Even liquor could not allay their fears. So they were placed on a vessel, taken to sea in a storm, and when desperately sea-sick, were told that only a treaty would appease the anger of the Great Spirit with them.

In terror they signed. Upon their return to Georgia, the Creeks tried McIntosh for treason and executed him. Thereupon the State of Georgia seized the gold lands under the pretext that the Creeks were guilty of violating the criminal laws, and not entitled to have their treaties with the state respected.

Following all this came the killing of Hamilton by Burr in a dual and the Burr Conspiracy in which Tammany was seriously implicated, to seize the lands of Spain beyond the Mississippi and found among the Indians an independent Republic such as Jackson sent Sam Houston to do later. Thus, as time went on, Tammany and the Yankees acquired an ever more evil name for under-cover and double dealing.

After Gen. Custer, the hero of the Civil War, who had been massacring the Kiowa in western Kansas, was sent west to provoke the Sioux into an act of hostility in the absence of Sitting Bull, a new scandal occurred. Riding into the camp of the Sioux on the Little Big Horn at night, in violation of the orders of his superior General Crook, whose plan was for his own and the army of General Miles to herd the Sioux back into their reservation without bloodshed, the single troop of the 7th Cavalry with Custer shot the old men and women down in the wigwams during the night. Sitting Bull gave orders to his chieftains, Red Cloud, Red Shirt, American Horse and Gall, to surround the troop and take Custer alive. To do this they had sacrificed hundreds of warriors and killed all the troops. Only Custer remained. Seeing that he would be court-martialled and dishonored if taken prisoner, according to the Sioux Sachems he blew out his own brains.[2]

As one of the original members of the Historical Section of the General Staff of the A. E. F. organized by his old friend, Brigadier General Oliver L. Spalding, soon after the Armistice, the writer found under him one Captain Eddy who had been an Indian agent among the Sioux and the Crow. In vain he had tried to gain aid in compiling the statistics of the 20,000 or more Indians in the Army as the personal friend of Lieutenant Red Cloud, the first officer killed in the A. E. F. in battle. With the writer's aid the work was achieved. Soon after the war Lieut. Eddy told Red Cloud's family that the writer was a descendant of Thomas Newport, who was exchanged by Capt. Christopher Newport and Capt. John Smith in 1608, as a hostage of James I for Namontacke, the brother of Pocahontas, and the first individual ever to receive a grant from the American Indians and also of the Rev. John Sergeant who had founded among the Housatonics the Indian school from which Dartmouth had evolved; of Henry Dunster, the first President of the Indian School founded by John Harvard at Cambridge, and that he was the great grand son of the Hon. John Sergeant who had represented the Cherokee in the great Indian cases of *Cherokee Nation vs. Georgia,* and *Worcester vs. Georgia,* wherein, as the associate of John Rose, "the swan," or the head sachem of the Cherokee, the rights of that Nation had been established under the basic Indian decisions of Chief Justice Marshall. After his unsuccessful candidacy for Vice President on the Clay ticket of 1832, and the service as the American Commissioner to the First Congress of Panama, Sergeant was employed by Ross to write the constitutions for the five Civilized Tribes of Cherokee who removed to the

wilds of Arkansas converted eventually into the Indian Territory which eventually was delivered over to the Territory of
Oklahoma.

When in 1920, Charles Evans Hughes, who had been employed to represent the Yankton Sioux, held them to be without a sound claim and withdrew from the case, Eddy sent Red
Bird's husband, Raymond T. Bonnin, to employ the writer.

To disclose the real meaning of the primordial shrine of
the Sioux, the writer brought to Washington the Seven Sachems
of the Yankton Sioux in March, 1925, and assembled 70 of
the leading members of the Government including Secretaries
Hughes, Mellon, the Solicitor General, James M. Beck, Speaker
Longworth, 18 ambassadors and ministers of other countries,
Admiral Simmes, Pershing, Bliss, Harbord, and other gener-
als, and numerous statesmen, scientists, scholars, and philan-
thropists, to hear Standing Bull as the successor of Sitting Bull,
and also Antelope, and Hollow Horn, as the three seniors,
narrate the story of the Custer Massacre in which as lads they
had engaged. All this was arranged by the writer's law clerk,
one of the seven Sachems, who had married Red Bird, the
granddaughter of Sitting Bull. And now it was for the first
time that the religious implications of the Messiah Dances
leading to the murder of Sitting Bull by a suborned Indian
scout was disclosed.

The Yankton Council now made the writer honorary head
chief of their tribe, giving to him the calumet and staff of Sitting Bull to preserve, and the name *Wambdi Kasapa*, "Eagle
Wise," a play on his military title in the Reserve (Colonel),
and his surname.

The court of Claims overruled the Yankton Claim. Thereupon the writer appealed to the Supreme Court of the United
States, arguing the case before Chief Justice Taft and a full
Court. A favorable opinion was rendered by Justice Sutherland
of Utah, a native born Scotchman. The Court of Claims de-
clined to find any damages. Again the writer appealed and the
Supreme Court ruled that the Court of Claims assess the dam-

ages in accordance with the rules of law. Thus at last, at the end of 60 years of litigation the rights of the Yanktons were established in the leading case of Yankton Sioux vs. United States (1927), wherein it was held that the Yanktons had a right of user in perpetuity in the Quarry, and as damages received $500,000 for the denial of their right of user during their exclusion, with the fee remaining in the United States and the right to maintain the Pipestone Indian School.

During a visit to the Northwest while taking depositions before the U. S. Commissioner of the Court of Claims, the writer had the novel experience of assembling the Yanktons to the number of a hundred or more including the Council, at the *Mountain of the Prairie* and through Captain Bonnin as interpreter reading to them Longfellow's *Peace Pipe*.

During the conduct of the case the writer wrote the constitution for the Council of United Indian Nations organized in his office, with Captain Bonnin as President, made possible by the contributions of Mrs. Ann Archbold of Washington, Senator Henry A. Dupont of Wilmington, and John Hays Hammond of San Francisco and Washington.

---

[1] A fact of great historical significance must here be pointed out. The predominance of the Che-yenne and the kindred Yanktons in ancient America by reason of their association with the Quarry, gave them a great reputation. So, just as the word Columbia originated in the concept of the Irish Colums of the pagan Milesians, Doodle originated in the concept of the Secret Order of St. Tammany that was organized before the revolution to nullify the Stamp Act by such masquerades as Indians as that of the Boston Tea Party. After the Revolution all the state organizations united in the Independent Order of Red Men, a purely eleemosynary association of mutual insurance, except the one in New York City, which in 1785 was converted by an Irishman into the Order of St. Tammany with Tammany Hall as its political headquarters, one of its purposes being to oppose Hamilton and another to make Aaron Burr President. In the writer's *Red Man in the New World Drama* (1930), he showed how Tammany undertook with the backing of Burr to steal the gold lands of the Creeks in Georgia and the resulting tragedy.

[2] The so-called Custer Massacre was never forgiven. It was easy to arouse the passions of the country with a suborned press. The politicians meant to have the Sioux treaty land. By 1890 the missionaries were branding the Oracle of Winnewassa as a mere heathen idol, and attempts were made to destroy E-e-ops-i-chi-pe as such with dynamite, and also the sacred tablets. The purpose of the whites was behind the Messiah dances of 1891. The Seventh Cavalry was sent

to round up a band of Sioux who left their reservation. Taking things in their own hands the men and younger officers massacred the band during a council. The event was being hailed as another victory in a great battle when an Indian scout was suborned to shoot Sitting Bull in the back. So the great Sioux Sachem perished just as King Philip had done through the treachery of a traitor to his race.

As a small boy the writer knew Red Cloud, Red Shirt, and many others who had taken part in the alleged massacre, as well as Annie Oakley, old Mammy Whitaker, and Nelson, the famous driver of the Deadwood Stage. He spent days in the camp of Buffalo Bill with Indian playmates in Richmond while Col. Cody was a guest in his father's house. His first pony was one given him by Col. Cody when he left for Europe.

APPENDIX "D"

THEORIES AS TO THE CHALDEAN, HEBRAIC, AND JEWISH ORIGINS OF AMERICAN CIVILIZATION.

It is especially important for the student of Civilization to note the theories of Chaldean, Hebraic and Jewish origins of American civilization, and the basis for them.[1]

Although a smattering of the works of Ari the Wise, of Iceland (c.1040-1100 A.D.), the writer of the first priestly scriptures called *Sagas,* implying texts of the sages, are now available to scholars, the others having been destroyed, or suppressed as was the *Flatayar Book,* containing the three redactions of the *Saga of Eric the Red,* eventually uncovered at Copenhagen.

Countless European eyes had beheld the evidence of antique civilizations in America, when in 1490 Martin Behaim accompanied Columbus to Guinea in Africa. Columbus and John Cabot had already visited England together in 1577 after Cabot's visit to Mecca where he was informed of the sea-way leading from Nova Zembla to Kamshatka.

Upon reaching England Cabot vanished with the Portuguese fleet while Columbus kept on to Iceland, explored the Gulf Stream to the west, met the English fishing fleet that had long been visiting Labrador, returned to Ireland, learned there of the lands in the West which it was said many Irish had visited, and whence had come people of the West to Ireland, thence returned to Portugal where in the employ of King John he was furnished by Toscanelli in the faculty of the Platonian Academy of Florence with a map of the world.

By Toscanelli it was explained to Columbus (Colon), that he could reach China either by way of the Pacific or the Northwest Passage of which Roger Bacon had written in 1266 while the Polos were visiting Peking whence they wrote to Venice of the enormous flow of gold into Japan and China from the East. To check Toscanelli's map, Columbus first visited Madeira, and after studying ancient charts of the South Atlantic, found there in the library of his wife's father, he went to Guinea with Behaim.

Toscanelli had died and been succeeded in the faculty of Florence by Leonardo da Vinci when Columbus returned to Portugal and Behaim proceeded to Abyssinia to study the zodiacal poles. When Behaim returned to Nuremburg to erect his terrestrial sphere, Columbus under the patronage of the Medici had abandoned Portugal and entered the service of Queen Isabella, the ally of Florence. There he was placed under the direction of Isabella's treasurer, the great Jewish Cabalist, Abrabanel, also called Barbenella, whose philosophic works display a vast knowledge of the past, and in which the labors of the prehistoric Nabatheans, the Chaldean patrons of agriculture are fully dealt with. Behaim uncovered his globe in 1490 and that year Lorenzo the Magnificent, as head of the Platonian Academy of Florence visited the court of Isabella and left there Amerige Vespucci who had been born in the province of Ameria in Italy, and had served as the Medici fiscal agent in Venice where Cabot had lived awhile, to build a fleet for Columbus. At last, in the spring of 1492 the Genoese Pope, Innocent the Eighth, an initiate like Columbus of the Order of Saint Columba which had been founded by Saint Columban in 605 A.D. at Genoa, won over by Lorenzo issued to Columbus a commission as an agent of the Vatican to plant a colony in the western world, although this commission has only recently been brought to light. Thereupon, Isabella and Ferdinand, who were being financed by Lorenzo through Vespucci, finally entered into a contract with Columbus making him the Grand Admiral of Spain and the Western Seas. The Borgias of Spain, however, had no idea of allowing the Medici to monopolize the western world through Columbus as their agent. Therefore, both the Pope and Lorenzo were poisoned, and with the greatest difficulty Cardinal Giovanni de Medici, the son of Lorenzo and the associate of Leonardo da Vinci managed to get Columbus off with a miserable expedition just as the Borgias elected Alexander Borgia as Alexander VI. Sailing from Spain the day after the papal installation, with crews including Borgia spies, Columbus narrowly missed Haiti in a fog, and before he returned to Spain in 1493, Torquemada as the Grand Inquisitor of Spain and the ally of the Borgias, had expelled the Jews from Aragon and Castile and driven Abrabanel to Leghorn under the protection of the Medici. Dying in 1508 his books were published posthumously at Venice two years after the death of Columbus. Meantime Columbus had reached the conclusion just as John Cabot had done while exploring Greenland and Labrador, that America was a part of the realm of the Grand Khan of Asia, implying the Mongol Emperor whose seat was then established at Karakorum in the Gobi at the old Abyss of Learning to which the Grand Khan had returned when about 750 A.D. La Ha Sa was turned over to the Lamaist Hierarchy.

Although in 1498, the year before he vanished, John Cabot had explored the entire North Atlantic coast, in 1505, the year before the death of Columbus, his original senior Captain, Cosa, who had visited Panama but lately, drew a map of America on which he placed the English flags showing the British occupancy of the North Atlantic, and that Cabot had erected a Fort at the site of the present Fortress Monroe. While Columbus had been in the West Indies on his third voyage, exploring Venezuela, and Panama, he had been recalled as governor of New Spain at the instance of the Borgias, and allowed to return to America in 1502, only under orders not to land in West Indies. Henry VII was maintaining a colony in New Foundland for which his predecessor, Edward IV had issued the original patent. Thus he had learned an immense amount, as Cosa had done, while Vespucci was exploring South America, and according to subsequent claims, rounded the

Cape and visited Peru. At any rate, soon after Columbus was finally recalled from Jamaica where he had been compelled to seek an asylum after being driven from Panama and Yucatan, in order to save him from the Borgias. Now Isabella died and Vespucci arrived at the Court of the young king, Charles I of Castile, to protect Columbus which he did until the Admiral's death at Valladolid as a pensioner of the Medici.

The year after his death in 1506 the German alchemist, Hylacomulus, the associate of Cardinal Giovanni deMedici, Leonardo da Vinci, and Vespucci, published at St. Die in France, under the auspices of Louis XII a map of the world placing on South America the name Americus. Although it has been commonly assumed that he gave this name to America in honor of Americus Vespucius, this was not the fact. In the text accompanying his huge map, after pointing to the fact that Vespucius had visited the mainland beyond the West Indies before Columbus, he went on to say that inasmuch as both Asia and Europe had been named after goddesses of antiquity, it was appropriate that the new world should be named after one, meaning the Goddess Amerika which for ages the Naga had been worshipping at Mount Amarakantaka, still their holy shrine in the Vidya Range of the Dek-k-ana of India. Moreover, at the time this map was published, among the Renape of Maine were the Amarakankanee who inhabited the region of the Scoggin River of which the name was changed by Governor Andros of New England in the reign of James II, to Andros Scoggin, to conceal the name of the Renape Tribe.

Vespucci died in 1512 as the Grand Pilot of Spain just as the Borgias succeeded in obtaining a patent for Ponce de Leon, the Governor of Porto Rico, to search out the mystical seven cities of Cibola in the land to which he gave the name Florida. Failing to find the gold that would mean eternal youth for the Borgias, the Spaniards were soon ravaging Texas under deVaca and converting the so-called land of peace into a veritable hell on earth. Such was the situation when Louis XII, backed by Giovanni deMedici who had been elected pope as

Leo X in 1513, undertook to end the holocaust in America, and by 1515 Sir Thomas More of England, the friend of the Pope, had published his Utopia dealing with the ideal republic which Plato had depicted. Thereupon Louis XII and Charles I of Castile both became candidates for the office of Holy Roman Emperor. Already when Charles I was elected Emperor as Charles V, he had dispatched the murderous Cortez who had destroyed the native population of Porto Rico as a successor of Ponce de Leon, to conquer Yucatan and Mexico. In order that the French and English might not establish prior claims to that of Spain, to the mainland of America, Cortez had orders to destroy every ancient record in Mexico, and even dug up graves to insure that none were preserved. Moreover, he took as his concubine the perfidious Marina, a Maya Princess, to help him.

By 1520, the year after Charles I became emperor, and Luther had instituted the Protestant revolt, the first Franciscans arrived in the realm of Queen Kalifa, now called California, to which references had been made in Spain in the time of the Cid (1004), showing that the Jewish Cabalists and the Moors alike, were familiar with the history of America. After Sebastian Cabot had visited Paraguay, and had been recalled, the Pizarros began the ravaging of Peru under the sanction of the Emperor Charles V, and even before Saint Francis Xavier was dispatched to India with a company of Jesuits, and began his explorations of the South Pacific of which the record has been suppressed, Magellan under the commission of the Emperor had been killed in the Philippines where he had been dispatched in 1519, just before Leo X was poisoned.

While Xavier was conveying Christianity to the Polynesians, the Portuguese Dominican, Ribiero, arrived in Mexico and wrote a history of America which was at once suppressed. Nevertheless, on the early Italian maps including that of Leonardo da Vinci in 1520, South America had appeared and on one of them the name Land of the True Cross was placed on this Continent. Thus it is obvious that even if Vespucci had not visited the Pacific Coast, the ancient history of America was known.

Sir Thomas More had been sent to the block in 1535, doubtless partly as a punishment for his *Utopia,* before the conquest of Peru was complete and Xavier, followed by Pinto, had visited Japan and died in China. Edward VI of England, with Sebastian Cabot as his Grand Pilot, had dispatched Richard Chancellor to Russia by way of Nova Zembla which Cabot's father probably had visited in 1477, when in 1555 Coligny undertook to found a republic of free worship at Rio de Janeiro in the region to which France laid claim as Antarctic France, only to have his colony destroyed when a second one was planted by him in 1564 at Fort Caroline in what was then the northern part of Florida. But inasmuch as de Allyon had founded the colony of San Michel somewhere near Jamestown Island in 1528, and already the Spaniards had founded Santa Fé in northern Mexico, Hernandez was dispatched to Florida to build the fort of St. Augustine on the ancient site of Selos, marking the horizontal arm of the True Cross, as the base from which to destroy Fort Caroline. Before this was accomplished Carillo had explored the Pacific Coast, Coronado had overrun the Central Continent and DeSota had ravaged Florida, Alabama, Mississippi, and Tennessee, also Oveido had ravaged the Amazon from Peru while the Portuguese had erected the City of Columbo at the base of Adam's Peak, showing that they were entirely familiar with the history of Peru.

Louder and louder had become the scoffing at the Bible because it had made no reference to America and the Red Men when in 1577 Drake rounded Cape Horn and laid claim to California as New Albion in the name of Elizabeth who had just been excommunicated as the ally of the Dutch. Returning to England, Drake as the Dragon of England and the other Elizabethan seamen finally compelled Elizabeth to grant Sir Humphrey Gilbert a patent to found a colony in America, and the year after he had done this at Newfoundland and perished at sea, the patent was renewed in Walter Raleigh, his half-brother, who at once dispatched Amidas and Barlow to locate the site of San Michel on the Powhatan River. Instead they located Roanoke Island by mistake, so that Raleigh's first colony was misplaced in 1584 just as William the Silent who had proclaimed the independence of the Dutch was assassinated, following the assassination of his father-in-law, Coligny.

To support the claim of Spain to America, the Dominican Father Duran in 1582 published his history of Mexico and the West Indies in which he ascribed the ancient civilizations of those parts to the Ten Lost Tribes of Israel which, he said had been deported by Shalmanesa II of Assyria. No such deportation had ever occurred, nor had the ten tribes of Israel been lost; instead scattered over the earth, they had been absorbed. Therefore, in 1585 the freemason Isaac Flemming of England republished the *Historia Varia* of Aelian (225 A.D.), dealing with the ancient peoples of the earth, concurrently with the analysis of the Platonian myth by Montaigne. By 1605 Francis Bacon had published his *Advance of Learning,* followed by his *Wisdom of the Ancients* (1609) and his *Atlantida Nova,* (1611), and in 1516 just before his mysterious disappearance Shakespeare had published his mystery play, *The Tempest,* in which he dealt with Andean God, Setbos of which Raleigh would have learned in Venezuela and Guiana when he visited those parts in 1591. Following Raleigh's second visit to Venezuela in 1617 where he learned still more about America, John Smith published his *History of New England, Virginia and the Summer Isles* (1620). No one today, however, knows what was in it, any more than what Raleigh wrote in his *History of the World,* (1618) while in the Tower a second time. Manifestly like the Sagas it has been hushed. Nevertheless it opens with a reference to Prince Madoc's mysterious voyages to the West of 1170-71.

Already Grotius was staggering western scholars with his revelations about the ancient world when in 1535 the mystic Andreae, the alleged head of the Rosicrucians, published his

Mythologia Christiana. In New England too, people were claiming that the Indians were descended from the Jews, and that, therefore, as declared by Governor John Winthrop they were without the pale of God's charity, when a Jew who had visited South America reported to the Jewish Kabalist Mannaseh ben Israel of Holland, the friend of the Cromwell, that he had found Jewish people among the aborigines of Venezuela. Thereupon the Freemason ben Israel, published his *Hope of Israel* (1644), wherein he set forth the claim of his informant, just as Roger Williams published his Dictionary of the Indian Language based on the findings of Grotius and what he had learned as an initiate from his friend Massasoit, Grand Sachem of the Renape in New England who, had been the warm friend of John Smith.

A violent altercation was raging in New England where Roger Williams had been exiled to the wilderness for defending the rights of the Indians, over the alleged Jewish origin of the Indians, when in 1652 Bishop James Ussher of Ireland, put forth on behalf of the Church of England the *Chronologia Sacra* to uphold the *Paschal Cycle* fixing the birth of Adam in B.C. 4,004. Spinoza as well as Grotius and Roger Williams had torn to shreds the popular ideas based on this chronology in its literal sense. The absurdity of Father Duran's claim had long since been exposed when in 1656 Carlos de Siguenza, Professor of Mathematics at the University of Mexico, was called upon to put forward a more reasonable explanation of the origin of the ancient civilizations of America. In his work he explained that the Egyptian *Naptuhim,* mentioned in the bible as the son of Chem or Shem, was in fact the same described in Genesis, the learned Naptuhim had come to Mexico by way of the vanished Atlantis of Plato. (See Bibliofilos Mexicanos for new edition of Siguenza's work, 1928.)

It was a futile attempt to bring the history of America within the so-called orthodox chronology.

Arriving in America in 1682 William Penn treated with the great Lenni Lenape Sachem, Tamenend, under the Sacred Elm of Sha-ka-max-on where he founded Philadelphia, (40° N. 75° W.) on the latitudinal circle of the old Abyss of Learning, Mount Olympus, the vanished Mount Atlas, and the great complex of religious Mounds at Newark in Ohio, and the Cone at Moundsville on the Ka-na-w-ha, also marking the meridian of the Gobi. Moreover he gave to his capital the name of Phila-delphus, 'the city of Brotherly Love,' which had been founded by the ancients in Syria. Undoubtedly initiated into the Renape mysteries of Nana-bo-za as Smith, Roger Williams, John Sergeant, and John Eliot had been, soon Penn vanished with Tamenend into the western wilderness and upon his return wrote that he had found much indicating a very ancient connection between the Indians and the peoples of the Old Testament. To-day it is known that the numerous geometric mounds he beheld in Ohio had been erected well on in the Christian Era, in all probability by the Islandingas who in 1122 had launched a crusade against the heathens of Vinland. (See *Mystery of Columbus,* Wise, 1947). It was upon this crusade that the poet Southey based his *Prince Madoc in Azitland.*

Penn was a contemporary of William Whiston, head of Cambridge University in England and the leader of the so-called Arian school of history. Already Penn had been recalled for proposing a union of the colonies similar to that of the Iroquois League of the Long House and for daring to enter into a treaty with the Lenni Lenape, when Whiston put out his *New Theory of the World* and his translation of Josephus upon which he based it. Having challenged the *Chronologia Sacra* he was dismissed from Cambridge.

Early in the 19th Century Elias Boudinot put out his *Star in the West* wherein he revived the whole Jewish theory whereupon the English Jew Evans set out to demonstrate that the Maya culture in Mexico and Yucatan was of Hebrew-Chaldea-Jewish origin, and expended a vast fortune on his Antiquities of Mexico (1835-45) for the compilation of which he was knighted at the instance of the elder Disraeli.

Meantime had occurred the great upsurge of Freemasonry

in American politics, during which Joseph Smith, a Freemason of northern New York, also an initiate of the Iroquois mysteries, put forth his *Book of Mormoni,* alleged by him to have been based upon the golden tablets which had been concealed by the ancestors of the Iroquois, and the whereabouts had been revealed to him by an angel. In that work he declared that Jesus had appeared among the peoples of America following his cruciform, and that a hierarchy of Apostles and bishops had been founded in America; that eventually, about 400 A.D. this civilization was destroyed in a great conflict such as that which about that time took place in Yucatan. In the text of this work reference to this alleged dream of Smith has been made.

The history of Yucatan shows that in 66 A.D., the year after Seneca, the patron of St. Paul in Rome, was compelled by his former pupil Nero, to destroy himself after referring in the *Media* to the peoples of the realms beyond Ultima Thule (Iceland) to which Strabo also had referred, and the very year that St. Paul and St. Peter are said to have been crucified on the Vatican Hill, during the burning of Rome, now ascribed to the Christians instead of to Nero, a company of blond Pythagoreans arrived in Yucatan from the North, calling themselves Chanes. Unquestionably they were the ancestors of the peculiar Sha-w-nees of the Atlantic Seaboard who eventually were driven into Kentucky and Ohio. Known to the Yucatecs as AH Zhais who were said to have come from Ah Zhai Land, or A-zl-t-land, comporting in its name with the realm of Plato's Twin *Azaeas,* of the Fifth Cycle of the mythical Kingdom of Atlantis, some of them called T-o-l-t-e-ca, 'Rubber People,' migrated to Mexico where they became the ancestors of the Tolteca. It was these Pythagoreans identical with the Miletans which Caesar had planted in Ireland, or the Irish Milesians, who caused Yucatan to become known as the Athens of the West because of the Ionian character of the architecture that appeared in Yucatan and Mexico, and that was plainly superimposed upon that of the great teacher Itzama (B.C. 3,000) who had caused Yucatan to be known as the Western Egypt. Mixing with the Mayavic Naguals of Mexico, or M-e-x-atla, the Tolteca eventually would produce the AH-Zhai-Tolteca, who came to be called A-z-tecs, whose civilization, ascribed by the Mexicans to a great white prince from the North, is traced back to about B.C. 800, when Ku-k-w-u-l-can, the second Que-t-za-l Coatl, or Serpent of the Queenland appeared in Yucatan where he is still revered along with Itzama.

In the Mystery of Columbus the writer has identified Kukulcan with the Danish Boreans in the reign of the pagan Canute who came to rule over England in 1014 A.D.

The first In-ca is now said to have appeared in Peru about 1,000 A.D. Inasmuch as the name Ti-ti-ca-ca indicates the superimposition of the Aryan upon the Sinitic cult of the Armaya peoples still inhabiting that part, it was only natural that Manco Copac, the first Inca, should have been said to have been begotten by the Sun out of Mamma Sin-ya-cu.[2] But as shown in the text the Inca had no more to do with the older civilization of the Ha-t-un Ru-na of Peru, than Mont-e-zu-ma, the first ruler of the Aztecs had to do with that of the Naguals and Mayas in Mexico and Yucatan. In truth the Peruvians in the time of Pizarro, like the Mayax and Aztecs in the time of Cortez, were merely the inheritors of the mysteries handed down to them, just as the cult of Nan-bo-z-ha common to the tribes of North America embodied the wisdom of the dim past.

Surely enough has been said to explain the persistent claims about Chaldean, Hebraic, and Jewish origins, and also of Welsh origins, for the American aborigines.

In addition to all that has been shown however, there is the claim of Aristotle that the Phoenicians visited the land west of the Azores, which in the time of Sertorius (B.C. 80) was known to the Lusitani as Antilles; the testimony of the Elder Pliny that the father of Nero was dealing with the King of the Western World; Plutarch's Greek colony in Labrador at the west of Greenland; the voyages of St. Brandan in

570, and the Portuguese record of the migration of the Arian Visigoths in 732 after the conquest of Spain by the Arabs; and the recent findings of the Snows that migrants from Europe undertook to colonize along the Sus-qe-ha-na-h and in Ohio during the lifetime of Plato. Also recently the Carnegie Institution of Washington has announced the discovery of the destroyed city of Ca-ra-k-mu-l in the jungles of Yucatan which is said to have been founded in 732. Finally there are the Vinland Voyages beginning in 1,000 A.D.

In all this is found a complete explanation not only of the *Book of Mormoni,* but of the Chaldean-Hebraic-Jewish theories, and of the origin of the Iroquois League of the Long House which came in 1577 to constitute the League of the Five Nations, just eight years before the alleged founding of the Powhatan Confederacy in Virginia. Ultimately the Tuscarora would migrate from the Carolinas (1714) and join the Five Nations as the Sixth Nation.

Also is found in it an explanation of the geometric Mounds, and of Fort Ancient at Portsmouth, Ohio. Therein is found the evidence of a terrific conflict in all probability tracing back to the Islandinga crusade. Finally, in the *Mystery of Columbus,* the writer has analyzed the great mound at Ka-ho-k-ia (38° 30' N. 90° W.), six miles southeast of St. Louis, and shown that two circles, drawn with radii in degrees corresponding to the measures of this huge truncated pyramid with a base four times as large as that of the Pyramid of Cheops, pass through nearly every port of importance in America.

From all this it is evident that the history of America must be radically revised.

The author hopes eventually to be able to publish the *Epic of Virginia* showing the facts about the colonization of America following the death of Columbus, in which will be fully explained the French colonies in Canada, Rio de Janeiro, and Fort Caroline, and the Spanish colonies of New Spain in Arizona, New Mexico, California, Newfoundland Colony of the British by Gilbert in 1578, and of the Roanoke Colony by Raleigh in 1582. The truth is, of course, North America was not a *terra incognita* when Jamestown was founded concurrently with the English colony at Kennibunkport in 1607 of which Raleigh's nephew, Raleigh Gilbert, the brother of Bartholomew Gilbert who had been killed in Virginia in 1603, was the head. In the records of the *Northwest Passage Foundation* of which John Gilbert was the head, was preserved all the vast knowledge of the past embodied in the countless works of the great Magician John Dee who had been the confidential teacher and adviser of Elizabeth, whose works have been left unpublished to the modern world. And here it is to be noted that he had vanished without explanation just as Jamestown was founded, about a decade before Shakespeare, Pocahontas, Raleigh and Thomas West, Lord Delaware, went the way of Lorenzo Medici, Leo X, Sir Thomas More, Coligny, William the Silent, Marlowe, and Henry of Navarre.

---

1 See *The Lost Ten Tribes of Israel,* Handbook of American Indians, Bureau Amer. Eth., Bulletin 30, Smithsonian Institution (1907).

2 M-an-co, 'Mia, Ana, the Celestial Serpent.'
Co-p-ac, 'the Celestial Serpent, the Papa of the Light.'
Thus, the two names together imply, 'an ever widening circle of Light.'

APPENDIX "E"

MONASUKAPANOUGH AND THE
UNIVERSITY OF VIRGINIA

It is well known, of course, that the treaty made by William Penn with Tamenend, the sachem of the Lenni Lenape, or Delawares, was made under the Sacred Elm of Sha-ka-ma-x-on.* Also it is known that a people called Sha-ka-ma-x of Siouan affinities once inhabited northern Virginia from the Valley to Chesapeake Bay. Here a bit of narrative is included by reason of its bearing on American history.

When John Smith arrived with Newport in Virginia, they found that among the Seven Hills of Po-w-ha-t-ta (37° 32' N. 37° 27' W.) on which Richmond eventually arose, was one called Sha-ko, and one called Chi-m-bo-ra-zo, below which were the falls of the Po-w-ha-t-ta, which marked the dividing line between the Mona-can Confederacy of Siouans at the west, and the Powhatan Confederacy at the East. Of the four principal towns of the Mona-cans who possessed Siouan affinities and whose blood was undoubtedly mixed in that of the Po-w-ha-t-ta of whom the young hereditary head man was the Taux. Thus his sister, as the daughter of Wa-hun-son-a-cock, a native of the West Indies, who undoubtedly had been imported by the Spaniards to head the Powhatan Confederacy when it was formed in 1595 after the massacre of the Roanoke Colony, bore the Siouan name Po-ca-hon-ti, "the Joyous One," and the Re-na-pe name Ma-to-a-ka, "dancing water," corresponding to the falls of the Powhatan. Inasmuch as the Spaniards in the time of d'Allyon had established a fort of San Miguel, at the present Jamestown Island in 1528 after the fort built by John Cabot in 1498 at the site of the present Fort Monroe had been destroyed, doubtless at the same time the Spanish mission

* Sha-ka-ma-x-on is interpreted by the Bureau of American Ethnology to mean "Place where chiefs are made."

[373]

of A-x-a-c-an on the Ra-pa-ha-n-o-c-k (1571). The presumption is that the Spaniards had formed the Powhatan Confederacy consisting of forty cognate tribes inhabiting the country from the Ra-pa-ha-nocks to Ro-an-o-ke Island, to prevent it from being seized by the Siouans at the west who, being from the north were more friendly to the French than to the Spaniards. Indeed it seems certain that even before the French despatched an expedition from Canada to the St. Mary's River in 1567 to punish the Spaniards who under Menendez had massacred the French colony at Fort Caroline in 1565, they had caused the Sioux to destroy all the Spanish forts in Virginia. For be it noted the Spanish mission of St. Mary's at A-x-a-can, by some placed at Port Royal on the Ra-pa-ha-n-nock, and by others at Fredericksburg, was destroyed the very year that the Guises, or the pro-Spanish party in France, caused the assassination of Coligny. He had founded the French colonies at Port Royal on St. Mary's River in South Carolina. On the other hand it was in 1577, or the year Menendez perished in the Netherlands, that the Rappahannocks were assailed and punished by the Spaniards.

Thus we see that instead of Virginia being an unknown wilderness when Newport was despatched in 1607 to found Jamestown, it had long been a battleground between the French and Spaniards, and had actually been occupied by Cabot and the English before Columbus was recalled from Jamaica in 1504 upon the joint demand of Henry VII and Louis XII of France. Indeed at that time there was a large British colony in Newfoundland although Cabot's Fort had been abandoned when Cabot vanished from the ken of men in 1499.

Before the death of John Smith the English had explored the Monacan country as far as Mona-su-ka-pa-nough which was in sight of the Mountain called the Watch Hill by the Monacans. Eventually William Randolph, the son of Thomas Randolph of Tuckahoe, who married the daughter of Thomas Bolling, the grandson of Pocahontas and John Rolfe, and the nephew of Sir John Randolph, patented the Watch Hill.[1] John Jefferson, as a teacher of surveying at William and Mary, descended from John Jefferson of the First Assembly in Virginia (1619), had surveyed Albemarle County with Col. Fry, a member of the College Faculty, and had made a map of Virginia. He bought the estate of *Shadwell* from the patentee, Wood, and named it after the great English poet laureate, Thomas Shadwell, who died in 1692. Inasmuch as the Jeffersons claimed to hail from Snowden in Wales where stands Mount Snowden, the highest peak in the British Isles, and a sacred Welsh shrine, undoubtedly the Jeffersons had inherited much knowledge about their Welsh ancestors.

To be sure John Jefferson, aided by the Indians, built his home with his own hands, but a man who had surveyed the state and made a map, was no clodhopper as he is often represented to have been, a mere crude commoner and frontiersman commonly designated as a Cohee as were the more crude Indians of the west, or the Sioux, to distinguish them from the Tuckahoes of the East. From William Randolph, the nephew of Sir John, who was his intimate friend and associate, he bought the "Watch Mount." After he had built his home he married Elizabeth Randolph, the sister of William and the daughter of the lordly Thomas Randolph of Tuckahoe. Thus he became the husband of the niece of Sir John Randolph, a friend of Shadwell, the poet, and one of the noblest men in the history of Virginia. John Jefferson's son was Thomas Jefferson, who was born at Shadwell in 1743. Hardly had he been born when his father, as the outstanding man in Albemarle, was appointed to command the Militia as the successor of Col. Fry on whose estate Patrick Henry's mother was born. For five years, therefore, Thomas Jefferson and his mother lived with her father at Tuckahoe where he received his first schooling in the little private school house still standing, at the hands of the Rev. William Douglas of Ayrshire, a kinsman of Lord William Douglas of Baads, and a first cousin of Col. William Douglas, the Laird of Garallan in Ayrshire, who had come over to Virginia with Colonel John Monroe in 1750, and settled with other Scotchmen in the Northern Neck. Moreover, it was Col. William Douglas of Loudon who patented the site on the south side of Point of Rocks in Loudon, to command the ancient trail of the Iroquois Senecas into Virginia, and who named it Garallan after his estate in Ayr which he had inherited from his ancestor James, Earl of Douglas.*

Entering William and Mary in 1767 there Thomas Jefferson roomed with Patrick Henry and was initiated into the Masonic Lodge of Apollo along with Washington, Patrick Henry, Richard Henry Lee, Edmund Pendleton, George Mason, and Dabney Carr, who had acquired Carr's Hall which included Monasukapanough. With the aid of Dabney Carr he resumed the explorations of the Monacan towns which they and Carr's father-in-law, Dr. James Maury, had made. Maury was the son of the first teacher of George Washington at Fredericksburg, and the brother of doctor Maury who founded the school at Gordonsville later attended by Madison, Monroe, and Lighthorse Harry Lee before Madison and Lee went to Princeton, the appellant in the famous Parson's Case in which Patrick Henry made his reputation as a lawyer after one year at college.

While Jefferson was building a new home on the Watch Hill which he named Monticello, "Little Mountain," because it had been the watch hill of the Monacans, he opened the great circular mound at Mona-su-ka-pa-nough but never disclosed in his *Notes on Virginia* (1798), what he discovered there. Still, however, the Monacans, who had been compelled by the whites to migrate to the West, made annual pilgrimages to the mound.

As a student at the University of Virginia, the writer was frequently the guest of Thomas Jefferson Levi's daughter, who resided at Monticello, and became deeply interested in Monasukapanough where a great growth of black walnuts lined the Riv-anna. Not until 1940, however, when the writer returned to live in Charlottesville, did he make a careful exploration of

---

* One of his tenants was Robert Burns, the poet.

Mona-su-ka-pa-nough where he located a black walnut tree with five of its original seven oriented branches still intact.

Expert botanists agreed that the tree might be 500 years old. At once the writer caused the parasitic growth of wild grape vines to be removed and the limbs to be sured with cables. He then asked the Bureau of American Ethnology for a translation of the name Mona-su-ka-pa-nough, which they admitted they could not identify by any language. Possibly, they said, the name implied a tree of food. Thereupon the writer arranged to have the tree and mound examined by the celebrated anthropologist, Ales Hřdlicka, Curator of the National Museum, and together they agreed on a scheme of exploration by cross-cuts of the mound from which apparently Jefferson had removed all the remains while exploring the surrounding kitchen middens of the Monacan country and the cairn still to be seen on Carr's Hill, said to be of great antiquity.

Having observed that Mona-su-ka-pa-nough marked exactly the meridian of Lu-ra-y cave in the Ma-sa-nu-t-ta Mountain to the north, the sacred shrine of Ac-co-ma-c on the eastern shore of Virginia which Verrazano had exposed in 1520, and the great complex of mounds at Ka-ho-ki-a at 90° W. in Illinois just six miles southeast of St. Louis, the writer knew that Su-ka-pa was a Siouan form of Sa-ka-pa corresponding to Ka-sa-pu, meaning eagle. The Bureau of Ethnology thought the *nough* meant "nut," or "food." What of Mona? They thought it might come from *Minne* as in Minne-so-ta and Minne-ha-ha, meaning "land of sky tinted Water," and "dancing water," respectively. The writer could get little aid from his Sioux friends but noted that the rock in the foaming surf of the northern point of Easter Island in the Pacific also bore the name Minne-ha-ha. In the end he traced down the mystical island of Mona in the Irish Sea, and the equally mystical island of Mona in the Bahamas. Then there was Mon-taux point on Long Island and Mount Mona-d-nock, an isolated height in New Hampshire.[2] This led to a study of Mona-co in the Riviera, Mona-s-tin in European Turkey, both plainly implying "Mona, the Serpent's Tree."

At last! The mystery of Leonardo da Vinci's Madonna— Mona Lisa. The name Mona proved to be the *Minne* of the Chon, implying the spiritual waters, or the heaven of co-na which is an abbreviation of co-narayana, giving Minne-Conarayana, abbreviated into M-o-na.

So we have at last not only the meaning of Sha-ka-cona, "the Spirit of the King, the Co, Narayana," but of Sha-ka-max-on which is derived from Sha-ka-ma-chi-co-narayana, meaning literally "the Spirit of the King and the Mother, Child of the Holy Spirit, the Serpent, Narayana."

In the same way F-r-a-n and Co-n-ia together give the meaning of France and "the Watcher," as 'Father, the Ru, the Ark of Nu, the Serpent of Nu, the Spirit of Itala, or the Itza Land of the Ethiopians.' Accordingly the Franconian word *mon-t* is to be traced to Minne-cona-T, "the Heaven of the Co, Narayana, the Taux." Therefore as we find Ana-conda, meaning the Serpent of Heaven, we find in Mont-ana a realm of spiritual high places.

Surely Jefferson must have known all this when he erected the University of Virginia below Mona-t-i-cello on the Rivanna river and embodied in his architectural design the symbolism of the Sephiroth. In his architectural design the Rotunda corresponding to the mound at Monasukapanough forms a symbol of the Python corresponding to the Pantheon of Rome. From the west it is approached by three terraces. On either side is a double line of students' quarters, called ranged, forming two infinity signs. In each range are ten original lecture halls and professor's quarters corresponding to the ten luminaries of the Sephuroth. The rectangle structure originally attached to the Rotunda at the North, symbolizing a terrestrial domain, was destroyed by fire in 1896. From it also one descended by terraces.*

* See Pamphlet, *The Legacy of Jefferson,* WISE (1940).

[1] From Elizabeth Randolph, the sister of Thomas, and the daughter of William Randolph of Turkey Island, the writer is descended.

[2] On Mona-d-nock the brother of the writer's adjutant in World War I, Lincoln MacVeagh, now Ambassador to Spain, a great-grandson of Simon Cameron of Lincoln's cabinet, and son of the Hon. Charles MacVeagh, a law partner of President Cleveland, and later Ambassador to Japan under President Coolidge, had lost his life in a snow storm.

APPENDIX "F"

COMPILED CHRONOLOGY

(Based on Adamic or Tamil Calendar of the Hindus; Genesis; Chronology of Berossus; Synthesis of Manetho; Dialogues of Plato; Maya Glyphs.)

18,000,000 B.C.	Separation of Sexes, Third Root Race.
5,000,000	Appearance of the present or Fifth Root Race.
2,596,000	Beginning of present Mahayuga.
2,506,000	Beginning of Adamic Cycle.
2,500,000	Destruction of Sin-ga-la; Separation of Africa and Brazil.
2,376,000	Beginning of the Cycle of Seth.
2,271,000	Beginning of the Cycle of Enos.
2,181,000	Beginning of the Cycle of Cainan.
2,110,000	Beginning of the Cycle of Mahalaleel.
2,046,000	Beginning of the Cycle of Jared (Aryans).
1,894,000	Beginning of the Cycle of Enoch.
1,819,000	Beginning of the Cycle of Methusaleh.
1,692,000	Beginning of the Cycle of Lamech.
1,574,000	End of Cycle of Adam.
1,519,000	End of the Cycle of Enoch.
1,484,000	End of the Cycle of Seth.
1,450,000	Beginning of the Cycle of Noah (Rama Balarama: Fifth Hindu Avatar.)
1,366,000	End of the Cycle of Enoch.
1,271,000	End of the Cycle of Cainan.
1,216,000	End of the Cycle of Mahalaleel.
1,154,000	End of the Cycle of Jared.
950,000	Beginning of the Cycle of Shem-Ham-Japheth
900,000(?)	Beginning of the Great Ice Age and the Quartenary Age.
855,000	End of the Cycle of Lamech.
850,000	End of the Cycle of Methusaleh. The Flood.
848,000	Beginning of the Cycle of Arphaxad (Akkadians: Founding of Akkad in Chaldea.)

813,000	Beginning of the Cycle of Salah.
810,000 (?)	Fall of Tower of Babel: Confusion of Tongues: Migrations.
783,000	Beginning of the Cycle of Eber: Founding of the Tree Cult by Hebrews.
749,000	Beginning of the Cycle of Peleg-Joktan. Hindus appear. Setting apart of the domains of the Gentiles. (Surveying of the two geodetic Chi.)
719,000	Beginning of the Cycle of Rea.
687,000	Beginning of the Cycle of Serug.
657,000	Beginning of the Cycle of Nahor.
618,000	Beginning of the Cycle of Terah.
558,000	Beginning of the Cycle of Abu-ramu or Abram.
528,000	End of the Cycle of Nahor.
510,000	End of the Cycle of Peleg.
500,000	End of the Cycle of Noah and the Paleolithic Age. Megolithic Age begins.
490,000	End of the Cycle of Rea.
458,000	Beginning of the Cycle of Isaac and Esau.
447,000	End of Cycle of Serug.
445,000	End of Cycle of Arphaxad.
432,535	First Divine Dynasty of Chaldea (Alorus).
428,000	Union of Isaac and Rebecca.
413,000	End of Cycle of Terah.
408,000	End of the Cycle of Abraham.
398,000	Beginning of the Cycle of Jacob.
396,735	Second Divine Dynasty of Chaldea (Alparus).
385,935	Third Divine Dynasty of Chaldea (Amilarus).
380,000	End of the Cycle of Salah.
348,000	End of the Cycle of Shem-Ham-Japheth.
339,135	Fourth Divine Dynasty of Chaldea (Ammennon).
319,000	End of the Cycle of Eber.
295,935	Fifth Divine Dynasty of Chaldea (Megalorus).
278,000	End of the Cycle of Isaac.
261,000	Beginning of the Cycle of Joseph.
251,000	End of the Cycle of Jacob.
231,135	Sixth Divine Dynasty of Chaldea (Daonas).
195,135	Seventh Divine Dynasty of Chaldea (Eudodereschus).
180,000	End of Cycle of Joseph.
130,335	Beginning of Eighth Divine Dynasty of Chaldea (Amenipsimus).
94,335	Beginning of Ninth Divine Dynasty of Chaldea (Ardates).

70,000	Destruction of Daitya, or the Land of Nod.
65,535	Beginning of the Tenth Divine Dynasty of Chaldea (Xisusthrus).
36,000	The Deluge of Xisusthrus.
30,000	Appearance of the present type of man.

The Neolithic Age

22,000	The Uighurs in Portugal.
20,000	The Dune Men in the Gobi.
14,000	Height of Uighur Empire. Ceramic Age of Egypt, and of the Zuni in Arizona.
12,000	Palace of Knossus in Crete, and the original Athens.
10,000	The Magnetic Cataclysm: Destruction of Pacific Continent. Migration from Mongolia to Alaska.
9,500	Destruction of Posidonis and Separation of Britain and Britanny.
9,500	Migrations from Asia Minor and Arabia to Egypt.
8,500	Hellenes found Säis in Delta of the Nile: Cult of Neith.
7,500	Rama Lunus, or Chandra, Sixth Hindu Avatar.
7,500	Union of Lower and Middle Egypt.
7,500	Migration of the Itzaes to North America.
6,000	Erection of the teocalli in Mexico and Peru by Maya and Naguals.
5.000	Mahabharata Age of India: Compilation of the *Veda*.
5,000	Age of navigation in Egypt and the Queenland of the Qui-ches.
4,004	Passing of Rama Chrisna, or Krishna.
3,200	The unification of Egypt; Fu Hsi in China, Sargon I of Assyria.
3,100	Itzama unites the Maya and Itzaes in Mexico; founds Itza-Maya state.
3,000	Building of pyramids of Gizeh begins.
2,500	Third pyramid completed in Fourth Egyptian Dynasty. The name *Europa* applied to Argos in Greece.
1,555	David, King of Judah, with capital at Jerusalem.
1,500	Rameside Empire founded.
1,350	Rameses II establishes capital at Delhi in India.
1,300	Moses and Exodus; Orpheus; Mediterranean world overrun by the Peoples of the Sea from the Isles of Israel (Celts).
1,100	End of Trojan War: Phoenecians found Cadiz; and the Greeks found Utica. Goidhals migrate to Ireland.

993   Reign of Solomon begins.
951   Ten Tribes of Israel secede from Judah: Kingdoms of Israel and Judah founded.
900   The Prophets Eli and Elisha or Elias.
850   Carthage founded.

The Golden Age of Greece

820   Lycurgus founds Sparta.
776   The First Olympiad.
753   Rome founded by Greeks of Latium and Etruscans.
750   The Theogony of Hesiod: Revised Myths.
735   Syracuse founded by the Corinthians.
720   The Prophets Isaiah and Micah.
715   Conquest of Israel by Sargon II: Deportation of the tribes of Manassah and Benjamin to Georgia in the Caucasus.
610   Anaxamander in Greece: Lao Tze in China; the First Mikado in Japan.
604   Nebuchadnezzar defeats Egyptians in Syria.
602   Necho II reopens Suez Canal: Solon Visits Egypt; Thales of Miletus and Pherecydes of Samnos.
600   The Phocians found Massilensis (Marseilles).
597   Nebuchadnezzar completes conquest of Judah; deportations of Hebrews from Jerusalem to Babylon begin.
597   Solon founds the Athenian Republic.
588   Jeremiah leaves Jerusalem for Spain and Ireland.
587   Jeremiah dies: Pythagoras born.
558   Death of Solon.
551   Confucius; Gotama Buddha.
535   Persian Conquest; Croesus of Lydia dethroned.
510   The Roman Republic founded.
500   Pythagoras dies; Egypt conquered by Cambyses II: Anaxagoras.
480   Aristophanes, Sophocles, Euripides.
450   Herodotus: Socrates; Isaeus. The Theocratic State of the Jews founded by Ezra and Nehemiah.
415   Ezra completes compilation of Jewish Testaments.
399   Death of Socrates.
388   Plato founds Academy of Athens.
375   Theopompus, of Chios; Aristotle; Demosthenes; Euclid.
356   Alexander the Great.

347   Death of Plato.
325   Death of Alexander the Great: Manetho and Aristotle found library of Alexandria; death of Aristotle and Demosthenes. The Synthesis of Manetho.
324   Ptolemy Soter; Colossus of Rhodes; Callimachus.
316   Manetho builds first light house at Alexandria.
314   Evemerus publishes the *Historia Sacra.*
250   Hyparchus of Rhodes; Archimedes; Pytheas of Massilensis surveys Scotland; Berossus of Chaldea compiles *Chronology.*
149   Carthage finally overthrown, becomes Roman province. Crates of Alexandria erects first known terrestrial globe. Gallia gradually designated as Europe while its three parts are being absorbed by Rome.
100   Posidonius of Rhodes reviews the Platonian Myth of Atlantis. Sertorius, Governor of Trans-Spadine Iberia, writes of the Land of Antillia beyond the Azores.
52   Julius Caesar visits Britain.
44   Seneca writes the Media telling of the western world beyond Ultima Thule (Iceland).
30   Strabo writes of the Western World. Virgil predicts the coming of the child of Jupiter.
15   John the Baptist begins his mission on the Jordan.

TOPICAL BIBLIOGRAPHY

Originally it was planned by the author to include a much more compendious bibliography. In view of the citations of authorities under the headings of this bibliography in the various encyclopediae available to scholars and readers, for practical reasons in the main the bibliography has been limited to authorities not commonly cited, upon which, with others the author has relied.

AMERICA

Anderson — America Not Discovered by Columbus (1874).
Bancroft—Native Races (1886).
Bourburg, Abbé Brasseur de — Le Manuscript Troano (1870).
Brinton — The Maya Chronicles (1882-85).
Burder—Welsh Indians (1797).
Cabiera—Exploration of a Newly Discovered City in Yucatan (1940).
Campbell—Migrations of the Hakka (1916).
Charney—Ancient Cities of the New World (1885).
Curtis—Children of the Sun (1898).
Cushing — Zuni Culture Growth (1888).
Cushing — Key dweller Remains on the Coast of Florida (1896).
Cushing—Zuni Folk Tales (1901).
Cushing — Outlines of Zuni Creative Myths (1896).
Dorsey — Study of Siouan Cults (1894).
Dorsey—Traditions of the Skidi Pawnee (1904).
Duran, Father—History of the Islands and Mainland of the New World (1579).
Fletcher—The Hako (1903). (Compare with the Red Hakka of China).
Frost—The American Egypt (1912).
Grotius—Dissertatio de Origine Gentium Americanarum (1642).

Hewitt—Ancient Civilizations of the Southwest (1930).
Hewitt — Iroquoian Cosmology (1903).
Hornius — Originibus Americannus (1652).
Janson—Stranger in America (1807).
Mallery—Israelite and Indian (1889).
Means—The Ancient Civilizations of the Andes (1932).
Morehead — Primitive Man in Ohio (1892).
Morgan — Ancient Society (1877). League of Iroquois (1861). Systems of Consanguinity and Affinity (1881).
Nadaillac, de — Nouvelles Découvertes Préhistoriques aux États Unis (1883).
Nadaillac, de—Les anciennes populations de la Colombie (1885).
Nivens—The Sunken Cities of Mexico (1898).
Nordenskjiold — Cliff Dwellings of the Mesa Verde (1893).
Powell — The Linguistic Families of North America North of Mexico (1891).
Rafinesque — The American Nations (1830).
Siguenza, Carlos de — in Bibliofelos Mexicanos (1928).
Tylor—Anahuac (1866).
Verrill—The Ancient Civilizations of America (1930).
Weiner—Maya and Brazilian Origins (1925).

Weiner—Africa and the Discovery of America (1922).
Willard—The Lost Empire of the Itzaes and Mayas (1932).
Williams, Roger — Dictionary of the American Language (1640).
Wise — America, The Background of

and Roman Antiquities (1842).
Thomson—The Archaeology of Easter Island (1875).
Warren — Underground Jerusalem (1876).
Windle — Remains of the Prehistoric Age in England (1904).

ARCHAEOLOGY AND ANTIQUITIES

Aerial Archaeology. See "archaeology," Ency. Brit. Current Edition.
Benziges — Hebraische archaeologie (1894).
Bezier — Anthropological Studies (1854).
Bliss and Dickie — Excavations of Jerusalem (1898).
Burgess — Cave Temples of India (1880).
Carthaillac — The Dolmens of Portugal (1886).
Columbus (1946).
Fergusson — Rude Stone Monuments (1872).
Fouquet — Des Monuments celtiques (1850).
Halévy, Joseph—Report on Archaeology of Yemen (1872). D'epigraphie et d'archeologie semitiques (1874).
Hewitt — Use of Stone in the Maya Hills (1898).
Josephus — Antiquities of the Jews (77 A.D.).
Kingsborough, Lord — The Antiquities of Mexico (1830-45).
Lhuyd — Archaeologia Britannica (1707).
Maitland—Works of the Old Men in Arabia (1924).
Mallet—Northern Antiquities (1770).
Michaud — Paleographie Universelle, etc. (1864).
Pausanias — Perigesis of Greece (c. 100-200 A.D.).
Prorok — In Quest of Vanished Worlds (1940).
Sayce—Archaeology of the Cuneiform Inscriptions (1907).
Schrader — Indo-European Antiquities (1907).
Smith, William—Dictionary of Greek

ARYANS

Boas — Mind of Primitive Man (1927).
Buhler and Keilhorn — Indo-Arischen Philology (1886).
Childe—The Aryans (1924).
Mitra—Indo-Aryans (1881).
Müller, Max—Bibliography of Words and Home of the Arya (1881).
Poindexter—The Arya Inca (1930).
Realexicon der Indogermanischen Alterktumskunde (1901).
Reinach — L'Origine des Aryans (1892).
Ripley—Races of Europe (1899).
Schrader — Prehistoric Antiquities of the Aryans (1890).
Sergi—Mediterranean Races (1901).
Spiegel—The Aryan Cycle (1888).
Taylor — The Origin of the Aryans (1890).

ASIA GENERALLY

Anderssen and Black — Paleontologica Sinica (1925).
Flutterer — Forschungen in Zentral-Asien und China (1896).
Humboldt—Central Asia (1830).
Idriantzeff—Sibirica (1886).
Junghuhn—Java, etc. (1852).
Koslof; Chara Chota (1922). (Karakorum in the Gobi). Mongolia (1923).
Marvin—Merv (1880).
Middendorf—Siberische Reise (1848-1875).
O'Donovan — The Merv Oasis (1888).
Przhe Valsky—Mongolia (1876).
Pumpelly — Explorations in Turkeystan (1888).
Stein—Ancient Kotan (1919).
Bell—Tibet Past and Present (1924),

Cahun—Turks and Mongols (1896).

Codrington — The Melanesians (1891).

Schultz—Siberien (1923).

Skrine and Ross — Heart of Asia (1899).

Vambéry — Travels in Central Asia (1865). Sketches of Central Asia (1868). Primitive Civilizations of the Turko-Tatar People (1879). History of Bokhara (1873).

ASSYRIA, BABYLONIA, CHALDEA, SYRIA, ARABIA, PALESTINE.

Charenensis, Moses — History of Armenia (c. 600-700 A.D.).

Chiera — Legal and Administrative Documents from Nippur (1914).

Clay — Documents from the Temple Archives of Nippur (1912).

Cumont—Études syriennes (1917).

Fisher — Excavations at Nippur (1907).

Haupt — Das babylonische Nimrodepus (1891). Beitrage sur Assyriologie (1892).

Hillprecht — The Library Temple of Nippur (1910).

Layard — Monuments of Nineveh (1848). Fresh Discoveries in Nineveh and Researches at Babylon (1853). Nineveh and its Remains (1848).

Lenormant — Lettres assyriologiques et épigraphiques (1872-73).

Loftus—Chaldea and Susiana (1857).

Peters—The Library Temple of Nippur (1897).

Rawlinson, George—History of Phoenicia (1889).

Renan — History of the Israelites (1887).

Sayce — Patriarchal Palestine (1898).

Sayce—Early History of the Hebrews (1897).

Sayce—Israel and Surrounding Realms (1898).

Wardle—Israel and Babylon (1925).

Zwemer—Arabia, the Cradle of Islam (1900).

ASTRO PHYSICS, GEOPHYSICS, AND GEOLOGY.

Carpenter—The Moon Considered as a Planet, a World and a Satellite (1903).

Cusa, Cardinal — De Quadratura Circuli (1344).

D'Alembert — Système du Monde (1754).

D'Alembert — Recherches sur la procession des équinoxes et la nutation de l'axe de la terre (1749).

Dubois—Nature (1896).

Gree, W. Lowthian—Vestiges of the Molten Globe (1875).

Holmes—Age of the Earth (1913).

Horbiger, Hans — The Cosmic Ice Theory (1911).

Humboldt, Alexander — Aspects of Nature (1814).

Humboldt, Alexander — Kosmos (1845-58).

Hutton—Theory of the Earth (1784).

Jeans—Nebular Hypothesis and Modern Cosmogony (1922).

Jensen — Kosmologie der Baylonier (1890).

Le Bon — The Evolution of Matter (1915).

Neumayr—Erdegeschichte (1895).

Ordonez—Historia de la creación del cielo et de la tierra (1650).

Ortelius — Theatrum Orbis Terrarum (1570).

Perrier — The Earth before History, Origin of Life and Man (1925).

Peschel — Geschichte der Erdkunde (1877).

Russell, Walter — The Russell Cosmogony (1953).

Suess—Des Antlitz der Erde (1883-1907).

Wegener—Die enstehung, der Kontinenti und Ozeans (1920).

Whiston — New Theory of the Earth (1696).

Winchell — Sketches of Creation (1870).

ASTRONOMY, GEODESY, MATHEMATICS.

Astronomy; First. See Classical Dictionary, Hindu Mythology, Dowson (1898).

Bailly — Historie de l'astronomie (1775-87).
Breasted—The Edwin Smith Papyrus (1922).
Cantor — Geschichte der Mathematik (1885).
Dicuil — Mensura Orbis Terrae (825 A.D.).
Epping and Strassmeir — Astronomische aus Babylon (1889).
Gruppe—Die Komischen Systeme der Griechen (1851).
Heath—History of Greek Mathematics (1921).
Lewis — Survey of the Astronomy of the Ancients (1882).
Mackey — The Mythological Astronomy of the Ancients Demonstrated (1828).
Maspero — Studies of the Mythology and Astronomy of the Egyptians (1893).
Montucla — Histoire de mathématiques (1802).
Neuberger — Die Technik des Altertums (1921).
Peat — The Rind Mathematical Papyrus (1923).
Row, T. Suba — "The Zodiac", in Five Years of Philosophy (1885).
Schaubach — Astronomy of Eratosthenes (1802).
Schiaparelli — The Precursors of Copernicus, etc. (1876).
Suter—Die Mathematiken und Astronomia der Arabe und der Werke (1900).
Tannery — Researches into the History of Ancient Astronomy (1893).
Wulekenauer — De Mensura (1907).

ATLANTIS AND LEMURIA

Babcock — Legendary Islands of the Atlantic (1922).
Bacon—Atlantida Nova (1613).
Blavatsky — Secret Doctrine (1886).
Donnelly—Atlantis; the Antediluvian World (1887).
Elliott — The Lost Atlantis and Lemuria (1930).
Florence of Worcester — The Chronicle (c. 1100. First printed 1592).

Judge—Ocean of Theosophy (1891).
Echoes from the Orient (1893).
Leslie—Submerged Atlantis, or Links and Cycles (1932).
Martin — Study of Atlantis (1850).
Montaigne—The Essays (1580).
Navano—Nuevas concide raciones sobre el problem de la Atlantis (1917).
Plato—The Dialogues.
Plutarch—The Lives (Solon).
Posidonius — Essay on the Timaeus (B. C. 100).
Proceedings of the Royal Irish Academy, Atlantis, Vol. XXVI (1907).
Proclus—The Orb (450 A. D.).
Scharf — Remarks on the Problem of Atlantis, proceedings, Royal Irish Academy (1903).
Spence — Problem of Lemuria; Problem of Atlantis; Story of Atlantis; Atlantis in America.
Steiner—Lemuria (1932).
Termier, Pierre — Atlantis, Translation, Bulletins of Oceanography, Monaco, Annual Report, Smithsonian Institute (1915).
Thompson — Atlantis, No Myth (1876).
Volquardsen—Der Mythen bei Plato (1877).
Voltaire — Philosophical Dictionary (1760).
Whishow — Atlantis in Andalucia (1930).
Wilson—The Lost Atlantis (1892).
BRITAIN, SCOTLAND AND IRELAND
Brink — Early English Literature (1883).
Bryant—Celtic Ireland (1889).
Geoffrey of Monmouth — Historia Regum Britanniae (1137 A. D.).
Holinshed — Chronicles of England, Scotland and Ireland (1578).
Joyce—Story of Ancient Irish Civilization (1907).
Joyce — Social History of Ancient Ireland (1903).
Lloyd — Ancient History of Cambria (1685).
Macalister — Ireland in Pre-Celtic Times (1921).

THE PHILOSOPHIC HISTORY OF CIVILIZATION

Macdari, Conor — Irish Wisdom (1940).

Nennius — History of Britain (800 A. D.).

Nutt—Cuchulainn, the Irish Achilles (1899).

O'Grady—Silva Gadelica (1902).

Ramsay—The Foundations of England (1894).

Thurneysen — Sagen aus dem alten Ireland (1901).

Turner—History of England from the Earliest Times (1799).

Wood-Martin—Pagan Ireland (1895).

CHINA AND JAPAN

Hirth — Ancient History of China (1906).

Masadero — La Chine antique (1927).

Matsumara — Cephalic Index of the Japanese (1925).

Munro—Prehistoric Japan (1911).

Parker — Ancient China Simplified (1908).

Richthofen—China (1852).

CHRONOLOGY

Africanus, Julianus—Chronology (A. D. 221).

Alexander Polyhistor — See Ante-Nicene Fathers (c. 100 B. C.).

Berossus—Chronology (250 B. C.).

Boekh—Manetho (1845).

Carlos de Siguenza y Gongora — Chronology (1656).

Durán — Historia de las Indias de Nuevo-Espagna y islas de Terra Forma (1582).

Florence of Worcester—Chronicon ex Chronicis (1117 A. D.).

Gregory the Great—Paschale Chronicon (602 A. D.).

Lenormant—Berose (1872).

Richter — Beros Chaldaerum Historiaeque Supersuitcum Commentationi (1827).

Siret — Questions de Chronologie et Ethnographie Iberique (1913).

Unger — Chronologie des Manetho (1867).

Ussher, James — Chronolica Sacra (1650).

Welcker—Der epische Cyclus (1835-49).

Zimmer—Nennius Vindicatus (1893).

CLIMATOLOGY OF THE ICE AGE

Agassiz — Système glaciare (1847).

Brooks — The Evolution of Climate (1922).

Croll—Climate and Time (1875).

Geikie—The Great Ice Age (1874).

Huntington—Civilization and Climate (1915).

Kendrew—The Climates of the Continents (1922).

Mathew — Climate and Evolution (1915).

Nadaillac — La période glaciare (1884).

Taylor — Climatic Cycles and Evolution (1919).

Wright—Man and the Glacial Period (1892). The Ice Age in North America (1889).

Wright — Glacial Boundary in Ohio, Indiana, and Kentucky (1884).

CROMLECHS

Petrie—Stonehenge in its Astronomical Relations (1888).

Stephens—Old Northern Runic Monuments of Scandinavia and England (1892).

Stukely — Avebury, A Temple of the British Druids (1743). Stonehenge (1740).

Wimmer — De Danske Runerindesmarker (1890).

EGYPT

Blackman — Rock Tombs of Meir (1914).

Davidson and Aldersmith—The Great Pyramid and Its Divine Message (1940).

Le Plongeon — Queen Moo and the Egyptian Sphinx (1884).

Masadero—Causerius d'Egypte (1907).

Masadero — New Light on Ancient Egypt (1908).

Otto—Priester und Tempel in Hellischen Agypten (1905).

Sayce — Egypt of the Hebrews and Herodotus (1895).
Smith, G. Elliot — Ancient Egyptians (1924).

ENOCH, BOOK OF

Book of Enoch—S. P. C. K. Translations of Early Documents (1917).
Burkitt—Jewish and Christian Apocalypses (1896).
Charles—The Book of Enoch (1912).
Forbes and Charles — Apoc. Pseudegraphia (1920). Slavonic Enoch, Secrets of Enoch (1896).
Leszynsky—Die Sadduzaer (1912).
Morfell and Charles — The Book of the Secrets of Enoch (1896).

THE FLOOD

Andree—Die Flutsagen (1891).
Hilprecht—The Latest Version of the Babylonian Deluge Story (1920).
Peak—The Flood (1930).
Prestwich — Traditions of the Flood (1895).
Usener—Flutsagen (1899).
Winternitz—Die Flutsagen des alterthums und der Naturvolker (1901).
Wright — Geological Confirmation of the Biblical Deluge (1902).

GENERAL

Aelianus, Claudius — Historia Varia (A. D. 225).
Cardinal Cusa—De Docta Ignorantia (300 A. D.).
Cooley—History of Maritime Discovery (1829).
de Capmany — Memorias Historicas, etc. (1779-92).
d'Olivet — Hermeneutic Interpretation of the Origin of Social State of Man (1814).
Eadmer — Historiae Novarum (1066 A. D.).
Evemerus—Historia Sacra (315 B. C.).
Frazier — The Golden Bough (1907-15).
Frederici—Scalping (1906).
Freeman — The Unity of History (1872).

Gardner—The Parthenon; Science of Forms (1925).
George—Historical Evidence (1909).
Leaf—Homer and History (1915).
Lenormant—Manuel d'histoire ancienne de l'Orient (1868).
Lenormant—Les Origines de l'histoire d'après la Bible (1882-5).
Libby—Radiocarbon Dating (University of Chicago Press, 1952).
Marianus Scotus—Chronicon Universale (1059 A. D.).
Müller, Johanne — Universal History (1811).
Nabatheans (See Abrabanel, Quatremère, Herbert Spencer, Chowlson— The Book of Q-tâmy.)
Rawlinson, George — Seven Ancient Empires of the East (1862-76).
Ray, John — Wisdom of God Manifested in the Works of Creation (1691).
Salmond — The Christian Doctrine of Immortality (1901).
Taylor — Plato, The Man and His Work (1936).
Timaeus—The Soul of the World (c. 400 B. C.).
Volney—Ruins of Empires (1791).

GEOGRAPHY AND PHYSICS

Babcock — Legendary Islands of the Atlantic (Am. Geog. Soc., 1922).
Beazley — Dawn of Modern Geography (1897).
Brugsch — Dictionary of the Geography of Ancient Egypt (1887).
Bunbury—History of Ancient Geography (1886).
Cassini, Jean Dominique — World Map (1696).
Cosmas Indicopleustes — Topographia Christiana (548).
Eratosthenes — Geographica (225 B. C.).
Field—Projective Geometry (1927).
Gerini — Ptolemy's Geography of E. Asia (1909).
Heidman—Founders of Oceanography and their Work (1923).
Hull—The Geography and geology of Arabia Patraea (1886).

Humboldt—Wichtige Stettin (1812).

Humboldt, Alexander — Vol. 2, Examen Critique de l'Histoire de la Géographie du Nouveau Continent et des progrès de l'astronomie nautique aux quinzième et sizième siecles (1836-39).

Jomard — Les monuments de la géographie, recuil d'anciennes cartes, Europèens et orientales (1842-62).

Kugler — Die babylonische Mondrechung (1910).

Leaf—Homeric Geography (1915).

Malte-Brun — Historie de la Géographie (1817).

Marinus of Tyre—Maps of. See History of Ancient Geography, Bunbury.

Pomponius Mela—De Choragraphica (c. 50 A. D.).

Ptolomaeus, Claudius — The Syntaxis (220 A. D.).

Quatremère—History and Geography of Egypt (1810).

Reclus—La Terre (1867). The Ocean (1872).

Ritter—Erdkunde von Arabien (1846-47).

Rose—The Mediterranean in the Ancient World (1934).

Ross, Sir John—A Voyage of Discovery (1810).

Ross, Sir James Clark—A Voyage of Research and Discovery in the Antarctic Regions (1839-48).

Saint Martin — L'Histoire géographique ancienne (1878).

Santaren—Atlas composé de Mappermonds et de Portulands (1842-53).

Schaff—Peoples of the Erythrean Sea (1912).

Schlangintweit — Researches on the Physical Geography of the Alps (1850). Scientific Mission to India and High Asia (1855-57).

Semple—Influence of Geographic Environment (1911).

Smith—Dictionary of Greek and Roman Geography (1885).

Tozer—History of Ancient Geography (1898).

Tozer—Selections from Geography of Strabo (1893).

Ukert — Geography of the Greeks (1816).

Warmington — Greek Geography (1934).

GERMANY

Aigner—Hallstatt (1921).

Grimm — Der Deutsche Heldensage (1829).

Grotius — Annals of the Low Countries (1644).

Larsen — Saxo Grammaticus, Nans Verk og Person (1925).

Sacken—Das Grabfeld von Hallstadt (1868).

Tacitus—De Moribus et Populis Germaniae (100 A. D.).

Waitz — Deutsche Verfassungsgeschichte (1844).

HEBREWS AND JEWS

Darmesteter — Cour d'Oeil sur l'Histoire du Peuple Juif (1895).

Delitzsch, Franz—Hebrews (1857).

Karpeles — History of Jewish Literature (1886).

HERMETICISM, MAGIC AND ALCHEMY.

Baumgarten-Crucius — De Livrorum Hermeticorum Origine atque Indole (1827).

Berthelot—Les Origines de l'Alchimie (1885).

Brauninger — Hermes Tresmegestos (1926).

d'Olivet—The Hermeneutic Interpretation of the Origin of the Social State of Man (1814).

Dufresnoy—History of the Hermetic Science (1735).

Ennemoser—Magistimus (1819).

Figuer—L'Alchimie et les Alchimistes (1854).

Hilger—Hermes Trismegeste (1855).

Hofer — Historie de la Chimie (1869).

Kopp—Die Alchemie in alterer und neurer Zeit (1886).

Levi, Eliphas — History of Magic (1860).

Levi, Eliphas—Transcendental Magic, Doctrine and Ritual (1856).

Lexa—La Magie dans d'Egypte antique (1924).

Lippman — Enstehungund Aubeitung der Alchemie (1919).

Magic, Balance, Speaking Stones. See Bibliography of, in The Secret Doctrine, Blavatsky (1886).

Mead — Thrice Greatest Hermes (1907).

Menard — Hermes Trismegeste (1866).

Mirville, de—Helgoat and other Magic Stones (1860).

Pietschmann — Hermes Tresmegestus (1875).

Pneumatology — de Mirville (1860).

Scott—Hermetica (1924).

Thompson—Semite Magic (1908).

Thorndike — History of Magic and Experimental Science (1923).

Wise, E. — Magic Stones of Great Britain (1876).

Wright — Narratives of Sorcery and Magic (1851).

IDOLATRY

Augustinius Hippolensis — City of God (c. 410).

Idolatry. See Evolution of Religion—Farnell. Also Ency. Biblica (1905) Cheyne.

Idols. See Primitive Culture — Tylor (1903).

Images and Idols. Ency. of Religion and Ethics—Ed. Hastings, Vol. 11 (1914).

Lactantius — De origine erroris (300 A. D.).

Mirville, de—Pneumatologie (1862).

Rose — Handbook of Greek Mythology (1928).

INDIA

Aburini — An Inquiry into India (1025 A. D.).

Battacharya—Hindu Castes and Sects (1896).

Brosse—L'Inde inconnu (1897).

Colebrook—Studies in India (1795).

Dutt—History of Civilization in Ancient India (1859-90).

Hopkins — India Old and New (1901).

Ketkar — History of Castes in India (1909).

Lassen — Indische altertumskunde (1844-61).

Manning—Ancient and Medieval India (1869).

McCrindle—Ancient India (1897).

Monier-Williams — The Wisdom of India (1875).

Oppert — Original Inhabitants of Bharatavarsa or India (1895).

Robertson, William — An Historical Disquisition Concerning the Knowledge which the Ancients had of India, etc. (1791).

Smith — Early History of India (1904).

Thurston — Castes and Tribes of Southern India (1930).

Wheeler—History of India from the Earliest Ages (1874-76).

KABBALA AND KABBALISTS

Abrabanel, Isaac—The Herald of Salvation (1529).

Bibliographica Kabbalistica (Leipsig, 1927).

Franck—La Kabbale (1843).

Ginsburg—The Kabbala (1865).

Hirsh—The Cabbalists (1922).

Meyer—The Philosophy of Ibn Gebirol, the Qaballah and the Zohar (1885).

Scholem — Encyclopaedia Judiaca (Adam Kadmon) (1927).

Waite — Literature and Doctrine of the Kaballah (1886).

Waite — The Doctrine and Literature of the Kaballah (1902).

LANGUAGE: ALPHABETS.

Amarakosa—The First Alphabet. See Classical Dictionary of Hindu Mythology—Dowson (1878).

Anderssen and Black—Paleontologica Sinica (1925).

Arntz — Handbuch der Runenslunde (1935).

THE PHILOSOPHIC HISTORY OF CIVILIZATION

Ball—The Akkadian Affinities of the Chinese (1910).

Bopp — Comparative Grammar of Sanskrit, Zend, Armenian, Greek, etc. (1833-52).

Buschmann—Aperçu de la langue des îles Marquises et de la langue taitienne (1843).

Champollion, Jean François—Système hiéroglyphique (1824). Grammaire égyptienne (1836-41). Dictionnaire égyptienne (1841-44).

Champollion, Jean Jacques — Paleographie Universelle (1839-41).

Deguignes — Tom. XXVIII, pp. 506-525. Mémoires de l'Academes des Inscriptions (1843).

Deimel — Sumerische Grammatik (1924).

Delitzsch, Friedrich—Assyrian Grammar (1877).

Diringer—The Alphabet (1950).

d'Olivet — La langue Hébraic restituée. (1810).

Donner—Origin of the Turkish Alphabet (1897).

Eichhorn, J. G. — Einleitung in das Alte Testament (1780-83).

Erh Ya — Chinese Dictionary (B. C. 1200?).

Evans—Further Discoveries of Cretan and Aegean Script (1909). Scripta Minoa (1909).

Gardiner—Rock Carvings in America (1898).

Gelzer — The Semitic Language (1784).

Grey—The Maya Glyphs (1896).

Grierson — Report of the Linguistic Survey of India (1927).

Grotius (Hugo deGroot)—Annals of the Low Countries (1657). The Language of the Western Hemisphere (1657).

Haupt — Die Akkadische Spracht (1898).

Haupt — Akkadische und sumerische Keilschrifttexte (1893).

Humboldt, Karl — The Kawi Language of Java (1836). The Heterogeneity of Language (1835).

Knight — Analytical Essay on the Greek Alphabet (1875).

Lacouperie—The Language of China before the Chinese (1886).

Laurent — Die Geschichtesschreiber der Deutschen Vorzeit (1893).

Layard—Cuneiform Inscriptions from Assyrian Monuments (1851).

Lenormant—Lettres assyriologiques et épigraphiques (1871-72).

Lenormant, Charles — Trésor de numismatique et de glyptique (1853).

Lepsius — A Standard Alphabet for Reducing Unwritten Language and Foreign Graphic Systems to a Uniform Orthography in European Letters (1855).

Marquart — Chronology of Ancient Turkish Script (1898).

Maspero — Inscriptions of the Pyramids of Saqqarah (1894).

Meillet and Cohen—Les Langues du Monde (1924).

Muir—The Language of the Parsees (1849). The Pahlari Language (1851).

Müller, Max—The Science of Language (1866).

Müller, Max—History of the Ancient Sanskrit Language (1864).

Pott—Die Zigenner in Europa und Asien (1844-45). Etomologische Forschungen (1833-36).

Rhys — Phonology and Manx Gaelic (1895).

Rouzick—The Russian Script (1924).

Schmidt, William — Die Sprachfamilien (1926).

Schnabel — Kidenas, Hipparch und die Entdeckung der Praession, Zeitschrift für Assyriologie (1926).

Shu Wen — Explanation of written words, China (120 A. D.).

Strandwold—Punic Rock Inscriptions Along the American Atlantic Seaboard (1939).

Stukely — Paleographia Britannica (1743-52).

Taylor — The Alphabet, Account of the Origin and Development of Letters (1883).

Taylor—Words and Places (1864).

Taylor—Greeks and Goths, a Study of the Runes (1879).

Vambéry — Turco-Tatar Languages (1873).
Vigfusson — Icelandic-English Dictionary (1869-1874).
Wright—Hamitic Language (1890).
Zimmern — Keilenschriften und das Alte Testament (1933).

MAN; RACIAL HISTORY AND EVOLUTION OF CULTURE.

Agriculture, institution of. (See Nabatheans).
Anthropological Researches by Jesuits in the Gobi Desert, Ency. Brit., "Archaeology". Current Edition.
Bender—Home of the Indo-Europeans (1922).
Boule—Fossil Man (1923).
Brinton—Races and Peoples (1892).
Burkett—Pre-History (1921).
Burkiett — Our Early Ancestors (1926).
Cartailhac — Les Âges Préhistoriques de l'Espagne et du Portugal (1886).
Dixon—The Racial History of Man (1924).
Dowd—The Negro Race (1906).
Dune Men of the Gobi. See Andrews —On the Trail of Ancient Man (1932).
Eliot—Prehistoric Man and His Story (1915).
Evans, Sir John — Ancient Stone Weapons, Implements, and Ornaments of Great Britain (1872-97).
Geiseler—Die Oesterinsel eine Statte Phahistorischer Kultur (1883).
Gunmere—Germanic Origins (1862).
Hewett — The Prehistoric Peoples of India, Southwest Asia, and Southern Europe (1926).
Huntington—The Character of Races (1923).
Jenness — Culture Waves from Asia (1937). A New Dorset Eskimo Culture in Greenland (1940).
Jordanus—De Summa Temporum vel Origine Actibusque Gentis Romanorum (550 A. D.).
Kunst—Paleolithic Kultur in Indien (1913).

Lubbock—Origin of Civilization and the Primitive Condition of Man (1870).
McCurdy—Human Origins (1924).
Morgan — L'umanité préhistorique (1921).
Morgan — The Consanguinities and Affinities of the Human Family (1871). Ancient Society (1879).
Myres—Dawn of History (1918).
Nadaillac, de—Moeurs et monuments des peuples préhistoriques (1888).
Nadaillac de — Le premier homme et les temps préhistoriques (1880).
Nadaillac, de — L'ancienneté de l'homme (1868).
Nadaillac, de — L'homme Tertiare (1886).
Obermaier — Fossil Man in Spain (1924).
Osborn — The Origin and Evolution of Life (1912).
Osborn—Men of the Old Stone Age (1921).
Osborn — The Dawn Man of Piltdown, Sussex, Old and New Standards of Pleistocene Division in Relation to the Prehistory of Man in Europe (1922).
Osborn — Man Rises to Parnassus (1928).
Perry—The Megolithic Civilization of Indonesia (1906).
Petrie—Tools and Weapons (1917).
Prichard—The Eastern Origin of the Celtic Race (1833).
Quatrafrages, de — The Pygmies (1895).
Radosavljevich—Who are the Slavs? (1919).
Rhys and Jones—The Welsh People (1900).
Rhys—Early Ethnology of the British Isles (1890-91).
Sarre—Kunst der Alten Perse (1925).
Sayce—Peoples of the Old Testament (1885).
Sergi — The Mediterranean Race (1901).
Shirokogoroff — Anthropology of Northern China (1923).
Smith—Migration of Culture (1917).
Smith and Howett—Native Tribes of

Australia (1900).
Sollas—Ancient Hunters (1924).
Taylor — Evolution and Distribution of Race, Culture and Language (1922).
Tylor—Researches into the Early History of Man (1864).
Tyler — The New Stone Age of Europe (1922).
Tylor—Primitive Culture (1871).
Voltaire — Discours sur l'homme (1784).
Willis—Age and Area (1922).
Winchell — Doctrine of Evolution (1874).
Winchell—Pre-Adamites (1880).
Winternitz—The Eskimo (1941).
Wissler—Man and Culture (1924).
Wood — Our Arboreal Ancestors (1916).

METAPHYSICS

Alexander of Aphrodisius—Metaphysica (175 A. D.).
Basel—Das Urreligionen des Amerikanischen (1888).
Bunsen—God in History (1857-58).
Charles — A Critical History of the Doctrine of Future Life in Israel, in Judaism, and in Christianity (1899).
Cumont—After Life in Roman Paganism (1922).
Dahle—Life after Death and the Future of the Kingdom of God (1895).
Dickey—One Man's Destiny (1942).
Farrar—The Eternal Hope (1892).
Harnack—History of Dogma (1904).
McIntyre—The Other Side of Death (1922).
Shedd—Doctrine of Endless Punishment (1886).
Williams—God's Great Plan (1910).

MYSTICISM AND MYSTICS

Cumont — Astrology and Religion among the Greeks and Romans (1912)
Cumont — Les religiones orientales dans le paganisme romain (1906).
Mirville, de — Pneumatologie des Esprits (1875).

Oman—Mystics, Saints, and Ascetics of India (1903).
Paracelsus—Works of (1580).
Petermann—Reisen in Orient (1861).
Teasey—Monastics (1898).

THE MYSTERIES

Aurich—Das antike Mysterien weisen in seinem Einfluss auf das Christentum (1894).
Black—Druids and Druidism (1920).
Boas — The Social Organization and Secret Societies of the Kwa-Kiutl (1875).
Boas—Die Tshimshian (1888).
Cumont — The Mysteries of Mithra (1903).
Cumont — Textes et monuments relatigs aux mystères Mithra (1894-1901).
Cumont—Fouilles de Doura Europos (1922-23).
D'Alviella—Eleusiana (1886).
Darmstat—Python (1878).
Doran—History of the English Stage (1898).
Dorsey — Mushinnongovi Ceremonies of the Snake and Antelope Fraternities (1902).
Dorsey — The Cheyenne Ceremonial Organization (1905). Orabi Trial Ceremonial (1901).
Faber—Dissertation on the Mysteries of the Cabiri (1801).
Foucart—Recherches sur l'origine et la nature des mystères (1895).
Heckethorn — Secret Societies in All Ages and All Countries (1875).
Iamblicus — The Mysteries (300 A. D.).
Kendrick—The Druids (1928).
Le Plongeon — Sacred Mysteries of the Mayax and Quiches (1876).
Loisy — Les Mystères Paiens et les Mystères Chrétiens (1919).
Nanabozha, the Cult of among American Aborigines. See Handbook of Am. Indians.
Plato—Dissertation on the Eleusinian Mysteries (380 B. C.).
Reitzenstein — Poimandres, etc. (1904).

Schuré—The Great Initiates (1912).
Secret Societies, Handbook of American Indians.
Skinner—Key to the Hebrew-Egyptian Mystery in the Source of Measures (1875).
Spence—Mysteries of Egypt (1925).
Stevenson — The Zuni Indians and their Secret Fraternities (1904).
Taylor — The Masque of the Gods (1872).
Thompson — The People of the Serpent (1922).
Webster — Primitive Secret Societies (1909).
Yarker—The Arcane Schools (1909).

MYTHOLOGY

Andreae — Mythologia Christiana (1630).
Boas — The Mythology of the Bella Coola Indians (1898).
Boas—Tshimshian Texts (1902).
Brinton — Myths of the New World (1868).
Brinton — American Hero Myths, a Study of American Religions (1885).
Conybeare—Myths, Magic and Morals (1910).
Cox—Polynesian Mythology (1856).
Curtin—Creation Myths of Prehistoric America in Relation to the Religious History and Mental Development of Mankind (1898).
Dowson—Classical Dictionary of Hindu Mythology (1879).
Florenz—Japanese Mythology (1878).
Gill — Myths and Songs from the South Pacific (1876).
Goldhizer—Mythology among the Hebrews (1870).
Grimm—Teutonic Mythology (1882).
Guerber — Myths of Northern Lands (1895).
Keith—Indian Mythology (1917).
Lang — Myths, Ritual and Religion (1886).
McKenzie — Myths of Crete and Pre-Hellenic Europe.
Meyer — Indogermanische Mythen (1888).

Murray, Alexander S. — Manual of Mythology (1897).
Preller—Griesche Mythologie (1854-56).
Reinach — Cults, Myths and Religion (1898).
Van Gennep — Mythes et légendes d'Australie (1890).

THE NAGAS

Hutton—The Angami Nagas (1921). The Sema Nagas (1921).
Mills—The AO Nagas (1916). The Lhota Nagas (1916).

PHILOSOPHY

Abel—Orphica (1885).
Abrabanel — The Philosophy of (1508).
Averroës—The Destruction of the Destruction of Philosophy (1171 A. D.).
Bakewell — Source Book in Ancient Philosophy (1909).
Berger—Geschichte der Wissenschaftlichen (1897).
Best—Bibliography of Irish Philosophy, etc. (1913).
Bois—Origines d. l. Philosophie of Philo Judaes (1890).
Bruce — Chin Hsi and His Masters (1923).
Callimachus — Causes (310-240 B. C.).
D'Alembert — Philosophie et Litérature (1761-80).
Fisher — Commentary on Orgigen's Theology and Cosmology (1846).
Gumperz—Greek Thinkers (1891).
Hegel—Vorlesungen über die Philosophie der Religion (1832).
Iamblicus — Life of Pythagoras (c. 300 A. D.).
Inge—Philosophy of Plotinus (1918).
Kern — Orphicorum Fragmenta (1922).
Legge—Life and Teaching of Confucius (1861-1872). Chinese Classics (1861-62).
Lobeck—Aglaophamus (1829).
Maritain — Philosophy of Nature (1950).

Mencius — Chinese Philosophy (c. B. C. 350).
Müller—Six Systems of Hindu Philosophy (1879).
Munk — Mélanges de Philosophie juive et arabe (1859).
Petersen — Der geheime Gottesdienst bei den Griechen (1848).
Plotinus — The Enneads (c. 250 A. D.).
Preller and Ritter—Historia philosophiae Grecae et Romanae (1836).
Russell — Mathematical Philosophy (1917).
Sarton—History of Science (1930).
Spinoza—Ethics Demonstrated in the Geometrical Order (1674).
Suzuki — Early Chinese Philosophy (1914).
Voltaire—Lettres philosophiques (Ed. 1784).
Zeller — Greek Philosophy (1883). Deutschen Philosophie (1873).

RELIGION AND CULTS

Barton—Semitic Origins (1902).
Bergaigne — La Religion Vedique (1888).
Bernouilli—Cult of Venus (1898).
Deimel — Pantheon Babylonien (1914).
Dhorne—La Religion Assyrie-Babylonienne (1918).
Eliot — Hinduism and Brahmanism (1921).
Faber—Horae Mosicae (1801).
Farnel — Cults of the Greek States (1924).
de Groot — Religion of the Chinese (1910).
Heussner, D. — Altchristlichen Orpheusderstellungen (1893).
Hyde—Religious History of Ancient Persia (1700).
Jablonski—Pantheon (1898).
Jastrow—Religion of the Babylonians and Assyrians (1905-12).
Jevons—An Introduction to the History of Religion (1902).
Keith—The Religion and Philosophy of the Veda and Upanishads (1925).

Langdon—Babylon Liturgies (1913).
Lepsius—Uber den arsten agyptischen Gotterkreis (1857).
Lidzbarski—Bel Sha-men (1888).
Lowie—Primitive Religion (1925).
Mainage — Religions Préhistoriques (1920).
Monier-Williams — Hinduism and Brahmanism (1876).
Moulton — Early Zoroastrianism (1913).
Müller—Natural Religion (1890).
Numenius — Biblical Allegories (c. 175 A. D.).
O'Raihally—Irish Religion (1920).
Renan — Etudes d'histoire religieuse (1857).
Réville—Religions of Mexico, Central America and Peru (1886).
Saussaye, de la—Religion of the Teutons (1890).
Sayce—Egyptian and Babylonian Religion (1903).
Scott—Gnosticism (1920).
Smith, William R.—Religion of the Semites (1889).
Teile—Religion in Babylonia and Assyria (1895).
Waring—Nature Worship (1874).
Wiedemann—Religion of the Ancient Egyptians (1897).

SCANDINAVIA, ICELAND AND GREENLAND

Brögger—Vinlands ferdene (1939).
Grammaticus, Saxo—Historica Danica (1250 A. D.).
Grimm — Der Gotterwelt der deutschen und nordischen Volker (1860).
Gustafsen—Nordski Oldtids (1906).
Headley—The Island of Fire (1875).
Judson — Hrosvitha of Gandersheim (1888).
Magnusson — Chronica Danorum (1695). Testamentum Magna regis Norvegiae (1719).
Nicol—Historical and Descriptive Account of Iceland, Greenland and the Faroe Islands (1844).
O'Reilly — Greenland, the Adjacent Seas, etc. (1818).

Otto—Denmark and Iceland (1881).
Philippi — Geschichte von Danemark (1846).
Snorre Sturleson—The Volsunga Saga (1271 A. D.). The Heimskringla.
Stefansson — Unsolved Mysteries of the Arctics (1935).
Taylor—Iceland and Egypt (1834).
Thomsen—Ancient Relations between Scandinavia and Russia (1906).
Torfaeus — Historia Vinlandiae antiquae, etc. (1705).
Vogt—Dublin Som norsk (1896).
York and Powell — Origines Islandidae (1905).

SCRIPTURES

Apollodorus — Bibliotheca (B. C. 140).
Apollonius of Rhodius — The Argonautica (B. C. 225).
Avesta—Translations of. (See Geldner).
Baumgartner—Das Ramayana (1896).
Beowulf — The Saxon Epic (c. 700 A. D.).
Bernhart—Vulfila oder die Goetische Bible (1875).
Blackeley — The Trithgofs Saga (1867).
The Book of Tao Tu—Lao Tze (B. C. 600).
Bunger—Theopompina (1878).
Caedman — English Bible (670 A. D.?). (See Morley).
Charles—The Book of Enoch (1898).
Cheyne—Sacred Book of the Old Testament (1898). The Two Religions of Israel (1910). Genesis, Critica Biblica (1904).
Clement of Alexandria—Codex Alexandrinus (250 A. D.).
Deseret News Co. — The Book of Mormon, Salt Lake City (1885).
Diodorus Siculus—Historical Collections (30 A. D.).
Dionysious Thrax. (See Sandys).
Dutt—Mahabharata (1883).
Easter Island Tablets. See Archaeology of Easter Island, Thomson (1874).
Edda—The Prose. (See Mallet and

Brodeur).
The Edda of Saemond the Wise (1156 A. D.).
Fauche—Translation of the Mahabharata and Ramayana (Paris, 1863).
Fleming—Collectanea Sacra Hibernia (1667).
Geldner—Avesta Literature (1897).
Griffiths — Translation of the Ramayana (Benares, 1870-74).
Grimm, Jakob — German Dictionary (1785-1863). Deutsche Sagen (1812). Deutsche Mythologie (1835).
Grimm, Wilhelm—Deutsche Heldensage (1829).
Halle — The Gothic Bible of Ulfilas (1875).
Haug—Aitareye Brahmana of the Rig Veda (1863).
Hecateus Miletus — Perigesis (476 B. C.).
Hecatacus, of Abdera—Zorn
Hermannsson — Icelandic Manuscripts (1929).
Herodotus—The Nine Muses (c. 400 B. C.).
Hesiod—Theogony (750 B. C.).
Holtzmann—Das Mahabharata (1892-95).
Homer—The Iliad and Odyssey.
Hopkins — The Great Epic of India (1902).
Hume—The 13 Principal Upanishads (1921).
Johnston—Bhavagad Gita (1908).
Knapp — Uber Orphensderstellungen
Kaeji—Rig'Veda (1886).
(1895).
Koht—Old Norse Sagas (1931).
Kusro Anoshirvan (Avesta) (531-579 A. D).
Lactantius — The Seven Books (325 A. D.).
Lappenberg — Scriptores Rerum Germanicarum (1876).
Lawrence — The Book of Enoch (1829).
Lichtenberger—Le Poème et la légende des Nibelungen (1891).
Lonnrot, Elias—Kalevala (1835-49).
Mills — Sacred Books of the East (1880-87).

Muir—Original Sanskrit Texts (1858-70).
Muspilli (900 A. D., Bavaria). See English Writers, Morley.
Nivelle — The Book of the Dead (1886).
Orpheus—The Argonautica.
Pherecydes of Syros — Classical Fragment (c. 500-600 B. C.).
Pherecydes of Leros — Fragments of Athens (c. 454 B. C.).
Philo Byblius — The Law of Chon (100 A. D.).
Philpott—Edda Addaga (1931).
Pindar—Odes of (522-443 B. C.).
Plato—The Dialogues (c. 375 B. C.).
Plutarch—On the Face of the Orb of the Moon (c. 100 A. D.).
Posidonius — The Timaeus (100 B. C.).
Proclus—Essay on the Timaeus (450 A. D.).
Quatremère — Mémoir on the Nabatheans (1835).
Ranade—Constructive Survey of Upanishadic Texts (1920).
Reinach—Orpheus (1898).
Richter—Greek Fragments (1825).
Roy — Mahabharata Translation (1883).
Sancthuniathon (The Whole Law Chon). (See Philo Byblius).
Schenkle — Corpus Scriptorum Ecclesiasticorum Latinorum (1896).
Schmidt — Egyptian Gnostic Texts (1892).
Schroeder — Pythagoras and India (1888).
Shu King — Historical Documents, Confucius (B. C. 531-478).
Sigfusson, Saemund—The Poetic Edda (1056-1133).
Smith — The Chaldean Account of Genesis (1878).
Thomas—The Codex Tro (1882).
Tschudi (Aegidius) — Chronicum Helviticum (1734).
Vendidad (See Avesta).
Vergil—Aeneid (c. 30 B. C.).
Wilamowitz — Works of Callimachus (1882).
Windischmann—Zoroastriche Studien (1863).

Ximenes—The Popul Vuh (1750).
Zorn — Hecatei Abderitae Fragmentia (1730).

SERPENT WORSHIP AND CULT

Buckland — Anthropological Studies (1891).
Fergusson—Serpent Worship (1873).
Frazer—The Golden Bough.
Muehly — Die Schlangenweit im Mythen und Cultur der Klassichen Volker (1867).
Sayce — Serpent Worship in Ancient and Modern Egypt (1893).
Tylor — Primitive Culture, "Serpent Worship" (1866).
Winternitz—Der Sarpabali ein altendischer Schlangenweit (1887).

SOUTH PACIFIC

Brown — The Riddle of the Pacific (1930).
Churchward, James—The Lost Continent of Mu (1930).
Churchward, James—The Children of Mu (1931).
Churchward, James — Mu: Cosmic Forces (1932).
Ellis—Polynesian Researches (1828).
Malinowski — Argonauts of Western Pacific (1922).
Mentroux—Easter Island (1940).
O'Brien—Mystic Islands of the South Sea (1920). White Shadows on the Pacific (1922).
Seligman — Melanesians of British New Guinea (1910).
Thompson — Te Pito Te Henna, or Easter Island (1889).

SPAIN, PORTUGAL, ITALY, ROME.

Espinosa, Friar Alonso — The Guanches of Teneriffe, etc. (1580-90).
Flach — Les Origines de l'ancienne France (1893).
Hercubano — Historia de Portugal (1279 A. D.).
Manuel de Faira y Sousa—History of Portugal (Madrid, 1628). Translated by Captain John Stevens (London, 1698).

Mariana — History of Spain (1592-1605).
Nogueira—Evolueoes da Civilization en Portugal (1893).
Ribiero — Estudos Prehistoricos en Portugal (1878).
Timaeus—History of Italy and Sicily (c. 264 B. C.).

SYMBOLOGY AND SYMBOLS

Borchardt — Des Alter der grossen Sphinx (1897).
Chipiez — Art in Ancient Persia (1892).
Churchward, Albert F. R. S. — Symbols of Primordial Man (1910).
Churchward, James—The Symbols of Mu (1932).
Clement—Legendary and Mythological Art (1861).
Cumont—Textes et monument figurés relatifs aux mystères de Mithras (1884-90).
D'Alviella—Les migrations des symboles (1886).
D'Aveenes—History of Egyptian Art (1878).
Dinosaur Eggs and Maya Symbols. See Kosloff in Mongolia.
Evans, Sir Arthur — Cretan Pictographs and Pre-Phoenician Script (1896).
Franz — Weiner Phahistorische Zeitschrift (1799).
De Genouillne — L'Art héraldique (1889).
Goodyear — Grammar of the Lotus (1920).
Gould—Mythical Monsters (1898).
Guillim — The Display of Heraldry (1610).
Hahn—Bibliotek des Symbols (1896).
Ilberg — Die Sphinx in der grieschinensage und Kunst (1895).
Jeuner—Christian Symbolism (1910).
Jones, Sir William — Asiatic Studies (1794).
Jubainville, D'Arbois de — The Animistic Symbols of the Druids (1885).
Knight — The Symbolic Language of Ancient Art and Mythology (1820).

Kuhn — Die Herabkunft des Feuers (1860).
Philpot — The Sacred Tree, or the Tree in Religion and Myth (1897).
Roscher — "Lotophagen" in Lexicon of Art and Mythology (1880).
Smith—Hindu and Arabic Numerals (1911).
Ward—Masonic Symbols (1924).
Wilson — The Swastika, the Oldest Known Symbol (1898).

TREE WORSHIP AND CULT

Boettecher—Der Baumkultus d. Hellenes (1856).
Evans — Tree and Pillar Worship in the Mediterranean Relations (1911). The Nycencaen Tree (1901).
Fergusson—Tree and Pillar Worship (1873).
Frazer—The Golden Bough.
Mannhardt — Der Baumkultus der Germanen und ihrer Nachbarstamme (1875). Antike Wald und Feldkulte (1879).
Philpot—The Sacred Tree, or Tree of Religion and Myth (1890).

THE UIGHURS

Humboldt, Alexander—Asia Centrale (1830).
Klaproth — Abhandlungen über der Sprache und Schrift der Uiguren (1820).
Schott—Uiguren Frage (1893).
Spiegel—The Aryan Cycle (1888).
Vambéry — Uigurische Sprachmonumente (1870).

WISDOM PHILOSOPHY

Agrippa—Occult Philosophy (1510).
Bacon—The Wisdom of the Ancients (1609).
Barua—Pre-Buddhistic Indian Philosophy (1912).
Blavatsky—Isis Unveiled (1877).
Blavatsky — The Secret Doctrine (1886).

Charles — Apocrypha and Pseudepigrapha of the Old Testament (1913).

Clay — Origin of Biblical Traditions (1920).

Garbe — Philosophy of Ancient India (1897).

Gupta—History of Indian Philosophy (1922).

Harrison — Prologomena to Study of Greek Religion (1903).

Judge—Ocean of Theosophy (1892).

Lenormant—Les sciences occultes en Asie (1875).

Outey — Doctrine of Incarnation (1896).

Petavel—The Problem of Immortality (1892).

Radhakrishum — Indian Philosophy (1923-27).

Sinnet—Esoteric Buddhism (1884).

Smith, W. R. — Religion of the Semites (1927).

Westermark — Ritual and Belief in Morocco (1926).

INDEX